MARTYRS AND TRICKSTERS

Princeton Studies in Muslim Politics

DALE F. EICKELMAN AND
AUGUSTUS RICHARD NORTON,
SERIES EDITORS

A list of titles in this series can be found at the back of the book

Martyrs and Tricksters

AN ETHNOGRAPHY OF THE
EGYPTIAN REVOLUTION

{⊱⋙⋘⊰}

Walter Armbrust

PRINCETON UNIVERSITY PRESS
PRINCETON & OXFORD

Copyright © 2019 by Princeton University Press

Published by Princeton University Press
41 William Street, Princeton, New Jersey 08540
6 Oxford Street, Woodstock, Oxfordshire OX20 1TR

press.princeton.edu

All Rights Reserved

LCCN 2019937190
ISBN 978-0-691-16263-8
ISBN (pbk.) 978-0-691-16264-5

British Library Cataloging-in-Publication Data is available

Editorial: Fred Appel and Thalia Leaf
Production Editorial: Brigitte Pelner
Jacket Image: Courtesy of the author
Production: Erin Suydam
Publicity: Nathalie Levine (U.S.) and Kathryn Stevens (U.K.)
Copyeditor: Kathleen Kageff

This book has been composed in Miller

Printed in the United States of America

10 9 8 7 6 5 4 3 2 1

For Lucie

Slap your disciple, Imam
Describe the redness of his cheeks to all the liars ...
And respect for those who are honest

—Graffiti from the wall of the Ministerial Council, December 13, 2011.
The lines were written by poet Ahmed Aboul Hassan to
accompany a mural painted by 'Ammar Abu-Bakr

The two men of this age are General 'Abd al-Fattah al-Sisi, on whom
the people have bestowed the title "Field Marshall 'Abd al-Fattah al-Sisi,
the leader of the Egyptian armed forces," and the television presenter Dr.
Taufiq 'Ukasha, on whom the people have bestowed the title 'detonator of
the June 30 Revolution and the leader of this nation.' To be perfectly clear,
Taufiq 'Ukasha is not the leader by himself, but rather Egypt today has
two leaders: al-Sisi and 'Ukasha.

—Broadcast on the al-Fara'ayn satellite television channel
in late August 2013. Uploaded to the internet on
August 25, 2013 ("Al-Sisi wa 'Ukasha Inqadhu Misr" 2013)

Lissaha thaurat Yanayir—*It's still the January Revolution.*

—Words printed on the jacket of activist Sana' Sayf,
worn in Tahrir Square on January 25, 2016,
the fifth anniversary of the revolution

CONTENTS

ILLUSTRATIONS

ACKNOWLEDGMENTS

IT WOULD BE AN UNDERSTATEMENT to say that I never expected to write a book about a revolution. Over the past couple of decades when I have been asked to describe my research interests I have normally responded, as briefly as possible, "mass media and popular culture, mainly in Egypt." I have written about nationalism, modernity, the history of Egyptian mass media, masculinity and gender more broadly, Ramadan riddle programs on television, and classic musical films, and I have often been asked to write about mass-mediated representations of Islam and other political issues. But it never occurred to me to write about revolution until I found myself living in the midst of one.

My partner, Lucie Ryzova, was also living in the midst of the January 25 Revolution with me. Lucie is at least as dedicated to all things Egyptian as I am; probably most of our friends would say even more so. I talked to Lucie at length about everything in this book. Lucie has her own interests in writing and teaching about revolution. This was her second revolution—her first was the Velvet Revolution in 1989. I will leave it to her, when she eventually writes more personal reflections on revolution than she has thus far, to reveal which of her two revolutions she considers more important. But while Lucie is a revolution veteran compared to me, I am pretty sure that prior to 2011 it had also never occurred to her to write about such events. We started reading, thinking, and talking about revolution together, and it is not an exaggeration to say that we reached a point at which we realized that the origin of ideas or opinions has became blurred. But one thing that is clear is that this book would not have been written without Lucie's constant encouragement, intellectual energy, and companionship.

My most important Egyptian interlocutors have all been anonymized. I will not unanonymize them by mentioning their names here. Some of them were hostile to the revolution, some indifferent, and some enthusiastically in favor of it. From those who were against the revolution or ambivalent about it, I learned the value of perspective. I believe the book benefits immensely from not having restricted myself to a bubble of activists and like-minded people. Those who did support the revolution taught me more than I can express. I am honored to have been present at and sometimes a minor participant in endless conversations about what was happening, what *should* be happening and often wasn't, and what events and personalities meant in particular situations. A number of my prorevolution friends were not just infinitely better attuned to the nuances of Egyptian politics than I could ever hope to be but were also much better read in political theory and better able than me to place the January 25 Revolution in the history of revolutions generally. My prorevolution circle in Cairo provided crucial moral and intellectual support. I would not have attempted to write this book without their support.

In the 2010–11 academic year I was in Cairo on an American Research Center Postdoctoral Fellowship, and I remained an ARCE affiliate in the 2011–12 academic year, when I was on sabbatical from Oxford. The purpose of the ARCE fellowship was to conduct research on the history of mass media in Egypt. While these years in Egypt did help lay the groundwork for my history of mass media project, publication has been greatly delayed, first by the turmoil of the revolution, and then by my subsequent efforts to write about it while my experience was still immediate. I have to confess with some shame that my initial thought was that I could write a "quickie" book on the revolution, and then get more seriously back to my "real" research. Clearly I was not cut out for such a task. However, ARCE did provide an excellent community of fellow academics whose research was affected in varying degrees by the events of 2011. Djodi Deutsch, ARCE's academic coordinator, deserves particular praise for keeping the center running smoothly through incredibly trying times.

Numerous colleagues and students overlapped with my stay in Cairo during 2011 and 2012. Jessica Winegar's intellectual brilliance and steadfast friendship were indispensable, particularly in the early months of the revolution. Our sons, Jan and Zayd, learned revolutionary chants together when they weren't playing at the Fun Tots nursery. Sinem Adar, Kira Allmann, Mohamed Bamyeh, Chihab El Khachab, Mohamed Elshahed, Dan Gilman, Elizabeth Holt, Aaron Jakes, Laurence Deschamps Laporte, Mark LeVine, Margaret Litvin, Yasmin Moll, Hussein Omar, Carolyn Ramzy, Sarah Smierciak, Nicholas Simcik-Arese, and Eric Schewe all shared the experience of conducting research in revolutionary conditions, and conversations with all of them contributed in various ways to my own research. Khaled Fahmy was seemingly everywhere in my two years in Cairo, in the actual world, in the virtual sphere, and through his incredibly brave writing and appearances in Egyptian media. My colleagues in Oxford Philip Robins, Eugene Rogan, Avi Shlaim, and Michael Willis were scheduled to take a Middle East Centre field trip to Cairo in the spring of 2011. Revolutionary turmoil pushed that visit back to February 2012, and when they did come their presence provided entry at a crucial moment in the revolution to a number of institutions and their associated perspectives that I would not have experienced on my own.

A number of academic conferences and conference panels between 2011 and 2017 provided opportunities to present early drafts of material that ended up in this book. Dozens of conference participants offered perceptive comments on my papers and enlightening perspectives through their own. They are too numerous to mention, but the organizers of these conferences at least deserve special thanks. They are Reem Abou-El-Fadl, Gianpaolo Baiocchi,

Paula Chakravartty, Julia Elyachar, Farha Ghannam, Sune Haugbolle (on two occasions), Neil Ketchley, Marwan Kraidy, Marc Lynch, Flagg Miller, Srirupa Roy, Judith Scheele, Andrew Shryock, Przemysław Turek, Jessica Winegar, and Madeline Zilfi.[1]

Several colleagues have read all or some parts of the book at various stages. Jessica Winegar and Gregory Starrett read the manuscript in full and gave crucial and extremely insightful input that greatly improved the final product. I greatly benefitted from Reem Abou-El-Fadl's reading of an early version of chapter 3. Reem also provided crucial translation advice on a crucial passage. Christa Salamandra's research and publications on *muslsalat* were an inspiration for chapter 8, and her comments on the first draft of the chapter were helpful in developing it into a chapter. Andreas Bandak and Lindsay Whitfield gave critical input to an early version of some of chapter 10. Sune Haugbolle, Bjørn Thomassen, and Miriyam Aouragh made incisive comments on the conference presentation version of that paper. Quite a few of my own students also gave detailed trial-run readings to early- and late-stage chapters. These included Miriam Berger, Krystel De Chiara, Oscar Edell, Calum Humphreys, Sarah Mohamed, and Nicholas Salter, each of whom read and critically analyzed portions of the book. This was immensely helpful in the long process of revising the text. Marwa Farag in particular had a sharp eye for both detail and general arguments and helped translate some lines in chapter 6 that I found difficult.

Several chapters evolved from articles or edited volume chapters that have been published previously. These are "The Iconic Stage: Martyrologies and Performance Frames in the 25 January Revolution" in chapter 3 (Armbrust 2015); "Sally Zahran: Ikunat al-Thaura" and "The Ambivalence of Martyrs and the Counter-revolution" in chapter 4 (Armbrust 2012a; 2012b); "The Trickster in the January 25th Revolution" in chapter 9 (Armbrust 2013); and "Trickster Defeats the Revolution: Egypt as the Vanguard of the New Authoritarianism" in chapter 10 (Armbrust 2017).

Finally, I must acknowledge the grim context of my book. I have no doubt whatsoever that revolution was the only choice that Egyptians who were not hardened by cynicism or ground down by circumstances could have taken in 2011. I have no doubt that the rest of the world should have learned from the Egyptian experience that it was time for profound changes in the global political order. And I have no doubt that the January 25 Revolution was defeated, helping to propel the ascendancy of exactly the political trends that the world can no longer afford. The agents of this defeat—the capitalist global superelites who can never have enough, who cynically use any means necessary to amass more wealth, and the political Tricksters they fund and enable—are responsible for a coming apocalypse. We are on the brink of mass extinctions that will include homo sapiens in a century, give or take a couple of decades. It may be that by 2011 the window to preventing a catastrophic future was already closed.

Or maybe 2011 was the last-gasp moment for us to choose a different path. We will never know for sure. What is beyond question now, in 2018 as I write these words, is that the window has been slammed shut. My son Jan, three at the beginning of the revolution, who once sat on my shoulders in the midst of vast crowds yelling *tahya al-thauwra*—long live the revolution—faces a dark future. Our responsibility for his predicament is variable. We should have no doubt that the titans of capitalism bear the most guilt for destroying the world. The rest of us should be angry. *Tahya al-thauwra!*

NOTE ON TRANSLITERATION

ARABIC TERMS HAVE BEEN TRANSLITERATED using a simplified version of the *International Journal of Middle Eastern Studies* conventions. I have not marked long vowels or emphatic consonants, but I have differentiated between the *hamza* (') and *'ayn* ('). I have also accommodated Egyptian colloquialisms where appropriate.

THIS TIME LINE gives a skeleton of events from just before the onset of the revolution up to the Rab'a Massacre in 2013. It is by no means a comprehensive list of events but rather focuses on key dates and incidents mentioned in my narrative.

2010

> June 6: Murder of Khaled Said by the police in Alexandria; subsequent formation of the Facebook group "We Are All Khaled Said," a major organizational stream of the revolution.
>
> December 5: Conclusion of Egyptian parliamentary elections; Mubarak's National Democratic Party (NDP) takes 420 of 518 seats, leading to widespread anger at the NDP's dominance.

2011

> January 1: Terrorist bombing of the Qadisayn Church in Alexandria; twenty-three dead and dozens injured; widespread suspicion of Mubarak regime complicity or deliberate negligence.
>
> January 14: The fall of the Ben Ali regime in Tunisia.
>
> January 25: Yaum al-Ghadab (the Day of Anger); nominally a protest against Minister of Interior Habib al-'Adli on the advent of 'Id al-Shurta (Police Day). Quick escalation to revolution against the Mubarak regime.
>
> January 28: Gum'at al-Ghadab (the Friday of Anger); a much larger mobilization against the Mubarak regime; countrywide protests.
>
> January 29: As a concession to the protestors Mubarak appoints head of Egyptian General Intelligence Services Omar Suleiman as his vice president, and Minister of Civil Aviation Ahmad Shafiq as prime minister.
>
> January 30: The Egyptian army takes control of the cities.
>
> February 1: Mubarak addresses the nation in an effort to quell the ongoing mass protests against his regime.
>
> February 2: The Battle of the Camel; ununiformed regime supporters attempt to drive the protestors out of Tahrir Square; a pitched battle takes place throughout the night; by the morning of the third it is apparent that the regime's counterattack has failed.
>
> February 6: Publication by the newspaper *al-Masry al-Youm* of a full-page feature on the martyrs of the revolution.

February 11: Mubarak resigns; governing power transferred to the Egyptian Armed Forces; Minister of Defense Muhammad Hussein Tantawi becomes interim ruler; Ahmad Shafiq is acting prime minister.

February 25: Gum'at al-Tathir (the Friday of Purification); mass demonstration in Tahrir Square.

March 3: Ahmad Shafiq resigns the prime ministership; Essam Sharaf appointed interim prime minister by Tantawi.

March 9: First clearing of Tahrir Square protestors by the military; protestors tortured in Egyptian Museum; "virginity tests" carried out on female protestors under the orders of Supreme Council for the Armed Forces (SCAF) member 'Abd al-Fattah al-Sisi.

March 19: Constitutional Referendum approves changes to the Egyptian constitution; first demonstration of Muslim Brotherhood and Islamist power in open elections.

April 6: Gum'at al-Muhakima wal-Tathir (the Friday of Judgment and Purification); a large demonstration attended by twenty-one uniformed army officers in support of the revolution.

April–June: Growing dissention between Islamist and non-Islamist revolutionary forces; increasingly open opposition by non-Islamists (and tacitly some of the Islamist youth) to interim rule by the military; increasingly vocal opposition to the military's practice of trying civilians in military courts.

July: Ongoing sit-in in Tahrir Square in the context of disputes within the revolutionary forces over whether elections should come before the writing of a constitution (the Muslim Brotherhood and Salafi position; also the position of SCAF) or the constitution should be written before elections are held (the non-Islamist position).

July 29: Gum'at Iradat al-Sha'b (the Friday of the People's Will), a show of strength by Islamists (nominally the Salafi parties, but possibly with substantial participation by members of the Muslim Brotherhood).

July 31–August 29: Ramadan; a lull in organized protests.

August 14: Publication of proposed "supraconstitutional principles" by Deputy Prime Minister 'Ali Silmi; principles to be agreed on by all political parties and forces prior to the formal writing of a constitution; most controversially, minimal oversight of the armed forces by civilians.

October 9: The Maspero Massacre, death of twenty-eight mostly Coptic protestors and hundreds injured at the hands of the military in front of the Radio and Television Building near Tahrir Square.

November 18: Gum'at al-Matlab al-Wahid (Friday of the Single Demand), mass protest against the Silmi Principles in Tahrir Square; late in the evening after most protestors depart the security forces attempt to clear a sit-in of martyrs' families from the square.

November 19–25: The Battle of Muhammad Mahmud Street; protestors rush back to Tahrir Square upon hearing that the security forces are clearing the sit-in; six-day urban battle against the security forces as protestors try to march on the Ministry of Interior.

November 28, 2011–January 11, 2012: Parliamentary elections across the country in three stages.

December 7: Interim prime minister Essam Sharaf resigns; Tantawi appoints Mubarak-era politician Kamal Ganzuri as prime minister; Ganzuri known to be particularly tough in security matters.

December 8–16: A sit-in forms on the street in front of the Ministerial Offices (Maglis al-Wuzara') a few blocks from Tahrir Square in an effort to prevent Ganzuri from taking up his office, and to protest the deaths of protestors on the Muhammad Mahmud Street the previous month.

December 16: Military forces (not the security forces) brutally clear the Maglis al-Wuzara' sit-in; assassination by an army sniper of Shaykh 'Imad 'Iffat, a prorevolution Azharite scholar and director of fatwas at the Dar al-Ifta' al-Misriyya (the office tasked with issuing official religious opinions). A video of soldiers dragging a female protestor on the ground and exposing her body (the "blue bra incident") goes viral.

December 16–20: Continued clashes between protestors and the military in Tahrir Square and the streets surrounding the Ministry of Interior.

December 23: Gum'at Radd al-I'tbar (the Friday of Restoring Honor) in Tahrir Square; Guma'at al-'Ubur (Friday of the Crossing) in al-'Abbasiyya Square, publicized by prominent counterrevolutionary Taufiq 'Ukasha.

2012

January 11: Conclusion of the parliamentary elections; Muslim Brotherhood's Freedom and Justice Party (FJP) wins 45 percent of the parliamentary seats; Salafis led by Hizb al-Nur receive about 25 percent.

February 1: Massacre of seventy-four Ahly Football Club fans in Port Said; security forces said to be complicit in the incident.

February 2 to about February 9: Demonstrations in the wake of the massacre; another round of street battles in the vicinity of the Ministry of Interior; streets around the ministry blocked off by massive concrete walls.

June 14: Supreme Constitutional Court rules the parliamentary election invalid, parliament dissolved.

May 23–June 17: Presidential elections in two multistage rounds; no immediate announcement of a winner at the conclusion of the voting.

June 24: Announcement by the Egyptian Electoral Commission that FJP candidate Muhammad Morsy has narrowly defeated old regime representative Ahmad Shafiq in the presidential election.

June 30: Muhammad Morsy sworn in as president in Tahrir Square.

August 12: Minister of Defense Muhammad Hussein al-Tantawi ordered to retire by Muhammad Morsy; SCAF member 'Abd al-Fattah al-Sisi appointed in his place.

November 22: Morsy issues a constitutional declaration arrogating all governmental powers to himself; the stated purpose of the declaration is to protect the ongoing writing of a new constitution by an Islamist-dominated Constituent Assembly; powers to be devolved back to parliament and judiciary upon ratification of a constitution.

December 5: Clashes between non-Islamist protestors and members of the Muslim Brotherhood outside the Presidential Palace; death of several protestors on both sides; conflicting narratives of how the clashes started and who initiated them.

December 15–22: Constitutional referendum in two stages; constitution approved by 64 percent.

2013

March–June: Increasing attacks on Muslim Brotherhood and FJP institutions and property; coordination and funding of the attacks alleged by members of the Muslim Brotherhood but denied by non-Islamists, who claim that all attacks were spontaneous expressions of antibrotherhood sentiment.

April 28: Formal founding of the Tamarrud (Rebellion) movement; collection of signatures demanding a new presidential election; calls for large demonstration against the Morsy regime to take place on June 30. Tamarrud later found to be clearly linked to military and old regime elements from the beginning.

June 30: Massive Tamarrud demonstration takes place with the blessings of the security forces and military.

July 3: Coup against Muhammad Morsy; 'Abd al-Fattah al-Sisi takes power.

July 26: Massive pro-Sisi demonstration takes place in Tahrir Square after al-Sisi asks the public to give him a mandate (*tafwid*) "to fight terror."

August 14: Clearing of pro-Morsy sit-ins in Rab'al-'Adawiyya and Nahda Squares; around a thousand Muslim Brotherhood supporters killed; widespread sectarian violence throughout the country for several days.

THE "LAST DAY OF THE REVOLUTION"?

Long ago we said to the tyrant: freedom has to come
"Liberta" was destined

> —From "Hurriyya," song of the Ahly Ultras

IT WAS VERY HOT ON June 24, 2012, the day that the results of the second round of Egypt's first postrevolution presidential election would be revealed. The announcement would nominally serve as a capstone of the tumultuous events that had begun the year before. The election had concluded a week earlier, but the Electoral Commission had left the country hanging, with no declaration of a winner. Unsurprisingly the entire country was aflame with rumors. Initial indications from the polling places were that Muhammad Morsy of the Muslim Brotherhood's Freedom and Justice Party had won. But the numbers were compiled by FJP observers, and hence discounted by many. Others were sure that legal challenges to the election process lodged by both Morsy and his opponent Ahmad Shafiq would result in a victory for Shafiq, and hence a return to the prerevolution rule of Mubarak's National Democratic Party. As the days wore on without an announcement, suspicions of a stitch-up in favor of the old regime grew. Why else should it take so long? Supporters of Morsy nervously occupied Tahrir Square. Counterdemonstrations promoted by Taufiq 'Ukasha, the archdemagogue of the counterrevolution, took shape in the northeast Cairo neighborhood of Madinat Nasr, at the foot of the *minassa*—"the podium"—where Anwar al-Sadat was assassinated by Islamists in 1981. Two days before the announcement, a Friday, was a day of dueling demonstrations, and the vast crowd egged on by 'Ukasha in support of Shafiq may well have been larger than the pro-Morsy crowd in Tahrir Square.

Whichever candidate won, it seemed that violence might occur. Consequently when it became certain that the announcement would be made on the twenty-fourth, the downtown Cairene preschool that my five-year-old son attended told me they would close early. I picked our son up dutifully at 1 p.m., and not knowing what else to do, we went to a café to watch the announcement on television. Our venue of choice was in the Bursa district, just down the street from the apartment we had been living in since August 2010. Bursa, named for the Egyptian stock exchange, was a pedestrianized area said to be a popular location for secular activists. Our favorite establishment was in an alley between the Mat'am al-Birins (Prince Restaurant) and a walled-off parking lot. We sat beneath a mural of famous January 25 Revolution martyrs and waited.

Somewhat to our surprise, we had to wait quite a long time. The crowd of our fellow elections spectators was large. Tables were set up as if for an important football match, which is exactly what it felt like at first. The people around us, some of whom we knew slightly, were festive or at least restless, fearful that the announcement would not name the candidate they preferred. Who they preferred was complicated. The second round of the presidential election featured an unknowable but undoubtedly immense amount of negative voting. Whichever candidate won would clearly be riding a wave of "not Shafiq" or "not Morsy" votes. We were unsure what the reaction of the people around us would be once the announcement was made.

On the television Faruq Sultan, the chair of the Supreme Presidential Election Commission, droned on for a good hour or more. The crowd grew fidgety and then just quiet. Sultan read very clumsily through the verdict on each and every one of Morsy's and Shafiq's challenges. Finally, with no change of tone and no build-up, Sultan announced that the winner was . . . Muhammad Morsy. The crowd of liberal activists around us erupted in wild cheers and joyful embraces. At that moment there was no question whatsoever who the revolutionary candidate was in that bitterly disappointing confrontation between Morsy's FJP and Shafiq's shadow representation of Mubarak's NDP: "not Shafiq." Our table was next to a group of Ahly Ultras—fanatical partisans of the Ahly football (soccer) club. The Ultras had become politicized against the regime in the years leading up to the revolution and had thrown themselves into battle against the state's security forces, decisively in some of the key early battles. Immediately after they cheered wildly at Morsy's victory over Shafiq the Ultras launched into a chant: *Yasqut yasqut hukm al-murshid*—"down with the rule of the [Supreme] Guide [of Morsy's Muslim Brotherhood]," an anti–Muslim Brotherhood slogan chanted in their victory celebration of the Muslim Brotherhood's candidate. Then the Ultras sang their iconic song, which had been heard frequently in demonstrations and gatherings over the past two years.

> Long ago we said to the tyrant: freedom has to come
> "Liberta" was destined
> Government, tomorrow you'll know
> You'll be cleansed at the hands of the people
> The tables are turned tonight
> They say trouble is in our blood
> How could we demand our rights?
> Stupid regime, understand my demand:
> Freedom . . . Freedom . . . Freedom . . . Freedom!
> I have no more fear of death
> Amid your terror my heart is clear

The sun will rise anew
Take our security, destroy our homes
That was before, when we were silent
The dream is finally near
What could the regime do?
The end is here
Understand this: leave now, the tyrant falls
Freedom . . . Freedom . . . Freedom . . . Freedom! ("Ihda' li-Shuhada'"
    2015)

The song was always moving. Over the past year and a half I had occasionally watched Ultras practicing it in the *saniyya* (the tray—the normally grassy spot in the middle of Tahrir Square) during sit-ins. It was doubly moving in this bittersweet victory celebration for the man that most of them thought was the second-worst candidate in the race.

Later I walked around downtown, of course to Tahrir Square, which was full of men (almost exclusively; there were very few women indeed) who were more genuinely enthusiastic about the election of Morsy, and not just delighted that the old regime's candidate was not allowed to steal the election. Here the chants were simpler and more visceral: *Morsyyy Morsy . . . Morsyyy Morsy . . .* Just Morsy's name chanted as if to an imaginary wedding procession. On and on in wild abandoned joy at a victory that nobody imagined could happen eighteen months ago. I wended my way from Tahrir to my home in Abdin. On Muhammad Farid Street opposite the Bank Misr headquarters I witnessed the passing of an astonishing garbage truck covered with over-the-moon Morsy supporters, waving Egyptian flags and still chanting the rhythmic and now familiar *Morsyyy Morsy . . .* I could not help thinking of the day after the regime fell, when Tahrir Square was full of earnest young middle-class men and women (more women than men on that occasion) with plastic trash bags and brooms, "taking out the trash" from the old regime, as one of my colleagues had astutely described it (Winegar 2011). The impulse to clean up, some of which was orchestrated by Islamists even in February 2011, had an unmistakable resonance with Morsy's "first 100 days" campaign platform, a conspicuous element of which was to remove uncollected trash from the increasingly disheveled revolutionary Cairo. But the celebration garbage truck I was seeing had another resonance inscribed on it. A small "Ros Roca" was legible on its side. Ros Roca—or Ros Roca Envirotec—is a private Spanish company apparently hired by the Egyptian government to remove and hopefully recycle trash, thereby threatening the livelihood of the *zabbalin* (trash collector) families who had formerly done the job. Contracting trash collection to private foreign companies was part of the economic liberalization programs that made the Mubarak regime so unpopular. Most observers expected Morsy's FJP to maintain or even intensify Mubarak's privatization agenda. The truck went by. I went home.

People often recount their "where was I on the first day of the revolution" stories. This was my story of the last day of the revolution. Or so President Morsy hoped. Actually, I had my doubts even then.

MARTYRS AND TRICKSTERS

CHAPTER 1

Introduction

REVOLUTION AS LIMINAL CRISIS

INITIALLY THE JANUARY 25 REVOLUTION meant just the first eighteen days after the beginning of the uprising culminating in the fall of the Mubarak regime. Tahrir Square in those first eighteen days was often referred to by participants in the revolution as a "utopia." A better way to describe the square in those extraordinary days is that it was a heterotopia, which we can think of as a spatialized formulation of liminality. Liminality allows us to connect revolution to a wide range of phenomena, both transparently political and, in less obvious ways not perceived by either observers or participants in the revolution, as politically motivated. Liminality also sheds light on the performative idioms and frames of revolution. Most importantly, liminality gives us a conceptual grasp of the potentially schismogenetic aspects of revolution: revolution can very easily result in unintended and even monstrous consequences.

Many other books about the January 25 Revolution are in fact also about what came after the "utopia" that so famously characterized the first eighteen days of the revolution, and often also in large measure about what came *before* the uprising, and hence about the conditions that made it inevitable. I am agnostic about the question of the revolution's inevitability. This is not to say that I dispute that there were material causes to the initial uprising that led to revolution. The grievances that led to revolution, largely formulated in negative terms rather than in positive demands, were undoubtedly incubated by the effects of economic liberalization in the three decades before 2011. Still, for an uprising to turn into a revolution so many things had to happen in exactly the right sequence and intensity that the question of causation is ultimately unanswerable, which is not to say that many scholars have not devoted themselves precisely to questions of causation, and from a wide variety of motivations.[1] The position taken here is that revolutions are unique occurrences,[2] but that once a revolution is accepted as such, it can be understood as *liminal crisis—*

entry into a social and political void, a heterotopic space, from which there is no apparent exit. Here the question of causation is secondary to seeking to understand what happened in that space.

I wrote this book primarily because I found the revolution inspiring, despite its ultimate defeat. I was in Egypt from October 2010 until August 2012 to research the history of Egyptian mass media. Many aspects of the January 25 Revolution were consistent with my long-term research interests centering on mass media and popular culture. My first trip to Egypt was in 1981, when I worked on an archaeological dig outside Alexandria. As an impressionable twenty-year-old I believed the social contradictions I thought I was witnessing made Egypt ripe for revolution. For a naive and not well-traveled young man, these contradictions were grounded in what seemed to me stark contrasts in wealth and poverty overlain with a tension between "Westernized" and "authentic" cultures. My simplistic views were underpinned by all the haphazard geopolitical discourse I could absorb, and liberally spiced with American panic at the rise of Islamism in the wake of the Iranian Revolution. A week after I returned to the United States from the dig, Anwar al-Sadat was assassinated. The revolution seemed to be starting! But then Mubarak became president and carried the country inexorably along the same free-market-oriented political path as Sadat. I learned not to trust my initial impressions, removed "revolution" from my analytical horizon, and set off on my own trajectory toward anthropology, a path that would, I hoped, enable me to better understand Egypt. I traveled to Egypt often starting in the mid-1980s. In my 2010–12 stay I was there to research the history of Egyptian mass media, but the revolution consumed me during those two years in which I observed it at close range. The political-economic roots of the revolution were in fact characterized by incredible disparities in wealth and power—my initial impressions were not entirely wrong about that. But the liminal void that opened up in 2011 deeply implicated my own society and government in ways I could not imagine in 1981. The iniquitous and antidemocratic effects of an evolving neoliberal order were more than an indispensible background to the January 25 Revolution. Aside from the specific "Washington consensus" market-oriented policy recommendations imposed on countries of the Global South, the neoliberal order is increasingly shared internationally. Neoliberalism makes the middle strata of the United States precarious just as surely as it does in the United Kingdom, the country that had been my place of residence over the past decade and a half. We had not yet rebelled against it as strongly as Egypt did in 2011, and I do not know if revolution *can* effectively oppose this order. The medium-term outcome of the January 25 Revolution has been grim. The old neoliberal order has been replaced with an even worse authoritarianism lacking even a fig leaf of political or cultural liberalism. Everywhere the trend is the same. In Britain the structured precarity of the middle class has been intensified by the vote to leave the European Union. America provided a launching pad for the would-be authoritarian Donald Trump, who gleefully betrays the precariat that brought him to office, to their unwitting applause. One encounters inexorable political and economic decline in revolution, as in Egypt, or decline without it, as in Britain, the United States, and really everywhere else. One can and should choose to go down fighting—whatever that might mean by the standards of one's time and place. But sustainable victories are few and far between. The downward spiral of the entire world appears irreversible. Nonetheless I admired then, and continue to admire, the impulse demonstrated in Egypt's revolution to stand at least for a moment and say "enough." Having witnessed this courageous and historic act, I had to write about it. I think it would have been irresponsible not to.

This is an ethnography of revolution, but not of revolutionaries. I knew and met many people who participated in the revolution, but I was not in any way "embedded" within a revolutionary movement. I attended numerous protests and sit-ins as an observer, and I was also attentive to the wider expressive culture that interpreted the revolution in mediated works of popular culture, mobilizational political art, and propaganda. But I also moved in circles that were less enthusiastic about the revolution, or even hostile to it.

I have three objectives in this book. First, I want to establish liminality as a productive concept for understanding revolutions. Liminality allows for flexible articulation between the political and social, artistic, or cultural spheres and is also attentive to the spatial dimensions of performance. My second objective stems from this last point. I want to explore the revolution through its spatial dimensions at a variety of scales, including the political-economic structuring of space throughout the country (and particularly in Cairo), the framing of Tahrir Square as a performance space both materially and historically, and some of the performances that were enacted in the course of the revolution. A thread that runs through much of the book is martyrdom, specifically its use in political performances. This was not entirely intentional; I only really became aware of how substantial martyrdom was in my notes, photographs, and memories when I was nearing the end of the first draft of my text. Martyrdom of course is an inflection on rituals of death. Ritual involves a departure from normative space into a space of liminality, and in that sense the ritual form lies at the core of the book. But I believe martyrdom also mirrors the phenomenon of liminal crisis more fundamentally. In the revolution, rituals of martyrdom, including the proliferation of representations of martyrs in urban space, consisted more of a suspension within liminality than an act of closure, as a funeral and burial in a cemetery would be.

My third and final objective is to explore the emergence of political Tricksters. In the uncomfortable condition of protracted liminality Tricksters—beings at home in liminality, common in folklore, mythology, and literature—can become dangerous in politics. I explore Trickster politics first through the rise of a counterrevolutionary propagandist, and subsequently through the eventual defeat of the revolution by the military, headed by 'Abd al-Fattah al-Sisi. Very likely Trickster politics is more common historically than we have previously recognized. Bringing liminality into the analysis of politics affords us a new and productive way to understand authoritarianism and populism. Moreover, I want to raise some questions at the end of the book about how liminality is increasingly structured in ways that generate Trickster politicians in nonrevolutionary conditions. The structuring of liminality as precarity enables the rise of Trickster politics on a global scale.

The book is organized in a roughly chronological sequence running from the beginning of the revolution in 2011 through to the consolidation of the Sisi regime in 2014. In terms of the book's thematic structure, the first chapter (or what remains of it from this point on) outlines the formal characteristics of liminality and its relevance to politics. Chapters 2 and 3 explore the performance frames of the revolution. Chapters 4–7 examine mobilizational rhetorics of martyrdom in a number of settings. Chapter 8 serves as a transition point between the martyrdom chapters and the Trickster politics chapters, by examining the mass-mediated framework of the single most violent episode in the revolution, namely the Rab'a Massacre. I argue that Rab'a was both an outcome of revolutionary politics, as well as preformed media discourses about the nature of the Muslim Brotherhood. Chapters 9 and 10 introduce and develop the theme of Trickster politics, starting from a relatively intimate scale and ending at national and international scales.

Liminality

The book explores revolution through the concept of liminality, which is understood as a condition characteristic of all transitions between normative social states. We depart from "normality"; enter a liminal state in which different possibilities can be entertained, a kind of subjunctive state; and then reenter a new normality. Entry into liminality is accompanied initially by a kind of euphoria, which the anthropologist Victor Turner dubbed "communitas"—a state in which one feels a deep sense of connection to everyone else undergoing the transition. Liminality is potentially dangerous, because the usual conventions that structure social relations are thrown open to contingency. Ritual (and sometimes other forms of social conventions) contain and manage the dangers inherent in transitions that we expect. The premise of my book is that the social form characteristic of transitions we expect can also help us to frame and interpret transitions that we do not expect, and for which no conventions or rituals designed to contain the dangers of liminality exist. Revolution is one such unforeseen transition.

As I am an anthropologist, the revolution made me think about liminality particularly at a moment in October 2011, when the "utopia" of Tahrir was becoming a memory, and all political outcomes still seemed possible though no trajectory was clear. I suspect most anthropologists will immediately know why I say this, though not many of them have articulated the idea.[3] To speak of revolution as liminality may sound odd to nonacademics, and to academics whose professional brief normally includes the study of revolutions, particularly historians, political scientists, and political sociologists—unlike anthropologists, who have given limited attention to revolutions, though much attention to phenomena associated with them.[4]

I invoke liminality because Egypt had either initiated or been plunged into a political passage when it left the Mubarak era, and this passage can be productively understood through Turner's "ritual process" (1977)—a passage out of normative social relations into a state of liminality, followed by reintegration of the ritual initiand into normativity, but in a transformed social state. In the narrowest terms rituals are rites of passage that require masters of ceremonies or at least accepted conventions. But the important aspect of ritual in this context is not ritual qua ritual (and there are many other ways to understand ritual than through Turner's approach).[5] It is rather that the ritual process carries greater social significance than a narrow focus on rites of passage marking birth, coming of age, marriage, or death, for example, might suggest. Rites of passage and rituals more generally have masters of ceremony not because there is an unwritten "rule" that for a ritual to be a ritual it has to have them, but precisely because liminality is *dangerous* and must therefore be managed if possible. While techniques for managing liminality vary tremendously across cultures, liminal conditions are independent of ritual, and the function of a master of ceremonies is incidental to the fact that transitions involving liminality are inevitable. Sometimes transitions manifest as "critical events" (Das 1996, 6), which are then institutionalized in collective memory. But such institutionalization happens only by means of a passage through liminality. Institutionalization is the end point of the process, the point at which initiands have *been* transformed, not the process of transformation. Critical events can include political cataclysms, but also natural disasters. Bjørn Thomassen, for example, suggests that the Lisbon earthquake of 1755, or to be more precise, the doubt and fear left in its wake, changed the course of European modernity by pushing Immanuel Kant to organize his philosophy of reason as "a heroic struggle against the chaos of the surrounding world" (Thomassen 2014, 99). The January 25 Revolution, a thoroughly unnatural event but certainly one that will be preserved in memory (despite the postrevolution state's policy of trying to erase it from the historical record), is an instance of a passage through liminality lacking a conventionalized conclusion. Such a lack is not a given in political revolutions, but it often is, at least in their initial stages. Because revolutions happen in modern states, the perpetuation of a "liminal crisis" (Thomassen 2012, 687–90), an uncloseable state of liminality, is intolerable, whether experienced as "incongruous" or "inappropriate" (Foucault 2005 [1970], xix), or as an "uncanny present" (Bryant 2016). The questions of who *seizes* the master-of-ceremonies role and how they do so are key issues for understanding revolution. If we see the January 25 Revolution as a political passage comprehensible through an unmediated liminal phase, then at the point of this chapter's scene-setting moment, October 2011, it was not clear where the country was headed. The feeling of transition was everywhere and inescapable. Questions of "how does this end" (Sabea 2013) were on everyone's mind.

The term "communitas" could have been invented to describe Tahrir Square in the first eighteen days of the revolution, up to the time of Mubarak's abdication. It was Turner who first conceptualized communitas as a general utopic euphoria that temporarily dissolves hierarchical distinctions (Turner 1977, 96). He introduced communitas to the anthropological lexicon in the 1960s. It is simply Latin for "community," but he was looking for a slightly displaced term to distinguish a characteristic social modality of the ritual process from the everyday sense of community as an "area of common living" (Turner 1977, 96). The idea was that communitas was precisely an *uncommon* experience. The concept must have been on many anthropologists' minds in the early days of the revolution. Anthropologist Hanan Sabea, for example, paraphrased Turner in describing Tahrir as "a time out of time" excised from the ordinary and the known (2013). She did not explicitly attribute this turn of phrase to Turner, but his understanding of liminality was predicated precisely on separation from the ordinary, and Tahrir's capacity for "making it possible to imagine other modalities of being" in the political and social spheres (Sabea 2013) was redolent of communitas.

Turner's communitas drew on previously underappreciated insights of French anthropologist Arnold van Gennep, who wrote a classic work in 1909, *The Rites of Passage* (2004 [1909]), which first elaborated a tripartite framework that Turner revived some sixty years later and reframed explicitly as a "ritual process" for negotiating transitions (Turner 1977). Bjørn Thomassen, an anthropologist working to reassess the legacies of Turner and van Gennep, describes the ritual process as more like the discovery of a pattern that is "both culture-dependent and universal" (Thomassen 2014, 5) than like a theory (Thomassen 2014, 2–3; 37–38). Anthropology makes few claims of universality, as the discipline is on the whole dedicated to exploring cultural variation. The ritual process is universal insofar as moments of transition are inevitable for all humans and must therefore be elaborated in all social systems (Thomassen 2014, 4). The ritual process, with liminality at its core, is a highly flexible form that neatly sidesteps certain of the dilemmas that anthropology and other social sciences have historically faced. It is not prone to fall into false distinctions between individuals and Durkheimian "collective representations." It potentially accommodates scales of social performance ranging from the intimately personal to the "civilizational." Nor were the intrinsically Eurocentric evolutionary assumptions characteristic of Durkheimian sociology or Marxism an element of the ritual process as van Gennep had envisioned it (Thomassen 2014, 26–27).

This way of thinking about liminality was largely out of fashion during most of my life as an anthropologist.[6] Van Gennep was a minor footnote in graduate anthropology core courses, and Turner was caricatured, misleadingly, as a warmed-over Durkheimian/Marxist functionalist even though his encounter with van Gennep's work in 1963 was actually the point at which he decisively *broke* with British social anthropology (Thomassen 2014, 78–79).[7] In a comparative vein, one notes that Foucault (who was and remains an indispensable source of theory for many) paralleled Turner in making a distinction between the liminal phase of a ritual or social drama (heterotopia in the case of Foucault) and a state of structured normality. For Foucault, heterotopias

> have a function in relation to all the space that remains. This function unfolds between two extreme poles. Either their role is to create a space of illusion that exposes every real space, all the sites inside of which human life is partitioned, as still more illusory. . . . Or else, on the contrary, their role is to create a space that is other, another real space, as perfect, as meticulous, as well arranged as ours is messy, ill constructed, and jumbled. (1986, 27)[8]

Turner, for his part, was by the 1950s already half a step outside of the work of his colleagues (Turner 1996 [1957]), many of whom actually were Marxist-inflected Durkheimians. It was a very different Turner who collaborated with Richard Schechner in the field of theatrical performance in the 1970s, or who argued in the 1980s through reading the philosophy of Wilhelm Dilthey that anthropology should be about trying to understand the nature of human experience. Yet his notion of "anti-structure" (a synonym for liminality in the ritual process) was written off as "the dialectical complement to structure" (Kelly and Kaplan 1990, 139) at a time when the discipline was in the process of discarding structure conceived as a totalizing phenomenon.[9]

By contrast Foucault's concept of heterotopia, presented in a brief but heavily cited essay titled "Of Other Spaces" (Foucault 1986),[10] has no formal connection to van Gennep's or Turner's formulations of liminality. But it serves well as a kind of secondary frame of reference that will be more familiar to some than liminality, given the long eclipse of Turner and van Gennep in academic writing. Foucault was emphatically not a theorist of liminality, and so putting him in this context might also seem odd at first glance. Yet if he had written "Of Other Spaces" as a term paper he might well have been accused of plagiarizing both van Gennep and Turner. He proposed six "principles of heterotopia" (Foucault 1986, 24–27), many of which had obvious harmonies with liminality as understood by van Gennep and Turner. Heterotopia is, first, universal, like the phenomenon of liminality and the form in which it is mediated; second, a heterotopia is a space historically subject to change; third, it is a space that can be occupied by multiple incompatible uses (reminiscent of the liminal phase in a rite of passage in which incompatible beings are joined together); fourth, it is linked to "slices in time" both as "repositories for time" such as museums and libraries, and as transitory time, such as festivals (just as the ritual process joins together space and time—both are crucial components of it); fifth, heterotopias "always presuppose a system of opening and closing that both isolates them and makes them penetrable" (almost a paraphrasing of the ritual process without attribution); and sixth, heterotopias "have a function in relation to all the space that remains," which is a way of saying that heterotopic space must be marked off from "normal" space, but without necessarily conceding any taken-for-granted quality to what we (or our informants) consider normal.

Foucault unsurprisingly put different emphases on his own formulation of liminality than van Gennep and Turner, and this is what makes putting the two concepts together productive. The concepts of heterotopia and liminality are complementary, each translatable to the terms of the other, but also each with different capacities. Heterotopia is a spatial concept that articulates with Foucault's conception of the power/knowledge relation as distributed through the subdivision of space, evident in everything from medicalization to urban planning. The ritual process is social, but only comprehensible through spatialization. It is predicated on time and movement through space. The ritual process is more performative, but less intrinsically connected to power than Foucault's heterotopia, yet it lends itself very well to political dynamics ranging from protest repertoires to graffiti.

How to Research a Revolution

My dilemma in 2011 was that I had experienced communitas in the early days of the revolution and heard people reiterate it endlessly thereafter. Some had been there, and others had not, but all of them acknowledged its power. It was that overpowering sense of the extraordinary that first made me want to write about the revolution. But very quickly after the fall of the Mubarak regime the more notable characteristic of the event was an ongoing state of liminality that was certainly *not* marked by a euphoric bond between all members of society regardless of class, gender, or religion. The revolution seemed like a passage into a liminal void; but not at first, of course, when so many people experienced Tahrir Square as the "recognition . . . of a generalized social bond that has ceased to be and has simultaneously yet to be fragmented into a multiplicity of structural ties" (Turner 1977, 96): the void came when the state of liminality became open ended and the bond was indeed fragmented. As Turner noted in one of his later writings, when the liminal phase of a social drama becomes protracted, a crisis ensues, and consequently "sides are taken and power resources calculated" (Turner 1988, 91). The calculation of resources inevitably requires a return to previous experiences and attempts to recombine them in new forms. The sort of crises he had in mind were precisely civil wars and revolutions—forms of "spontaneous events" writ large, as opposed to predictable "planned events" (Lewis 2013, 10). The inability to reenter a socially consensual state of normality was a striking feature of the January 25 Revolution (and perhaps of revolutions generally). In Foucault's brief essay on heterotopia one finds no glimmer of Turner's concept of communitas—the feeling of euphoria and bondedness that initiands in a ritual feel upon first entering a state of liminality. But more interestingly in this context, one of Foucault's other brief references to the concept of heterotopia, in *The Order of Things*, describes heterotopias as disturbing, "a worse kind of disorder than that of the *incongruous*, the linking together of things that are inappropriate . . . things are 'laid,' 'placed,' 'arranged' in sites so very different from one another that it is impossible to find a place of residence for them, to define a *common locus* beneath them all" (Foucault 2005 [1970], xix).

Some regard the original 1966 *The Order of Things* as a masterpiece of structuralism (Mangilier 2013, 114), which is to say a system in which the meanings of terms resulted from their opposition to other terms. The terms themselves had to be taken as given—a conceptual precondition that tends to preclude consideration of liminality. Turner's ritual process was predicated on the opposite condition: that the categorical boundaries between terms, objects, and the systems formed from relations between them inevitably are transgressed. Transgression requires cultural work precisely because it presents the discomfort, disorientation, and even danger that Foucault alludes to in his brief meditation on heterotopia. Social conventions mediate these dangers when they are predictable. In the context of category transgressions that are unpredictable and protracted (since there may not be a conventionalized means for mediating them) Turner sounds more like Foucault. As he said in one of his later writings, when the liminal phase of a social drama becomes protracted, the euphoria of communitas ends, and a crisis ensues, and consequently those who experience communitas sort themselves into groups, and strife begins (Turner 1988, 91). In many ways the revolution began after the eighteen days of Tahrir communitas ended with the fall of the Mubarak regime.

Broadly speaking the concept of crisis can also be seen as central to history (Koselleck 2006, 371). In this sense crisis signifies "an epochal concept pointing to an exceptionally rare, if not unique, transition period" (Koselleck 2006, 371). The centrality of transition to this mode of historical understanding of crisis resonates with the emphases that van Gennep, Turner, and Thomassen place on liminality, which is marked off from normal time by (or as) precisely a crisis. Crisis is often discussed in terms of "calculable forms of indeterminacy (risk) versus non-calculable forms of indeterminacy (uncertainty) (Roitman 2013, 74). One might transpose these highly abstracted concepts to the more generalized terms of the ritual process. Ritual is a cultural form for managing the calculable (in other words, transitions in social states that are predictable). But the indeterminate is inevitable in the form of such phenomena as natural disasters, war, and of course revolution. The temporality of crisis can be thought of in terms of "critical thresholds" (Bryant 2016, 21–24). We do not normally sense the present, but rather we anticipate an unknown future by implicit reference to past experiences. Anticipation is "a comportment and mode of action oriented towards the future" (Bryant 2016, 25). "Crisis" is what happens when we cannot anticipate the future. In that case we sense the present acutely; we cross a threshold, or a limen (Bryant 2016, 23). Bryant refers to it as an "uncanny present" of a future that *cannot* be anticipated (Bryant 2016, 20). When we find ourselves in such a situation we reach back into our pasts to find orientation, but by definition when we do so we are using the past in a new way. People in crisis reorient themselves through return and repetition (Bryant 2016, 26).

This understanding of crisis resonates in many ways with the ritual process. Events are perceived as such by the crossing of thresholds. The way back to "normal" is not scripted or managed as a ritual, but it does run through the past; not necessarily a "normal past," but possibly past experiences of trauma. Revolution is different. First, it is a form of crisis, but not necessarily experienced as such in the beginning. The "uncanny present" for those who supported the revolution was strongly marked by crossing a threshold, but the initial sensation was of euphoria and communitas, not of fear and anxiety. Of course others may have experienced it precisely as fear and anxiety, but many other phenomena are similarly polyvalent. The second aspect of revolution that differs from many other crisis experiences—and this is more broadly applicable to all parties affected by the event—is that it is protracted, or even open ended. In Egypt once communitas faded, there was no question of immediate reorientation. The postcommunitas process of "calculating power resources" (Turner 1988, 91) may well be a political inflection on what Bryant describes as return and reiteration—new uses of the past in other words.

Turner's ritual process was conceived as a social means for containing uncontrollable forces unleashed in crises, which one can broaden to include other kinds of transformative contexts that also mark off the present by the perception of having crossed a limen. Normally such transformations are elaborately managed precisely because conditions of liminality are unsettling and dangerous. It takes no great leap of imagination to view revolutions as transformative events, but for a revolution to emerge as such, control of the process must be at least thrown into doubt, if not altogether absent. This is not to say that revolutions can occur without the conscious will of agents. The point is rather that revolutions intrinsically require at least a moment of doubt that a definable agent controls events, or that "normality" persists, and the contours of this moment are extremely elastic. In the case of Egypt's January 25 Revolution the moment of doubt initiated by the fall of the Mubarak regime was long; it lasted at least until the coup by 'Abd al-Fattah al-Sisi in the summer of 2013. Whether or not the rise of the Sisi regime really marked the end of the revolution remained a matter of debate for some time. This is not because opposition to his regime continued (though it did among some Islamists and, less openly, in various non-Islamist sectors of society), but because in some ways Sisi himself remained in a liminal position, halfway between the SCAF and the civilian state.

The disciplines most concerned with contemporary revolution—political science and sociology—distinguish structural approaches from process-oriented analyses, the latter allowing for contingent action by social agents, particularly in a "revolutionary situation," which bears some resemblance to what I have called (following Thomassen) a liminal crisis.[11] Not all social scientists would even acknowledge the Egyptian events that unfolded from 2011 to 2013 as a revolution. Theda Skocpol's 1970s vintage definition of social revolutions as "rapid, basic transformations of a society's state and class structures . . . accompanied and in part carried through by class-based revolts from below" (1979, 4) is still viable for some.[12]

Revolution is not necessarily easy to frame anthropologically. The discipline was, for most of its history, "united in its quest to discover the regularities of social life" (Niehaus 2013, 651), or a "science of the ordinary" (Malkki 1997, 89). Attempts to research such matters occurred less often.[13] Anthropological studies directly focusing on revolution as a social category are fairly rare. There is no question of applying for a grant to write an ethnography of a revolution, though one might get funding to pursue other topics in a revolutionary society, or to research the aftermath of revolutionary events, assuming grant-giving agencies, institutional review boards, and departments can be convinced that research is safe and feasible. But while field research *on* revolution might be institutionally difficult, anthropologists sometimes do happen to be doing fieldwork *during* a revolution. Donald Donham, for example, conducted fieldwork in Ethiopia over two decades of revolutionary turmoil. He went to research the political economy of labor in Maale but could hardly avoid the fact that revolution and civil war affected every facet of his informants' lives (Donham 1999).[14] Because of the necessary serendipity of conducting field research on revolutions, anthropological approaches to revolution per se are not highly developed.[15] Anthropology is, however, very attentive to the causes and background of revolutions, particularly in its extensive literature on social movements, secularism, and liberalism.[16] But there are some formidable obstacles to engaging directly with some revolutions, or at least with certain phases of revolutions. Anthropologists work slowly, preferring to embed themselves in field sites for long periods, and this to some degree mitigates against the analysis of sudden events. But whether or not a revolution actually has to be understood as a sudden event is a highly complex issue. By some standards "the revolution" in Egypt lasted for just eighteen days, though this is not of course the standard applied here or in most serious analyses of the January 25 Revolution.

There is one excellent ethnography of the January 25 Revolution, or we can perhaps call it a de facto ethnography of revolution. This is Samuli Schielke's *Egypt in the Future Tense* (Schielke 2015). Schielke does not offer the book as an outright "narrative of the revolution." Indeed, he is ambivalent about whether the events of 2011 and subsequent years even deserve to be called a revolution. *Egypt in the Future Tense* emerged from long-term research focused on the lives of young people, mostly men, in a delta village near Alexandria. The book is in some ways about being pious (or not) in the modern world, but piety is framed as a "grand scheme" among others such as "persons, ideas and powers that are understood to be greater than one's ordinary life, located on a higher plane, distinct from everyday life, and yet relevant as models for living" (Schielke 2015, 13). Schielke's analysis is in large measure about ambiguity in the context of (mostly frustrated) great expectations. The last chapter deals with self-consciously revolutionary young men. But given that the research took place mainly between 2011 and 2013, all grand schemes were heavily inflected by the revolution. *Egypt in the Future Tense* brilliantly evokes both the immense hopes pinned on the revolution as well as the bitter disappointment in its suppression. Unsurprisingly given the book's title, it also articulates with the temporal issues raised in anthropological studies of future-oriented temporality such as Rebecca Bryant's work (2016). In its analysis of the poetics of anticipation *Egypt in the Future Tense* evokes anticipation of a disappointing future, but also the experience of crossing a threshold from normality, "an urgent desire to live in a different world—a sense that needed only the revolution of Tunisia as an example to transform to the realization that rather than coping with the condition of normality, it is, after all, possible to change that condition" (Schielke 2015, 172).

Texts

My goal in this book is to write about the revolution directly. It is a personal account inevitably, but one that articulates with the already extensive literature on the revolution, and one that can be read equally well from any disciplinary perspective. It is in no sense a "classic" ethnography that seeks to keep the analytical frame as close to a group of informants' perspectives as possible. I have deliberately sought to include textual and mass-mediated sources in my narrative, woven into the lives and routines of informants in some cases, but in other cases contextualized with events and higher-level discursive trends.

Such texts (by which I mean also audio-visual productions) often caught my attention simply because they fit into long-term research agendas. For the past twenty-five years I have published on Egyptian media—films, television (both terrestrial broadcasts and satellite-era broadcasts), music, the print media, and digital media—not always strictly as an anthropologist, but sometimes in more historical or political writing.

Some of the texts featured in this work were artistic or literary, and they served to index the politics and class of the people who used them in revolutionary contexts. For example, lines of poetry written by Ahmad Fu'ad Nigm, Amal Dunqul, and Nagib Surur recur at several points in my account of the revolution because they appeared on walls, on Facebook and blog posts, and in political mobilization efforts that made use of the rhetoric of martyrdom. They were figures of the 1970s leftist student movement, with the exception of Nigm, who had been prominent since the late 1960s but (unlike the others) was alive at the beginning of the revolution in 2011. Not everyone who encountered such lines in 2011 "got" the references, but at the same time the reiteration of them expanded their scope. It was not necessary for a millennial Egyptian activist to know that "the flowers that bloomed in the gardens of Egypt" was written by Nigm when he was a political prisoner in 1973 to understand what the line meant when it was attached to the faces of a group of young martyrs to the cause of the revolution. Their faces, often accompanied by Nigm's line of poetry, were reproduced on hundreds of thousands of martyr images ranging from expertly painted street murals to commercial paraphernalia, and always with some trace, whether large or small, of a sentiment to continue the unfinished project of a revolution that had not yet achieved its aims.

Many other kinds of texts can be seen as social "actants" as Latour (2005) would call them. If a kettle, knife, basket, hammer, or bar of soap can be granted agency (Latour 2005, 71) in an actor-network predicated on a sociology of associations, then surely so can a YouTube video. For example, in chapter 5 I describe Kamal Abu Eita, a prominent labor activist, invoking a martyr in a May Day speech in Tahrir Square. The martyr's name was significant because Abu Eita mentioned it within earshot of army officers who were present "standing guard" over the event, and it was precisely the army who killed the young man a week before the speech. I believe that many in the audience (unlike me at the time) understood why Abu Eita was invoking the martyr's name—as an implicit challenge to the military. But I doubt that many of them (possibly none of them) witnessed the killing directly. They knew about it through either seeing YouTube videos documenting the young man's death, or through talking to someone else who had. It was those same YouTube videos that allowed me, much later, to recover the political significance of Abu Eita's statement, which I had recorded on my phone standing in a crowd in which dozens of other people were also recording the speech. Hence this YouTube video, and many others I have cited plus numerous other texts of varying types, can be understood as having a certain agency—they were part of social life, not incidental to it; they were also there on May Day shaping Abu Eita's speech as surely as the glowering red-capped military police looking on and listening. In my book such texts as the implicitly present YouTube video at Abu Eita's May Day speech do double duty, as both social actants in specific circumstances, and also as more conventional sources that others can consult to extend or challenge my interpretations.

Location

Contemporary norms of anthropological fieldwork put greater emphasis on location as a political construct than on sites bounded either geographically or socially (Gupta and Ferguson 1997, 36–37). This book is based on having lived in Cairo during 2011 and most of 2012. Two years before the revolution, my partner, Lucie Ryzova, and I had purchased an apartment in Cairo, just off of Tahrir Square in the neighborhood of Ma'ruf.[17] Just before the revolution began we had purchased another very small flat in Abdin, also on the margins of downtown Cairo, with the intention of using it to store research materials—mainly books and magazines from roughly the 1920s through 1950s, too many to transport to England, and we thought the materials in any case should ideally stay in Egypt. Both apartments were undergoing renovation in 2011–13, and our interactions with the various men who worked in them was often enlightening and valuable.

Our apartments in Cairo were not home in any legal, cultural, or citizenship sense, but neither was Cairo simply an "other" society chosen as a research site because of its maximal difference from "my own" society. I was not in Cairo because of the revolution, but because I have been researching, writing, and teaching the history, politics, popular culture, and mass media of Egypt since the mid-1980s. In the decade prior to the revolution I had been going to Cairo during most of my vacations, as much because I liked Cairo and had friends there as to do research, though it would be untrue to say that friendship and work did not blur into each other—a common occurrence in anthropological research. Older conventions of what location and space meant in anthropology would have envisioned separate histories between "different peoples" that could be bridged only by the anthropologist (Gupta and Ferguson 1997, 16). That vision of completely separate societies no longer makes sense. Cairo is a highly networked city, globalized and subject to neoliberal politics and economics, just as the United States and Britain are. No doubt the political-economic similarities between Egypt and the United States and UK can be overstated. Nonetheless if "tracing lines of possible alliance and common purpose" (Gupta and Ferguson 1997, 39) is part of fieldwork situated within shifting locations, then one might not want to *under*emphasize the neoliberal political-economic macroframework that encompasses so much of the world today. Within the global order there is no question that Cairo and London occupy different locations in a hierarchy of power. Egypt was open on a very casual basis to virtually anyone from Europe or the United States, but because of the politics of migration the reverse was decidedly not true—ordinary Egyptians could travel to Oxford at best only by subjecting themselves to comparatively immense scrutiny and regulation. Only a small number of Egyptian elites enjoyed the same freedom of movement that we had.

Given our capacity to be in Cairo, specifically downtown Cairo, my narrative is structured by both an event (the January 25 Revolution) and a geography that was in fact bounded in locally meaningful ways. Downtown Cairo is a roughly triangular urban area approximately a kilometer to the east and a bit further to the northeast from Tahrir Square.[18] This does not mean that all my informants or all the events, texts, and interactions discussed in this work were restricted to downtown. Downtown was my base; it is also as much "the neighborhood of Tahrir Square" as anything. My narrative will weave in and out of downtown, but this is where it begins and ends.

Downtown can claim a certain amount of local and international cachet as "Khedivial Cairo," a label that greatly understates its historical complexity, though it is true that the plan for its grand boulevards and node-like squares dates from the nineteenth-century Khedivial era. The original name for the area was Isma'iliyya, after the Khedive Isma'il (who ruled from 1863 to 1879). In contemporary Cairo a commercial development consortium called Al Ismaelia for Real Estate (Al Ismaelia 2015) trades on nostalgia for the colonial era in a still (as of the 2010s) fledgling attempt to remake the area along private-sector neoliberal lines. In reality the area has gone through multiple demographic and architectural shifts since the nineteenth century. In the four or five decades prior to the revolution, downtown's population, both transient and resident, had become more Egyptian, meaning that both the British and Egyptianized migrant populations (Greeks, Italians, Armenians), as well as some local minorities (Jews) had left. Foreigners in the area were predominantly cultural tourists, for whom the Egyptian Museum on Tahrir Square (exhibiting pharaonic artifacts, including from the tomb of Tutankhamun) was a powerful magnet. The American University in Cairo, also located on Tahrir Square until it moved to a suburban site in the mid-2000s, brought foreign students and academics to the area. And some foreign researchers, like Lucie and I, frequented the area because it was a gathering place for artists and intellectuals, many of whom were also interested in politics as observers or activists.

That aspect of downtown was a characteristic of the area for quite a while. Since roughly the 1960s downtown had taken on a distinctly bohemian character, as the centers of commercial and political power migrated to other parts of the city, while overlapping circles of writers, artists, intellectuals, and journalists increasingly frequented the area, forming impromptu "salons" in cafés, restaurants, galleries, or bookstores. The latter institutions, galleries and bookstores, diversified over the past two or three decades as the increasingly liberalized private sector began to invest in the area. Certain downtown streets also functioned as theater districts, for both live theater and cinema, predominantly

commercial in both cases, but always including a smattering of more artisti-
cally ambitious or avant-garde productions.

In the decade leading up to the January 25 Revolution downtown was frequented by at least six distinct groups, which interacted with each other only
marginally, and yet collectively made up the most socially diverse population
in Cairo. This was the key to downtown as heterotopia: "a space 'in-between,'
a space of otherness, simultaneously physical and mental . . . [which] can only
be understood in relation to other spaces outside of itself" (Ryzova 2015; n.d.).
The overlapping and interpenetrating socialities of these groups within a common space, the area's temporal rhythms, and the movement of people in and
out of it all contributed to downtown's heterotopic character. It was a kind of
liminal beachhead prior to 2011, preparing the ground for the more generalized
liminal crisis of the revolution.

The constituent groups in the area were the long-term intelligentsia; the
newer private-sector arts community linked to neoliberal capital; lower-
middle-class and lower-class youth drawn to the area for its entertainment
potential enabled by the high concentration of theaters, cafés, and commercial
venues (selling clothes mainly, which afforded window-shopping opportunities), and by the fact that the area did not really "belong" to anyone; tradesmen
and workers whose livelihoods were linked to workshops, many of them in the
informal economic sector, all around the margins of downtown and to some
degree within it;[19] middle-class office workers who staffed businesses and bu-
reaucracies in and around the district; and merchants, a few of whom lived in
the area. The non-Islamist activists who were central to sparking the revolution and sustaining it in the first two years, mainly youth (both male and female), were substantially drawn from the first two groups—the long-term intelligentsia, many of whom were older respected figures from earlier periods
of activism, and the neoliberal arts community. But collectively the overall
atmosphere of downtown, heterogeneous on the surface but substantially socially disconnected in its various parts, was crucial as an incubator of (non-
Islamist) political socialities before the revolution, and as a quasisafe revolutionary hinterland once the revolution began.

Downtown was a "field site" for me in a very loose sense. As the reader will
see, my narrative will dip in and out of downtown as a literal space. But the
experience of living in downtown Cairo, not just during the first two years of
the revolution, but periodically over a much longer period, is integral to my
overall vision of the January 25 Revolution.

Conceptual Organization of the Book

The theoretical scaffolding of the book operates at different intensities
throughout the work. I deploy a suite of linked conceptual tools that can be
arranged hierarchically. Liminality is at the top, the master theme of the whole

work. Below that are heteroptia as it relates to space in some chapters, and Richard Schechner's performance theory as it pertains to the overall framing of the main performance space of the revolution. Performance is a thread that runs through the middle chapters—4, 5 and 6—in the sense of special events that are not routinized and that are publicly staged; nonreducible emergent phenomena (Hobart and Kapferer 2005, 11), but linked to martyrdom and the revolution.[20] "Performativity" can have a variety of meanings—for example, in connection to language (Bauman and Briggs 1990; Butler 1997), theater (Schechner 1988 [1977]), or the gendered embodiment of the self (Butler 1999; Morris 1995). But all performance turns on a zone of contingency in which human subjects exercise some degree of agency. Turner generalized his ritual process into what he called "social dramas," which were predicated on measures taken to heal a breach in the normal affairs of a society (Turner 1980, 150). In the broadest terms how one defines what was "normal" Egyptian life in the early twenty-first century is an open question. By many standards the "norms" of Egyptian political life by the first decade of the twenty-first century were constantly evolving and hence by no means fixed.[21] But caveats aside, there was a "political normal" in the decades leading up to the January 25 Revolution, even if it may have been shifting. The revolution was a palpable event. All political forces could at least agree on that.

In more specific terms, martyrdom is the chief performance theme running throughout the book. It was inscribed in the revolution's most prominent performance space, Tahrir Square, as commemoration. This is important to understand in terms of how the space was defined, but it is even more important to appreciate the difference between the commemoration of death by martyrdom and martyrdom as a performative idiom. Death of course is an important occasion for a rite of passage, but in the revolution death in martyrdom was less about passage than about *suspension* of the passage. The point of martyr performances was to keep the martyr alive rather than to mark his or her death. One could often discern a dissonant pull between nationalist commemoration on one side, predicated on the completion of the passage to death, and revolutionary political claim making linked to mobilizational strategies on the other, in this case predicated on a continued liminality that resonated with the more general liminal crisis of the revolution.[22]

Also on this secondary tier of linked concepts is schismogenesis (Bateson 1936), the normalizing of "deviant" patterns that had been previously unthinkable or even undesirable, and the spread of such new patterns through imitation. Thomassen's reformulation of Bateson's concept in political theory, and linking it to liminality, is crucial for bringing schismogenesis into productive focus (Thomassen 2012; Horvath and Thomassen 2008). A further implication of this bundling together of liminality and schismogenesis is the importance of Tricksters to politics—also brought out by Thomassen. Tricksters are creatures of liminality found in all cultures, written about extensively in folklore, mythology, literary studies, and anthropology, but before Thomassen's intervention rarely thought of as a political type. This is the subject of chapters 9 and 10. Chapter 9 examines a television talk-show host named Taufiq 'Ukasha—a Trickster if there ever was one—who emerged as the public focal point of the counterrevolution. Chapter 10 interprets 'Abd al-Fattah al-Sisi as a Trickster politician.

A third tier of concepts consists of neoliberalism, precarity, and hegemony. In an earlier draft of this work I included a brief chapter on the history of neoliberalism in the Middle East and Egypt. In the end I opted to remove that chapter because it interrupted the unfolding of the main themes of the book— liminality, martyrdom, and Trickster politics. But readers will see that at a number of points, particularly in chapters 2, 6, and 10, I do invoke neoliberalism as the underlying cause of the revolution, if not necessarily a straightforward grievance articulated by revolutionaries. There is nothing exotic in this. Virtually all books on the January 25 Revolution put considerable emphasis on how economic liberalization in the decades prior to the revolution created the conditions necessary for its outbreak.

But aside from my general agreement with the existing literature on the revolution, neoliberalism is of more direct concern in this book in chapter 2, which discusses the material frame of Tahrir Square as a performance space as a product of political economy. Neoliberalism is also of direct concern to chapter 6, which discusses class, and chapter 10, which looks at the rise of 'Abd al-Fattah al-Sisi and the final defeat of the revolution. Part of Sisi's governing strategy is predicated on a resumption and expansion of neoliberal development projects that, prior to the revolution, had starved Egypt of capital devoted to the needs of ordinary people (for education, health care, infrastructure at the neighborhood level) in favor of speculative real estate development that benefitted primarily elites.

This is where precarity comes into my analysis. Precarity (Lorey 2015) is an effect of neoliberal political economy with which most of us are increasingly familiar. It refers to a reformulation of the state's social contract such that the protection from various forms of risk that states formerly offered to all citizens, unevenly in practice, but comprehensively in theory, should be restricted to only a small circle of elites. Everyone not encompassed within this circle of elites will be suspended between certain material limits. The nonelite population exists above the limit of starvation, because they cannot care for themselves if they starve, and cannot serve as productive labor. And they are kept below an upper limit, which is rebellion. Within these thresholds the nonelite population is offered only the hope that by diligent individual effort they can pull themselves into the charmed circle of the elite—a "cruel optimism" (Berlant 2011) in which the individualized desire for the good life acts as an impediment to achieving it. Prior to the institution and maturation of neoliberalism, the disorienting affects of capitalism and modernity—both of them predicated on unending change (Thomassen 2014; Berman 1988)—had been mitigated by hegemony. Hegemony made people feel that they were living in a world of solidity anchored by conservative values, custom, and religion. But precarity pulls the rug out from hegemony, "leaving man compelled to face with sober senses his real conditions of life" (Marx and Engels 1975 [1848], 476), or more precisely, reduces hegemony to the dimension of ownership; man is not quite "left to face his real conditions of life," but is rather reduced to *"homo oeconomicus"* (Brown 2015, 10). "The promise of the good life no longer masks the living precarity of this historical present" (Berlant 2011, 196). And so with all illusions but that of self-reliance stripped away, we get, on the one hand, a politics of anger focused on the benefits accruing to "those people" who "aren't as self-reliant as me," and on the other hand, an ever-expanding wasteland of zero-hours contracts, a "gig economy," and casualized labor without recourse to collective representation. This is a fertile environment for the emergence of Trickster politics.

At the end of chapter 9 I observe that if Sisi can be seen as a Trickster politician who emerged from the uncloseable liminality of a revolutionary situation, then we might note that he is hardly alone. We appear to have entered the Age of the Trickster—and not just of Sisi, but of Donald Trump, Silvio Berlusconi, Boris Johnson, Nigel Farage. In the Czech Republic Miloš Zeman. My Russian and East European colleagues heard me give a lecture on Trickster politics, and they immediately nominated Vladimir Putin as worthy of the title. Turkey's Recep Tayyib Erdoğan, often described as a populist, may come into better focus as a Trickster. And below the level of the most famous politicians, there is a vast network of quasipoliticians and yellow journalists made from the same mould as 'Ukasha—the talk-show host/politician who is the subject of chapter 9. When I published an article on 'Ukasha (Armbrust 2013—the forerunner of chapter 9) it was published in translation and was widely discussed in Egypt, including by 'Ukasha himself, on air, on at least two occasions. A newspaper article on my translated article was given the headline "Taufiq 'Ukasha: The Glenn Beck of Egypt" (Barakat 2015).[23] Beck, 'Ukasha, Limbaugh, the British tabloid press, the phrase "fake news" suddenly on the lips of every would-be strong man: a shattered public sphere is either a symptom or a cause of Trickster politics.

A number of questions might be posed. One is whether "Trickster politics" is a form of authoritarianism that has simply gone unrecognized until now. But more urgently, why is it so salient at this historical juncture? In chapters 9 and 10 we trace the rise of Trickster politics in Egypt from within the protracted liminality of revolution. But why are we seeing Tricksters and authoritarians (usually one and the same) emerging all over the world? Chapter 10 will suggest some tentative answers to these questions, centered on the notion that precarity—holding people within limits of uncertainty—has begun to function as a kind of artificially permanentized liminality. It is, however, a form of liminality devoid of the creative potential (and danger) of revolutionary liminality.

In artificial permanentized liminality, Tricksters, who are always with us in a certain marginal part of our social imaginaries, become audible outside the margins. This is because to live in precarity is to live entirely *within* the protracted liminality of the margins. Hence the January 25 Revolution can be understood as an instance of a country going beyond the threshold of rebellion, and the violent repressive actions of the Sisi regime after the defeat of the revolution can be seen as a project to reestablish the threshold at all costs, because the entire political-economic system depends on its maintenance. And this is why the United States could elect Donald Trump, the American Taufiq 'Ukasha, as its president. Egypt went into the January 25 Revolution rising up against the effects of neoliberalism on the global periphery. It emerged from the revolution in the vanguard of a dark new global authoritarian order. Liminality has come back full circle to precarity.

My Eighteen Days

THE FIRST EIGHTEEN DAYS OF the revolution culminating in the downfall of Mubarak were important because they created a fund of symbolic re-sources—stories people told about where they were and what they did, and mass mediation of narratives and images, both during and after the events. I too will tell some of my stories. They resonate with the widely felt process of entering into a liminal void, and they help establish some of the places and people who will feature in subsequent chapters.

At the very beginning of the revolution I often spent my days working in a rented flat—not the one I lived in, because that was too small for us all to live and work comfortably. The office flat was not far from Tahrir Square. I spent my days there attempting to read various materials relevant to my research on the history of Egyptian mass media. After January 25, trying to glean insights on the history of radio and television from old magazines was an exercise in futility, not because the magazines weren't rich sources for my research, but because the revolution taking place in the streets below was a constant distrac-tion. Indeed it was more than a distraction. Even before the onset of revolution everyone I knew was abnormally absorbed in politics. Once the revolution began ordinary things like moving boxes of my research materials into my of-fice took on a political hue. My landlord in the office building, a confirmed revolution skeptic from the beginning, saw boxes going up the stairs and thought I was storing political pamphlets. He feared I was turning his flat into a headquarters for the foreigners that were, according to some media voices, directing the ongoing revolution. It took the intervention of a friend who lived in the building (a university professor much respected by the landlord), and the demonstrable sight of old books and magazines actually coming out of the suspicious looking boxes, to calm his panic.

On the street outside the building I lived in, a few blocks from my office, an elderly woman sat in a chair every day on the edge of a stretch of pavement where men worked assembling bicycles. She embarrassed me one day, asking loudly in front of everyone whether I was a foreign operative. They all knew me, had seen me coming and going for months. In fact I had rented that flat two years before the revolution, out of a desperate need to store the ever-growing collection of books and magazines that my partner and I had acquired on regular trips to Cairo. Our prerevolution pattern had been to inhabit our flat during vacations only. Then, just before the revolution began in early 2011, we were suddenly living in it full time. Our sudden constant presence, just as the revolution commenced, had to have seemed suspicious, given the ebbs and flows of political news, including periodic campaigns to pin instigation of the revolution on foreign agents. The woman must have been voicing what all the bicycle assemblers were also thinking: what *were* we doing there?

Meanwhile many friends and acquaintances—Egyptian students, writers, educators, and artists, all of them non-Islamists—actually were deeply involved in revolutionary protests and other political activities. Downtown Cairo, where we lived, is the most directly contiguous neighborhood to Tahrir Square. It is a socially porous space that facilitates a greater degree of mixing between different classes and genders than is typical for most of the city. Before the revolution downtown was an incubator of diverse though generally non-Islamist political tendencies. During the revolution it became the natural hinterland of the iconic Tahrir Square, a place of respite from the rigors of asserting an ongoing revolutionary presence in public space and culture. One of the trials of this mode of politics for protestors was enduring harassment by agents of antirevolutionary political forces during the day, and attacks sometimes carried out by the security forces or the military, and sometimes by anonymous *baltagiyya* (thugs in the pay of various antirevolution forces) using firearms, particularly in the wee hours of the morning. Since our apartment was not far from Tahrir Square, on several occasions (this was long after the first eighteen days) we were awakened at home during this "graveyard shift" of the sit-ins a few blocks away by the sound of gunfire, which was sometimes fatal, and marked the next day on the street by impromptu memorials to the newest martyrs. This pattern crystallized very quickly after the fall of the Mubarak regime, and downtown's many cafés functioned as semisafe zones for weary activists determined to sustain their revolution at all costs. By October the more politically engaged prorevolution parts of our social circle were either resolutely working to sustain sit-ins in Tahrir Square, or hotly debating whether that tactic was right for the evolving political struggles that absorbed all their attention.

But that was yet to come. During the most intense parts of the eighteen days my small family—Lucie Ryzova and our son Jan, then three years old—spent much of the time on the rooftop of a five-story building near our flat. The building was about a ten-minute walk to Tahrir, and less than five minutes to our apartment. We went to this rooftop partly for company while the curfew was on, and partly so that Jan would have a place to run. Our link to the building was not through the inhabitants of its spacious apartments, but through the much more marginal people on the roof. One of them, Sharif, was the foreman of a crew of painters. They had painted our apartment, and thereafter we became friends.[1] Around him were gathered a crew of mostly young workers who he treated like an extended family, which some of them actually were. The most important of these was Zizo, a tall, handsome man in his twenties, from Bulaq al-Dakrur, an immense network of informal neighborhoods on the western side of Cairo (more precisely Giza, the governorate on the opposite side of the Nile from the Cairo governorate, in effect half of the Greater Cairo metropolitan area). Zizo was the only member of Sharif's crew with a relatively high degree of education. He had a college degree in hospitality management from a private university with suspect academic credentials. The degree gave him no advantage on the job market. Like the others, the only work he could get was so intermittent, low paying, and so insecure that he was effectively unemployed.

When the revolution began the crew had no work, but they still came every day to downtown Cairo and congregated on the rooftop with Sharif. While our nominal purpose for being there was for Jan to be able to run a bit, the real reason was that we were desperate for company and insight on what was happening. Our friends in the intelligentsia during those days had little time for us. Some of them were participating in the demonstrations, and the places we normally met them were closed. Our apartment, just down the street from Sharif's rooftop, was tiny, and Jan's preschool had been closed after the first day of the revolution.

For the first few nights of the revolution I went through the motions of continuing to work in my office. Every night when I came home the streets were mostly empty. The few people visible were furtive, and on one occasion the security forces were chasing after someone and shooting at him. My route was along Muhammad Farid Street, between 'Abdin Square, which was used as a rallying point for security forces vehicles, and Rushdi Street, where we lived. What struck me most on the evenings of the twenty-sixth and twenty-seventh of January were the immense convoys of troop transport trucks shuffling security forces around the city and the country. Later it occurred to me that contrary to the ideology of nonviolence espoused by the most articulate revolutionaries, the revolution actually had no chance of succeeding without the continuous violence that was happening throughout Egypt on those two nights. That was what exhausted the security forces far more than the middle-class protestors marching to Tahrir chanting "silmiyya, silmiyya" (peaceful, peaceful). At the time I simply wondered how long the security forces could keep this up. Of course I got my answer within days, on the Friday of Rage, January 28, when the security forces were broken by unprecedented demonstrations all over the country. The security forces tried to suppress them to no avail.

My first memory of the Friday of Rage was panic at the internet outage that the government imposed in an attempt to limit channels of communication. It was not just that we would be deprived of communication and news, but also that we had no alternative source of information outside our suddenly shrunken circle of friends. We had no television in our apartment. We had been meaning to get one, but we had not yet done so. In the morning I took a walk to Tahrir Square. A brief look told me that trouble was on the way: there were lots of security personnel, and groups of plain-clothed tough-looking men being unloaded from trucks and briefed by uniformed officers. These were presumably the proverbial baltagiyya being prepped for battle—thugs, basically hired political muscle (or criminals freed from prison on the condition that they make themselves available for doing the regime's dirty work). I dashed down the street to Bab al-Luq, about halfway between Tahrir and home, and found that one of the many electronics stores in the area was still open. Although I did nothing remarkable during the legendary first eighteen days of the revolution, I think I might at least be able to claim that I made the very last television and satellite dish/receiver purchase in downtown Cairo before everything shut down. After that I went home and watched long lines of protestors march down our street from 'Ataba toward Tahrir. People in the apartments above threw down anti–tear gas kits—onions, handkerchiefs, water, and sometimes Coca-Cola, though I read later that these homemade tear gas remedies probably actually did nothing to counteract the effects of the gas. The fighting was visible and audible from our balcony. The tear gas down below in the street became so intense that it gassed us all the way up in our eighth-floor apartment.

I had the television and the dish, but unfortunately I needed someone to install the dish and tune the receiver. By that time we were regular visitors to Sharif's rooftop. One of Sharif's friends thought he could get someone from his neighborhood to come do the job. It took until the afternoon of the thirtieth, but he delivered the promised technician. We turned on our new television just as air force jets made a series of terrifyingly low passes over the city to awesomely announce the arrival of the army (which had actually begun the day before), to secure the city and . . . what would they do? Whose side were they on? Whatever the orders given to soldiers were, people in the street could not be sure of the army's intentions until they were actually there on street corners and in public squares. Sociologist Neil Ketchley suggests that a kind of popular insurance policy went into effect—fraternization, "an intuitively familiar idiom of contentious street politics that dates back to at least the eighteenth century" (Ketchley 2014, 157). I remember watching a video from that day that a friend, Butros, who worked in the publishing business, had made on his phone. He had marched on the twenty-fifth in a demonstration that started from Muhandisin on the west bank of the Nile and moved toward Tahrir. I could hear his private conversations with his comrades, referring to the security forces as *murtaziqa*—"mercenaries"—but then, when they came close to some soldiers just before they attacked, calling out to them to join the revolution—an invitation to fraternization that the security forces generally rejected, but hopefully not the army. In retrospect it seems that once the army moved in, it is highly unlikely that they had orders to attack the protestors, though presumably they had scope to respond to attacks if necessary. But the initial reaction of the revolutionaries, once the brief feeling-out ritual that Ketchley describes had taken place, was to interpret the army's entry as a victory for their side. That, at any rate, was very much the reaction on Sharif's rooftop, where jubilation reigned, and I heard my first chants of "al-sha'b wil-gaysh 'id wahda," "the people and the army are one hand," which no more than two months later turned into "yasqut yasqut hukm al-'askar," "down with military rule." Sharif and his neighbors were yelling the *'id wahda* chant into the street from the low wall at the edge of the rooftop. "The army comes from us," he said, face beaming. "This is fantastic. It means the revolution will win!"

Lucie and I were less confident of the army's good intentions. Our apartment was right around the corner from the main headquarters of Bank Misr, a key institution that had to be protected. Tanks and armored personnel carriers appeared on the street corner, and the soldiers were looking at all passersby very closely. Lucie had the extremely smart idea of introducing ourselves to the unit on our street corner by posing Jan for a picture on one of the army vehicles. Everyone was doing it, and the tanks and personnel carriers were covered in prorevolution graffiti. Later someone told me a joke about it: "The armed forces have issued a new communiqué to the people: 'the army will not return to its barracks until every child in the country has been photographed on a tank.'" But Lucie went one step further and made sure that before we were finished we had introduced ourselves to the officer in charge. The wisdom of that became clear a few days later. As the situation became dire for the regime, orders were issued to try to control the international flow of news about the revolution. Below our balcony we could see every passing car being stopped and searched, and if tools of the journalism trade were found with anyone who had recently entered the country, the driver and passengers were detained on the street corner. But the *khawagat* (foreigners) with the blond kid? They could not possibly be journalists. So we were left alone.[2]

Initially the army's presence elated everyone who was prorevolution. In the brief lull we made visits to Tahrir Square, which, in the heat of its communitas phase, was delirious with positive energy. But shortly thereafter, on the afternoon of February 2, we got a brief taste of the struggle that was yet to come. We were sitting in a café on the edge of a pedestrianized café district. Everyone around us was prorevolution, still marveling at the apparent success in shaking the regime to its core. The revolution nobody had dared to imagine seemed to be happening. Suddenly the mood changed. A procession was making its way up the street, moving toward Tahrir Square. It was mainly men but included some women, many of them carrying posters of Mubarak, and chanting pro-Mubarak slogans: "iw'a timshi ya rayis; ihna binhibbak ya rayis" (don't you dare leave, president; we love you, president); or "ya Gamal, 'ul li-abuk; al-sha'b al-Masry biyihibbuk" (Gamal, say to your father; the Egyptian people love you). They were an ugly sight, at least to us. The women seemed to be snarling at the angry onlookers. The men were armed with crude metal weapons. We grabbed Jan and hustled him home as quickly as possible. It was, we discovered over the next couple of days, the beginning of the "Battle of the Camel," the regime's last-ditch counterattack, which famously began when camel- and horse-mounted Mubarak supporters rode into the square slashing and beating at people from atop their animals. This was the first sortie in what would become a pitched overnight battle that resulted in heavy casualties—eleven dead and up to eight hundred seriously injured.

Revolutionary narratives about the attack inevitably focus on the ubiquitous "thugs" hired by the regime, or speculation about which regime allies organized the assault. But a less comforting truth is that while the attack was certainly organized and vicious, not all the attackers were joining in strictly for pay. A writer I met several months later told me that she had been living just off of Champoleon Street, near our Ma'ruf apartment, in a rented flat at the time of the revolution. She was passionately prorevolution and had used her apartment to feed and provide respite for those fighting the battles. On the evening that the Battle of the Camel began suddenly the neighborhood was turned into a rallying point for angry antirevolution forces. Businessmen in the area—not NDP high fliers, but local men who owned car repair shops—were organizing this campaign. She and her daughter had to flee.

Those men may in fact have been paid, as revolutionaries often alleged. But others were not. Four years later Hamdi al-Khashab, a used book and magazine vendor from whom Lucie and I often purchased research materials, let it slip inadvertently that he was a soldier for the antirevolution side. "I never saw any problem with Mubarak," he said in a heated political conversation with me. "That's why I joined in the Battle of the Camel." Then he looked embarrassed and changed the subject. Whether or not pay for attacking revolutionaries was offered, he hardly seemed to need extra incentive to fight. He was never anything less than a vociferous regime supporter. Hamdi's in-laws were residents of 'Ataba, a neighborhood that was like a second home for him. The snarling procession that was passing by us as we sat in the café was coming from 'Ataba. If we had not felt a need to move Jan to safety we might have witnessed Hamdi coming by with a Mubarak poster and a *singa* (long knife, or handmade sword) on his way to Tahrir.

He was not the only member of my social circle who was proregime. 'Id and Hisham al-Bakri, two lawyers I knew who lived on Pyramids Road, were also vehemently proregime. I had known them since the 1980s but made no effort to contact them (or Hamdi for that matter) during the first year of the revolution, because I thought that political friction would make talking to them rather unpleasant. Finally, after Muhammad Morsy became president, I reestablished connections with them. I was curious, particularly about 'Id and Hisham. Hisham in particular had always struck me as overbearingly pious. Their homes were austere, without any form of decoration other than quranic verse. I wondered if they were Morsy sympathizers. Not at all, as it turned out once I reconnected with them. The essential irrelevance of piety to attitudes about the Muslim Brotherhood was never starker than when they engaged in spirited verbal assaults on Morsy and the brotherhood. I should have expected as much. There are pro–Muslim Brotherhood lawyers, but institutional success in the legal profession—and both Hisham and 'Id were quite successful—tended to come through social circuits closed to the brotherhood.

Our other social network centering on downtown consisted of intellectuals and artists. They were journalists, theater professionals, publishers, novelists, and academics, and also the most prorevolution people I knew, some of them actively involved in the protests. They are not easily anonymized, so given their affiliations with the now-criminalized revolution, I leave their details vague. For the most part we saw little of our better-educated friends during the first eighteen days of the revolution. But of course events kept happening without them. Once the Battle of the Camel was over on February 2 it was a matter of time before the Mubarak regime would have to resign. Much of the public had still supported him prior to the Battle of the Camel. He had appointed long-serving head of the General Intelligence Directorate Omar Suleiman vice president, and Civil Aviation Director Ahmad Shafiq his prime minister. Then Mubarak made a speech on February 1 in which he promised not to run for another term of the presidency, and for many these were sufficient concessions. But immediately after the ostensibly conciliatory speech the Battle of the Camel was launched, and everything Mubarak had just said appeared to have been deceitful. As the days went by there was general excitement but also extreme anxiety on Sharif's rooftop. Everyone was glued to the television at night during curfew time, watching the Arabic BBC and the Saudi-owned al-'Arabiyya channels. They would have tuned in to al-Jazeera, which was then assumed to be presenting the straight unvarnished truth about events, but it was usually jammed, and accessible only to those who knew how to redirect their dishes to unblocked satellites. Shortly after the Battle of the Camel the internet came back on, and I started getting requests to comment on events in the Western media. I did a few of these, initially appearing on BBC via Skype from my bathroom, where it was quiet enough to make myself heard. Later I managed to make it to the BBC studio on the corniche just over the Nile. On the night of February 11 the BBC called me again, while I was at Sharif's, asking me to make another short comment on current events. I agreed to go and even managed to get a taxi that was able to take me over the October Bridge north of Tahrir Square and drop me off on the corniche. As soon as I got out of the car I knew something had happened. People were excited, they were running around and yelling, and car horns were honking.

By the time I got up to the studio I knew that Mubarak had resigned. I cannot remember exactly what I said when I went on the air. It was something along the lines of "First, profound congratulations to the Egyptian people on this momentous occasion. This, in my opinion, will be remembered as the most important moment in modern Egyptian history." It sounds incredibly clichéd in retrospect, though I remain convinced of its truth, even if I later was not sure whether "important" necessarily meant the bright future that everyone captivated by the revolution hoped for.

After my thirty seconds of fame were over I found my way back to the street. It was complete pandemonium. There was no way to get a cab back to downtown, so I walked into downtown at a crawl. Once I made it back to Sharif's rooftop we all went out, Jan hoisted up on my shoulders yelling *tahya al-saura*—long live the revolution—albeit with a bit of prompting from us, and descended to the street to savor the moment. There was no question of trying to get into Tahrir Square. We satisfied ourselves with staking out a spot on a nearby street and just stood there grinning and reveling in the invisible bond joining all the happy people together.

CHAPTER 2

The Material Frame

*A society, as its history unfolds, can make an existing heterotopia
function in a very different fashion; for each heterotopia has a precise and
determined function within a society and the same heterotopia can,
according to the synchrony of the culture in which it occurs, have one
function or another.*

— Michel Foucault, "Of Other Spaces" (1986, 25)

WITHIN DAYS OF THE REVOLUTION'S outbreak Tahrir Square became
known globally as the central theater of the uprising. While Tahrir Square's
fame was primarily symbolic, its significance was underpinned by widespread
political mobilization across the country. The square would never have been
captured by activists chanting "silmiyya" (peaceful) if intense attacks on police
stations and other government buildings had not taken place throughout the
nation. Battles that took place outside the media frame ultimately overthrew
the regime, but of course by the same token those battles would never have
been joined without the symbolic and ideological initiatives taken by activists,
for whom the march to Tahrir was a primary tactical goal once the revolution
became perceived as such. Tahrir Square was, to be sure, also the location of
pitched battles as well as several "million-man" demonstrations.[1] But most
importantly, it became famous as a place of communitas, where social cleavages of class, religion, and gender were eclipsed in the liminal moment. Communitas is meant to be an intimate social state, redolent of an almost physical
face-to-face connection between people. But nothing could have been less intimate than Tahrir Square *outside* the scope of political happenings. Given the
post-2011 fame of Tahrir, its intense romanticization and aestheticization, it is
easy to forget that before the square became a revolutionary swan, it had been
a neoliberalized ugly duckling.

Neoliberalism

Very early on, analyses of what caused the revolution centered on the Mubarak-era neoliberal political economy. However, to say that neoliberalism was a necessary condition of the revolution is quite different than saying it was a revolution against neoliberalism. For some it *was* a revolution against the excesses of capitalism. Others were motivated to go into the streets by other causes, including the implementation of *shari'a*, or simply a chance to fight the police after years of abuse at their hands—abuse that was intrinsic to neoliberalism, even if many of those fighting the police could not articulate the link between Mubarak's security state and abstracted political economy.

Neoliberalism refers in the first instance to "privatization, cutbacks to social spending, the reduction of barriers to capital flows, and the imposition of market imperatives throughout all spheres of human activity" (Hanieh 2013, 14). As a term, "neoliberalism" had no standing in the everyday language of protest in Egypt, and only slightly more in the press. In dozens of demonstrations and sit-ins that I observed in 2011 and 2012, even "capitalism" named as such was rarely a specific object of criticism. Angry rhetoric against the much more amorphous term *fasad* (corruption) was more common by many orders of magnitude. A lack of specific focus on capitalism in contentious events was mirrored among my more politicized friends and acquaintances, who ranged from passionate socialists to economic liberals. Scholarly accounts of the January 25 Revolution likewise can quite easily discuss the effects of neoliberalism without extensive recourse to the actual term (e.g., Kandil 2012; Achcar 2013), though the political-economic analyses of these works inevitably point to the same set of policies and global processes leading to revolution as the works that do conjure specifically with "neoliberalism" as a term.

Tahrir Square, the most prominent political theater of a revolution that was to a substantial degree caused by the effects of neoliberalism, was also profoundly shaped by antihuman and elitist neoliberal policies over the previous four decades. Neoliberalism is, at its most basic level, simply a label for late capitalism. In practice it leads to privatization and commodification of public goods, "financialization" of all types of human activity, the manipulation of crisis, and upward redistribution of wealth by the state (Harvey 2005, 159–64; Ortner 2011). But while neoliberalism is nominally an economic policy that emphasizes the efficacy of markets over that of the state, many scholars insist that it is more than that. Harvey emphasizes that it is a philosophy of freedom, and as such it has proved an attractive ideology (Harvey 2005, 5). After all, who wants to be in the position of arguing against freedom? The devil, as one might expect, is in the details. Neoliberalism privileges the freedom to own property above all other possible concepts of freedom.[2] Hence the state, in theory, becomes an enemy of freedom as much as any other "ism" that might pose a threat to it, such as fascism, or communism, or Islamism. The corollary to this is that while one might expect neoliberal ideology to demand the smallest possible state in order to weaken its potential for compromising the "hidden hand of the market," in practice neoliberal states are often very interventionist, but specifically interventionist on behalf of those who are the largest property owners. Neoliberal states arrogate to themselves the right to impose their vision of freedom by force if necessary (Harvey 2005, 6–9). But more than that, market rationality cannot be taken for granted. Neoliberalism "does not presume the ontological givenness of a thoroughgoing economic rationality for all domains of society but rather takes as its task the development, dissemination, and institutionalization of such a rationality" (Brown 2005, 40–41).[3]

Neoliberalism is, in the end, a quite utopian philosophy, but it may be its interventionist character that gives it its greatest political traction. This is because "intervention" can be tailored to local circumstances. Mitchell unpacks the trajectory of Egyptian neoliberalism in the 1990s, examining the financial arrangements that made neoliberalism possible, and the system's overall irrationality (T. Mitchell 2002, 272–303). The result was nothing like "laissez-faire economics" that neoliberalism might seem to imply if one just stops at the market-over-state formula: "The 'free market' program in Egypt was better seen as a multilayered political re-adjustment of rents, subsidies, and the control of resources" (T. Mitchell 2002, 277). In other words, the state did not shrink so much as it allocated its resources for the benefit of a small, politically connected "private sector."

To cite a particularly consequential example, virtually all the ostensibly private sector real estate development in Egypt in the decades leading up to the revolution was predicated on massive expenditure by the state to build infrastructure (Sims 2014, 267–70). Much of this development took the form of luxury housing estates in vast new neighborhoods and satellite cities. These were inaccessible to the majority of the population and housed only a tiny percentage of the total population of Greater Cairo. Given the effect of this massive diversion of both public and private resources into real estate speculation that benefitted very few but sapped the country of its capacity to address more pressing issues such as education and health care, in a sense the January 25 Revolution was a revolt against luxury housing. As we will see in the remainder of this chapter, Egyptian political-economic policies of the four decades before the revolution also reshaped the inner city (including Tahrir Square) by chopping it into disconnected neighborhoods and linking inner-city urban islands not to their contiguous neighborhoods, but to the far-flung frontiers of real estate speculation.

Neoliberalism is, however, considered by many observers to be more than a set of political-economic policies. It is also a quasi-ideology of fetishizing the "magical" (or mystified) distributive powers of markets. As such, neoliberalism is more ascribed by its critics than embraced by its adherents, many of whom adamantly oppose the notion that neoliberalism even *is* an ideology. For them neoliberalism is simply an expression of the freedom that all human beings should enjoy; they simply are not interested in arguments that neoliberalism presupposes a hierarchy that puts the freedom to own property at the top, or that doing so has implications for how individuals articulate with society. But critics of neoliberalism are themselves divided over both the parameters of the phenomenon and its effects. Hence neoliberalism has been described as "a rascal concept promiscuously pervasive, yet inconsistently defined, empirically imprecise and frequently contested" (Brenner et al. 2010, 182).[4]

Whether neoliberalism produces a specific mode of subjectivity or agency comparable across many complex societies is an important issue, but not my main focus in this book. What concerns me here is what neoliberalism has done to the urban fabric of Cairo and many other cities, as a tangible product of history. Therefore, while economic liberalization over the three or four decades prior to 2011 was clearly implicated in forming the political grievances that made the revolution possible, for present purposes my emphasis will be on what these market-oriented liberal policies did to Cairo, instantiated by Tahrir Square writ a bit larger than it has been in most accounts of the revolution. Tahrir exemplifies larger processes that took place in Cairo and the rest of the country, but it was more than a metonym for Egypt under neoliberalism. Liminality, a phenomenon of transitions and thresholds, is intrinsically spatial. Formally, public space in prerevolution Egypt was systematically divested of political potential. But because neoliberalism elevates the freedom of private ownership above all other forms of freedom, it tends to be antidemocratic and is hostile to nonprivatized spaces in which alternative forms of sociality might flourish. Consequently, the transition from Tahrir as a politically sanitized space, dominated by privatized automobility, to a brief moment of radical heterotopia animated by at least a flicker of the Paris Commune, made this square qualitatively different than the rest of the country.

Tahrir's political luminescence was not born ex nihilo. The "second principle" of Foucault's "Of Other Spaces" stipulates that the function of heterotopic spaces can change (1986, 25). He was not thinking about a place like Tahrir Square, but of the repurposing and relocation of cemeteries, heterotopic by virtue of their capacity to mix the living and the dead.[5] Nominally Tahrir was more like a "non-place" (Augé 2009), or what Lefebvre (2003, 128–29) called a "cut," or a "suture"—a transit zone between urban places—than a space of repurposing and relocation.[6] We will, however, encounter a rather different repurposing of space in Tahrir Square here and in the next chapter. The square was heterotopic in that it served as a transportation hub, martyrological space (dominated by the state but contested by revolutionaries), and theater for political performance. But these functions were cyclical rather than simultaneous, and this does resonate with Foucault's point about the repurposing of heterotopic space. It must be acknowledged that in the imaginary of city planners Tahrir was always thought of as potentially more than just a place to pass through—as an area of gardens, culture, and governance (Elshahed 2011). It never achieved those goals, but even aside from such ambitions the long periods in which Tahrir Square was used as nothing more than a transportation hub were still shaped by political-economic forces linked to politics, both for and against the state.

The roots of the revolution were deeply embedded in the material frames of its performance. These frames were not "just there," therefore some attention is due to how Tahrir Square as an urban space emerged historically. Sketches of the symbolic and political-economic character of Tahrir have been done before (e.g., Gunning and Baron 2014, 241–55; Winegar 2006, xv–xvii), and of course since the revolution a vast outpouring of scholarship and journalism has described the square in various ways. But despite the already considerable salience of Tahrir in scholarship on the revolution, there is no question that its symbolic weight must be acknowledged. Hence I will walk the reader through this exercise yet again, but hopefully from an unfamiliar angle.

In considering Tahrir as a performance space, it must be emphasized that there are both material and social parameters determining the scope actors have to improvise, or in the context of a revolution, the agency afforded to protestors to express their grievances. Performance scholar Richard Schechner formulated the shaping of performances spaces in terms of frames (Schechner 1988 [1977], 17–18). Schechner was a friend and collaborator with Victor Turner. Schechner's book *Performance Theory* is now a classic, and it draws out explicit analogies to performance and the ritual process, and not just formal theatrical performance, but other types of human activities that functioned along the same lines. He specified a whole range of magnitudes of performance that went from a bar mitzvah to hostage crises and wars. One of Schechner's ideas was that there is an "axiom of frames": "The looser the outer frame, the tighter the inner, and conversely, the looser the inner, the more important the outer" (Schechner 1988 [1977], 17–18). His point was that the area of "freedom" in a performance—his translation into theatrical terms of the liminal phase in the ritual process—was defined by a relation between space and rules. His model included several different layers of rules—conventions, drama, and director. If one adapts this idea to political performance, then it can be simplified. Both space and rules, or conventions, can be historicized. Here we consider space; in the next chapter we examine conventions.

If we think about Tahrir Square as a performance space, then its immediate boundaries are the boundaries of the square itself, the space that people could fit into—about two hundred thousand maximum, if you filled all the nearby major thoroughfares and counted them as part of the square. But the interesting thing about the square is that it has a history, and as a material place, it is the history of how neoliberalism has reshaped the area over the past four decades. The square itself is heterotopic in the sense that several functions occupy the same space, though not exactly simultaneously. Neoliberalism made it increasingly what you might call a "nonspace," a place that one passes through, but not a place that has any function in and of itself. If we expand the outer frame a bit more, then the effects of state policy on the material frames of Tahrir will become more evident.

In formal theater the frames consist of conventions, direction, *and the delimitation of space.* The next chapter examines the question of conventions. Here it is the materiality of political economy—specifically its capacity to delimit and define Tahrir Square as a performance space—that I seek to bring out. Crucially, the contemporary form of Tahrir Square cannot be fully appreciated apart from the larger political economy of the country. The materiality of Tahrir therefore enabled the revolution's contentious performances and at the same time serves as a spatialized point of entry to some of the material factors underpinning the revolution.[7]

"People Power" in the Antipeople Zone

Tahrir Square, a space of approximately five hundred acres (AlSayyad 2011), had been a focal point of collective protest before, particularly in 2003 (the American invasion of Iraq), 1972 (the student movement against Sadat's "corrective revolution"), and 1967 (the June War and Nasser's offer of resignation). Many smaller demonstrations targeted Tahrir less memorably. The square had also been the site of prominent public funeral processions, such as for the singers Umm Kulthum and 'Abd al-Halim Hafiz, President Gamal 'Abd al-Nasir, and the "martyr general" 'Abd al-Mun'im Riyad. Until the late 1940s Tahrir had been the location of the Qasr al-Nil barracks for the British army, and redevelopment of the area commenced with independence in 1952 (Elshahed 2011).[8] The *midan,* "square," we now know as Tahrir used to be called Midan Isma'iliyya, after the Khedive Isma'il. In 1954 Tahrir (liberation) replaced Isma'iliyya in commemoration of the long-running battle to force the British out of the Suez Canal zone following World War II, culminating in the massacre of approximately sixty policemen in the canal town of Isma'iliyya on January 25, 1952. In the January 25 Revolution Tahrir Square became globally famous for the exercise of so-called people power. But by 2011, outside its moments as a theater for contentious political performance, Tahrir Square was remarkably inhospitable to people. More precisely, it was inhospitable to people whose presence in the square was not mediated by private automobility.

Since the 1980s, when Metro construction turned the square into a giant crater for several years, Tahrir has not been a particularly pleasant place to look at, though much depended on the speed or height at which one experienced it. Speed could be more or less graphed as a relation of one's access to vehicular transport as one axis, and the quality of transport as the other. In other words, it looks better when one moves through it at vehicular speeds, but depending on whether one's vehicle is an air-conditioned private automobile or a jam-packed bus. Foot passage through Tahrir is sometimes excruciating, and almost unacknowledged in the material parameters of the space because it barely counts in the motorized hegemony within Cairene mobilities. The "locomotory practices" of Cairo are sharply hierarchical and consequently are productive of social identities and statuses that remain largely unarticulated (Elyachar 2011, 96).

Certainly in the Mubarak-era phase of its history, Tahrir "Square" was not in any sense a public square in which people gathered for purposes of leisure, nor was it even remotely a spatial analog to the concept of a "public sphere" in which civil discourse between bourgeois subjects could take place. There is only one small green space in Tahrir—a circle about 70 meters in diameter, raised above the traffic by a little less than a meter. It is situated roughly in the center of the square. The closest landmark to it is the Kentucky Fried Chicken restaurant inserted into the area in the mid-1990s, which became the punch line of many jokes during the revolution after state media put out rumors that the protestors were staying in Tahrir because they had been bribed by the promise of KFC meals. A few shrubs and small trees grew on this modest circle, but it was otherwise an empty grassy space. Protestors referred to this circle as the "saniyya" (the pan), and it became the key space in the many attempts to maintain long term *i'tisamat* (sit-ins) in the square after the first eighteen days culminating in the fall of the Mubarak regime. This was the best place in the square to pitch tents, and they were set up for a good bit of the six months following the eighteen days.[9] The saniyya was really the only colonizable subsection of the midan, but outside Tahrir's sporadic use as a political theater, nobody used it for anything (see figure 2.1).

Aside from its symbolic status as a political theater, the language of Tahrir Square prior to the revolution was movement. It was a place that people traversed, though the modes of doing so were highly unequal. This was what made Tahrir a nonplace in normal times: "What reigns there is actuality, the urgency of the present moment. Since non-places are there to be passed through, they are measured in units of time" (Augé 2009, 104). In Tahrir it was not just units of time that functioned as the measure of a nonplace, but degrees of comfort. At the top of the hierarchy of passing through Tahrir were privately owned motor vehicles, which are the major cause of urban congestion in Cairo, even though only around 11 percent of the public owned private cars (Sims

FIGURE 2.1. Aerial view of Tahrir Square. Map data: Google Maps.

2010, 235). Comparison with Beirut, another massively crowded city in which class dynamics are expressed in mobility hierarchies (Monroe 2013), is instructive. In Beirut 68 percent of all motorized trips are taken in private automobiles (Monroe 2013, 30). In Cairo the figure is 20 percent.[10] The fact that the automobile is the implacable enemy of Cairo will be obvious to any first-time visitor in ways that are rarely articulated by people who live there all their lives. A true neoliberal ideologue loves the private automobile, despises public transportation's collectivism, and wants everyone to forget that the maintenance of roads (and always at some level the building of them) is conventionally an infrastructural responsibility of governments rather than private enterprise. By such standards Cairo is a neoliberal urbanist's dream.[11]

Trying to suppress automobile use and ownership would be hugely unpopular with the politically dominant middle and upper classes. And yet even though the prerevolution lives and transport needs of 89 percent of the population were continually and progressively blighted by the 11 percent who clogged the roads with private automobiles, it was and remains (at least in my experience) surprisingly rare for anyone to articulate the obvious link between Cairo's ever-present sense of overcrowdedness and the dominance of the private car specifically, as opposed to the more general crush of motorized traffic. Conceivably lower-class people with no prospects of obtaining an automobile feel differently than the middle class. Millions of people in Greater Cairo have never even ridden in a private automobile according to Sims (2010, 235). But my experience of complaining about cars to even the most minimally middle-class-aspiring people was that my complaints were met with incomprehension. Admittedly those conversations took place in the 1980s, when the immense volume of Cairene traffic was still new to me, and hence remarkable and something I thought I needed to better comprehend. Possibly attitudes have changed.

To be sure, complaints about overcrowding in general were *very* common throughout the thirty years I have been going to Egypt, and not just on the level of everyday conversation. *Zahma*, "crowdedness," was a key justification for the many unsuccessful desert development schemes that have been championed by governments from Nasser to the post-Mubarak era (Sims 2014, 35–64). Overcrowdedness was both a popular complaint (often formulated as a sense of being *makhnuq(a)*, or suffocated), as well as the Mubarak regime's primary driver of the imperative to build vast new suburbs on either side of the Nile delta, which sucked the state's resources away from where people actually lived into a vast complex of lucrative real estate speculation. Complaints about the daily transportation agony inevitably reinforced this centrifugal dynamic. In everyday life overcrowdedness was likely to be attributed to either a general lack of *nizam* (order) in *driving* behavior (as opposed to the massive number of parked cars that regularly reduce wide thoroughfares to one lane), or to the "backward" mixing of nonautomotive modes of transport such as donkey and horse carts with cars. Pedestrians, who were routinely forced to share streets with cars because parked cars made the sidewalks useless, were rarely blamed for congestion, but cars for the most part ignored their presence. Consequently, there were no politics of automobility in Egypt other than the state's efforts to find ways to increase car ownership. Walking is actually the main form of mobility in Cairo by a substantial margin; the prevalence of walking has actually *increased* as the dominance of private automobility has risen.[12] Julia Elyachar explores the implications of this dominance for walkers and, more generally, those consigned to the less privileged forms of automobility. She notes an implicit mitigation of the risks and discomfort faced by walkers (and patrons of cheap forms of automobility) through "gestural resources" that enable them "to recognize and respond to one another without making themselves vulnerable to outsiders or slowed down by explicit formulation of ideology or verbal meaning" (Elyachar 2011, 96).

To put it bluntly, Tahrir during the era of *infitah* (spanning both the Sadat and Mubarak regimes) became increasingly an immense traffic interchange rather than a public square in any presence-on-the-ground social sense, even in the simple sense of being able to walk. On a bad day Tahrir Square resembled a giant slowly moving parking lot. Of course a bad day for those in cars translated to a slightly better day for anyone compelled to attempt crossing the midan above ground on foot, as traffic jams made movement through idled cars less dangerous than in the moments when cars were moving at close to highway speeds.

Vehicles entered and exited primarily from six substantial streets, several of them converted to one-way thoroughfares by the ever-pressing need to keep automotive traffic moving. In the years leading up to the revolution a large construction site on the west side of the square, hidden behind impenetrable steel sheets, took up more than half the midan's space. The purpose of the project was to serve automobiles through the construction of a substantial underground parking structure. During the revolution activists breached the wall and were surprised to find that no construction was ongoing, though the site had been barricaded for years. Some suspected that the construction site was actually little more than a stratagem to reduce the size of the space in which demonstrators could congregate.[13] The centrality of Tahrir as a traffic interchange made sit-ins an effective tactic because protestors could disrupt traffic far beyond the square. The revolutionary forces were never able to mount a general strike to paralyze the country and force the state to bargain for their demands, but shutting down the busiest transportation hub in the city at least made the protests palpable to a substantial portion of the public. At the same time Tahrir's crucial place in the city's mobilities put a limit—of indeterminable but undoubtedly limited duration—on how long a sit-in could last before it became counterproductive. All revolutionary acts of protest involved the presence of people on the ground either walking in the many marches that converged on various symbolic destinations (usually Tahrir in the case of Cairo) or stationary specifically for the purpose of immobilizing automotive traffic. Walking provides "trajectory, direction, connection, and [it creates] a bridge between distanciated spacetimes" (Bonilla 2011, 316), and it is therefore an element of political protest almost everywhere. The spatiotemporal status of Tahrir— its centrality to protests in earlier events—made it a particularly salient destination in the history of protest in Egypt. But in a protracted political crisis constant mobilization becomes impossible, and walkers must eventually come to rest. The struggle becomes one of holding space rather than moving through it, and when that happened in Cairo the hegemony of automobility—the unstated almost unverbalizable acceptance of a hierarchy that favored private automobile owners—inexorably came into conflict with the will to protest. The point of counterproductivity was reached at the moment when the impediment to automotive movement outweighed the clarity and popularity of the protestors' demands in the opinions of the various publics that make up Cairo's political field. Nobody could know for sure when that moment had been passed, or for whom. But the question of "how long is this tactic effective?" was debated in all sit-ins, and for good reason.

Landmarks

A number of distinctive buildings had been constructed in the area since the late 1940s, when the British vacated Egypt. These included the Arab League Headquarters, the Mugamma', the Nile Hilton Hotel, and the Egyptian Museum, home of the country's most iconic pharaonic artifacts and a massively important tourist attraction. One of the main Cairo Metro stations lay underneath the square.[14] On the northwest corner of the midan, abutting the Nile Corniche, was the National Democratic Party headquarters, built in the 1960s originally to house the Cairo municipality, but immediately converted into first the headquarters of the Arab Socialist Union under Nasser, and later the ruling National Democratic Party (AlSayyad 2011).[15] During the revolution the NDP headquarters were burned on the Friday of Anger (January 28), and there was subsequently much speculation about what would happen to the site.[16] Someone in an official position had an answer: the NDP never existed. In the Metro station below Tahrir a large poster appeared about a week after the fall of the Mubarak regime, showing three patriotic faces cheering the revolution as one would cheer the national football team, painted in the colors of the Egyptian flag, a man, a woman, and a child (see figure 2.2). The child was depicted in Tahrir Square superimposed over exactly the spot where the blackened hulk of the NDP headquarters stood. "Builders of the future" was the caption—revolution over, now everyone should get back to work. By the end of 2015 the nameless official's vision came true. All the revolutionaries' ideas were ignored: no preservation of the blackened building as a warning to future tyrants; no Hyde Park–style speakers' corner; no public library. The building was torn down and its land assimilated to the grounds of the adjacent Egyptian Museum. The museum itself was, by that time, slated to become a historical footnote to a much more massive Grand Egyptian Museum under construction somewhere far out in the desert on the Giza side of the Nile where, it was hoped, a much larger volume of tourists could be bussed once the tumult of the revolution was ended.

The museum's migration to the suburbs was part of a pattern. On the eastern edge of *wust al-balad*, downtown Cairo, a significant institutional presence for almost a century had been the main campus of the American University in Cairo (AUC). By the time of the revolution it was used only for continuing education programs and a few other special programs that needed to be downtown to function properly. The actual university had moved to the desert suburb of New Cairo City in 2008.[17] AUC's move to the desert was emblematic of a larger urban transformation—an attempted "Dubaisation" of Cairo (Abaza 2011). Moving the most exclusive private university in the country to a remote desert location was justified on grounds of space and cost. But the economic viability of the move depended on the availability of cheap land on the suburban desert

fringe. However, the availability of affordable desert land far from the center of Cairo was entirely contingent on huge and tragically wasteful public subsidies for infrastructure (see figure 2.3 on pages 42 and 43 to get a sense of the scale of greater Cairo in relation to the inner city).[18]

A large proportion of the land allocated to new developments in Cairo had been devoted to exclusive gated communities (Kuppinger 2004, 43; Sims 2014, 128; Denis 2006, 49). Khaled Adham estimates that the total area of development on the peripheries designated for luxury housing exceeded the entire Greater Cairo region that had developed over a millennium (Adham 2005, 24). All these developments were planned as low-density housing with a large proportion of land devoted to green space (Sims 2010, 171). Water for this greenery, which grandiose private or public visions for the new Cairo carefully refrained from depicting as ecologically inappropriate for the area, had to be moved uphill and over long distances by means of electricity-powered pumps. Moreover, the new towns were situated in areas where the runoff would not replenish aquifers, hence the resources used to water lawns and golf courses in the new cities has been entirely lost, and will continue to be as long as desert development schemes remain tethered to visions of greenery in the desert (Sims 2010, 200–201). Also the fuel used to power the private automobiles that were absolutely fundamental to Egypt's desert development schemes was among the most heavily subsidized in the world (Wagner 2012–13, 6–7).

In a nutshell, whether or not AUC had remained in its Tahrir Square location, the economic calculations for moving it would have been utterly different if the institution had had to bear the true cost of developing the new desert location, and if students and faculty had had to pay unsubsidized prices for fuel so that they could drive to it. This underscores the fact that the economic liberalization that underpinned changes in Cairo's urban fabric in the decades leading up to the revolution was not a doctrine of laissez-faire economics, but rather a "programme of deliberate intervention by government in order to encourage particular types of entrepreneurial, competitive and commercial behaviour in its citizens" (Gilbert 2013, 9). "Marketplace decisions" such as where to locate a private university, were decisively structured by the actions of a state that officially extolled private-sector entrepreneurialism, but in fact diverted public resources for development that benefitted only a few.

The political-economic factors that structured AUC's decisions were intimately tied to the revolution's demands for social and economic justice. In fact, continuation of the new cities as conceived during the Mubarak and Sadat eras was completely incompatible with social and economic justice for the simple reason that they required the provision of public subsidies used for the benefit

---

FIGURE 2.2. *Top*: The burned-out hulk of the NDP headquarters, April 2011. *Middle and bottom*: "Builders of the future," with the young girl erasing the NDP building. Author's photographs.

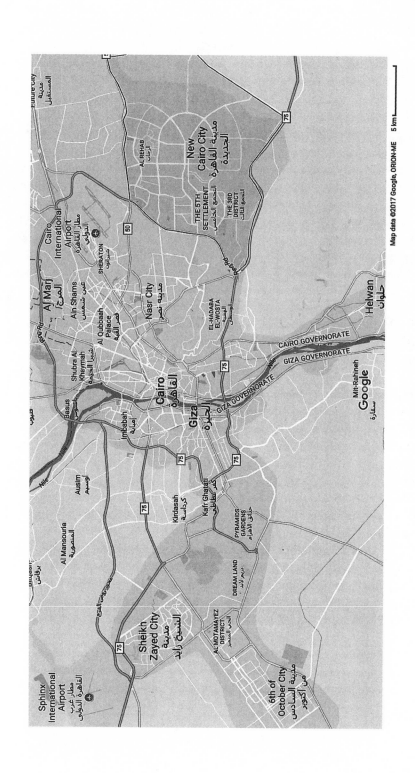

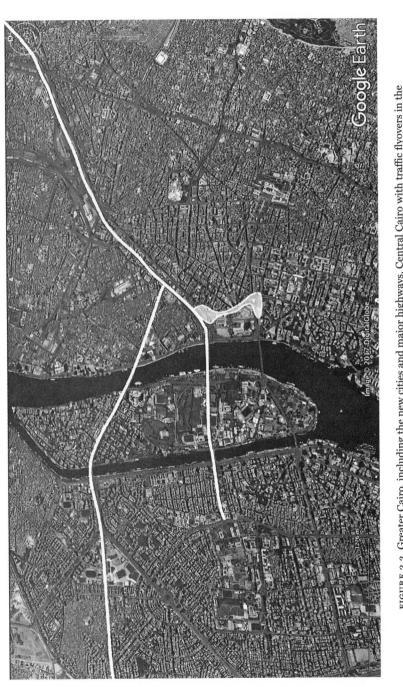

FIGURE 2.3. Greater Cairo, including the new cities and major highways. Central Cairo with traffic flyovers in the magnified satellite map. Main map about 70 × 40 km, magnified area about 7 × 5 km. Map data: Google Maps.

of a wealthy few (Sims 2014, 146–50). Such issues often were unacknowledged or essentially unthought by individuals. Many AUC students and faculty were enthusiastic participants in the revolution, oblivious to the fact that true fulfill-ment of the revolution's demands was totally at odds with the residential (and by extension political-economic) decisions that they and their elders had made, effectively in collusion with the political regime that many of them came to oppose.

The abdication of AUC from downtown Cairo was emblematic of the state and private-sector forces reshaping Cairo in the decades prior to the revolu-tion. While some institutions were relocating to the desert, other forces were trying to lure suburban money and foreign investment back into the old "belle epoch" downtown center. Isma'iliyya (or Ismaelia in this context), the former name of "Khedevial Cairo," was also the name of a group of wealthy investors who, in the years leading up to the revolution, were buying numerous down-town properties with the ostensible aim of gentrifying the area (Al Ismaelia 2015). The quasibohemian character of downtown Cairo and its reputation as a cultural magnet increased the district's marketability. The Ismaelia Group knew this and consciously invested in the art scene (Argaman 2014, 118–19; Ryzova 2015; n.d.). The explicit aim of Ismaelia's gentrification was to bring the sort of wealthy clients into downtown who have been purchasing property in the automobile-dependent state-subsidized gated communities of the "new cities" currently under construction on both sides of the Nile val-ley—precisely the destination of the Egyptian Museum's world-famous col-lection of pharaonic artifacts and the exclusive American University in Cairo.[19] The notion of new cities clients getting out of their cars to live in downtown Cairo is actually fairly preposterous. If the Ismaelia project truly depended on attracting such clients, then it would surely fail, because the entire downtown area is immensely complex, hence Ismaelia's purchases, while substantial, were very far short of acquiring a sufficient amount of downtown to dictate the removal of people considered "undesirable" by the standards of the target market for gentrification. For the residents and habi-tués of the area Ismaelia was a magnet for suspicion. The lawyer for one of my own apartment purchases specialized in real estate and took cases chal-lenging the big developers (including some opposing one of the Ismaelia pur-chases). He speculated that the project was really a money-laundering scheme. An academic who was born in the area expressed fears to me that the business group's ultimate goal was to carry out the kind of sterile gulf con-sumer–oriented building project for which Beirut's Solidere project (a recon-struction of the war-torn central Beirut district after the end of the civil war) is often criticized (Makdisi 1997). Fears that Ismaelia wanted to carry out a similar agenda of destroying downtown to create a gulf-style leisure play-ground were probably never realistic, but for at least a time the group's pur-chases did at least raise downtown real estate prices. Such developments were part of the political economy of the area in which Tahrir sits, and also of the larger national political economy. The political economy of property adjacent to midan al-Tahrir is, in turn, an important aspect of the social hierarchies that form the "pre-swan" ugly duckling image of the place; the structure, in other words, from which the antistructure of the revolution departed in a revolutionary passage to the unknown.

Steel Fences

Once we widen our focus enough to include neighborhoods surrounding Tahrir as part of the performance frame, the logic of the political economy that shaped the area over the past few decades becomes clearer. A different part of Foucault's oeuvre becomes relevant, namely the linking of power and knowledge through the subdivision of space most clearly instantiated in *Discipline and Punish* (1979). The subdivisions create invidious binaries in which the sick are quarantined from the healthy, or more generally, inferiorities are defined by contrast to a superior Other, for example "the East" to "Europe" as dissected in Said's *Orientalism* (1978). With respect to central Cairo, in the first instance—the space closest to the midan itself—subdivisions of urban space enable a mobilities apartheid. The eastern and southern edges of the midan—precisely the parts of the area that articulated with the city, unobstructed by impassable roads—were hemmed in by massive steel fences. The eastern fence ran along the edge of downtown; the southern fence cut off the area in front of the Mugamma' from the traffic moving through the middle of the midan. The fences facilitated crowd control in times of demonstrations simply by carving up the midan's space. But in the periods between revolutionary or other political events the fences were there to separate foot traffic from automobile traffic. This was notable mainly because of their abject failure. Like everywhere else in Cairo, automotive traffic and people mixed in Midan al-Tahrir. This was simply because walkers had no choice but to enter into the drivers' space, since there was no infrastructure for pedestrian movement and few sidewalks because they were mostly occupied by parked cars. Moreover, what looked on the surface like a rationalizing attempt to separate functions (walking and driving) actually worked punitively against walkers by making walking more unpleasant for those who had to do so. There were usable sidewalks on the city edge of Midan al-Tahrir (the eastern side of the square). But walking across the midan in any direction was an excruciating experience.

Disregard for pedestrians was systematic and completely normal everywhere in the city. I mention it because what was normal in Tahrir contrasted so sharply from Tahrir's revolutionary time, when people owned the square and automobiles were banned. Normal-time Tahrir reiterated a hegemony salient throughout the city: the majority who walk were always at the mercy of the wealthier minority who drove, and yet the walkers' pain could not be articulated. The right of pedestrians to the city was certainly not a political demand and could barely be articulated as a grievance. And yet the invidious political economy of physical mobility powerfully symbolized the notorious inchoateness of the revolution.

The Northern Periphery

If we widen our focus on Tahrir Square to encompass the surrounding neighborhoods we see the spatial transformations of the previous four decades reiterated and enhanced. In the area's configuration at the time of the revolution the Egyptian Museum separated Tahrir from Midan 'Abd al-Mun'im Riyad, just to the north. Midans 'Abd al-Mun'im Riyad and Tahrir were to some extent one continuous area, though walking from one to the other was an arduous experience. Named after a "martyr general" killed in the War of Attrition fought against Israel in the years following the 1967 June War, Midan' Abd al-Mun'im Riyad, like the more famous Midan al-Tahrir, was the site of intense battles between prodemocracy protestors and the state security forces. It was dominated even more depressingly than Tahrir Square by the functional imperative to distribute motor-vehicle traffic into a series of traffic arteries and elevated highways without the slightest regard for pedestrians. In traversing 'Abd al-Mun'im Riyad on foot one simply dodged traffic often moving at high speeds on all sides of a center area that hosted a major bus stop. Sidewalks, such as there were, terminated in the middle of nowhere. A series of fences compelled long detours and inevitably forced one back into the automobile traffic. One could change busses in 'Abd al-Mun'im Riyad and depart for other parts of the city, but there were *no* designed facilities for transferring pedestrians from the bus stop to any of the surrounding areas, including downtown Cairo, the Nile Corniche, Ramsis Street leading to Cairo's major train station, Tahrir Square, or the deliberately precarious nineteenth-century neighborhood of Bulaq Abu al-'Ila (see figure 2.4).

This is where the quarantine logic of *Discipline and Punish* was inscribed most deeply into the fabric of the city. Bulaq, the southern part of which is sometimes referred to as "the Maspero Triangle" (named after a European Egyptologist, and associated usually with the state's Radio and Television Building on the corniche), is the northern periphery of the linked Midans Tahrir and 'Abd al-Mun'im Riyad. Bulaq is home to mostly very poor people and has been made almost impassable to the surrounding city. There is literally no pedestrian articulation with either the adjacent downtown Cairo, or with the Nile Corniche, which is essentially a highway. The state's policy for several decades had been to empty Bulaq of its longtime residents to make way for exclusive developments on the corniche (hence accessible only by automobile).[20] The result of state policies in place since the 1980s, favoring the largest and most powerful developers, was to effect a "structural and systematic process of evacuation of the social, economic, and physical being of the residents"

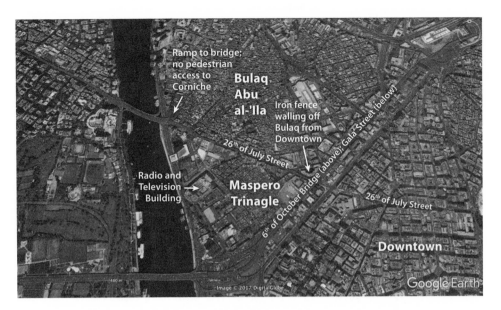

FIGURE 2.4. Northern border of Tahrir Square. Map data: Google Maps.

(O. Khalil 2015, 209). In the case of one area at the northern tip of Bulaq, beneath the tall shadows of two imposing gold-domed skyscrapers,[21] the new developments offset this "systematic process of evacuation" by providing some employment in such fields as construction and security for residents of the area. Consequently, in the early days of the revolution these residents protected the very projects that were displacing them (O. Khalil 2015, 212). But a string of postrevolution governments consistently supported the developers and did not hesitate to use police and Ministry of Interior forces against the residents. Hence by 2013 the same Bulaq residents who had defended the skyscrapers were joining protests against the ongoing forcible evictions from their neighborhood (postrevolution, 218–19).

The sides of Bulaq facing the city to the east and north (as opposed to the Nile Corniche on the west) were cut off from surrounding areas by fences and traffic flyovers, and increasingly by grandiose state development. The remaining residents of Bulaq could communicate with the city only through what should have been (and was until the 1990s) a major traffic corridor running east-west from the elite neighborhood of Zamalek to downtown straight through Bulaq. However, during the three decades prior to the revolution, that corridor was almost completely blocked to foot traffic at either end of Bulaq. On the west end of Bulaq pedestrians were forced to cross the corniche, essentially a two-lane highway constricted at strategic intervals by unofficial microbus stops which disgorged passengers into the middle of nowhere, after which they had to walk uncomfortably and unaccommodated by urban design to somewhere. The old bridge that used to continue from Bulaq into Zamalek was torn down, and vehicular traffic heading west through Bulaq instead emptied onto the ramp of a traffic flyover—essentially a highway into the sky that traversed Zamalek in the air, leading to upscale neighborhoods, or to the distant reaches of Cairo's ring road and the still largely uninhabited new cities. It seems like a great irony that a poor and beleaguered neighborhood like Bulaq should be better connected to the distant elite neighborhoods of the desert, until one remembers that the long-term plan for Bulaq is extinction of the existing neighborhood in favor of high-end development.

At the east end of Bulaq vehicles were also funneled into ramps elevating drivers onto flyovers that whisked vehicular traffic off to distant neighborhoods. When pedestrians—the vast majority of Bulaq residents—tried to leave the area they encountered a steel fence on the downtown edge of the neighborhood. Or to be more precise, the steel fence would have prevented pedestrian movement if "people power" had not succeeded in knocking a few gaps in it, through which residents and other pedestrians could infiltrate in the interest of moving between downtown and Bulaq. Enterprising microbuses could take a plucky resident of Bulaq only toward flyovers. Most Cairo streets had been converted to one-way thoroughfares in the interest of keeping private automobiles from standing still. One could escape from Bulaq in any direction only by filtering through the gaps in fences or dodging across fast-moving traffic.[22] The intentional isolation of the Maspero Triangle southern end of Bulaq—walled off by massive skyscrapers on the Nile Corniche side, and closed off on the other two sides by impassable roads and fences—led some developers to nickname it "the Bermuda triangle" (Abaza 2011, 1075). But there was no mystery about why unlucky travelers into Bulaq seemingly disappeared. The developers themselves have spent decades trying to make the entire area disappear.[23]

The Southern Periphery

The south end of Tahrir is similar, and yet utterly different: similar because the area is cut off from its surroundings; different because the logic is security of the inhabitants *inside* the quarantined area. "Security measures transformed not just the city's built environment but also the mobility practices of its residents, as motor vehicles and, in some sites, pedestrians were deemed a potential threat to a select group of people, namely political figures, while they were at home, work, leisure, or in transit themselves" (Monroe 2013, 80). That statement refers to Beirut, but it applies equally to Cairo, and particularly to the southern end of Tahrir Square (see figure 2.5).

The southern periphery of Midan al-Tahrir abuts Garden City, an early twentieth-century neighborhood laid out in a curving art nouveau plan that is quite long, but rather narrow, running from Midan al-Tahrir on the north to the Qasr al-Aini Hospital on the south, parallel to the Nile. Garden City is an elite neighborhood, though one much altered over time, as the generous gar-

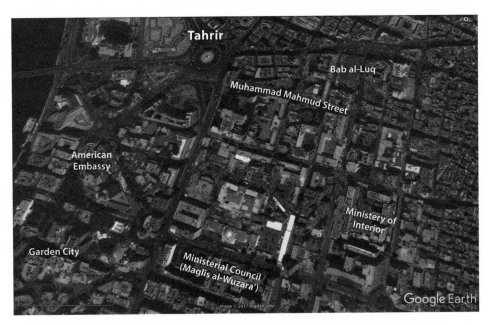

FIGURE 2.5. Southern border of Tahrir Square. Map data: Google Maps.

dens of the original design have largely been filled in with lucrative apartment buildings. It was and remains the location of many embassies, including those of Great Britain and the United States. Starting in 1979, with the signing of the Camp David peace treaty between Israel and Egypt, Egypt became the second-largest recipient of US foreign aid,[24] and consequently the American diplomatic mission to Egypt became one of the largest in the world. The US embassy is located at the northern end of Garden City, about a one-minute walk to Midan al-Tahrir.

The political status of the US embassy in Cairo was sufficient to give it a high profile. For the past two decades the United States had been the most forceful (literally) proponent of the "Washington consensus," which broadly espoused free-market-oriented political-economic policies associated with neoliberalism (Williamson 2004). Egypt was an important test case of free-market ideology in the Middle East, and as many have pointed out, by the time of the revolution it had been considered a success story in economic liberalization. The political role of the United States in promoting economic liberalization and privatization was well known in Egypt for decades.

But the US embassy also made a significant mark on the physical space of Cairo—a mark indelibly associated with the policies it espoused. Before the expansion of the American embassy in the 1980s, it had previously been housed in a nineteenth-century villa. This was torn down, to be replaced by two enormous towers, each around ten stories high, and designed for security, with few windows and none at ground level, hence easily sealed off in the event of a breakdown in control of the embassy's perimeter. The iron fence that had surrounded the US embassy was replaced with a very high and very thick wall, and truck-bomb barriers were placed outside the walls. The crowd-resistant architectural style (minus the walls and truck-bomb barriers) will be familiar to anyone who has toured American college campuses, many of which adopted the same basic design for key administrative buildings in the wake of the 1960s student movement. No doubt the Iranian hostage crisis of 1979 played a role in the redesign of what had been a fairly accessible and modest embassy, and even more so the bombing of the US embassy in Lebanon in 1983, in which sixty people were killed. But locally the new defensive posture of the embassy was associated more with the unpopular American-sponsored support of normalizing relations with Israel. Having been in Egypt myself in the summer of 1984 when the walls were going up (the Darth Vader towers came later), I remember reading then-president Ronald Reagan's loud proclamation that the United States was "standing tall" in the wake of the Lebanese debacle, even as the embassy was actually hunkering down behind high and hopefully impregnable walls. Thereafter I always thought of the new fortification as "the standing tall wall." It was of course in reality an implicit admission of fear. After construction of the Cairo embassy's "standing tall wall," higher walls became US policy throughout the region, regardless of the message it sent to populations already inclined to be suspicious of American political agendas. The infamous five-square-mile fortified "Green Zone" in Baghdad, following the 2003 American invasion and heavily contested occupation, became the most elaborated expression of American neoliberal-colonial architecture. But its logic was familiar to anyone who had been in Cairo in the 1980s.

For Egyptians the real affront came after 2003, in the wake of the invasion and occupation of Iraq and the 9/11 attack on the United States two years earlier. In response to American security concerns the Egyptian government assented to a plan to shut all the streets around the US embassy, effectively closing off the north end of Garden City (and southern border of Tahrir Square), and as a consequence weirdly mirroring the urban planning apartheid imposed on Bulaq at the northern end of Tahrir Square. Closure to traffic that might have passed into or through Garden City imposed significant impediments to movement throughout the area. Garden City became an island with fast-moving traffic moving around it, essentially traffic sewers, like the flyovers taking traffic out of Bulaq. The urban planning crime committed against Garden City was in truth of far less magnitude than the atrocity visited on Bulaq. The more powerful residents of Garden City rarely walked, hence the pedestrian problems caused by the embassy street closures were scarcely noticeable to them. In their cars they could always pass through the checkpoints designed to keep outsiders at bay. Bulaq, by contrast, was slated for extinction, cut off from both pedestrian and vehicular communication with its surroundings, whereas Garden City, though unpleasantly besieged by traffic, remained one of the most exclusive districts in Cairo.

Nonetheless, in the political imaginary the crime against Garden City was much more serious. In 2003 novelist Sonallah Ibrahim delivered an electrifying speech rejecting a LE 100,000 literary prize given by the Supreme Council of Culture. He denied the legitimacy of the Egyptian government, at one point focusing on its collusion in the closure of streets around the American embassy: "the American ambassador occupies an entire quarter [i.e., Garden City] even as his soldiers spread throughout every corner of the nation that used to be Arab" (Ibrahim as quoted in "Tasfiq Had" 2003). For intellectuals Ibrahim's denunciation of the Mubarak regime was a key step on the road to the January 25 Revolution. It cannot be doubted that the most committed core of secular activists occupying Midan al-Tahrir in the eighteen days were all well aware of his calling out of the American embassy. Many observers of and participants in the early days of the revolution remarked on how little emphasis there was in the rhetoric and chants of the protestors on foreign intervention. All attention was focused on the regime in Egypt, and little was said about its links to foreign powers, or its place in the hierarchy of America's empire. That would not be the case in the longer term.

Conclusion: The Revolutionary Stage

The social organization of space is intrinsic to the ritual process (Thomassen 2014), and by extension to performance, which draws heavily on the same universal processes and forms (Schechner 1988 [1977]). Schechner discusses performance space in terms of what he called an "axiom of frames": by this he meant a relation between how space was delimited, and the conventions of performance. This relation governs the freedom of actors to improvise, or restrictions against it as the case may be. Schechner intended his insights to have relevance beyond formal theatrical performance, and his axiom of frames can accordingly be adapted to Tahrir Square. I do not see myself as "stretching" Schechner's performance theory here, but as following it where it actually should lead.

This chapter has examined the material frame of Tahrir. As a space it has been shaped by the political-economic policies of the past four decades, which essentially turned it into an antihuman space, nominally suitable only as a "nonplace" that people passed through. A liberalized economy under the umbrella of a state that systematically redistributed income upward shaped demands for "bread, freedom, and social justice" as surely as it walled off Bulaq from communication with its urban surroundings, segregated Garden City to protect the imperial agents of the "Washington consensus," and prepared downtown for private redevelopment. The causes of the revolution were inscribed in the urban fabric of its primary theater. It should be emphasized that the revolution-era character of Tahrir Square is incomprehensible without linking it to the growth of the *formal* parts of the expanding city, specifically the suburbs and their gated communities. But it is equally incomprehensible without similarly linking it to the even more significant growth of the *informal* parts of the city, and indeed the more general character of informality in many spheres of life, most significantly labor, which was systematically made precarious by the same design that poured resources into the new cities and slated Bulaq for extinction. But as we will see, the quotidian antihuman Tahrir Square depicted in this chapter has greater depth as a performance space than one might think.

CHAPTER 3

The Martyrological Frame

The heterotopia is capable of juxtaposing in a single real place several spaces, several sites that are in themselves incompatible. Thus it is that the theater brings onto the rectangle of the stage, one after the other, a whole series of places that are foreign to one another; thus it is that the cinema is a very odd rectangular room, at the end of which, on a two-dimensional screen, one sees the projections of a three-dimensional space.

—Michel Foucault, "Of Other Spaces" (1986, 25)

Trustworthy men hold the reins of power.

—Caption on the poster of the "Prince of Martyrs,"
Brigadier General Ibrahim al-Rifaʻi, shown saluting the
statue of ʻAbd al-Munʻim Riyad, January 25, 2012

FRAMING, THE SUBJECT OF THE previous chapter and the starting point for this one, has a long history in the social sciences.[1] It is a common analytical device used in many different ways. For example, anthropologist Gregory Bateson defined a psychological frame as "a spatial and temporal bounding of a set of interactive messages" (1987 [1972], 147). Media scholar Todd Gitlin understood frames as "persistent patterns of cognition, interpretation, and presentation, of selection, emphasis, and exclusion, by which symbol-handlers routinely organize discourse" (1980, 7).[2] For both of them, frames either enable or constrain intelligibility. The principle applies to performance as well.

In the previous chapter I introduced Richard Schechner's classic *Performance Theory* (Schechner 1988 [1977]). Schechner did not push his analysis into politics very much, but he did consciously articulate his approach to performance with respect to what Victor Turner called "social drama" (Turner 1980, 150)—a later reformulation and expansion of the ritual process—which Schechner paraphrased as "macro-drama": "large-scale social actions viewed performatively . . . where whole communities act through their collective crises" (Schechner 1988 [1977]), 326).

One characteristic of a performance space is that it is periodically "fallow"— it sits empty in other words, when it is not being used for performance (Schechner 1988 [1977]), 14). Tahrir Square is of course used all the time but is only periodically employed as a *political theater*. Secondly, a performance space is "organized so that a large group can watch a small group—and become aware of itself at the same time" (Schechner 1988 [1977]), 14–15). Mass mediation makes this possible, and we all know that there has been a tremendous amount of speculation about the importance of media to the January 25 Revolution. Earlier "new media" such as the press or the radio could gesture at this specatorial dimension of performance, but the simultaneity of live television broadcast or connection through social media gave Tahrir a bond between audience and spectator akin to live theater. Moreover, the essence of a "large group watching a small group" is the act of watching or even the impulse to watch more than the relative size of the groups watching or being watched. Hana Sabea mentions "the oscillation between [the square's] appearance as a space of revolution and a space of carnival, which attracted many 'to come and see,' to consume and be consumed by the moment and the place" (2013). The point is that the principle of a relation between the watched and the watching is more elastic than Schechner's passage suggests.

Thirdly, a performance space is an area of "play," not in the sense of children's play, but in the sense of "free activity" bounded by loose frames, where one makes one's own rules (Schechner 1988 [1977]), 15–19). This is suggestive for politics, and specifically for political processes understood through liminality. The sphere of "play" in Schechner's analysis is the phase of liminality within a political performance patterned on the ritual process. If the "frames" that determine the space of play are physical—for Schechner stages, sets, and props; in our context the space of Tahrir Square as it evolved over four decades of neoliberal restructuring of urban space—then they must also be conventional: rules for performance, whether scripted, directed, or improvised.

The liminal space within the frames is where actors are free to improvise; yet the space itself is also heterotopic—like the stage or the screen on which a film is projected, as invoked in the epigraph of this chapter. But whereas Foucault imagined the endless chain of "places foreign to each other" within a framed space, Schechner refines the implications for performance. Expansive flexible performance spaces necessitate precise rules for controlling what the actors do. The opposite extreme is that tight outer frames facilitate loose inner frames. Improvisation occurs most readily in the context of tight outer frames.

The contentious performances in Egypt's most symbolically prominent performance space were famously improvisational, at least at first glance. Countless observers marveled at the clever signs made, astonishingly, by novice activists with no previous history of protesting; at the creative use of history in invoking political resistance movements of earlier eras such as the student movement of the early 1970s, the 1919 Revolution against British imperialism, or cultural icons of the Nasser era; poetic slogans; "tweets from Tahrir"; or in some moments, the flexible tactics used to organize battles against regime forces.[3] But at the same time there were common themes; "repertoires" as sociologists of contentious performance call them (Tilly 2006). In the absence of formal directors (though protest leaders and organizers fulfill that function to a degree), these repertoires constitute a fund of conventions—the "inner frame" of Schechner's axiom of frames. The conventions of Tahrir were shaped by its history, which was connected to anticolonial struggle and rituals of death—both official commemorative rituals, and in the revolution, mobilizational rituals of martyrdom.[4] Martyrdom became one of the most salient idioms of the revolution, but it did not emerge from a vacuum. Tahrir Square had what one might call a martyrological frame, which is an important part of what made this particular space effective for political performance insofar as it provides at least a partial answer to a question many observers of the revolution asked (e.g., Sabea 2013): why Tahrir Square in particular, and why at that particular moment in 2011?

The Importance of Death

Death serves as one of the most powerful occasions for a rite of passage. In the revolution death of a comrade was always labeled as *istishhad*, martyrdom. However, martyrdom in the active process of political contention is less a rite of passage than a *refusal* of passage. Those who remembered the martyr sought to keep him or her suspended between life and death, or even considered "still alive" as long as the cause that endows a death with meaning remains unfulfilled.[5] Just as the material form that shaped Tahrir Square as a political theater acted as a performance frame, so too did the commemoration of martyrdom.

Martyrdom in the revolution was often contested by the state or by opponents of the revolution. Commemoration, by contrast, was more often a bid to legitimize the authority of the state. Public memory aims to promote values rather than facts (Volk 2010, 4), and particularly when memory is connected to dead bodies—particularly bodies that have died in highly significant circumstances—it enters into "struggles to endow authority and politics with sacrality or a 'sacred' dimension" (Verdery 1999, 36). "Sacrality" in the case of Tahrir Square was not so much a quality of religion per se as a powerful activator of nationalist affect that makes the nation the "limited imagining" that nonetheless causes "so many millions of people, not so much to kill, as willingly to die" for it (Anderson 2006, 7).

Tahrir Square functioned as an icon of the revolution, and so did martyrs, both revolutionary and officially commemorated. All popular icons in the mediascape tend to be provisional because they emerge through an "iconic process" analogous to Turner's "ritual process." The emergence activates a threshold, like a crossing into the "uncanny present" (Bryant 2016). A popular icon emerges from the ordinary in particular situations and for many reasons—because of the prominence of the martyr in society, the circumstances of the death, or the role the person played in the cause. But in all cases it is particularly the *moment of separation* from the ordinary that draws the eye— the primary function of the icon. The moment of separation between the icon and the ordinary is a border, a "limn." Thereafter the popular icon may lose its power and recede back into the ordinary unless it can perform a longer-lasting mediational role, which is no mean feat in a contemporary mediascape that constantly generates eye-catching spectacle.[6] Elvis Presley, for example, retains his iconic status because he mediates between our contemporary condition and a lost moment—the "birth of rock and roll," or the ethos of a particular age. Thus he occupies a contradictory position on the edge between two things; he become an "iconoclash" (Latour 2002), inspiring passion because his icon is both infuriatingly not "the thing," while at the same time functions as a necessary link to it. But for every Elvis Presley there are a thousand Peter Framptons—eye-catching for a brief mass-mediated moment, before they recede into the category of ordinary performers. Or in the context of Egypt one might say, provocatively, that for every Sayyid Qutb—a massively salient martyr in Islamist circles—there are a thousand "ordinary" martyrs whose contested grievability becomes secondary to their obscurity. The obvious partiality of an iconic person's devotees is intentional. Sayyid Qutb, the Muslim Brotherhood ideologue executed by Nasser, is decidedly iconic only for some, and a deeply polarizing figure over the long term. Many other martyrs, as we will see in the next chapter, proved likewise to be both a focus of contention and a bid for mobilization.

The provisional, emergent, and productively unstable nature of iconicity resonates with an understanding of revolution as liminal crisis. Tension between provisionally iconic martyrs that unify and mobilize, and martyrs as a focus of contention facilitates contentious political performance. The important thing is not what martyrs or icons *are*, but rather *how* they are. But my aim here is not to discuss the performances so much as to focus instead on what defines the space in which January 25 Revolution icons take place—space that, in the case of Tahrir Square, was marked by martyrologies long before the January 25 Revolution. Hence I turn my attention to the "legitimate" side of revolutionary commemoration through martyrdom. Over the long term commemorations shape Tahrir Square as a space for political performance, while the performances themselves are often wildly at odds with the significance of the commemorations.

For the Sake of the Martyrs

In the wake of the January 25 Revolution countless political speeches, demands voiced at demonstrations, or newspaper editorials were predicated on the sometimes directly stated notion of "for the sake of the martyrs." Martyr graffiti was already all over downtown and many other parts of the city before the most spectacular canvasses of revolutionary wall art drew global attention.[7] Martyr music videos filled the mainstream video clip channels and the dead air time on all the mainstream television stations (Gilman 2011).

All these unsanctioned and revolutionary memorials to martyrs blended easily into the novelty of the new-media tactics employed by activists in 2011. However, the objects of these commemorations articulated not just with like-minded people, but also with a "martyr-scape" of the past. Wars of course inevitably shaped Egyptian memory culture, serving as generational markers. This was true to varying extents of the 1919 Revolution, the student revolt in the mid-1930s, the Suez War (1956), and the October War (1973). The disasters of the Palestine War of 1948 and the June War of 1967 are not directly commemorated but have instead been assimilated to their respective *aftermaths*, thereby enabling a kind of de facto commemoration.[8] In the case of 1948, the military fiasco suffered by Egyptian forces in Palestine was not so much assimilated as it was eclipsed by an ensuing guerrilla war fought against the British in the canal zone. The conflict in the canal zone was commemorated in art and public culture, thereby creating a kind of nationalist catharsis after the disaster in Palestine.

Within Egypt's larger martyrological history, it is precisely the campaign against British occupation of the canal zone in the late 1940s and early 1950s that stands out in the context of the January 25 Revolution. Tahrir Square gets its name from the liberation from the British resulting from this campaign; and January 25 was chosen as the opening date of the revolution specifically after an event that took place during the Battle for the Canal.

Conflict with Britain began escalating after the end of the Second World War in 1945, spurred by an upsurge in nationalist sentiment that saw British infringements on Egyptian sovereignty in the postwar era as intolerable.[9] In the canal zone fighting became very fierce in 1951, and paramilitary actions against the British were a popular cause in the late 1940s and early 1950s. The massacre of a unit of Egyptian policemen in Isma'iliyya on January 25, 1952, forms a genealogical link between this period and the present.[10] In 1952 it was the beginning of the end of the monarchy—" for some . . . an incident in which ordinary Egyptians reclaimed urban spaces from which they had been previously excluded . . . for others . . . a clarion call for revolution" (Reynolds 2012, 181). The Free Officers coup removed the king in July, and shortly thereafter Midan Isma'iliyya became Midan al-Tahrir. The massacre led the next day, January 26, to intense riots in Cairo, which spun out of control and resulted in acts of arson that severely damaged many downtown buildings, very near to the square.[11]

The martyrs of this massacre were commemorated by the designation of Police Day on January 25. In 2009 the Mubarak regime gave added emphasis to Police Day by decreeing that it would become an official holiday observed by the closure of public institutions. As the Ministry of Interior's own website put it, this was done "in appreciation of the efforts of the men of the police, and in acknowledgement of their sacrifice in achieving the security and stability of the nation" (Markaz al-I'lam al-Amni 2009). Given the Mubarak regime's ever-increasing dependence on harsh security tactics, upgrading Police Day to an official public-sector holiday can only be seen as a provocation, as the organizers of Yaum al-Ghadab (the Day of Rage) on January 25, 2011, were very well aware.

A link between martyrs of the 2011 Revolution and history was emphasized in a photo feature of youths killed in the early days of the revolution published by the newspaper *al-Masry al-Youm* (see figure 3.1).[12] The images published by the paper were culled from the martyrs' Facebook photos, accompanied by text that endeavored to link the martyrs of 2011 with those of earlier events. In the first instance the most prominent link with history was not with the 1952 massacre of the police, but with the student movement of the 1970s, which was evoked pointedly by a line from a poem by a prominent leftist poet: *il-ward illi fattah fi ganayin Masr*—the flowers that bloomed in the gardens of Egypt (Nigm 2005 [1973]). The text originally published along with these images consciously ties them to 1952:

> Fifty-eight Egyptian martyrs from the police fell by the bullets of the occupation during the battle for Isma'iliyya in defense of their country on January 25th, and on another January 25th dozens of Egyptian youth fell as martyrs to the bullets of despotism, in defense of a new future for the same country. Between 1952 and 2011 a blood-tinged "Egyptian tale" traces its features in the faces of the martyrs of a revolution of youth that is now entering its thirteenth day. ("Shuhada' 25 Yanayir" 2011)

The massacre of fifty policemen in Isma'iliyya had not occurred in a vacuum. The central figure in that long-ago drama was a peasant woman named Umm Sabir from a village near the large British supply base in Tel El-Kebir near Isma'iliyya. Now semiforgotten, the Umm Sabir incident was a prominent cause célèbre at the time.[13] She was an innocent bystander slain in 1951 by a panicky British soldier during a botched inspection of a public bus and became instantly labeled a martyr in the press coverage of the time. A lurid cover of the November 19 issue of the weekly magazine *al-Ithnayn* depicted her death agony with the caption, "Umm Sabir: Martyr of Tyranny" ("Umm Sabir, Shahidat" 1951; and see also "Umm Sabir . . . wa Madha" 1951, from the same issue).

FIGURE 3.1. *Al-Masry al-Youm* martyrs feature from February 6, 2011.

Two years later a 1953 issue of *al-Ithnayn* depicted Umm Sabir in a more dignified (even provisionally iconic) portrait: a noble peasant woman's face, eyes focused on distant horizons, with a village painted in smaller scale below (see figure 3.2). This was not meant to be her own village, but rather one named in her honor. An article explaining the cover image described her as "the first martyr" of the *ma'rakat al-tahrir* (battle of liberation) and reported that the first new village of Tahrir Province would be named Qaryat Umm Sabir.

FIGURE 3.2. "Umm Sabir, the Martyr of Tal al-Kabir," on the
cover of *al-Ithnayn* 1006 (September 21, 1953).

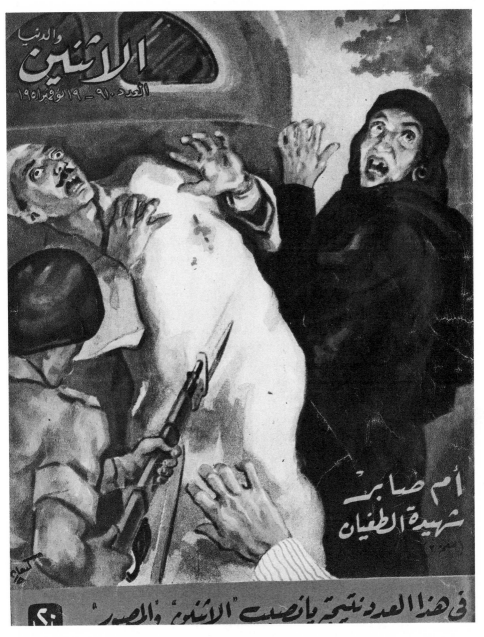

FIGURE 3.2. (*continued*) "Umm Sabir, Martyr of Tyranny" on
the cover of *al-Ithnayn* 910 (November 19, 1951).

The point of an article inside the issue was not to glorify Umm Sabir, but rather to reveal that while Umm Sabir had become widely celebrated, her image being carried in demonstrations and her name put on a village, her survivors were doing poorly. Her niece's husband had been wounded in the same incident, her sister was blind, and her daughter sick, and no meaningful compensation from the government had been paid ("Inqadhu" 1953).

The state had in fact carried through on its promise to name a village in Tahrir Province after her. Tahrir Province itself was a major public-sector venture of the Nasser era, in which the state's investment into infrastructure, particularly land reclamation, was to result in production of fruits such as strawberries and mangoes, and considerable employment opportunities for university graduates.[14] The Tahrir Province project is remembered as a technopolitical venture that "mobilized an armature of metaphors of factories, steel, and a vanguard of soldiers" (El-Shakry 2007, 210). Indeed, Magdy Hasanayn, the Free Officer who initially headed the project, dedicates his book on Tahrir Province to "thousands of noble anonymous soldiers of our eternal people who sacrificed their souls and blood" (M. Hasanayn 1975, 6). The "liberation" that was the namesake of Tahrir Province was, of course, the same battle for liberation that culminated in the Free Officers' seizure of power, as is the now much more famous Tahrir Square.

The theme of the state's failure to recognize martyrs resonates with the present. The rhetorical claim made through idiom of martyrdom is redressive: *"you can't argue with this; something must be done."* Redressive action for martyrs of the Battle for the Canal in the 1950s was prominent in the campaigns waged around the figure of Umm Sabir. This was also the case in the January 25, 2011, revolution, when retribution was a prominent demand in many of the demonstrations that occurred after the fall of the regime. Such demands were both literal (though never met by the state), and an idiom, a means for asserting that the revolution was unfinished, in direct opposition to state campaigns, starting with the interim military government and continuing right into the Morsy era, to slam the door shut (see figure 3.3).

For example, one could see an image war waged in public space immediately after the fall of the Mubarak regime. Almost the instant the regime fell, Cairo was festooned with posters encouraging closure in the interest of "building Egypt," or "building the future." All the state-owned media echoed the sentiment of embracing the revolution implicitly for the purpose of declaring it over. On the other side, the revolutionary forces wanted very much to *avoid* closure. Consider, for example, the genre of "build Egypt" posters placed in many public places. There were thousands of them. One in Ramsis Square, for example, soothingly said, "We all love Egypt; your hand in mine we will build and reconstruct." Below ground that sentiment was counteracted by "micrograffiti" in the metro trains. The Metro stop at Ramsis Square had been named after Mubarak. For months citizens waged a campaign to change the station's

FIGURE 3.3. Nominally prorevolution government posters near Ramsis Square. Left: "We all love Egypt." Right: "O Lord, protect Egypt." April 2011. Author's photos.

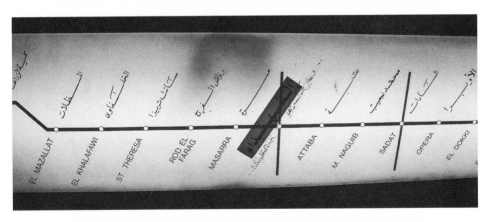

FIGURE 3.4. Metro guide in an underground train. The Mubarak stop (Ramsis Square) has been written over with "Shuhada'" (martyrs). Author's photo.

name by scratching out "Mubarak" on the station guides above the doors in the trains, and writing in *shuhada'*, "martyrs." This underground "write-in" campaign was successful, and the name of the Mubarak station was indeed changed to Shuhada' (see figure 3.4).[15]

The struggle over public space echoes a historical dynamic in which martyrs present incontrovertible arguments, implicitly stating that "you may disagree with my political demands, but you can't oppose *this*," "this" being the image of someone who paid the ultimate price for the cause. In practice martyrs, like all political "dead bodies," function as points of political contention

FIGURE 3.5. "First Martyr from the University." Cover
of *Al-Musawwar* 1423 (January 18, 1952).

rather than as points of closure. "All that is shared is everyone's *recognition* of
this dead person as somehow important. In other words, what gives a dead
body symbolic effectiveness in politics is precisely its ambiguity, its capacity to
evoke a variety of understandings" (Verdery 1999, 29). Older martyrologies
reflect the same dynamic. An image from the press coverage of the Battle for
the Canal in the early 1952 shows this well and can again be put in a historical
genealogy linked to the revolution in 2011. The January 18, 1952, edition of
Al-Musawwar ("Awwal Shahid" 1952) memorialized "the first martyr from the
university," 'Adil Ghanim, a medical student killed when he and eleven other
students attacked a heavily defended British position near al-Tel al-Kebir. They
set off a mine and came under fire. 'Adil, manning one of the group's machine

guns, drew the British fire so that his friends could escape, and he was killed as a result of his act ("Misr Tushayyi" 1952; see figure 3.5).

Ghanim's martyrdom was packaged in *Al-Musawwar* with that of three other students who died in the Battle for the Canal. Three of the four, including Ghanim, were members of the Muslim Brotherhood according to the brotherhood's own wiki site, which presents its alternative version of modern Egyptian history ("Ihtifal," 2011). *Al-Musawwar*'s profiles of the martyrs say nothing straightforwardly about brotherhood connections. In 1952, when the feature was published, tensions were high between the brotherhood and other political groups. The Muslim Brotherhood had been banned by Wafdist prime minister Mahmud al-Nuqrashi in 1948, leading to the assassination of al-Nuqrashi by a member of the brotherhood, and then Hasan al-Banna's assassination in 1949. The article did carry an oblique acknowledgement of the student martyrs' brotherhood affiliations. A photograph in the article on the bottom left of the two-page spread depicts a group of brotherhood-affiliated notables attending their funerals, including Hasan al-Hudaybi, the Murshid 'Amm, "General Guide" of the Muslim Brotherhood's Guidance Bureau, Hasan al-Banna's successor.[16]

However, the subtitle of the section in the article describing Ghanim's heroics was "min huna nabda" (from here we begin), which surely evoked a book by the same title written by Khalid Muhammad Khalid (Khalid 1974 [1950]). Khalid was an former member of the brotherhood. *Min Huna Nabda'* was a strong and popular denunciation of the brotherhood's ideology, and it had been published little more than a year before the university students were killed in the Battle for the Canal. Later in life Khalid recanted and joined the Islamic trend, but in the early 1950s his book was well known and was said to have been a key influence on Nasser. Hence by invoking Khalid Muhammad Khalid and also acknowledging the Muslim Brotherhood by including the photograph of the Murshid attending the students' funeral, the magazine article steers a delicate path through a minefield of "ownership claims" of the martyrs.[17] This is a distant but strikingly similar echo of similar contests between Islamist activists and those of other ideological convictions in the January 25 Revolution. Non-Islamist political forces argued that the Muslim Brotherhood "rode the wave" of a revolution made by others, and that the Islamist political agenda was in no sense revolutionary, or even in many ways politically reactionary. Islamists of course hotly disputed this narrative, partly on grounds that they had formed a counterpublic to the regime over many decades, often at great personal cost; partly on grounds that they saw the revolution as an ethical project more than as a more prosaic struggle for democracy; and partly on much-disputed grounds that they actually were active participants in overthrowing the regime in the early days of the revolution—crucially in the Battle of the Camel, the Mubarak regime's last-ditch attempt to drive the protestors from the square—despite public statements by the senior leadership that the movement should stay on the sidelines.

In 1952 *Al-Musawwar* described martyrs in heroic terms emphasizing their martial prowess. An anonymous wounded *fida'i* (guerrilla) interviewed at the beginning of the article from his hospital bed, claimed that Ghanim had killed fifty British soldiers before his heroic death: "Suddenly we heard his voice yelling "Allahu Akbar! I've been hit guys!" We turned toward him quickly and saw blood gushing from his chest, and his hand still had an iron grip on his gun'" ("Misr Tushayyi'" 1952, 13). Shahin was one of the activists claimed as a Muslim Brother on the Ikhwan wiki site, which hosts a very lengthy article on him, referenced to multiple sources ("al-Shahid 'Umar" 2014). At the same time, he was memorialized in the Nasser era by having a village named after him in none other than Tahrir Province—the second village, after Qaryat Umm Sabir as mentioned above. Both were meant to be model villages, planned to exacting scientific and technological standards, and peopled by "New Peasants." Magdy Hasanayn, the Free Officer in charge of the project in its early years, described the naming of the village as follows: "the first battalions of these new peasants were sent to the village of 'Umar Shahin, the great student who was martyred with his friend Ahmad Mansy [also claimed as a Muslim Brother on the Ikhwan-wiki site], both of whom were among the groups of fighters I trained for one of the battles against British imperialism at Tal al-Kabir" (M. Hasanayn 1975, 127).

The contrast between *Al-Musawwar*'s and Hasanayn's larger-than-life depiction of martyrdom makes a striking contrast to the understated way *al-Masry al-Youm* depicted January 25 Revolution martyrs in 2011. The newspaper's memorials to citizens killed in peaceful demonstrations against a violent regime were written almost like a resume: "The martyr Islam Muhammad Abd al-Qadir Bakir: 22 years old; bachelor's degree in the Faculty of Arts, Department of European Civilizations; died after being hit by live ammunition on the 'Friday of Rage' of January 28" ("Shuhada' 25 Yanayir" 2011). Or "the Martyr Ahmad Basiouny; 31 years old; teacher in the Faculty of Arts Education, Helwan University; father of two children, Salma and Adam; killed in Tahrir Square" ("Shuhada' 25 Yanayir" 2011). Just like 'Umar Shahin their images then became either a bone of contention or a political prize, though it seems unlikely that anything will be named after them.

Dueling Icons

Political martyrs often function as "bio-icons" which "bear an indexical charge for collectivities that place social demands through them" (Ghosh 2011, 12). In these circumstances the process of martyrology works by making claims through the idiom of the martyr—claims for independence from colonialism for example, or for retribution against those who killed the martyr. Claims are predicated on the fact that the martyr paid the ultimate price for a cause, and on the assertion that the "grievability" (Butler 2009) of martyrs is a given—an assertion that may form the basis of contention rather than of transcendental unity. In this situation a martyr is presented as an irrefutable call for re-dressive action. *"You can't argue with this; something must be done about it."* However, the irresistible force of the martyr will often be met with an im-moveable object of contention. In this revolution-as-liminal-crisis, martyrs were used as unifying symbols, but their mobilizing force was also used by the state against revolutionaries in a kind of commemorative jujitsu.

It very quickly became obvious that the apparent potential of the January 25 Revolution to inaugurate a less authoritarian social and political system in Egypt would not be quickly realized, or may even have been illusory. Conse-quently, in the interest of examining not just the "irresistible force" of the revo-lution, but also the "immovable objects" that opposed it, we might focus not just on the popular (but contested) iconization of martyrs, but also on the rela-tion of martyrology to commemoration, or in other words, on the dynamic between *official* use of martyrs and mobilizational martyrdom. The state's use of martyrology was already inscribed in Tahrir Square long before the January 25 Revolution. It is part of the materiality of Tahrir Square as a space for politi-cal performance.

Thus far the only lasting "legitimate" icon of the January 25 Revolution is not a human "bio-icon." It is rather Tahrir Square itself that forms a material sign standing for the January 25 Revolution in all representations of the revo-lution within spheres controlled by the state. "Legitimate" representations of Tahrir do feature humans, but they are strictly anonymous. It is the square itself that people are encouraged to "know" in official discourse, extending often to fictional films and television programs. Bio-icons of specific individual martyrs were plentiful in graffiti and private commemorations,[18] and they were pointedly named: Coptic activist Mina Daniel, Azharite official Shaykh 'Imad Effat, and Gaber "Jika" Salah, among many others.[19] But putting a name and a *biography* on a bio-icon inevitably evoked emotions and controversies that undermined the martyr's capacity as a unifying symbol. As the contested status of virtually all these martyrs suggests, commemoration responds to an imperative to say something about those who have fallen for the cause—a par-ticularly brutal imperative when the cause itself is hotly disputed. Indeed this chapter is premised on the notion that the "raw semiotic material" (Ghosh 2011, 10) used to propel the January 25 Revolution forward often consisted of martyrs. A discussion of martyrs and martyrology is a de facto discussion of provisional iconicity.

Protestors may harness the raw and unformed energy of provisional iconic-ity, the insistent claim that only a dead body can make to "do something about this" an imperative that can at least temporarily mobilize political action in the absence of anything that qualifies as an elaborated ideology. The state answers

FIGURE 3.6. *Left*: Statue of the martyr in the War of Attrition ʿAbd al-Munʿim Riyad (killed on March 9, 1969, in an Israeli artillery barrage). Placed in ʿAbd al-Munʿim Riyad Square adjacent to Tahrir Square in 2002. Author's photo. *Right*: A photo montage of the funeral of the martyr General ʿAbd al-Munʿim Riyad in Tahrir Square, *Images*, March 15–21, 1969.

with the power of commemoration. What protestors do with images of course is *also* a form of commemoration, but unlike the state, protestors usually cannot inscribe their commemorations permanently into the city's fabric and may in practice be more interested in *not* commemorating their friends' and comrades' deaths so much as in investing their deaths with meaning by symbolically keeping them alive and "in play" in political contention. Commemoration channels emotion in very different directions. Consider a commemorative marker that sat in the vicinity of Tahrir Square throughout the January 25 Revolution without anyone, as far as I know, ever commenting on it. This is the statue of ʿAbd al-Munʿim Riyad sited in ʿAbd al-Munʿim Riyad Square, which is for all practical purposes the edge of Tahrir Square—really, part of the same space. The statue was placed in this location only in 2002.[20] ʿAbd al-Munʿim Riyad was killed in 1969, in the War of Attrition fought after the defeat of 1967, during which the Egyptian army began to reestablish its credentials as a military force. His funeral was attended by many thousands ("Adieu Riad" 1969), the crowds completely filling Tahrir Square in scenes that now remind us of the January 25 Revolution (see figure 3.6).

FIGURE 3.7. Poster of *Amir al-Shuhada'* (Prince of Martyrs) General Ibrahim al-Rifaʻi, killed in the October War in 1973. Placed on a building facing the statue of ʻAbd al-Munʻim Riyad, as if saluting him. Author's photo.

If we think of Tahrir Square as a political performance space, then martyrdom features prominently in the frame as well as the performance. The statue of ʻAbd al-Munʻim Riyad is a historical part of the frame expressed materially. The very name of Tahrir Square is part of the performance frame. Liberation was the culmination of a long struggle, but the events that culminated it were rich in martyrology. The date chosen for the onset of the demonstrations that turned into the January 25 Revolution was a commemoration of martyrdom, and also a challenge to the state's control of its legacy; likewise the statue of ʻAbd al-Munʻim Riyad. Battles were fought in its shade. But the statue was not an innocent bystander; and like all other representations of martyrs, it was not an irrefutable fact that united disparate political positions but, on the contrary, stood for something that produced contention.

The military itself was part of the martyrological dynamic. Shortly after the Supreme Council for the Armed Forces (SCAF) took power, a poster of a second military martyr was placed on top of a building that faced the statue of ʻAbd al-Munʻim Riyad. This was Major General Ibrahim al-Rifaʻi, who was killed in the October War in an Israeli ambush. In the military's iconography he is known as *Amir al-Shuhada'*, the Prince of Martyrs.[21] This poster of him was used by SCAF in an attempt to firmly assert its domination: the phrase "Trustworthy men hold the reins of power" was emblazoned on it (see figure 3.7).

Revolutionaries did not necessarily agree. On March 9, 2011, SCAF began its first attempt to declare the revolution over, by arresting activists who remained defiantly in Tahrir Square despite orders to leave. Some of the activists were tortured on the grounds of the Egyptian Museum, which sits just a few meters west of the statue. This was the occasion for the notorious "virginity tests" carried out on female protestors and justified by General 'Abd al-Fattah al-Sisi, then considered a relatively junior member of SCAF (Abouel-naga 2015; Seikaly 2013). Just as the revolution was initiated on a day commemorating martyrs, so was SCAF's action against the revolution timed by martyrdom; March 9 is the day on which 'Abd al-Mun'im Riyad was killed. As events unfolded, March 9, 2011, turns out also to be the day that brought into the open the decline of the military's almost unquestioned prestige, a decline that had begun almost immediately after the fall of the Mubarak regime in February.[22]

The attempts of SCAF to create an immoveable object in the path of the revolution was met by an irresistible force. A statue asserting unity became instead a palette of contention. By the first anniversary of the revolution initial reluctance to confront SCAF was in full retreat. Tahrir Square resounded with *yasqut hukm al-'askar* chants. The pedestal of the military's immoveable object was covered with anti-SCAF graffiti (see figure 3.8).

Conclusion

The history of martyrdom inscribed in and around Tahrir Square constitutes one frame for the political performances that were the idioms of revolution. Indeed, martyrdom was an idiom of the performances themselves. Martyrs are very common in commemoration, though not necessarily iconic in the sense that they inspire veneration or attract the eye. As Lucia Volk puts it in the context of Lebanese Civil War monuments:

> Public memorials need to be considered as "events" with a life of their own. They keep changing along with the physical and cognitive landscapes around them, some are intentionally vandalized or accidentally damaged, others mysteriously disappear and reappear, are wounded and healed, and most of them keep expanding. (Volk 2010, 2)

Icons are also events insofar as they become iconic in the moment they stand out from the ordinary, but the capacity of icons to continually generate that moment is highly variable. The statue of 'Abd al-Mun'im Riyad was at best quasi-iconic. It *might* be eye-catching to someone moving through that part of the city on the way to Tahrir Square, and it would be foolhardy to deny that the military it symbolized can act as an object of nationalist veneration. The military, like Tahrir Square, is a "nonbio-icon"—a complex concatenation of narratives and images not reducible to a single human being.

As a part of Tahrir Square's performance frame 'Abd al-Mun'im Riyad presents a conundrum. Martyrology frames the space, and the statue subsumed within it, but by itself the statue is like thousands of streets, squares, and vil-

FIGURE 3.8. 'Abd al-Mun'im Riyad Square on January 25, 2012, the first anniversary
of the revolution. Calls to free blogger Michael Nabil and activist 'Ala' 'Abd al-
Fattah from military prison on the pedestal of the statue. Author's photo.

lages in Egypt that commemorate martyrs. One cannot always be confident
that a passerby would understand the significance of the name. There is a
street in Omaha, Nebraska, named Armbrust Drive, not because any of my
ancestors died for a cause, but because it runs through land that used to belong
to my father, who sold it to a developer, who somewhat fancifully commemorated my family. Someone riding a bus through Qaryat 'Umar Shahin might
think no more deeply about the name than a person passing through Armbrust
Drive.

However, it would be a mistake to dismiss the cumulative weight of commemoration as irrelevant to the political performances that took place in 2011
and its aftermath. The revolutionary political alternative, ideologically diverse
(or incoherent in a more critical vein), was enacted on a stage composed partly
of a much less ambivalent commemorative martyrological history that could
always potentially be mobilized against it. And it was mobilized with a ven-
geance in overthrowing Muhammad Morsy in the summer of 2013. Possibly

FIGURE 3.9. 'Abd al-Fattah al-Sisi in the company of dead presidents
Gamal 'Abd al-Nasser and Anwar al-Sadat. A poster handed out in the
weeks before the Tamarrud demonstration on June 30, 2013.

the real seizure of power by SCAF came not on June 30, the day of the Tamarrud (rebellion) protest against Morsy, but on July 26, when 'Abd al-Fattah al-
Sisi openly called for a popular tafwid (mandate) to "fight terrorism," making
an open accession to rule, ratified later by a patently fixed election, inevitable.
July 26, 2013, was al-Sisi's iconic moment, when he separated from the ordinary, drawing all eyes to himself (see figure 3.9). Tens of thousands of the
people thronging Tahrir Square and its surrounding streets on July 26 carried
posters of al-Sisi in that demonstration, essentially appointing him president

long before he would admit publicly that he wanted the job. Many of these posters visualized him in the company of Nasser and Sadat, essentially admitting him in advance to a kind of "dead presidents club." At that moment his name was literally on everyone's lips. But it should be emphasized that even though al-Sisi was backed by powerful individuals and institutions, and even though his emergence on the political scene indisputably drew all eyes toward him and inspired genuine veneration, his icon-hood was provisional, which is to say that it was inherently unstable. In the ritual process, communitas, a characteristic of the state of being in between normative social conditions, is full of endless promise, and inevitably attempts are made to institutionalize it (Turner 1977, 132). And so it is with the iconic process. Sisi and his backers have tried mightily to institutionalize his iconic moment, but such a project is very difficult to carry off. Putting him in the company of dead presidents may be jumping the gun. If he ends up on Egypt's figurative Mount Rushmore beside Nasser and Sadat (and one notes that the inclusion of either the latter or the former in the tableau already introduces an element of instability to the edifice, as quite a few people consider the veneration of Nasser to be incompatible with venerating Sadat) then he will prove to be a political genius. But in my opinion under the circumstance one may as well try to bottle lightning or juggle hummingbirds as to institutionalize the communitas of July 26, 2013. It seems more likely that Sisi's provisionally iconic image will end up a thousand times more contentious than any of the January 25 Revolution martyrs.

CHAPTER 4

The Disputed Grievability
of Sally Zahran

As long as Egypt is fertile
With labor pains and menstrual blood
Its sun will continue to rise
In spite of the Citadel and its jail cells

—Ahmad Fu'ad Nigm, "Sabah
al-Khayr," 1973 Sign al-Qal'a
(Nigm 2005 [1973], 312)

FOR ME THE STORY OF Sally Zahran began in Midan al-Tahrir on Friday February 25, 2011, billed as the "Day of Purification" ("'Gum'at al-Tathir'" 2011), one of what seemed then like an inexhaustible stream of revolutionary mass demonstrations.[1] The objective of that day's demonstration was removal of Prime Minister al-Fariq (Lieutenant General) Ahmad Shafiq, the Mubarak crony appointed early in the revolution in a desperate attempt to quiet the rebellion by reshuffling the cabinet. The actual demise of General Shafiq's prime ministership came about a week later, after he imploded on national television in an astonishing spat with novelist Alaa Al Aswany ("Khinaqat Ahmad Shafiq" 2011).[2] On the twenty-fifth Shafiq's fateful encounter with the bulldozer-like Al Aswany was not in anyone's crystal ball, but even if it had been, gauging the mood of the protests was as interesting to me as the demonstration's actual objective for the day. So accordingly I went to the "Day of Purification" to take some photos, look, and listen.

At one point I was standing in front of a bulletin board on which manifestos, artwork, and graffiti were posted. While I was trying to decide if it was worth photographing the small print of the manifestos, suddenly the voice of a man standing behind me rose angrily: "Look what the Muslim Brothers have done! Those sons of bitches—they've wiped out her picture just because she isn't wearing a hijab." At first I had no idea what they were talking about. Then I noticed which bit of paper on the wall they were referring to: the famous *al-Masry al-Youm* poster of January 25 martyrs, with the addition of Khaled Said, the young computer programmer who had been beaten to death by the police in Alexandria in June 2010, sparking a protest campaign that eventually became one of the main organizational streams of the revolution. The problem with this poster, and the reason for the outrage of the men behind me, was that one of the twelve faces on the poster had been scribbled out by a blue felt-tipped pen. The scribbled out face was the only woman in the poster's assemblage of martyrs: Sally Zahran (see figure 4.1).

The "famous poster," already introduced in the previous chapter, was not yet famous to me. This was my first conscious encounter with the *al-Masry al-Youm* martyrs' canon. To my lasting regret, I had not purchased the print edition of the paper that originally published the images, and consequently I was still unfamiliar with this collection of faces that was, by that time, spreading like a virus. I had not even noticed the disfigurement of Ms. Zahran's face until the argument about it broke out. Arguments appear to have been anticipated, as the poster had a guardian, a mustachioed middle-aged man in a sweater with just a small hint of a *zabiba* (a "prayer mark" cultivated by many pious men) on his forehead. Apparently he had been charged with defending and explaining his poster or perhaps had taken up the task on his own. The guardian of the defaced poster mumbled to the two angry men that Ms. Zahran had been a pious woman who wore the Islamic head scarf, and that all the un-hijabed pictures of her on the internet were being replaced by a new one of her as a *muhajjaba*. The angry men appeared disgusted, but not enough to start a fight. They moved on, leaving the defender of the disfigured poster to carry on with his mission.

Women and the Revolution

Sally Zahran was the only woman in the *al-Masry al-Youm* martyrs assemblage, and the fact of her gender must be a starting place in any analysis of her political significance. The revolution initially supercharged existing initiatives to advocate agendas of women's rights. These initiatives themselves took shape within tensions and contradictions of considerable historical depth, structured by postcolonial discourses in which women were potent symbols of national identity, active participants in a wide variety of feminist projects, but also subject to an ever-present weight of the West as both a model to be emulated and a yoke to be thrown off (Abu-Lughod 1998). In the two decades before the revolution all these historical tensions were present in, on one hand, a surge in activism engaged in defending and furthering women's rights, but on the other hand, co-optation of women's issues through state feminism, in which the Mubarak regime posed as the sole guardian of women (Abouelnaga 2015, 37), much as it had for Christians.[3]

FIGURE 4.1. The *al-Masry al-Youm* martyrs with Khaled Said added, but Sally Zahran scratched out. Tahrir Square on February 25, 2011. Author's photo.

Initially activists believed that the overthrow of the Mubarak regime could result in the breaking of tensions and the removal of political impediments. Yet throughout the revolution and its immediate aftermath there was never a moment in which "an androcentric value system that cherishes hierarchy and obedience and is blind to women" (El Said 2015, 110) was not the dominant power at the highest levels of Egyptian politics. This dominance extended over the "interim" rule of SCAF, the year of Muhammad Morsy's rule, and the subsequent seizure of power by 'Abd al-Fattah al-Sisi. Below the level of high politics, the basic dynamic of women's participation in the January 25 Revolution was that the revolution initially "seemed to have a feminist face, with prominent women activists at the forefront, [but that] as the events progressed women were relegated to the sidelines and, even more seriously, were aggressively violated" (El Said 2015, 109). Such figures as activist Mona Seif, April 6 Movement cofounder Isra' 'Abd al-Fattah, or human rights lawyer Mahienour El-Massry were key organizers and promoters of the revolution.[4] A video blog by Asma' Mahfuz, another cofounder of the April 6 Movement, was credited as an important spark in setting off the revolution (Mahfuz 2011). Yet once the revolution began women's leadership was continually cast in doubt, and women were subjected to a rising spiral of violence that pulled focus away from the agency of female activism and toward the symbolism of women's bodies, which in turn provided an opening for questioning women's participation in the revolution. A shocking incident in December 2011, in which a woman was beaten by the army in the breakup of a sit-in at the Ministerial Council and dragged on the ground until her body was exposed, acted as a kind of threshold for women in the revolution. Before the "blue bra" incident, as the December beating was called, women fought a rising tide of counter-revolutionary propaganda and brutality, but they retained some sense of political momentum; after the incident women were put on the defensive, as they were increasingly targeted for sexual violence in protest spaces (El Said et al. 2015; El Said 2015; Abouelnaga 2015). The story of Sally Zahran was a minor footnote among the prominent watershed moments in the revolution that were consciously connected by observers to the status of women.[5] But as we will see, she nonetheless achieved a level of iconicity that no other female figure enjoyed. Her iconicity was, however, controversial. What follows tracks the contours of these controversies and unpacks their significance to the course of the revolution.

Martyrdom: The Immovable Object and the Irresistible Force

Chapter 3 showed that martyrology was inscribed into Tahrir Square as commemoration—the state's immovable object. Martyrdom was also the revolution's irresistible force. It is easy to fall into the linguistic habit of describing many of the posters, stencils, and art works appearing on Cairo's walls as commemoration, but in the revolution the process of deciding which lives were grievable (Butler 2009) was distinct from the more specific tension between mobilization and closure. Commemoration in memorials and war cemeteries constitute rhetorical spaces of a particular kind, space "to imagine community that transcends ethnic, racial, and religious boundaries" (Volk 2010, 25). But commemoration can also be an aggressive assertion of unity when it is imposed on socially and politically fractured people. In the January 25 Revolution commemoration can be described as a form of closure intended to invoke and implant a transcendent unity that covers over or even erases differences, and ultimately history itself. Throughout the revolution the state and counterrevolutionary forces sought that kind of closure, often with direct appeals to forget politics, get back to work, and "build Egypt." Transcendent commemoration was not the goal of revolutionaries. Rather it was unity within the ranks of revolutionaries *against* their opponents, chief among them a state that continued to marshal its resources against them. Martyrs were less objects of mourning and remembrance than comrades to be kept "alive," because as long as they remained in the struggle "the revolution continues"—a phrase repeated endlessly whenever the revolution suffered reverses—and by definition this was meant agonistically. Making martyrs was revolutionary work, and indeed, work of a performative kind, which goes particularly well with the notion of revolution as liminal crisis in a protracted ritual process. "Performances need to be constantly reaffirmed, and they require an audience—one that might change over time and that might pull the interpretation in different directions" (Mittermaier 2015, 588). They are "tools for holding the state accountable" (Mittermaier 2015, 591).

While martyrs were often promoted as an issue in their own right, their high profile in the revolution owed much to their capacity to submerge issues on which there was no consensus—calls for socialism, for example, or imposition of shari'a. Other issues were less difficult for disparate revolutionaries to synthesize, and in this case martyrdom acted as a unifying symbol rather than an obfuscatory necessity. For months campaigns were waged to bring the Mubarak regime to justice, to curtail the arbitrary exercise of power by the interim Supreme Council for the Armed Forces, to repeal the emergency law that remained in effect long after the expiration of the regime, to challenge the culture of authoritarianism that had been nurtured by the regime, to reform structures of governance so as to facilitate the rule of law, and to reimagine institutions as more transparent vehicles for carrying out the people's will. Before the emergence of Sisi it seemed that these campaigns might have continued for years. But in February 2011, for the localized theaters of revolutionary contests to be comprehensible as true outcomes of the revolution (and hence sustainable and worth pursuing), they had to be expressed not just as a struggle of wills between individuals "on the ground," but also in symbolic terms linked to the larger cause(s) for which the revolution was fought. After the battle to overthrow the regime, symbols became a means of "scaling up" from local contests to a revolutionary project, against which all members of society were obliged to reckon a social position.

An image of a martyr projected into discourse or public space is an affective construct—a "pre-personal" experience of intensity (Shouse 2005), and therefore more visceral than emotion. Not everyone can experience the martyr so directly. For those more removed from the viscerality of martyrs, their images constitute an implicit invitation to declare a position on what these particular deaths signify. It is undoubtedly true that the meaning of martyrs for a given cause can become homogenized—locked in a matrix of consensus that limits interpretive scope, though it never kills it completely. But such fixing of the meaning of martyrs in the public imaginary emerged over time. In February 2011, and for most of the next two years, martyrs remained points of contention. This was clear from the beginning particularly in light of the brief history of Sally Zahran, one of the key martyrs of the early days of the revolution. The Sally Zahran case, particularly her contested status as a female martyr, demonstrates how martyrdom emerged as a key symbol for mobilizing affect and action, and how ambiguities in what martyrs signify can actually be productive in concrete political struggles over such issues as religious identity, gender, and nationalism.

The Rise and Fall of Sally Zahran

FAME

As mentioned above, by the time I discovered her, Sally Zahran's face had already become very famous as the only female figure on *al-Masry al-Youm*'s canonical February 6 martyrs' issue. Her image, with a vibrant smile and wild hair, was the largest, most central, and the most eye-catching on the page. The image was instantly adopted in protests, and marketed in revolution paraphernalia by an army of street vendors who had nothing to do with the political activists who organized the revolution. As time went by it became clear that at least some of the vendors were informants for the various security services, or baltagiyya—"thugs" in the pay of antirevolution forces—inserted as provocateurs who would ruin the reputations of the prodemocracy activists or even, in some cases, stir up trouble that would provide a pretext for the authorities to forcibly remove the protestors.

The same faces that appeared on paraphernalia sold in the square dominated representations of martyrs in other media, such as commercial music videos. In posters there were many variations on the martyr theme, some more truncated and others lengthier, but long after the fall of the regime remarkably few of the assemblages of martyrs' faces were completely devoid of the original *al-Masry al-Youm* martyrs' feature. In the months after Mubarak's fall one could see martyr paraphernalia on display in shops, in car windows, on buildings, and on cardboard amulets and quasi-official-looking "revolution badges." Within a few months most of this first wave of martyr posters grew tattered and damaged and were gradually removed from public space. But they only completely disappeared when the representation of martyrs became officially discouraged and eventually forbidden (see figure 4.2).

FIGURE 4.2. The *al-Masry al-Youm* martyrs reproduced on posters.
A protestor carrying a framed copy of the newspaper on January 25, 2012.

FIGURE 4.2. (*continued*) Poster based on the *al-Masry al-Youm* martyrs hanging from the pedestal of a statue of Tal'at Harb, a few blocks from Tahrir Square, on February 11, 2011, the night Mubarak resigned.

FIGURE 4.2. (*continued*) Poster using the *al-Masry al-Youm* martyrs with Sally Zahran in hijab, from July 2011.

The original selection of eleven martyr images was made by ʿAmr al-Hadi, a staff member of *al-Masry al-Youm*, "according to what was published by activists and friends of the victims on the internet" ("Shuhada' 25 Yanayir" 2011). One might surmise a logic of selection guided by social inclusiveness, though al-Hadi only hints at such an agenda, and he gives no indication of the degree to which the activists who supplied lists of martyrs guided his choices. Sally Zahran was the female representative. Ahmad Basiouny, another of the eleven, was a fairly well known artist and independent musician, who was later to be memorialized at the Venice Biennale (M. Hamdy 2011; Noshokaty 2011).[6] Mustafa al-Sawi was a representative of the Muslim Brotherhood in the poster.[7] Sayf Allah Mustafa was a youthful innocent bystander killed by a stray police bullet in Madinat Nasr. Muhammad ʿAbd al-Munʿim Husayn and Husayn Taha, killed in Raʾs Sidr and Alexandria respectively, provided regional diversity.

As mentioned in the previous chapter the original tableau was given a leftist resonance by titling the martyrs' page *al-ward illi fattah fi ganayin Masr* (the flowers that bloomed in the gardens of Egypt). It was a line from an Ahmad Fu'ad Nigm's poem, "Sabah al-Khayr" (Good morning). The last lines of the poem appear at the beginning of this chapter. Here is how it begins:

> Good morning to the roses that bloom in the gardens of Egypt
> Morning of the nightingale that chants songs of the *subu'*[8]
> Morning of the midwife, the swaddling cloth, casting salt in the
>   wedding procession
> A morning dawning with our flags from the Citadel to Bab al-Nasr
>   (Nigm 2005 [1973], 314)

Repeated references to the Citadel, more precisely the Citadel prison, index the work's politics. But these references are nonetheless relatively understated. In the context of visual commemoration in mass-produced posters of the youth destroyed by a corrupt state in the January 25 Revolution a quotation of the first line of the poem—"Good morning to the flowers that bloom in the gardens of Egypt"—was enough to convey the gist of Nigm's poem, even to those who might not have been intimately familiar with the full text or its provenance.[9]

Placing Nigm's poem on the martyrs' pantheon amounted to a salute from the 1970s generation of secular youth activists to that of the January 25 Revolution. It was Nigm himself who put his poem back into circulation in 2011, when he recited it during an al-Jazeera interview around February 1 ("Kalimat al-Sha'ir" 2011). Hence it was unsurprising that both the youth activists and perhaps the *al-Masry al-Youm* staff would have had it on their minds when the February 6 martyr feature was published. Nigm is known as a poet of the Left, and for his specific association with the student movement that crested in 1972 (Badawi 2007). Islamists were also tortured in the Citadel in that period, and even though the visual references of the *al-Masry al-Youm* selection of martyrs was consciously inclusive in this regard—the Muslim Brotherhood was pointedly represented in the figure of Mustafa al-Sawi—the application of Nigm's poem to the pantheon of martyrs was nonetheless a small foreshadowing of the coming contests over who "owned" the martyrs and, by extension, the revolution. In early February the flash of communitas in the early days of the revolution was already giving way to a contest for power carried out on multiple fronts, including the symbolism of martyrs.

By the time I almost landed in the middle of a fight over Sally Zahran's image on February 25, controversy over her narrative had been percolating for a while. It became known that she was a twenty-three-year-old activist. She had a BA from Sohag University, where her father was employed as a professor. Her major subject was English, and she had done some work as a translator. All accounts of Ms. Zahran's death agree that she died on January 28, the "Friday of Rage" that left the Central Security Forces broken after four straight days of trying to brutally suppress the demonstrations. By February 3 the regime's attempt to push the prodemocracy movement out of Tahrir Square with mercenaries had also failed, and shortly thereafter the work of creating revolutionary icons was in full swing. *Al-Masry al-Youm*'s martyrs' feature carried the caption "She was on her way to Tahrir Square when she was stopped by thugs, and hit on the head by a club. She died from the effects of a brain hemorrhage."

This version of Sally Zahran's story went "viral," elevating her not just to fame in Egypt, but to global iconic status within a few days. Many Facebook users substituted Sally Zahran's face for their profile pictures. A prominent artist painted her image, anointing Sally Zahran the "Egyptian Jeanne d'Arc" ("Sally Zahran: Jeanne d'Arc" 2011)—a phrase and image repeated on many a web page. She became "the bride of the white revolution" (Fayed 2011). Numerous poems were written in her honor.[10] *Al-Masry al-Youm* reported that an Egyptian American employee of the National Aeronautics and Space Agency had requested that Sally's name be inscribed on a microchip placed on a future mission to Mars.[11] That story mutated into reports that NASA would actually name the spaceship itself in her honor.[12] There were said to be plans for a Sally Zahran movie ("Mona wa Hilmi" 2011).

DOUBTS

Just as Sally Zahran's martyrdom was becoming a phenomenon, the contours of her story began to change dramatically. *Al-Masry al-Youm* reported on February 7—the day after publishing the famous martyrs feature—that Ms. Zahran had actually *not* been in Cairo, let alone Tahrir Square, on January 28, when she was supposed to have died ("Fallen Faces" 2011). She was instead in the Upper Egyptian town of Sohag, where her parents lived. The article still maintained that Ms. Zahran died as a result of being clubbed on the head by one of the regime's mercenaries. Shortly after *al-Masry al-Youm* corrected itself on the whereabouts of Sally Zahran when she died, additional details emerged that conflicted with the published narrative. The discrepancies made her an object of contestation between various parties—the regime and the revolutionary forces, as well as between nominal revolutionary allies.

So did her appearance. By February 11 a "Sally Zahran" Facebook group was started (or more precisely, the first and largest of several groups dedicated to the memory of Zahran), and by the fourteenth it was mired in disputes over how Sally looked. In the iconic image she was always shown with free-flowing hair, but it transpired that for at least some part of her life she wore the hijab (the Muslim head scarf worn by most Egyptian adult women). Pictures of her in hijab surfaced, and campaigns were waged to replace the un-hijabed Sally with the ones of her as a muhajjaba. Ms. Zahran's family was said to have initiated the requests to change the original picture used on Facebook and other internet sites to one of her in hijab ("Usrat al-Shahida" 2011).[13]

The claim that Ms. Zahran was a muhajjaba quickly attained the status of fact for many, and the campaign to replace images of the un-hijabed Sally with those of her as a muhajjaba was swiftly underway. On some Facebook groups any posting of the old un-hijabed Sally Zahran image was met with a snippy posting asking to have it removed. For example, in an exchange on a different matter one member of the "Sally Zahran" group used an ID image of the old *al-Masry al-Youm* martyr page with Sally Zahran front and center. Another member of the group posted "ya gama'a leeh nashart li-ha suwar wa hiyya bi-sha'riha ba'd wafatiha kida haram lamma hiyya muhajjaba aslan" (guys, why did you publish pictures of her with her hair [showing] after she died; this is haram when she's a muhajjaba originally). In some cases a picture of a muhajjaba Sally Zahran was photoshopped into the original *"Masry al-Youm* eleven" feature.

Some of the many Facebook groups that used the words "Sally Zahran" in their titles complied with the endlessly repeated (but unverifiable) "request by her family" to use the muhajjaba pictures. As of April 2011 there were approximately seventy-five such Facebook groups using Arabic characters, and twenty-five using the English alphabet. Many of the groups had the same titles but with different pictures, hence there were hijabed and un-hijabed versions of "Sally Zahran Bravest Egyptian Girl," and of "We Are All Sally Zahran." Some groups were entirely devoted to the hijab issue, such as "Together We Will Publish the Picture of Sally Zahran in Hijab" and "Call to Change the Picture of Sally Zahran" (using the hijab photo as the group's masthead). The effect of the campaign to put Sally Zahran in hijab was not only waged on Facebook. The masthead of the online version of the *Shorouk* newspaper briefly featured the old martyr montage with Ms. Zahran un-hijabed, and then, by March 3 at the latest, had photoshopped in a replacement image of her in hijab. Eventually hijabed Sally began to filter into the ubiquitous martyr products sold in the streets, though the majority of the posters and bumper stickers featuring martyr montages always used the old un-hijabed photo. Some people did so in conscious opposition to the hijab campaign. One of my former students, an Egyptian citizen who actively participated in the revolution, responded to a query I posted on Facebook about the hijab issue angrily:

> The *hijab* thing is absolutely not true. There was a massive uproar against it on twitter amongst her activist friends. She was in the Complaints Choir at Townhouse [a prominent private art gallery], friends of many of my friends. The *hijab* thing was completely fake to discredit her. some gov't articles (I havent seen) also suggested she was MB. This is just a horrible attempt to discredit her.

The same student forwarded some tweets by the famous contrarian blogger Sandmonkey[14] in which he quotes "a relative of Sally Zahran who doesn't wish to be named":

Believe it or not but her family mainly cares about her hegab photo is used in the press more than anything else in the world." #Sally (Sandmonkey)

"They really and sincerely do not care about the demos and do not want her to be associated with it.

. . .

"The girl was totally different from her immediate family & they didnt like at all the fact she removed the veil 2 years b4 she died" #sally (Sandmonkey)

"her veil was the main (and probably the only) thing they cared about when her photo was used."#jan25 #sally ("@Sandmonkey's" 2011).[15]

Various testimonies to the nature of Ms. Zahran's life and her actions in the revolution appeared on the internet, some obviously false, others clearly authentic.[16] But controversies over Ms. Zahran's status as a muhajjaba, which had been percolating from the day of her death on January 28, were to be overtaken by new twists to the story—information that had been known to people close to Ms. Zahran, but not to the general public.

On February 24 a popular television program broadcast an interview with Sally Zahran's family ("Baladna" 2011).[17] The report began with a narrator reciting the original story, that Sally Zahran was considered a martyr of the revolution, killed on the "Friday of Rage" by a truncheon blow from a thug on her way to Tahrir Square. During the introductory voice-over the camera panned over the iconic images of Sally Zahran: the *al-Masry al-Youm* print edition that showed Ms. Zahran's face as the centerpiece of a martyr montage; the famous photograph of Sally with her free-flowing hair; the "Sally Zahran as the Egyptian Jean d'Arc" painting being used as a computer screen's desktop image (later in the interview it becomes clear that it is the family's own computer in the living room). Then Ms. Zahran's mother began speaking:

> Suddenly there she was in newspapers being called a martyr; NASA names a spaceship after her; *ustaz* Mustafa al-Tuni [it was actually Ahmad al-Tuni] draws a caricature of her titled "Jean d'Arc"—"the Egyptian Jean d'Arc." Our Lord honored her in life; God willing He will honor her in the afterlife as well ("Baladna" 2011).

Then the narrator says that when they came to talk to Ms. Zahran's family they were met with a big surprise, and the mother continues:

> She called her friends in Sohag and found that they were organizing demonstrations. . . . Then she came in [on the day of the demonstrations] and had her cup of Nescafe—she hadn't eaten for two days; she didn't try to eat or anything, just had a Nescafe and then went into the

bathroom. And I found her getting dressed. "Where are you going Sally?" I asked her. "I'm going to the demonstrations. I want to partici- pate no matter what." I let her go down. There was no way to stop her. She just had to go down at that time. [Later] I found her coming back in all wet from being sprayed [by fire truck hoses] and smoke from the [tear gas] bombs. Her face was yellow, a horrible yellow—like she was dying. She was coughing, choking. She came in to change so that she could go back down [to the demonstrations] again. Of course as a mother I just couldn't let her, and I told her no way, you've done enough Sally. She went into a rage, to the extent that she was grabbing the table like it was in her way, yelling, "Leave me alone, Mama, leave me. Let me do something, not for myself, but for my brothers." She was in a rage and angry; she could have done anything. She went into her room say- ing, "If you won't let me go down then I'll go down from the balcony." I was standing in the doorway, and she was on the balcony, saying "open the door and let me go please." Then she made as if . . . she was getting dizzy . . . and she fell ("Baladna" 2011).

After the revelation that Ms. Zahran had fallen to her death, her brothers testi- fied to her character. An older brother in his teens or early twenties empha- sized her determination to change the social circumstances in which she lived; a younger brother around the age of ten focused on her participation in the demonstrations and her status as a martyr. One of Ms. Zahran's friends also appeared in the program. She was the most emotionally affected of all those interviewed, strongly asserting that Sally was no less important than those who were killed in Tahrir Square, that her actions would affect her throughout her life, and that if they breathed the air of freedom it was because of Sally's sacrifice.

For many, the OnTV interview was the definitive word on the manner of Sally Zahran's death. A few believed that her family was compelled by elements of the old regime to issue a denial of the heroic martyr story, under threats that something would happen to her brothers if they didn't.[18] But suspicious or not, the OnTv interview undeniably poured oil on the fires of debate over the mean- ing and status of Sally Zahran's martyrdom. It amounted to a public debate over whether or not Sally Zahran was "grievable," an ethical and political issue (Butler 2004, 12), and one at the core of Sally Zahran's unintended fame. From the very beginning counterrevolutionaries claimed that martyr stories were made up. One could easily access a shocking YouTube video of General Hasan al-Ruwaini visiting Midan al-Tahrir on February 5, just after the most violent battles had ended, and telling incredulous doctors who had treated the wounded and dying that "there was no revolution," and the whole thing was just "play acting." The discrediting of Sally Zahran, the most recognizable face of the martyrs in the early days of the revolution, played a starring role in antirevolution propaganda to the point that her actual life barely mattered—to those who used her against the revolution at any rate.

The OnTv interview also intensified debates over the significance of Sally Zahran's hijab or lack thereof. Sally Zahran's mother was the author of the requests forwarded to Facebook that her daughter's un-hijabed pictures be struck from the public record—or at least this is what those who promoted the *tahjib* (putting on the hijab) campaign believed. But throughout the entire interview in her own home Sally Zahran's mother sat surrounded by precisely the iconic images of the un-hijabed Sally that had become so familiar to the world. There was not a single picture of Sally Zahran in hijab visible in her family's home during the interview. Some took this as further evidence that the family was compelled to go on television. The circumstances of her death undermined the secular activists who organized the revolution; the confusing stories of her family wanting her to be known as a muhajjaba, and then appearing on television amid pictures of her without a hijab, fuelled *fitna* between the liberals and the Islamists.

The Afterlife of Sally Zahran

Sally Zahran was probably the most prominent martyr in the early stages of January 25 commemoration campaigns. The fact that Ms. Zahran was a woman animated social and political tensions. On the other hand, her effectiveness as a symbol was completely separate from her actual political role in the revolution. Nobody claimed her as a key player. However, the coin of political struggle against the regime could not necessarily be easily converted to a currency of feminist politics, or even simply to a more prominent role for women in public life. Not long after Mubarak's abdication, a "million-woman march" on the occasion of International Women's Day provided something of a reality check for anyone inclined to see "freedom" as the most efficiently stated aim of the revolution translated straightforwardly to greater freedoms for women. Marchers were grotesquely harassed by male onlookers ("Al-Taharrush" 2011), in stark contrast to the utopian ideal of equality that Midan al-Tahrir was said to have exemplified during the communitas phase of the revolution. The incident was buried in the press, which was preoccupied with rising sectarian violence at the time.[19] Such questions as "What can revolutions do for women? Or, what do women need from revolutions?" (Shayne 2004, 3) are universal. Nonetheless the emerging mythology of the revolution in early and mid-2011 largely focused on the heroism of men. There were no significant female political figures in the transitional government, and it goes without saying that SCAF was intensely male. The largely male character of politics in the public sphere, notwithstanding the demonstrable effectiveness of female activists, makes the prominence in revolutionary symbolism of a nonactivist such as Sally Zahran noteworthy.

One of the most thought-provoking essays on Sally Zahran was written by Umniyya Tal'at, a journalist and novelist ("Umniyya Tal'at" 2011).[20] For her the Sally Zahran case was an infuriating exhibition of patriarchal control. It did not matter so much whether Ms. Zahran "was or wasn't" (a muhajjaba or a martyr), but that women like Sally Zahran had so little control over what they did and how their actions were interpreted:

> In truth whether or not she wore the hijab wasn't the real issue. It was rather this: in whose interest was it to impose the hijab on her after her death? I do not believe that the campaign to posthumously put the hijab on Sally was done with good intentions or that it had any dimensions of political Islam. Nor do I believe that it is incumbent on those of us who do not belong to the political Islamic trend to be magnanimous and say it's a trivial topic that we should ignore, for the simple reason that the attempt to put the hijab on Sally after her death is an odious declaration promoting the idea that women who are not muhajjabat are not suited to be martyrs or that they have any serious national position. This is what we can never be silent about. . . .
>
> After all the clamour about her death, I firmly believe that Sally was the martyr of a society that harshly judges women, insisting on putting them in a specific mold, and forbidding them from going out of it. . . . The truth is that she died in a country that does not know how to acknowledge a woman and her freedom to do as she pleases. God have mercy on you, Sally. In my view you are the martyr of a stupid and hypocritical society.
>
> And do we now have the capacity to acknowledge the personalities of all the other female martyrs? Amira from Alexandria; Christine from Cairo; Amira Muhammad Isma'il and Rahma Muhsin Ahmad from Rod al-Farag in Cairo; Rasha Ahmad Gunaydi from al-'Umraniyya in Giza. (Tal'at 2011)

Tal'at's intervention emphasized that the only way, it seemed, for a female martyr to be noticed was negatively, for all the wrong reasons. If she had been allowed to behave as the adult she was, Sally Zahran may well have lived on for years after the revolution. Tal'at's essay also alleges that the rumor that Ms. Zahran's family was pressured into publicly disavowing their daughter's participation in the revolution is unsubstantiated, though Tal'at is not the only person to raise such suspicions.[21] But the depressing reality for Tal'at is that aside from Sally Zahran, women's sacrifice for the cause of the revolution would have been completely invisible. One can read her essay as a refutation of all patriarchal customs that deny women's agency whatever their source.

But Sally Zahran was never confined strictly to negative terms. Rather the controversies surrounding her demanded continual revision. For some she could be an Egyptian Jeanne d'Arc, but she would never do as an Egyptian

Marianne, symbolically rallying the people to action, or standing for a unified state (Agulhon 1981).[22] For others her iconicity was never compromised, even if they had to go through a process of reasoning why she should remain iconic. Following the previous chapter, if iconicity can be thought of as a process analogous to the ritual process, in which the image coming into view forms a temporal threshold as it enters the consciousness of the viewer, then Sally Zahran's contentiousness extended the effect, at least for a time, before the accumulation of additional events eventually made her recede—but never completely disappear—until the revolution itself could no longer be expressed openly.

During the months when the window of Sally Zahran's iconicity was still open her case came up often. For example, when I attended an exhibition by the Revolution Art Union at the Giza Culture Palace in mid-April 2011 she was there.[23] The exhibition consisted of around 150 paintings and drawings made by amateur artists, many of whom were participants in the most violent phase of the revolution. Some of the works displayed had actually been painted in Midan al-Tahrir. The exhibit was poorly publicized—I knew about it only from having seen a poster in a nervous early-morning demonstration in Midan al-Tahrir a few days after two or more protestors had been killed in clashes with the army following a large demonstration.[24]

When I went to the exhibit about a week later nobody at the culture palace seemed aware of the event, though the same poster I had seen in Midan al-Tahrir was displayed in the lobby. However, I finally found a young employee of the institution who was willing to figure out where the exhibit was (in a closed dark room right behind the poster as it happened). He was happy to serve as my personal guide and indeed knew many of the amateur artists who had contributed work to the exhibit—he had been there with them as a protestor, though not as an artist (his academic field was anthropology). One corner of the exhibit featured drawings of martyrs, emphasizing, as usual, the *al-Masry al-Youm* eleven. With no prompting from me, my guide commented on two of the images. One was Mustafa al-Sawi, who he flatly identified as a member of the Muslim Brotherhood, with no further elaboration. The second face that he commented on was Sally Zahran—an artist's rendition of the hijabed Sally that had been circulated on the internet after the original un-hijabed version published in *al-Masry al-Youm* had gone viral. I told him that I was well aware of the controversies surrounding her. For him the most important aspect of Ms. Zahran was not whether or not she wore the hijab, and he had no doubts that she should be considered a martyr. In his view the importance of Sally Zahran was that she symbolized a rejection of backward traditionalism, specifically the conservative treatment of women associated in metropolitan Cairo with Upper Egyptian (*sa'idi*) customs.

On another occasion, in May, I found myself in Manshiyet Nasr, an informal neighborhood, attending a "Day of Culture" organized by a friend who worked as an actress. She and other performers and artists, conscious of the criticism that Islamists had deep roots in neighborhoods while the non-Islamist intelligentsia confined themselves to safe bourgeois spheres such as downtown Cairo, had begun their own individualized initiatives to move out of their comfort zone and reach out to people who were not like themselves, but whose political loyalties and engagement were seen as crucial for the success or failure of the revolution.[25] At the event I made the acquaintance of a prominent man from the area. When I went back to talk to him alone he turned out to be a low-level member of Mubarak's NDP.

Near the end of our conversation he asked questions about my work. I told him I wanted to write about the revolution, and that I was interested in those who were being called martyrs. He immediately leaped to the attack and started talking about Sally Zahran. In his case he ignored the hijab controversy and insisted that she was a false martyr simply because she was not killed in battle. "I think they're all like her," he said. "How many were really killed in Tahrir Square? Four? Eight? What you should be researching is the truth or falsity of each "martyr," and you'll find that they're all phony."

When the OnTV interview with Ms. Zahran's family began making the rounds on the internet I shared the following post to my Facebook friends:

> Is there something very odd about the Sally Zahran affair? First she's the international icon of the revolution (http://bikyamasr.com/wordpress/?p=26661) and lots of people adopt her picture in their profile. Then there's this t.v. interview in which a similar picture sits behind her mother; she says her daughter wasn't even in Cairo when she died, and didn't die in fights with government thugs, but rather fell or jumped from the balcony. Then a campaign starts, supposedly initiated by her family, to persuade people to only use photos of her in hijab (e.g., http://forums.fatakat.com/thread1242959) on facebook. The video strikes me as phony. Maybe not quite Mubarak in Sharm al-Shaykh photoshopped by al-Ahram phony, but in the same ballpark. Or am I being overly suspicious? (February 27 at 8:56pm)

The first response to this was a slightly defensive reaction to my having put the spotlight on the hijab issue, coupled with a rather jaded comment on how the regime might have manipulated the issue:

> M: Why would portraying her in hijab be phony? It seems to be her in the picture. . . . As for the falling from a balcony—well that suggests murder rather than suicide if you take into account the history of Egyptians and balconies i.e. suad hosny, ashraf marwan etc (February 27 at 9:35pm)[26]

A more extensive comment followed from a different Facebook friend—a writer who strongly supported the revolution:

S: I think there's nothing odd in the story of Sally. The only odd [thing] is how people react to the issue of her photo with no hijab. And this is due to so closed minded who we are suffering from. I'm also not surprised that she wasn't in Tahrir. I . . . remember the first time I saw Sally's pic was published on FB along with some other pics of young Egyptians who killed or seriously injured after Gomaaet el Ghadab. And I remember I read a lot of comments by members questioning if Sally was still alive or not. And then after hours the admin assured that she was killed in Tahrir. I remember one particular comment by someone said that a friend of Sally said that she died at her home not in Tahrir. But then the news of her horrible killing in Tahrir was widely spread and that particularly comment was completely ignored. I myself thought that maybe this comment was mistaken and I went to believe more about the other story. About two weeks ago I was tagged with or was sent a note with a pic of Sally in hijab and the guy of the note urged everyone to replace her wide spread photo with the one with hijab. I, in fact, ignored this note. But amazingly, many notes have been widely spread about the importance of reposting Sally's pic with the one with hijab. I remember I read some comments suggested this is so important as they thought she was a Christian at the beginning!!! But now they were relieved!!! I think that the family didn't offer such thing and doesn't care much about which photo of Sally should be posted. This is an offer by closed minded people who are many!! And I agree with you Dr. that she might wear it recently!I think "our" media (which in many cases is copying what is going on FB) waited for the appropriate time to make the sabk. Before now, it was impossible to interview her family and revealed how she died! (February 28 at 12:32am)

The person who made this comment was a journalist, and someone I knew well in the actual world; very prorevolution, and she herself wore a hijab. Clearly she was appalled by the *tahgib* (en-hijabing) campaign. Aside from a slight defensiveness among some of my interlocutors provoked by my outsider's query, the tahgib campaign was real, and the stakes of it were of strong local significance. Off-the-cuff opinions expressed on my Facebook page typified the essential—and productive—instability of Sally Zahran as a symbol of the revolution. With her story in full public circulation, it was difficult to take a neutral stance on what she signified. In terms of her capacity to mobilize the political, social, and even artistic imagination, she was among the most potent symbols of the first months of the revolution, albeit in a polarizing rather than unifying way. In the early postcommunitas discourse on Sally Zahran polarization crystallized most clearly in opposition between Islamists and partisans of a left-leaning cultural formation anchored in literary symbols of the 1970s. These latter symbols will reappear later in my narrative. But first let me delve into a fully articulated Islamist polemic about the affair.

THE SALAFI

The campaign to posthumously put the hijab on Sally Zahran for the most part left implicit the dividing line between those who wanted her to be a muhajjaba and those who insisted that she was not—a firm directive to "honor her family's wishes" by substituting a muhajjaba picture for a *safira* (unveiled) one, despite a lack of evidence that the family had actually expressed such sentiments. This was countered by indignation or outrage, particularly by those who actually knew Ms. Zahran, at the attempt to fundamentally alter her personality in death. There is no way to know how many of the hijab campaigners were casual Facebook users simply imitating a trend without investigating its origin, or even "trolls" paid by the state to spread chaos. But there were, of course, people all too happy to state their opinions blatantly. Khalid Harbi, an Islamist and prominent campaigner in Coptic-Muslim sectarian issues, was one such person. Director of a website called "The Islamic Observatory for Resisting [Christian] Proselytizing" ("Al-Marsad" 2011), Harbi is identified as a Salafi on numerous forums and blogs. Salafi internet forums reported that in April 2011 the authorities forced him to surrender himself by incarcerating his pregnant sister ("I'tiqal Shaqiqat" 2010)—a tactic frequently used by the state to compel at-large suspects to turn themselves in to the authorities. Here is an excerpt from his analysis of the Sally Zahran phenomenon:

> Everything about her was vague. Nobody knew anything more than that she was an Egyptian girl who the thugs of the NDP and state security officers killed in the vicinity of Tahrir Square. . . . Then in the heart of the square with the revolution still burning one of the brothers carried an image of an Egyptian newspaper that had published photos of the martyrs in which he had erased the photo of Sally Zahran because she was showing her charms [*mutabarrija*—making herself pretty], leaving just her name with no picture. . . . As soon as the news spread . . . they have all attacked and stormed against not the person who erased the picture of Sally, but against the entire Islamic trend. Some of them called for expelling people in beards and *niqab*s [full face veils] from Tahrir Square. One mercenary wrote in his blog that the beard and the hijab and the niqab are the shame of the revolution [*'aurat al-thaura*], and not Sally Zahran. . . . If Sally were alive she would refuse to have her picture published without a hijab. This is the simplest of the rights, which anyone who belongs to the human species should respect. But you cannot hope for that from the secular extremists, liberal mercenaries, and lords of the church. Their one goal is to fight Islam, even in a picture of a hijab worn by a martyr killed by Mubarak. (Harbi 2011)

Harbi's polemic is easy to pick apart on factual and logical grounds, but it is nonetheless a productive and revealing text. Sally Zahran's martyrdom reveals the contours of a new Salafi trend in the formal political sphere, distinct from the long presence of Salafism in the social sphere (Lauzière 2010). And to be sure, it is a fault line between the Salafis and others that was there long before the Sally Zahran phenomenon. What Ms. Zahran's martyrdom did so efficiently was to activate Harbi's agenda publicly.[27] It was precisely controversy that set the stage for political performances open to the scrutiny of all. Sally Zahran's martyrdom had the capacity to do this precisely because she became a contested symbol.

THE PROVINCIAL INTELLECTUAL

Sally Zahran's martyrdom was elaborated and contested on other grounds than the polemical hammer blows of Khalid Harbi. One of the most extensive memorials to Sally Zahran was created on a Facebook page by a doctor in a provincial Delta city who I will call Muwatin X—"Citizen X"—or just "X" for short. Muwatin X puts Sally Zahran in a literary context. He called his memorial "The Secret beyond Sally Zahran; or, The Perfect Martyr," his own English translation of "al-Sirr wara' Sally Zahran." Except for the title, the site was all in Arabic. By sometime in 2012 he took it down.[28] "X" put Sally Zahran in a specifically leftist literary context that echoed more fragmentary allusions to the same sources that would shortly be appearing in Tahrir and the surrounding neighborhoods as revolutionary graffiti and other forms of public martyrology over the next two years. His memorial, "The Secret beyond Sally Zahran; or, The Perfect Martyr" (Muwatin X 2011), was also a memorial to the 1970s poet Amal Dunqul. Dunqul (1940–83) was a pioneer of free verse in Arabic poetry starting in the 1950s. He reached a new level of fame for his political poetry written after the 1967 Naksa, particularly "La Tusalih" (Dunqul 1986b) (Do not make peace), a key resistance text written in the late 1970s aimed at opposing Sadat's peace overture to Israel. X's text began with a quote from a different Dunqul poem, "Death of the Moon":[29]

> They spread the painful news through the sun's mail
> To every city
> "The moon has been killed"!
> They saw its stiffened body with its head hanging from a tree
> Thieves stole a priceless diamond necklace from his chest
> They left him in the sticks
> Like the black legend in my blind eye
> My neighbor says
> "He was sacred, why did they kill him?"
> Our neighbor the young girl says
> "He liked my song in the night
> And gave me bottles of perfume
> For what crime would they kill him?

Did they see him at my window, before the dawn, listening to music!"
(Dunqul 1986c, 68)

Dunqul's poem creates no explicit resonance with Sally Zahran, but the death theme sets an impeccably somber tone, and the moon is a common simile for beauty in literature and everyday speech. After some additional literary references,[30] he launches into his real subject: the revolution, and Sally Zahran's place in it. The first section sets a scene between January 29 and the epic "Battle of the Camel" on February 2 to hold the midan against the thugs. This is when the story of Sally Zahran begins. All manner of police have disappeared, and of course looting and attacks on the people (*sha'b*) rise alarmingly, in accordance with the regime's strategy to turn public opinion against the revolution. Sally Zahran, "a girl of bronze complexion" (*khamriyyat al-laun*) is given a mission to bring food to the protestors occupying the midan, and killed by thugs while carrying it out. X then turns to the campaign waged by the regime to sow seeds of doubt about the revolution and the revolutionaries:

The regime was firing everything it had in the psychological war, the last arrows in its quiver:

> It was up to the revolutionaries to respond. They brought out their famous publication: "The flowers that bloom in the gardens." The selection of the martyr pictures was done carefully, with extraordinary focus on a brilliant girl who occupied the undisputed center of the page. The revolutionaries had given it their best shot, gambling that people would be sympathetic to these martyrs whose appearance shows them as "respectable people with a future" [*wilad nas wa ladayhum mustaqbal*]. The picture of our heroine carried out the mission completely, with her vibrant smile, her wild hair, and her beguiling eyes.

X unpacks all the complications in the Sally Zahran story—her surprising global fame; the view from Sohag, revealing the narrative of her jumping or falling from the balcony; the hijab issue, about which he quotes several Islamist sources, including Khalid Harbi; the straightforward facts about her life (to the extent that they were available on the internet); the appearance of an unsolvable riddle about who she really was and what she was doing; and then the video of Sally's mother, which seems decisive to him. "It would have been possible for the mother to avoid the scandal that touched her family if she had just said that her daughter had been in Midan al-Tahrir. But she didn't, because she had learned that a lie like this would be shameful. Indeed, the mother hadn't lied, and all of Sohag knew it."

Then in his seventh and final section ("Mood"—*Al-Mazj al-Akhir*), he attempts to resolve the contradictions in the Sally Zahran story through his own poetic ode to her martyrdom:

> There were two martyrs.
> Their martyr

In Sohag
In her hijab and with her fall
Her name was Sally Zahran
As for our heroine—our martyr
She was coming to the Midan
When her path was blocked by thugs
With a club they smashed her head
Her head that was not covered by a hijab
She resembled Sally Zahran
But she never was Sally Zahran
Who was she? What was her name?
I don't know
She has many names
Maybe it was Fatma, or Amal, or Christine
Perhaps it was
Perhaps it was
Where is she?
I don't know
Maybe she is lying in a morgue with no name
Perhaps her family will know her
Perhaps
Perhaps
But this I know: she now looks down over the midan
With her gypsy hair
Her tanned complexion
Her beguiling eyes

> Vigilant against tyrants with her spirit that she
>   surrendered while dreaming
> Dreaming of freedom

At the bottom of his Facebook memorial to Sally Zahran X appends a composite image: Midan al-Tahrir at the height of the revolution, vast crowds, ecstatic at the astounding achievement of toppling Mubarak in eighteen days. And over that image, the "original" un-hijabed Sally Zahran, benevolently vigilant and dreaming of freedom (see figure 4.3).

Conclusion

The disputed grievability of Sally Zahran proved to be a microcosm of the major fault line within the revolutionary camp, particularly between the Muslim Brotherhood in uneasy alliance with Islamists more generally, and the non-Islamist protestors, but also a fault line between men and women. The Left were undoubtedly the most articulate among the non-Islamist revolutionaries, or if not Left in a hard ideological sense, then at least those who saw

FIGURE 4.3. Sally Zahran's image superimposed over crowds in Tahrir
Square. From the Sally Zahran tribute of "Muwatin X," on Facebook.

themselves as inspired by the generation of the 1970s. To be sure, Sally Zahran's death also touched on the rage of the old regime against the revolution,
evident through the undercurrent of suspicion that someone, or some political
force, was trying to cover it up or negate its meaning. Whether or not old regime elements were trying to manipulate Ms. Zahran's death, the mere suspicion of manipulation was a foretaste of vicious pro-regime polemics against
the revolution that had, at that juncture, receded into the background, but
would again come roaring back in challenges to every single event that had
been taken as a "fact" by the revolutionaries. Sally Zahran's death also highlighted the confluence of gender politics with revolutionary politics. The participation of women in protest became a constant target of provocateurs and
propaganda. Sit-ins were condemned as cover for licentious behavior. "Virginity tests," a tactic used by 'Abd al-Fattah al-Sisi in March 2011 when he was still
the head of military intelligence, were used to intimidate and humiliate female
protestors. Systematic harassment and, eventually, rape became weapons in
the counterrevolutionary repertoire.

But Sally Zahran's case was different in several respects. She was iconic in
ways that no other woman was—as a symbol of the *revolution* rather than as
a symbol of the status of women *within* the revolution. As we have seen, her
symbolism became embroiled in tensions, but for all the ambiguities and
ambivalences of her iconicity, as long as the revolution could be promoted in
public spaces through representations inscribed on walls and posters, or carried in demonstrations, she was never absent. To a degree she transcended
tensions more than any other female symbol of the revolution. To a considerable extent the most heavily circulated images of the revolution were male:

gas-masked youth hurling tear gas canisters back at the police; a brave man putting his body in front of a water cannon; youthful determined men with raised fists. Scholarly attention to gender in the revolution often focused on male youth, such as the role of Ultras football fan clubs in fighting the police (e.g., Woltering 2013; Rommel 2016). Despite the evanescence of her unchallenged iconicity, in the longer term perhaps precisely *because* of the challenges to her status, she serves well as a point of entry into precisely the issues of women's agency in politics and revolution that became obscured by the incessant focus on women's bodies activated by many of the more prominent watershed moments in the revolution.

Without a doubt Sally Zahran revealed a flicker of just how explosive the politics of martyrdom would become in Egypt's revolution. Although Sally Zahran was far from the only woman killed in the revolution, she was practically the sole female figure in this political dynamic. Her ambivalent position in the pantheon of martyrdom was both productive and emblematic of a state of suspension characteristic of a liminal crisis. In the wider scope of the revolution the apotheosis of grievability as an index of political affiliation came roughly two and a half years later, after the coup against Mohammad Morsy, when hundreds of Muslim Brotherhood supporters were massacred at the Rab'a al-'Adawiyya Mosque and Midan Nahda sit-ins. It would take an act of schismogenesis—the normalizing of what had previously been considered unthinkable—to bring violence past a point of no return.

But before that happened, when grievability was still a possibility, not so much for one's obvious opponents, but for one's uncomfortable allies, then embracing it might still become a powerful means for suturing affect to political action. Friends and relatives of martyrs sustained sit-ins when nobody else could be counted on. They were sometimes flashpoints in violent episodes. Such events were foretold in the death of Sally Zahran. Her brief separation out of the ordinary into iconic view, followed by a collapse into bitter conflict, encapsulated all the political dynamics that were to unfold over the next two years.

The death of every single martyr was felt intensely by families of the victims, and their friends and comrades. The sort of online shrines and Facebook groups that sprang up to commemorate Sally Zahran were replicated for virtually every person who died, and these were often sustained by people for whom the deaths of others bound them viscerally to ongoing struggle. I knew few such people in 2011 when I first encountered the Sally Zahran affair, but a few years later I became acquainted with several of them.[31] They sometimes spoke of their dead comrades in an inverse way, insisting that their slain friends were still alive and that they were the dead ones. This bound them to the revolution even when it had clearly become, at least in the short term, a hopeless cause. For them and for many others who had known the dead in life, liminal crisis was personal. The death of others was a life-changing event.

CHAPTER 5

Martyr Milestones

PROTEST ON BEHALF OF THOSE who died in the revolution's cause was one of the most productive strategies for expressing grievances and demands, and also simply as an ambivalently political (but not apolitical) means for rallying protestors. The commemoration of martyrs could, however, lay bare disputes among the revolutionary camp rather than mobilize unified action against the revolution's opponents. This chapter recounts four stories of protests presented as photo essays. All four essays articulate with issues raised elsewhere in the book. Space and martyrdom are threads that run through all the stories here. As previously mentioned, the death of a comrade in the midst of fighting for the revolution was always labeled as *istishhad*—martyrdom. And yet for martyrs in a mobilizational context the passage from life to death was, by design, suspended. The protracted not-dead/not-alive state of the martyred comrade mirrored the protracted liminality of revolution.

Martyrdom more generally can of course be used in commemorative bids for transcendent unity, as opposed to the mobilization of unity *against* the forces that control the state in the context of an ongoing revolution. Throughout the revolution one could discern a tug-of-war between rhetorics of closure and rhetorics of mobilization. This rhetorical battle took place on multiple fronts, not all of them spatialized in the ways that protests and sit-ins were. Aside from protests, it was often an asymmetric battle. The counterrevolutionary state could create its own martyr narratives through music videos for example, that conflated deaths among the security forces with deaths of revolutionaries, and suggested a false equivalence by refusing to depict the cause of the revolutionaries' deaths. The conventions of that kind of martyr discourse were established early on in the revolution (Gilman 2011), and amplified as time went by to the point that one eventually lost a sense that there even was an agent of violence against revolutionaries. That evolution in revolution imagery of course neatly tracks the process of court cases against Mubarak and members of the security forces, all of which eventually collapsed for "lack of evidence."

Temporally this chapter traces the progress of the revolution in the post-communitas liminality that began by about the middle of February 2011 and lasted until the rise of 'Abd al-Fattah al-Sisi in 2013. The events depicted are all performative in the sense that meaning emerged through the interactions of people in space. They begin with an account of the dynamics of closure and mobilization around the attempts of the army to retake Tahrir Square for good, and the resistance of protestors to the army's incursion into "their" space. That dynamic took place throughout 2011, but my narrative focuses on the period between mid-April, when the army resodded the saniyya in an attempt to declare the revolution over, and the breakdown of the new military order on May 1, when organized labor and leftist groups staged a celebration of International Workers' Day. A second episode recounts a protest at the Ministry of Interior on June 6, the first anniversary of the death of Khaled Said, the young computer programmer beaten to death by the police in 2010. His death initiated social-media-fueled protests that coalesced into one of the most potent streams of activism, helping to spark the revolution in 2011. The commemoration of Said's death, and (re)birth as a still-potent martyr, pointedly linked him to the heritage of leftist resistance through the quotation of poetry by Amal Dunqul, the same poet invoked by Muwatin X in the previous chapter. Then a third episode turns to "Fangari's finger." Mohsen Fangari was a member of SCAF and served as their official spokesman. In July he delivered a speech harshly criticizing an ongoing sit-in of Tahrir Square, which elicited blisteringly sarcastic responses from protestors, enacted in graffiti. This too was linked to martyrdom, as Fangari had produced an iconic moment in February, when he delivered a televised military salute to the civilian martyrs, a moment interpreted then as a symbol of the revolution's ultimate victory. And finally, a fourth episode examines the sit-in at the Ministerial Council in December, following the savage weeklong Battle of Muhammad Mahmud Street in the previous month. The sit-in featured rows of mock coffins bearing the names of martyrs, and again, lines of poetry linking them to the longer history of protest that animated leftist activism.

War of Position, War of Maneuver

In politics . . . the war of manoeuvre subsists so long as it is a question of winning positions which are not decisive, so that all the resources of the state's hegemony cannot be mobilized. But when, for one reason or another, these positions have lost their value and only the decisive positions are at stake, then one passes over to siege warfare; this is concentrated, difficult, and requires exceptional qualities of patience and inventiveness. In politics, the siege is a reciprocal one, despite all appearances, and the mere fact that the ruler has to muster all his resources demonstrates how seriously he takes his adversary. (Gramsci 2000, 230)

The government began pushing back against the revolution overtly on March 9, 2011—the date of the first clearing of an ongoing sit-in in Tahrir Square. On that occasion protestors were tortured on the grounds of the Egyptian Museum, and 'Abd al-Fattah al-Sisi ordered the infamous "virginity tests" of female activists. A tense month ensued, in which the first cries of *yasqut hukm al-'askar* (down with military rule) were chanted. On the morning of April 14 SCAF made another symbolic bid to close off the revolution by landscaping and resodding the saniyya in Tahrir Square under the watchful eyes of army officers. The unsightliness of endless sit-ins was already very unpopular with drivers and broad portions of the middle class, who cursed the protestors as prostitutes, baltagiyya, and street children. Clearing the midan was undoubtedly good politics with respect to the steadily growing portion of the public that had either never supported the revolution or were becoming skeptical of it. But there was a much more important reason for SCAF's firm attempt to close down the revolution on the fourteenth. A week earlier, on April 6, a large demonstration titled Gum'at al-Muhakima wal-Tathir (the Friday of Judgment and Purification) had pushed very hard for putting Mubarak on trial. But what made this demonstration different from any other up to that point was that a group of twenty-one uniformed army officers had appeared on one of the stages set up that day to speak in favor of the revolution. That raised the specter of a split in the military's ranks—SCAF's ultimate nightmare. The reaction was swift and violent. The protestors who tried to remain in the square that night, including the officers, were brutally attacked, with loss of life—reports varied between one or two protestors killed and dozens arrested, to one or two protestors *and* one or two of the officers killed amid general mayhem ("Shahid 'Ayan" 2011; Mar'i 2011). Whether or not any of the protesting officers were killed, there is no doubt that the rest were immediately arrested. A month and a half later SCAF was forced to concede to demands to put Mubarak on trial.

On the fourteenth the saniyya was resodded and landscaped. All the grass and shrubbery would turn to dust in the coming months, as thousands more protestors would pitch their tents there in future i'tisamat (see figure 5.1). But at that point the army ringed the temporarily verdant saniyya with several signs that tried to spin the military's seizure of the protestors' de facto barracks as a prorevolution act: "Continuing the success of the January 25 Revolution" on one; on another, "we are your Egyptian Armed Forces, we express our love, pride, and esteem to our beloved Egyptian people and its righteous martyrs." Or "the January 25 Revolution brought down a regime; the people and the Egyptian army must now face the challenge of efforts to bring down the state." The replanting was businesslike but had an air of volunteerism, rather like the spontaneous Tahrir cleanup immediately after the fall of the regime that was, at the time, a remarkable exhibition of civic spirit, and also a forthright appropriation of basic control that had been denied to citizens by the Mubarak

FIGURE 5.1. Resodding the saniyya after the army had cleared the sit-in,
April 14, 2011. On the poster: "Continuing the success of the January 25
Revolution is a trust borne by the armed forces." Author's photo.

regime.[1] But that notion was dispelled when I asked one of the workers if he
had taken on the beautification project of his own accord. No, he said, this was
his job. He seemed uninterested in elaborating, and the presence of army officers made me feel that pushing harder for a response was probably unwise.

Throughout the first two years of the revolution, until its final defeat by Sisi
in 2013, protestors engaged both the state and, more specifically, the military,
in a protracted war of position and maneuver over control of symbolic space,
most prominently Tahrir Square, but also extending to other symbolic prizes.
Gramsci's position/maneuver metaphor invoked frontal military attack against
an enemy as opposed to siege tactics. But as the passage above suggests, in a
long battle "the siege is a reciprocal one" in which the question who is attacking

and who is defending becomes secondary to the capacity of each side to marshal enough resources to keep fighting.[2] The position/maneuver distinction
provides an excellent means for thinking about the relationship between the
regime (or the interim government together with more deeply sedimented formations within the state) and the activists. Holding public space (particularly
Tahrir Square) was the most prominently publicized tactic of the revolution.
But in countless less well known engagements it was the state trying to hold
its ground, for example, against initiatives to make institutions more democratic, or to defend walls against graffiti or more elaborate murals.

In Egypt following the collapse of the Mubarak regime the political sphere
was marked by a mixture of both tactics. The revolution boiled on for some
time within civil society. For months, small strikes were waged against myriad
government institutions throughout the country. Universities, government offices, factories, and small towns all engaged in fevered debate and action over
how the revolution should compel change—at first the question of whether it
should or not was less considered than the direction change should take. Everyone sensed an opportunity "to change local politics and spread a new political consciousness" (Schielke 2015, 198). In small towns far from Tahrir this
might mean trying to extend a spontaneous cleanup campaign into a complete
reform of local public services (Schielke 2015, 199).

Closer to the political center it often meant purging institutions of Mubarak
appointees and rethinking the way the institutions were structured. On one
occasion I sat in the living room of Faruq, a university professor, with a group
of his friends, all of them well-established figures in various aspects of the
cultural field. The subject of the conversation was the appointment of a new
minister of culture, the third since the revolution began. They all had direct
experiences of the new appointee ('Imad Abu Ghazi), who was a patrician
nephew of one of Egypt's most venerated sculptors, and a longtime power broker within the Supreme Council of Culture, which was one of the favored institutions within the Ministry of Culture, but also one that was deeply embedded within the patronage system of the Mubarak era. For my friend he was far
too associated with the old regime. He was "the ultimate mediocrity" according
to another who worked as a theater director. Another, who worked as a musician, thought the best way forward would be to break the Ministry of Culture
into *mu'assasat* (separate institutions), one for cinema, another for fine arts,
one for theater, and so forth. Such was a plan being bruited at the time for the
Ministry of Information, which had briefly been abolished altogether. It
seemed like a good model to all of them. On the other hand, nobody was quite
sure how arts budgets (which Faruq described as nonexistent at the time)
would be formulated or allocated to the various institutions. Most of them
flourished during the revolution years. And yet all discussions of purging or
restructuring were eventually eclipsed, first by the electoral success of the Muslim Brotherhood in the summer of 2012 and its attendant *ikhwanat al-daula*

(brotherhood-ization of the state), and then by the cold indifference of the Sisi regime after the coup in 2013. That long-forgotten conversation in 2011 between artists and academics was a small snippet of much larger and more heated debates over the fate of civil society as Gramsci defined it. But the ambivalent process of trying to take over the state from within (how does one keep from simply becoming the state that one opposes?) amounted to very little in the end.[3]

The thousands of often heated debates over reforming or purging institutions of civil society were ambiguous as either wars of maneuver or wars of position. With the ruling regime smashed, the distinction between a frontal assault on the state and the seizure and holding of positions within it was often hard to discern. But one could be certain that the front in this war was virtually every state institution. Two weeks after the replanting of the saniyya I took a long walk on the peripheries of downtown and Tahrir Square. The fabulous graffiti that commemorated martyrs and kept the revolution front and center in everyone's purview was in its first exuberant phase. I wanted to photograph as much of it as I could, but I also simply wanted to walk in some neighborhoods outside of downtown. My feet took me across the Nile into Gezira and Zamalek, which boasted a great deal of martyr graffiti, though not in the neighborhood itself, which is very elite, though also surprisingly rich in graffiti on its margins at that time, particularly the pillars of the traffic flyovers and beneath the bridges.

I recrossed the Nile from Zamalek on the May 15 Bridge, named in honor of the "corrective revolution" against Nasser by Anwar al-Sadat in 1971—essentially a purge of state institutions that resonates with the theme of this chapter. Beneath the May 15 Bridge lies the entombed Twenty-Sixth of July Street, named for the revolution that brought Nasser to power, or more precisely, renamed after Fuad al-Awwal (the Khedive from 1917 to 1936). Since some time in the early 1990s, Twenty-Sixth of July Street was cut off at both ends by iron fences and flyovers, but it used to be the major thoroughfare from Zamalek to downtown Cairo, running through the doomed neighborhood of Bulaq Abu al-'Ila, which was slated for eventual extinction by the forces of neoliberalism, a processed touched on in chapter 2. There was much less graffiti in Bulaq then there had been in Zamalek, but the army had been there and painted the pillars holding up the flyover in half camouflage and half Egyptian flag colors.

At the eastern end of Twenty-Sixth of July Street, just before one was forced to infiltrate through a gap in the iron fence that protected downtown from the residents of Bulaq, I encountered a demonstration (see figure 5.2). It was protesting the Niyabat al-Murur—the Traffic [Violations] Agency—which is the arm of the state that regulates vehicles and hands out fines to those who infringe on traffic laws. In general traffic laws are not highly respected in Egypt,

FIGURE 5.2. Demonstration at the Traffic Violations
Bureau, April 14, 2011. Author's photo.

but drivers do try to toe the line at points where they actually see a traffic
policeman controlling intersections. In the Mubarak era the Traffic Agency was
held to be spectacularly corrupt. If the traffic tended to be *ʿashwaʾi* (haphazard
in this case rather than "informal" as the word is glossed in the case of housing
and unregistered trade), then the application of fines was downright arbitrary—arbitrary, but not random. Traffic police deliberately singled out drivers
of taxis and minibuses for punitive fines, lack of licenses, and both moving violations and infractions of the mechanical standards that were supposed to
apply to vehicles for hire—standards that were almost impossible to adhere to
by vehicles constantly in motion in the harsh Cairo traffic.

Though the atmosphere at this demonstration was unusually tense, I asked one of the men in the crowd what the purpose of the demonstration was. He said it was almost all taxi and microbus drivers:

> A car costs somewhere between sixty and ninety thousand pounds. Say the average is seventy thousand. What are you going to pay in fines? Should you just give the government your car? The car costs seventy thousand and you owe fines of ninety thousand! What are you going to do? Give them the car, or work for them? Or worse, you have to give them your car and still pay the fine.

Often the owners of the vehicles are not the drivers, but the drivers are the ones who pay the fines. To make matters worse, the police themselves are said to be major investors in microbuses.[4] At first glance it seems odd that the police would undercut their livelihood by punitively fining their own vehicles. But it amounts to dual rent streams: the driver pays rent to the owner of the vehicle (a policeman) in order to earn his own living from it, and traffic fines can be "fixed" by the same policeman-owner, who may take less than the official fine into his own pocket in return for expunging the record of the infraction. The demonstration against the Traffic Agency was surely a "war of maneuver"— a frontal attack rather than a holding action. On the other hand, the demonstration was happening at that particular moment precisely because the protestors sensed that they had leverage over the institution. They had real hopes that they could change its internal structure and ways of doing business. The siege was indeed a reciprocal one, just as Gramsci said.

A few days later I witnessed the first stage of a reversal in SCAF's own war of position. The resodding and landscaping of the Tahrir saniyya on April 14 described above was meant to close off the open-ended liminality that had governed the Square since January 25. On May 1 the chasm of antistructure began to reopen. A substantial and very vigorous demonstration was held on the occasion of International Workers' Day. The square was festooned with the banners of communist, socialist, and Nasserist parties, as well as numerous fledgling independent unions representing particular trades or sectors. Since uniformed police and security forces could not possibly appear at a protest, the government's presence was fulfilled by the ostensibly more prorevolution army, mainly military police. But given the brutal clearing of the sit-in following the Day of Purification three weeks previously, including the arrest and possibly the murder of some of the army officers who had joined the protestors, the speakers at the May Day event must have been highly conscious that they were within earshot of uniformed army officers.

Among the speakers was Kamal Abu Eita, a legend in the Egyptian labor movement who had fought the state-controlled Mubarak-era union for years before the revolution, and a prominent member of the Nasserist Karama

(dignity) Party. He spoke from the main stage set up in front of the Mugamma',
but his speech initially focused not on labor issues, but on one highly significant martyr:

> Our country is full of bounty. Listen, listen; in our country there are
> youth, and there are people. . . . Let me tell you about something. We
> have with us today my colleague from college. He was in the same co-
> hort as me, Ustaz Mahir. Where is he? The *last* martyr of this revolution
> was *al-shahid* 'Ali Mahir [his friend's son]. He was a martyr of the Fri-
> day of Purification. Listen Mahir. This revolution is for all of us. [Some-
> one in the crowd breaks out into *la ilah illa Allah . . . il-shahid habib
> Allah*—"there is no god but God . . . the martyr is the friend of God.]
> Haven't we been singing that anthem throughout the revolution as we
> carry the bodies of our martyrs?

'Ali Mahir, the martyr Abu Eita referred to, was a teenager, the last martyr of
the revolution only up to that point of course. As the speech says, Mahir died
in the breakup of the sit-in following the Friday of Judgment and Purification
on April 8, six days before SCAF's firm attempt to close down Tahrir as a protest space by resodding the saniyya as described at the beginning of this section. Abu Eita did not need to mention the military in order to convey what
many revolutionary activists believed: that Mahir was killed by the army, who
were there listening.

The workers were not about to attempt establishing a new *i'tisam* in Tahrir
Square on that May Day. They were there with their families. The speeches
after Abu Eita made little attempt to do more than cheerleading for the revolution. The most interesting part of that day was less the speeches than the reactions of the soldiers who where there ostensibly to keep order. "Keeping order"
meant waging a losing battle to keep people from spilling onto the newly resodded saniyya. There was a stark difference in the body language of the lower-
rank soldiers and the officers. The officers were military police in their distinctive red caps. Military police were among the toughest and most loyal units in
the army, often used to commit violence against protestors. In the wake of the
April 8 officers' fraternization with the revolutionaries, they looked very uneasy
as they tried to cajole the many workers spilling onto the grass to move away.
The soldiers, by contrast, looked bored and tired, as if they would have preferred to join the picnic-like atmosphere of the protestors rather than chase
them away. These images stuck in my mind far more than the May Day
speeches (see figure 5.3). It was impossible to tell who was under siege. Maneuver and position were one. But whether they were the attackers or the de-
fenders, SCAF was in retreat that day. It did not last, but for me that was, in
some ways, the high point of Tahrir Square's mystique, even though hardly
anyone noticed.

FIGURE 5.3. Army soldiers and officers nervously confronting citizens filtering back onto the saniyya, on May 1, 2011, during a rally held to celebrate International Workers' Day. Author's photo.

FIGURE 5.3. (*continued*)

The First Birthday of Khaled Said

One could mark the temporal flow of the revolution through martyrdom already in the revolution's gestation stage, when Khaled Said, the young computer programmer beaten to death by the police in Alexandria, became a rallying point for protest against the Mubarak regime. Martyrs' websites established by their friends and relatives often listed the date of death instead the person's birth date, in keeping with the logic that the death of a martyr should not be marked by a rite of passage, but by the *suspension* of the rite of passage, holding the dead in a liminal state—a condition that mirrored the liminal crisis of revolution. By that standard, Khaled Said was born on June 6, 2010.

On the first anniversary of the martyrdom of Khaled Said the security forces that had murdered him were still far from recovered after their defeat in the early days of the revolution. The sight of uniformed policemen in the street was still rare. Many neighborhoods were largely unpoliced, which was welcomed by young men whose experience of policing was largely as the targets of punitive action. But middle-class anxiety at the ongoing security vacuum was steadily increasing. The new passivity of the police was partly by necessity, caused by the degradation of their infrastructure (around a quarter of the police stations in the country had been burned during the initial phase of the revolution) and the refusal of many people to accept resumption of the sort of harsh security measures that had characterized the later years of the

Mubarak era. But the absence of a more overt police presence was also a strategy designed to feed the anxieties of those who were unenthusiastic or opposed to the revolution. On several occasions I heard stories about waves of automobile thefts. When the owners tried to report the loss of their vehicles they would be told to "go tell it to your revolution." Traffic snarls were blamed on the revolution. The papers were full of stories about all kinds of criminals running amuck. There was a steady erosion of the narrative that the Mubarak regime had ordered the prisons to be emptied when it knew it was going to fall, in favor of a narrative that the prisons had been emptied by Muslim Brotherhood operations to free its members.

A demonstration against the Ministry of Interior on the first anniversary of Khaled Said's birth/death was announced for June 6, 2011. It was an extremely angry event, not large enough to threaten taking over the fortress-like ministry, located a few blocks from Tahrir, but organized to take place primarily at the main gate of the ministry, on Shaykh Rihan Street, a location that could never have been the focus of a protest in the wildest prerevolutionary dreams. Security forces looked down menacingly on the protestors from windows but made no attempt to interfere. In addition to the chants against the police and signs denouncing torture, some of the protestors designed and cut stencils, on the spot, which were then used to tag the wall of the ministry itself and the wall on the opposite side of the street. The stencil reproduced the outline of a famous photo of Said after his death in which the bottom half of his face was grotesquely mangled. But in place of his smashed jaw, the stencil substituted lines from a poem (see figure 5.4). "Does my blood flow like water before your eyes? Do you forget my blood-spattered garment?" It was a line from "La Tusalih" (Do Not Reconcile), the most famous work of the poet Amal Dunqul (1986b). "Do Not Reconcile" was an angry rejection of normalization with Israel in the wake of Anwar al-Sadat's trip to Jerusalem and the ensuing Camp David accords. The work of Dunqul and other leftist poets, mainly from the period of the 1970s student movement, was used often in revolutionary graffiti and street art. Connoisseurs of such works tended to be long-term committed non-Islamist activists of middle-class or more broadly intelligentsia backgrounds, and that was clearly the social profile of most of the protestors in the crowd that day.[5] But one need not have been devoted to leftist poetry to appreciate the powerful denunciation conveyed by the stencil, framed by the very well known outline of Khaled Said's head, and in that location. Unsurprisingly, few passersby were destined to encounter this stencil, at least in that location. While it had been previously almost unimaginable to hold a protest right at the front gate of the Ministry of Interior, simply holding the protest had been enough. There was no question of trying to establish at sit-in there. By the next morning when I strolled down that street as casually as I could, all traces of the stencils were gone.

FIGURE 5.4. Stencils of Khaled Said painted onto benches and walls just outside the main gate of the Ministry of Interior, on June 6, 2011, the first anniversary of his murder by the police. Author's photo.

هل يصير يمر
بين عينيك
ماءً
اتنسى ردائى
المنفخ
بالدماء

From Fangari's Salute to Fangari's Finger

From Communiqué Number 3, announcing the abdication of Hosny Mubarak on national television the night of February 11, 2011. Delivered by SCAF spokesman General Mohsen al-Fangari:

The Supreme Council for the Armed Forces offers full salutations and appreciation to President Muhammad Hosny Mubarak for what he has done in the course of patriotic work in war and peace, and for his patriotic stance in giving priority to the higher interests of the nation. And with regard to this subject, the Supreme Council for the Armed Forces gives its full salutations and esteem to the souls of the martyrs [he pauses, looks straight into the camera, and gives a military salute] who sacrificed themselves for the sake of the freedom and security of their country. ("Bayan Raqm 3" 2011)

When General Mohsen al-Fangari, SCAF member and designated spokesman for the group, assistant minister of defense, and head of the Organization for Regulating and Managing the Armed Forces, saluted the martyrs of the January 25 Revolution his act was taken as a sincere indication of respect and a sure sign that the protestors had won. Al-Fangari's salute to the martyrs became iconic. It appeared on commercial revolution paraphernalia almost as much as the *al-Masry al-Youm* martyrs (see figure 5.5). His image was the perfect vehicle for coupling patriotism with revolutionary idealism and, for the military, a powerful statement of closure.

Closure, of course, was a long time in coming, was never accepted by many, and to the extent that it became a reality, was imposed through a defeat engineered by the same military for which al-Fangari spoke. "Closure" did not mean reconciliation but rather was an expression of power: whoever closed the revolution's protracted liminality seized the right to define what emerged from it. In July 2011 al-Fangari became prominent again, though for very different reasons. By this time military rule was being denounced across the spectrum of revolutionary forces, or at least by the rank and file; the Muslim Brotherhood and Salafi leadership pointedly refrained from any harsh criticism of SCAF, fuelling the anger of non-Islamists at the presumed secret deal made between their nominal allies and the military. That anger cut right through the revolutionary forces, dividing Islamists from non-Islamists irrevocably, no matter what the Islamist rank and file might have said off the record about SCAF rule.

July was the time of fierce debates between Islamist proponents of the "constitution first" school and the non-Islamist "elections first" alternative. The non-Islamists had reestablished a continuous sit-in in Tahrir, though they themselves were divided about the wisdom of pursuing this tactic. Long-running sit-ins were, by that time, thoroughly infiltrated by provocateurs and often attacked at night. In the summer heat many of the protestors looked di-

FIGURE 5.5. The iconic salute of SCAF spokesman Mohsen al-Fangari to the
martyrs of the January 25 Revolution on a box of tissues. Author's photo.

sheveled, and some of them (or possibly the provocateurs) were beginning to
block entrance into the Mugamma', the massive government office building on
the south side of the square, which had become a palette for revolutionary graffiti. I increasingly heard longtime committed activists saying that they did not
know who these protestors were, and wanted no part in maintaining a sit-in.

Into the teeth of these multifaceted rising tensions, on July 12 an obviously
angry al-Fangari read out a new communiqué from SCAF, firmly stating that
SCAF had no intention of stepping down until a civilian government was ready
to rule, and that the country would remain on the elections-first course that
had been ratified by a referendum that the Islamists had handily won. He
stipulated that there would be a committee to discuss "guiding principles"
(*mabadi' hakima*) governing the writing of a constitution, an issue that would
come back to haunt the country a few months later. Then, wagging his finger
several times for emphasis, al-Fangari launched into a three-part denunciation
of protestors:

> [Shaking finger] 1. Deviance by some from a peaceful manner in dem-
> onstrations and protests, leading to harming the interests of the coun-
> try and its citizens, and hindering the country's public utilities, causing

FIGURE 5.6. Graffiti satirizing al-Fangari's finger, on the
Mugamma' in Tahrir Square, July 2011. Author's photo.

significant damage to the national interest [takes a deep angry breath];
2. The spreading of rumors and false information, which leads to division, disobedience, ruining the nation, and casting doubt on measures
taken to bring stability to the country. 3. Putting special interests above
the higher interests of the country and the reputation of the armed
forces, with their historical responsibility. And in view of their national
role, they call on all honorable citizens to stand against anything that
impedes the return of normal life to our great people, and to challenge
harmful rumors. The armed forces are aided by the confidence of the
people, and emanating from its national foundations they assure you
that they will not allow anyone to seize power or to exceed legitimacy,
and it will take all necessary steps to confront the threats that surround
the nation, or to affect its citizens or national security by any wickedness

FIGURE 5.6. (*continued*)

they may desire. This is all within the framework of constitutional and legal legitimacy. God protect Egypt from the evils of strife and save it from all harm. God's peace be on you and his mercy and blessings. ("Khitab al-Liwa' Muhsin al-Fangari" 2011)

Al-Fangari's speech played well to those who were already inclined against the revolution, or who simply feared chaos and wanted stability at any price. But the reaction among the substantial numbers of still-committed protestors was absolute scorn. Al-Fangari, the erstwhile icon of revolutionary legitimacy became an object of ridicule (see figure 5.6). Graffiti on the Mugamma', precisely the institution that al-Fangari insinuated was being blocked by

FIGURE 5.7. Fingers on a piano on the other side of Tahrir Square
from the Fangari's finger graffiti. July 2011. Author's photo.

protestors, showed the SCAF spokesman angry, sweaty, and with a huge red
finger shaking at the disobedient youth who dared to continue their revolution.
Fingers were everywhere. On the north side of the square another graffito displayed a series of giant fingers playing the piano (see figure 5.7). I encountered
a protestor in a Palestinian *kuffiya* standing in the traffic with a crude cardboard sign saying "Aha ya Fangari" ("fuck you Fangari" using the Latin letter
code for transliterating Arabic characters on non-Arabic keyboards).

When he saw me take out my camera he posed and flashed the finger just
to make sure I got the point (see figure 5.8). I did not talk to him very much.
At the time I did not fully appreciate what I was photographing—it was only
later that I found the Fangari image on the Mugamma', and it started to sink
in that the finger symbolized the speech, which I had heard about but not yet
listened to. Symbols distill the position of initiands in a ritual with respect to
their past social commitments (Turner 1977, 94). But in uncloseable liminality
the community of initiands constantly shifts, and so can the significance of
symbols that might have previously been understood as unifying. The Fangari-
inflected sit-in struggled on through the heat, with the skepticism from within
the ranks of the protestors, attacks from thugs and infiltrators, and the increasing hostility of the nonrevolutionary public. Al-Fangari's finger in July was
connected to martyrdom through his famous and much-admired salute to the
revolution in February. But the two Fangaris were joined at the hip. There is
no question that the outrage and sense of betrayal at his haranguing speech
was predicated on his salute to those killed by the state he represented, even if
only on an interim basis, or so his speech emphasized. Unfortunately. many
more deaths lay over the horizon.

FIGURE 5.8. Protestor carrying a sign saying "Aha" ("fuck you," in internet Arabic characters) to Fangari. July 2011. Author's photo.

December 2011: Coffins at the Maglis al-Wuzara', a Wall on Muhammad Mahmud Street

In many ways the decisive period in the revolution was between October 2011 and February 2012. It was the period of urban battles and national parliamentary elections. The first salvo in the battles was fired by the military, when a group of Coptic protestors who were largely independent of the patriarchate and implicitly refusing the political role that had been allotted to them in the Mubarak era, marched to the Radio and Television Building at Maspero and were attacked by the army, with dozens killed and hundreds injured. After that, in quick succession, came the Battle of Muhammad Mahmud Street in November, in which protestors fought a five-day war of attrition against both the security forces and the military on the main street leading from Tahrir Square to the Ministry of Interior's primary headquarters, taking the brunt of shotguns aimed deliberately at the eyes, military-grade tear gas past the expiry date, and sometimes live ammunition. That was followed by the resignation of interim prime minister 'Isam Sharaf, who was nominally prorevolution, and the appointment of Kamal al-Ganzuri, a Mubarak-era dinosaur, who had been a particularly security-minded prime minister in the late 1990s. The appointment of al-Ganzuri was abhorrent to the revolutionary forces, and some of them (non-Islamists) initiated a sit-in at the Magils al-Wuzara' (Ministerial

Council building) in December to block him from taking office. That protest was broken up violently, again with deaths, injuries, and much brutality, in mid-December. Finally, on February 1, 2012, seventy-four members of the Ultras Ahly football fan club were killed in a stadium riot in Port Said.[6] The police stood by and watched while it happened, and worse, someone had chained shut the exit doors to the stadium. Dozens were killed from asphyxiation in the corked up stampede, in addition to others killed by members of the rival Port Said football fan club. The Ahly Ultras blamed the police for planning the massacre, even if the instrument of the violence had been football fans. And there followed "the Battle of Muhammad Mahmud II," much of which took place on other streets leading toward the Ministry of Interior, as Muhammad Mahmud Street had been blocked off with a wall made of giant concrete blocks after the first battle. By the end of February almost all the streets leading to the Ministry of Interior were blocked off by similar walls.

At the same time, parliamentary elections went ahead on schedule, between December 2011 and January 2012; SCAF was deaf to appeals by the non-Islamist revolutionary forces to delay elections until the violence had been ended. Islamists came out of the elections with a huge parliamentary majority, at least if one combined both the Muslim Brotherhood's political wing (the Freedom and Justice Party, which was nominally independent of the Muslim Brotherhood itself, though it was plainly beholden to the brotherhood in practice) and a number of Salafi parties that seemed to have come out of nowhere. Some of the Salafi vote, in retrospect, appeared to have been a de facto protest vote against the Muslim Brotherhood. Certainly the two groups did not see eye to eye on all issues, and by the summer of 2013, when the coup against Morsy took place, relations between them were poisonous indeed. But prospects for cooperation between the Muslim Brotherhood and the Salafis looked bright in the beginning, and to non-Islamists the Salafi agenda appeared even more unacceptable than that of the Muslim Brotherhood. Hence the parliamentary election left both non-Islamist political forces and people sympathetic to the old regime in a state of panic. In summary, the October to February period began with the most intense anti-SCAF activity of the revolution, a sentiment shared by much of the Islamist rank and file, if not by the Islamist leadership, which continued to make conciliatory statements about the military in public. But the period ended with all eyes on the alliance between the Islamists and SCAF, a parliament completely dominated by Islamist agendas, and the non-Islamist political forces widely discredited by street battles that made much of the public who were not politically mobilized uncomfortable.

In November when the Battle of Muhammad Mahmud Street occurred I was out of the country with my son, attending conferences. Lucie, my partner, was to join us later. By the time she did, she had experienced the battle at fairly close hand and wrote about it (Ryzova 2011; n.d.). One of her observations, which was not emphasized adequately in most accounts of the battle, was that the committed activists fought in alliance with many young men who were not highly politicized in a formal sense, but who wanted to exact a price for the years they had suffered at the hands of the Ministry of Interior's forces. Many of the men who joined the battle "to hit and be hit" by the police were under-employed youth, often from informal neighborhoods labeled in Egypt as 'ashwa'iyyat. The alliance of the relatively articulate activists and these socially and economically precarious youth had the disadvantage of further jarring the sensibilities of the unpoliticized or antirevolution public. Middle-class people began muttering about "street children" in Tahrir Square, and this was echoed in both print and television media.[7] But beyond such class-inflected rhetoric, the dynamic was quite different. What appeared to be vicious street battles from afar, particularly the Battle of Muhammad Mahmud Street, were, from the perspective of many of those in the fray, more like a carnival—a liminal phenomenon in which social rules are suspended or inverted (Ryzova; n.d.). Articulate political demands, underpinned by the rejection of an initiative to exempt the military from civilian oversight in any constitution-writing exercise that might be undertaken, fused with an exuberant determination by a youth-ful and very male "precariat" to seize their rights by fighting the security forces. The fight was an end in itself, and the battle was, to be sure, grotesquely un-equal; many of these young men died from shotgun pellets, "nonlethal" rubber bullets, tear gas inhalation, and live fire from the security forces. Yet the battle was experienced not only as grim combat, but also as pure joy. In that sense this key moment in the revolution, encapsulating the crucial end of 2011 and beyond that the revolution itself, was a thing of liminality.

By the time I got back to Egypt the Maglis al-Wuzara' sit-in had been es-tablished. It was in large part an extension of the Battle of Muhammad Mah-mud Street. Its purpose was to block al-Ganzuri from taking up his office. Ganzuri was appointed to bring order after the Battle of Muhammad Mahmud Street. The battle was triggered by the breakup of a sit-in by martyrs' families, and the reason for the sit-in was to extend a demonstration against the attempt by SCAF to get all the political forces to agree in advance to "supraconstitu-tional principles" that would have exempted the military from civilian control (see the previous chapter—the same issue is mentioned in al-Fangari's com-muniqué reproduced above). But both the trigger and the reason for the dem-onstration became secondary to the battle itself.

The Ministerial Council building, where the sit-in had been established, is on Maglis al-Sha'b (the People's Assembly) Street, about a block from Tahrir Square. Down the middle of the street in between the protestors' tents a row of mock coffins marched, each with the name of someone who had died in the Battle of Muhammad Mahmud Street (see figure 5.9). Each coffin had poetry attached to it. Amal Dunqul was prominent, as he had been at the Ministry of Interior protest in June—both "Do Not Reconcile" and "The Last Words of Spartacus" were used, but also many others. A few coffins were embellished

FIGURE 5.9. Posters and mock coffins commemorating the
martyrs of the Battle of Muhammad Mahmud Street in front of
the Maglis al-Wuzara'. December 2011. Author's photo.

with lines by the Palestinian poet Mahmud Darwish ("The most beautiful of
mothers who waited for her son as he returned martyred cried two tears and a
rose, and never yearned for the mourning robe"), 'Abd al-Rahman al-Abnudi
("Kill me. My death will not bring back your state. With my blood I write a
second life for my nation"), Faruq Guwayda ("Mother, I came to ask for my
wedding clothes, and with your hand, to my joy, you gave me my funeral
shroud"), and the Quran ("Think not of those, who are slain in the way of Allah,
as dead. Nay, they are living. With their Lord they have provision").

The first time I went to the Ministerial Council sit-in many of the people
there were battered, wearing eye patches or on crutches, obviously fresh from
Muhammad Mahmud. As often happens at such protests, strangers were nose

to nose in heated political arguments, with onlookers all around, many of them with their telephone video cameras out recording. In one of these knots of people a tiny woman, obviously very poor, was talking to a much more middle-class-looking young man and a rather stylish woman in hijab, also clearly more middle class than their interlocutor. The older and poorer woman was trying to find her son, who had gone to join the battle and had gone missing. "He's gone every day, to a million places. He doesn't sleep Mr. tough guy (*ya gada'*)." It seemed she was angry at the protestors rather than at the government. The young woman in hijab intervened, though rather apologetically, telling her that if someone has made a mistake she should give them a second chance. "You shouldn't insult them. If you give these people a chance, they might change for the better." But the man wasn't having it and started trying to convince the middle-class woman (ignoring the older woman looking for her son) that the problem was the appointment of Kamal al-Ganzuri, and that of course they had to block him from taking up his office because it was unjust. Then everyone started talking at once. Another man started talking to the woman in hijab about how the country desperately needed one man to take charge, while the young middle-class man began to argue with the poor woman about the dangers of the Ikhwan. A woman in niqab (a full face veil) with an Egyptian flag–colored headband standing behind the middle-class man tried to intervene, was talked over, gave up, and moved to a different conversation. So did I. In another conversation knot I found an old man, obviously poor like the woman, wearing an eye patch and with a bandaged head, shouting in a slightly Upper Egyptian accent about how Ahmad 'Izz, one of Mubarak's senior cronies, had corrupted the parliament, and killed eight hundred protestors. As he spoke he gestured toward the parliament building across the street from the Ministerial Offices. Everyone started talking at once and turned toward the parliament for a moment. The old man started yelling again and got their attention back. "Here, these people are a mafia, and they've ruined the revolution." I had seen such conversations going on for hours in Tahrir when the adrenaline was flowing. That was certainly the case here. Everyone knew it was just a matter of time before the army moved against them.

Maglis al-Sha'b Street was lined with tents from the intersection with al-Qasr al-Aini Street at the Tahrir end of it for about a block, until it hit an army checkpoint secured with barbed wire. That end of the street led toward 'Abdin and downtown, with several smaller streets off to the side leading to various apartment buildings and government offices. Those streets were still partially open, because residents and workers in the offices had to get through. In the days before the inevitable breakup of the sit-in I tried going through those back streets once. What I found was quite alarming. The streets were cut down to a narrow pedestrian corridor surrounded by barbed wire. On the other side of the barbed wire, sometimes on top of walls when they were available, very angry looking soldiers glared down on the passersby. The atmosphere was thick with menace. The people walking through those streets were mostly just bureaucrats trying to get to their offices. Protestors were all coming and going from the Tahrir/Qasr al-Aini direction, which was controlled by them. But I felt extremely uneasy walking through those barbed-wire corridors, and everyone else seemed to be scurrying as fast as possible to get away from the wrath radiating from the soldiers. The attack did indeed come a day or two later, touched off some said by one of the protestors trying to retrieve a football that had sailed over the parliament building's fence. Unsurprisingly given the state of the soldiers, it was a shocking attack, coming in full daylight and well recorded on videos.

Meanwhile Muhammad Mahmud Street, the root of the sit-in at the Ministerial Offices, was already becoming a shrine, a status it would hold until well into the Sisi era, and for those who fought there a permanent reminder of both pain and exhilaration. At that time, in December 2011, the wall blocking off access to the Ministry of Interior from the Tahrir direction was still a novelty. The street had been a palette for graffitists and street artists already for months. They were just getting started on the wall itself. After my return from attending conferences, before going to the Maglis al-Wuzara' sit-in, I had made my own small pilgrimage to the Muhammad Mahmud wall. It was early in the morning. The only people there were some young men, possibly veterans of the battle, one of them spraying some graffiti, and a woman in niqab with a camera in her hand, obviously there for the same reason I was there. If one came right up to the wall, through some of the gaps in the stones one could see lines of soldiers standing at attention (see figure 5.10). No wonder they were angry. I would have been angry also if someone had made me stand at attention at 8 a.m. just to guard a wall. And yet angry soldiers guarding a wall from a handful of kids was a potent distillation of the moment.

Conclusion: Martyr Performances in Time and Space

Through these vignettes we see the history of a crucial swathe of the revolution told through performances of martyrdom. These link to important political events in the revolution, but also to a dense network of textual and spatial anchors far beyond the scope of discrete acts of political contention. The experience of uncloseable liminality in the revolution was disorienting and uncomfortable, but it was also truly liminal in the sense that it enabled new forms of agency, or one might just say that "thinking outside the box" becomes obligatory when the status of the box itself is thrown into doubt. For some this absence-of-the-box agency was a source of creativity. When a contest for power ensued after the collapse of communitas it did not mean that all forms of history and prior social attachments disappeared, but it did allow revolutionaries much greater license as bricoleurs who could do things in performance spaces that could not have been previously thinkable, and join things

that SCAF was incapable of running the country in the long term. Revolutionary demands were well articulated by this time, but largely unmet. But neither did it appear certain that the interim government or a vaguely conceived "deep state" had the upper hand. Demonstrations and sit-ins, large and small, continued across the country. The exuberant communitas of the early days was long gone, if still fondly remembered. The revolutionary forces struggled to formulate a coherent master strategy.

In this context the political debate of the hour was whether to push for elections first, or for writing a constitution followed by elections. A constitutional referendum in March had already specified that it would be elections first. Islamists, who expected to do well in the elections, and SCAF both preferred this sequence. Non-Islamists (usually referred to in the media deceptively as "liberals") were desperate to reopen the issue on the assumption that they might not come out of the elections with decisive control of the political agenda. Throughout the second half of June debate raged over what should be the theme of a *milyoniyya* demonstration that was to be held on July 8. In the end it was to be "the revolution first," in view of the unmistakable fact that no consensus could be reached on whether or not the "elections first" followed by constitution could or should be changed.

In the midst of this highly charged debate Abu al-Ghayt, a medical doctor, published a blog post that attempted to cut through the fog of contention over the sequence of the transitional process in politics, and consequently to refocus attention on core goals that everyone agreed the revolution should try to achieve. The post was titled "The Poor First You Sons of Bitches (*Al-Fuqara' Awwalan ya Wilad al-Kalb*).[1] "The Poor First" was widely read and discussed and resulted in Abu al-Ghayt making a career change into journalism. The political chasm between Islamists and non-Islamists was far too wide to be bridged at that point, but Abu al-Ghayt's blog post stands as an excellent and in some ways prophetic synthesis of the political moment. Up to that point there had been very little open acknowledgment of the debt the revolutionary elite owed to nonelites who had thrown themselves into battle with the security forces in the early days of the revolution. Without them, the more articulate activists marching to Tahrir Square could not have brought down the Mubarak regime. And yet all attempts to embody the revolution in human representations systematically pushed the more "unsightly" and less politically articulate faces of the revolution aside. The post specifically criticizes the *al-Masry al-Youm* martyrs' middle-classness. Moreover, by June disgust at the often disheveled *appearance* of the revolutionaries who were still defiantly occupying public space was being voiced more loudly by those inclined to be dubious or hostile to the revolution—and there was no doubt that the number of such people was growing.

The core of this chapter consists of a translation of Abu al-Ghayt's post. I have abridged only a section containing pictures and short biographies of a

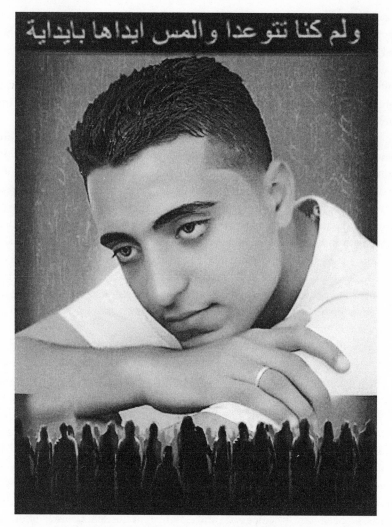

ولم كنا نتوعدا والمس ايداها بايداية

FIGURE 6.1. The martyr Muhammad 'Abd al-Hamid, in Muhammad Abu al-Ghayt's blog post "The Poor First You Sons of Bitches." July 2011.

number of martyrs. Since I cannot reproduce all the pictures here, the text of that section would not come across very effectively. The pictures Abu al-Ghayt refers to in the beginning of his post are of young male martyrs from nonelite mostly working-class backgrounds. They come from martyr commemoration web pages. The friends and relatives of the martyrs depicted on these pages intended them to be seen, hence I have reproduced the first image Abu al-Ghayt refers to but left out the rest.[2]

Also, in the first few lines he refers to a term rendered as *sirs* or *sirsagi* (pl. *sirsagiyya*). There is no convenient gloss for this in English. It is a derogatory term for certain types of youth. One could say "dead-end kids," or "feckless youth," but these terms aren't exact equivalents to *sirs/sirsagiyya*. The etymology of *sirsagi* may be "a boy who collects cigarette butts." But the contemporary image is of a young unemployed man, unmasculine, having an obsession with fashion. The sirsagi is only vaguely classed ("definition" pages often distinguish between "rich" and "poor" sirsagiyya), but in Abu al-Ghayt's post the association is with young men very likely from 'ashwa'i (informal) neighborhoods who are a prominent component of the neoliberal "precariat."[3]

The Post Translated

What is the first thing that comes to mind when you see this picture [see Figure 6.1]. Usually it's a flood of sarcastic comments such as "who's that king of romance [*min king al-rumansiyya da*]?" "Who's the prince, king of the sirs [*min il-birins malak al-sirs*]?" A great many of us on Face[book] have seen the picture of Sha'ban and Sabah, with all the reactions that they evoke.[4] There are even Facebook pages dedicated to depicting the images and actions of those in this sirsagi milieu such as "The National Campaign against Sirsagiyya ... the Bloody Fist [*Al-Hamla al-Qaumiyya didda al-Sirsagiyya ... al-Qubda al-Damiyya*]," which has over twenty-three thousand members.

The pleasant and slightly different surprise this time is that the subject of this picture—the king of romance, the prince king of the *sirs*—is the martyr Muhammad 'Abd al-Hamid, [killed] by a police bullet on the Friday of Rage at the Zawiya al-Hamra' police station. He was known among his friends as "Kamba." He worked in a petrol station for tips. He had two sisters and a brother, all of them married; he was the youngest, and lived on Sixth of October Street, branching off of Ahmad Hashad Street. He was brought [i.e., after funeral services] from Masgid al-Nadhir in Manshiyyat al-Gamal and buried in Turab al-Ghafir:

I had been thinking myself, and feeling a burning resentment in my heart when going over pictures of martyrs, seeing that a large proportion of them were "sirsagiyya kids" [*'ayal sirsagiyya*], youth from popular or poor 'ashwa'i neighborhoods as revealed by their cheap clothes, their attempts to look elegant, or their pretensions to romance through contemplative looks resembling what they had seen on television or on the streets of wealthy areas. Let us look together:

[There follows a series of pictures and text on the sort of martyrs he has in mind: a mix of youth bearing the "sirsagiyya" diacritica, as well as just plain lower-middle-class or working-class men.]

Why don't we see pictures of any one of them, or of those like them? Why does the discussion of "youth of the revolution" or "martyrs of January 25" only ever focus on people like us, youth of the middle or petite bourgeois class, educated and elegant, from the youth coalitions or from the April 6 movement? Why wasn't a picture of a single one of them in *al-Masry al-Youm*'s historic article, from which the pictures of martyrs became visual icons? Was it because they were from a [lower-class] "environment," or sirsagiyya, and hence it's not right for them to be "the flowers that bloomed in the garden of Egypt"? In any case, they hadn't been concerned with flowers throughout their entire lives because they were concerned with something more important: bread.

> We love the rose
> But we love wheat more.
> We love the essence of the rose
> But the spike of grain is purer
>
> —Mahmud Darwish[5]

I am always provoked by the silly argument made from time to time about the role of each political power or youth organization in the revolution; and there has to be a fight over the role of April 6 and the day the Ikhwan joined, and whether they delayed and then rode the wave of the revolution, and what was the extent of their role on the day of the Battle of the Camel, and whether if they hadn't been there the midan would have fallen and the revolution would have ended, and so on and so on. But almost nobody talks about a more important role, and that's the role of the *sirsagiyya* in protecting the revolution, challenging the police, and burning their vehicles and stations, particularly on the day of [January] 28, even though without them truly the *dakhiliyya* [Ministry of the Interior—a synonym for the security forces under its command] wouldn't have fallen in a few hours.[6]

Unfortunately I wasn't there in Cairo on the Day of Rage, as I was off getting arrested at that time. But my cousin told me about what he had seen on that day. For sure what he saw was repeated all over Egypt. He had gone to a peaceful demonstration as usual with a small group of friends, who had prayed the Friday prayer in the Sayyida ʿAisha Mosque. By merely beginning to chant slogans, [they caused] the security forces [to come] down on them, hitting them, shooting tear gas bombs, and shooting. "My friends and I ran, looking for a place to hide. The shooting and tear gas entered people's balconies, and we found the people of the area coming with us shouting "—— *ummak ya Mubrarak*," "*hukuma wiskha ya wilad il-wiskha*," and "*wilad il-—— batil*"; "your mother's ——" [a vulgar expression not given explicitly in the text]; "a filthy government you sons of filth"; "sons of —— you're worthless." Everyone who came had a sword or a knife, and whoever came across a soldier or officer attacked him. I thought they were bringing vinegar [for the tear gas], but it turned out to be bottles of gas, which the youth turned into Molotov cocktails, and threw at the trucks and the soldiers. In less than two or three hours all the trucks had been burned. The officers ran, and the stations were burned."

Another friend from Giza told me a similar story: "I said [to myself] I have to go down [to the demonstrations] today, to hit and be hit. I found the kids from the neighborhood going after prayer, so I went with them. They turned out to be *sis* kids;[7] as soon as the soldiers hit them and [and came to] take some of them [arrest them presumably] and shoot tear gas at them they [came] back running. After a while I found kids coming from Talibiyya—a nearby sha'bi neighborhood. Just them. One boy from this group was taking tramadol—narcotic pills—he jumped onto an armored car, grabbed the soldier in it, and brought him down! After a while they learned that the soldiers were withdrawing from the area, and in seconds they surrounded them from the front and back, and kids from the rooftops pelted them with stones and Molotovs. In less than an hour the entire dakhiliyya fled, and the officers were removing their uniforms before running bare naked!"

Dr. Muhammad Salim al-'Awa told almost the same story in front of me about the youth of Shubra who brought staves and knives and broke up the paving stones to defend their friends from the youth of Madinat Nasr at the entrance to Tahrir by the Ramsis Hilton. And there were others who also told me about the participation of the kids from Shubra and Duwaiqa in defending the midan on the day of the Battle of the Camel.

These kids didn't go out to demand a constitution—whether first or last—or elections; they didn't go out so that Egypt could be liberal or civilian or Islamic or whatever [*islamiyya wa la mahalabiyya*]. They went out only for the reasons that touch their reality: the price of food and clothes and housing, which have been going up insanely; the police officer who stops his brother's microbus to steal fifty pounds from him; the officer who arrests him in an investigation and tortures him for days for no reason; his sister who has no money with which to marry; his uncle who is put into retirement early because his factory was privatized; his cousin who lost everything in the land [because of] young graduates['] scheme in which plants died from thirst after preferential irrigation for the land of big owners; his aunt who died of cancer while they couldn't find a bed for her in the government hospital; and so on and so on.

In a scene from this video ["Gum'at al-Ghadab" 2011] summarizing everything [at 5:50], which shows the burning of the Sayyida Zaynab police station, the videographer—who appears from his voice and his

way of speaking to be middle class and educated—asks one of the
youths, who appears to be from the neighborhood, to "watch out for the
gunfire." The spontaneous response is "It's normal . . . makes no difference if I die or not." He didn't say "it's all for Egypt," or "I die a martyr
fighter for Islam." He makes no comparisons or "big talk" of any kind—
not the nation, or religion, or even dignity, just nihilistic feelings that
his life in these miserable circumstances is no different than his death.
Could he have imagined that the day would come when some would say
that not putting the constitution first was a betrayal of the blood of
martyrs, to be answered by the "elections first" team that they gave the
most blood and made the most sacrifices in defense of the revolution!

> I tell you the truth:
> The living have no rights
> If the rights of the dead are forsaken
> The dead have no rights
> If the sanctity of the word is violated!
> And if the pain of the dead
> Has been made into a commodity,
> A veil, an icon,
> A slogan, a prize
> Then cursed be the age
> The Flood is near!
>
> Heroes,
> In the true meaning of the word
> Died expecting not even a single word
> Not one of them thought
> —when he was martyred—That martyrdom is heroism
> Or that he was giving something
> To the next generation
> For he was a martyr, not a philosopher
> And what can one hope to gain
> Who has given the last he had
> In a fit of anger or of love. (Naguib Surur)[8]

For them—the 40 percent of Egyptians below the poverty line, including twelve million who live in 'ashwa'i neighborhoods and 1.5 million living in the cemeteries—the entire struggle over the constitution
and the elections and the system of rule in the country is just "newspaper talk" [kalam garayid] that represents nothing but the extent of its
very direct influence on their opportunities for work, their salaries, and
their livelihoods. The constitution versus elections debate doesn't seem
to concern them more than a wrestling match. The result is that a large

number of people now curse the revolution, the revolutionaries, and the politicians all together after a rise in the prices of just about all products these days, and this is what causes the greatest disappointment in the general public, which thought that if prices didn't come down then it would maintain, after so much blockage of the means of livelihood, what the microbus driver I wrote about in my last blog post [Abu al-Ghayt 2011b] said: "*Wallahi* there are people who are exhausted, and most of them can't make enough to eat. Ten pounds means a lot to them, but you [elites] have no idea. I can get by, but older people over the age of sixty or seventy and retired, where are they going to get their medicine? And there are people who were living hand to mouth [*'ayshin arzqiyya 'ala bab Allah*], and now after the revolution—God forbid!—they can't even manage that [*hatta bab Allah ma'adush laqiyinuh*]!"

We haven't heard a single voice from the "elites" objecting to the rise in prices. People kick up a fuss at a rumor of an activist getting beaten, but we don't hear a word of solidarity from them with the protestors of Madinat al-Salam at the Radio and Television Building.[9] Perhaps some would condemn these protestors as "special interest"[10] demands. It should be incumbent on them to accept their losses and wait in the street or in tin shacks until we finish with our own disputes, which are more important than their trivial ones!

In the 1990s Turkish prime minister Erdoğan attended a conference for representatives of Islamic organizations. Instead of saying that he would work to "impose shari'a" or "spread Islamic spirit into the social fabric," he said that he was going to work to solve the problem of Istanbul's water drainage system. The audience burst into laughter. But that's exactly what he did, and he brought Turkey from dependency to what it is today. The Turks didn't elect his party because it was Islamic, but because it proved its ability to solve real daily problems. Up to now we have no Egyptian Erdoğan unfortunately. We have dull old elites who are still immersed in the binaries of Islamist/secular, and "constitution first" or "elections first." To all of them I say: The poor first you sons of bitches!

'Ashwa'iyyat and the Precariat

"The Poor First" twice invokes the term *'ashwa'i*—in the original text *'ashwa'iyyat*. It is an important term in the essay, and important also in the context of the revolution more generally as a way of talking about class. *'Ashwa'i* literally means "haphazard," but in urban studies it is glossed as "informal housing," in the sense of housing built without planning permission. Some 60 percent of the population of Greater Cairo lives in 'ashwa'iyyat (Sims

2010, 96). 'Ashwa'iyyat were essentially the citizens' response to a housing crisis that had developed by the 1970s, which the state was unable or unwilling
to address.[11] In other parts of the world such areas might be called "shanty-
towns," but such neighborhoods are not very shanty-like in Egypt.[12] Discourse
on 'ashwa'iyyat often defines them in terms of abnormality; they are the perfect instantiation of what Foucault called "heterotopias of deviance"—"those in
which individuals whose behavior is deviant in relation to the required mean
or norm are placed" (1986, 25). In reality 'ashwa'iyyat as distinct neighborhoods outside the formally planned areas are for the most part simply that—
not where the extremely rich live, but nonetheless socially stratified, sometimes fairly close to the center of Cairo, sometimes situated far away in the
peri-urban edge of the city in Qalyubiyya or Giza Provinces, as are the vast
planned developments of New Cairo and New Giza. Most people know someone who live in 'ashwa'iyyat. On my street in the centrally located neighborhood of 'Abdin many of the clerks and workers commuted to work from
'ashwa'iyyat.

The "deviance" of 'ashwa'iyyat is discursive, and a consequence of this was
that in the years before the revolution a mythology of 'ashwa'iyyat had crystallized. *Ashwa'iyyat* became a word that symbolized a problem. Cairo is over-
crowded? It is because of the growth of 'ashwa'iyyat, even though objectively
the oppressive congestion of the city has far more to do with the domination
of private automobiles owned by the relatively affluent eleven percent of the
population who can afford them. Poverty? 'Ashwa'iyyat, even though the social
stratification and occupational profile of these areas differ only slightly from
the "formal" parts of the city. Drugs? 'Ashwa'iyyat, but also encompassing
other marginal areas such as Bulaq Abu al-'Ila, as described in chapter 2.
Gangster culture? 'Ashwa'iyyat, romanticized after the revolution through the
rising stardom of an intense and sinewy young actor named Muhammad Ramadan. His "vulgar" (in middle-class stereotype) and sometimes violent films
such as *al-Almany* (Al-Sharif 2012), *'Abduh Mauta* (I. Faruq 2012), and *Qalb
al-Asad* (Al-Subki 2013) were set in 'ashwa'iyyat, inevitably shown as squalid,
lawless, and drug infested, and marketed through *mahragan* music videos, a
genre described by some as "electro sha'bi" (heavy on synthesized rhythm
tracks and strongly attuned to the 'ashwa'i origins of the singers, rather like
American hip-hop music in the class connotations it projects, if not in its sonic
character). Before the revolution it had been "social realist" films of Khaled
Youssef such as *Hina Maysara* (Youssef 2007) or *Dukan Shahata* (Youssef
2009) that built an image of 'ashwa'iyyat as a particularly virulent site of social
pathologies.

In the early months after the fall of the Mubarak regime I was struck by
references to the notion that 'ashwa'iyyat were a form of social pathology, a
problem to be solved, in two very different conversations. One was with Mariyam, a strong-willed politically active female novelist, resident of central Cairo,

widowed, and struggling to make ends meet on an inadequate day job in a public-sector publishing house. The other was the owner of an elite preschool in Zamalek that my son attended for a year. She was a relative of Gamal Mubarak's wife. Although they spoke from utterly different sociopolitical worldviews, both of them formulated postrevolution priorities in remarkably similar terms. "The government should immediately do something about the 'ashwa'iyyat"—almost identical words though the writer spoke in Arabic and the preschool operator in English. The preschool operator said that she simply meant that poverty caused the revolution, and that it should be alleviated by more activist state state-led housing construction. For the novelist the solution to 'ashwa'iyyat was the same: "move them to the desert." But for her what elevated the 'ashwa'iyyat to the status of a serious problem, and top priority for a postrevolution government, was that they constituted a political and cultural vacuum, and that this vacuum was inevitably filled by both the regime and by Islamists—the two relatively organized political forces in the country. A primary requirement for reforming politics for her was to eliminate the 'ashwa'iyyat problem.

Periodically after 'Abd al-Fattah al-Sisi had consolidated power, he too reproduced a virtually identical rhetoric about "ending the problem of 'ashwa'iyyat. This, he said in 2016, would be accomplished within two years. It was utter fantasy, at most a strategy for directing ever more of the state's resources toward wasteful (but lucrative for those within the charmed circle of the state's protective umbrella) desert development. Even if the two million housing units he, and Mubarak before him, promised would be built almost overnight could materialize, so many of Greater Cairo's roughly twenty million inhabitants lived in informal housing that the promise itself was ludicrous. Yet the correspondence between Sisi's 'ashwa'iyyat and the way my interlocutors spoke was striking. The "problem of the 'ashwa'iyyat" was very deeply rooted in political discourse.

One might link the term *'ashwa'iyyat* to a different term, one not mentioned in Abu al-Ghayt's essay: *precarity*. In everyday usage "precarity" of course conveys a sense of unpredictability. But in the context of contemporary politics it is a specific post–welfare state construct, often in the nominal form, "precariat." The precariat has been the focus of organized politics in Europe since the early 2000s (Standing 2011).[13] They are post-Fordist "flexible" workers with no benefits and an increasingly shredded social safety net. A precariat differs from the Marxist category of "lumpenproletariat," who are unemployable workers with little hope of social integration (Standing 2011, 9). Precarious workers are, on the contrary, "normal" laborers in a system predicated on individuals marketing their skills with no guarantee of long-term employment.

Precarity is a condition of all life (Butler 2004), but one subject to a socially and governmentally distribution of mitigation (Lorey 2015). In other words,

states choose who deserves protection and who does not. From the late nineteenth century until roughly the 1980s the logic of modern nation-states—including the postcolonial state in the case of Egypt—was to extend protection
to all citizens. "The great achievement of the welfare state, . . . consisted in its
capacity to protect, to a certain degree, even those not safeguarded through
property: that unprotected 'strata of the population' permanently affected by
social insecurity, by unforeseeable dangers such as illness, accident and unemployment, and therefore exposed to the constant danger of poverty" (Lorey
2015, 51). It is precisely the effort by states to mitigate "unforeseeable dangers"
for a substantial portion their citizenry that neoliberal governance under-
mines. Moreover, the "unprotected 'strata of the population'" has steadily expanded over the past five decades or so. Nominal property ownership is no
longer sufficient as a criterion of sheltering under the state's steadily shrinking
protective umbrella, and consequently the hierarchy of protection is now much
more complex than a simple dichotomy between owners/nonowners suggests.
The phrase "the 99 percent" (and by extension, "the 1 percent"), coined by the
American Occupy Movement, is a rhetorical formulation of the new logic of
governance. There is no precisely definable threshold between the charmed
circle who have access to the state's full protection and those who do not, but
the trend of states facilitating almost unlimited accumulation for a few against
the interests of the many is clear virtually everywhere in the world.

In Egypt, just as in the United States, "middle class" no longer means "protected by the state" in the sense that the state would expend substantial effort
to mitigate the risks of life crises. "Middle class" is as much an expectation, or
an aspiration, as a material reality. It is difficult to pinpoint exactly when the
middle class lost its belief that the state would help them to achieve its expected "middle classness" in the old sense implied by the welfare state. Assume
that this loss of faith was (and remains) an uneven process both across nations
and within them. What takes the place of the dream of security that the welfare
state once seemed to offer? Lauren Berlant suggests an ideology of attachments to fantasies of a good life that is no longer achievable for the vast majority of the population—"cruel optimism" (Berlant 2011). One can perhaps sense
cruel optimism in the face of the martyr Muhammad 'Abd al-Hamid, the
"prince of the sirsagiyya" invoked by Abu al-Ghayt at the beginning of his essay.
In Egypt the objects to which he and others are meant to want to attach themselves are everywhere, literally, in the marketing of "the good life" to be
achieved by migrating to luxury housing compounds. Highways are lined with
billboards for these projects, and television advertising is saturated with it.
Once he became president, 'Abd al-Fattah al-Sisi flogged endless grandiose
visions of it (Morsy, in his year, not so much). "The good life" envisioned in
these fantasies is achievable only by the enterprising individual; it is a vision
of *escaping* the state, not of fulfillment *within* the state.

Precarity, 'Ashwa'iyyat, and Liminality

In terms of governance precarity is something different. Government of the precarious withdraws the umbrella of the welfare state and puts in its place thresholds for containing the unprotected population. Starvation is the lower limit; rebellion the upper limit (Lorey 2015, 65). The resources of the state are therefore redirected to policing these limits rather than to mitigating life crisis risks for those who live within them.

Abu al-Ghayt's blog post alluded to class dimensions of the revolution that were largely missing in most mass-mediated commentaries at the time. His intervention was at least partly a response to an editorial published by Ibrahim 'Isa, a very prominent journalist and television presenter.[14] 'Isa's comment on the "elections versus constitution" debate had scornfully dismissed economic arguments in a way that carefully avoided linking economic issues to organized labor or to ideologies that might challenge the way Egypt's economy was structured:

> It was not a revolution of the poor, or of the hungry, or of the old philosophy that some of us reiterate these days, claiming that people do not care about elections or the constitution, and that the important thing is the poor first, and consequently, we must work to raise the economic standard of the people because it is the most important demand and the highest priority. The awful thing is that this exaggeration is repeated as if the January 25 Revolution actually ended in February, that we've returned to the same line as Hosny Mubarak with even more idiotic enthusiasm and foolish sincerity. ('Isa 2011)

The revolution was, he said, about freedom, dignity, and self-respect, "not merely advancing requests for raising salaries" or demanding a minimum wage ('Isa 2011). 'Isa's intervention was implicitly addressed to a middle class that no longer existed—a welfare state middle class.

In a different way 'Isa had his finger on the pulse of public opinion. Already in March 2011, mere weeks after the fall of the Mubarak regime, similar sentiments were being voiced. One day when I was at Sharif's apartment (our host during a large portion of the first eighteen days of the revolution) his wife came home in considerable consternation. "I was talking with some women and some shopkeepers in the Bab al-Luq market," she said. "They told me the revolution has failed!" I was curious and skeptical and asked for more elaboration. "They said we had a revolution, and prices are still high! What went wrong? Wasn't the revolution supposed to make things better?" She seemed skeptical in her turn when both her husband and I told her that of course a revolution could not bring prosperity so quickly, and indeed might make daily life harder for quite a while. By summer such sensations of disillusion, however unreasonable they may have been, were growing. 'Isa was skilled in manipulating such false hopes; Abu al-Ghayt's intervention highlighted entirely different aspects of the revolution's articulation with class.

Academic explanations of the revolution do not ignore political economy (e.g., Hanieh 2013) but are vague about class. Alexander and Bassiouny's *Bread, Freedom and Social Justice* (2014) focuses on organized labor, devoting only three pages to discussion of informal or precarious labor. They also do not quite touch on the class contrast that Abu al-Ghayt attempts to articulate. His text is anchored in the same leftist activist culture that animated so much of the revolution's artistic performance (Darwish and Surur in his case), but unusually he endeavors to highlight friction between those who saw themselves as politically articulate, and the "voiceless" who joined the revolution for reasons that are less audible to scholars writing on the revolution. Abu al-Ghayt's intervention was a kind of organic formulation of "Can the Subaltern Speak?" (Spivak 1988). He "breaks with the immunizing defensive discourse of the bourgeois centre about the 'threatening precariat'" (Lorey 2015, 111), dissolving the layers of mystification between the "polite" and politically articulate middle class, and "the poor," who are marked—for rhetorical purpose in his essay—by a certain masculine style and an 'ashwa'i location.

One could go further. His "poor" are no lumpenproletariat, socially undigestible and unable to work. Abu Ghayt's martyrs work at gas stations; they drive microbuses; they work in factories (until they get privatized); they get cheated in government development schemes, fail to find medical care in hospitals. His pictures of martyred men (now a series of dead links; possibly gone from the internet forever by the time this is published) included a student, a married man with children, a graduate of an Italian institute for accountancy, and another half dozen men who for the most part lacked the diacritica of sirsagiyya that Abu al-Ghayt highlights at the beginning of his essay, precisely to make the point that despite their appearance they are just like the others. What differentiates Abu al-Ghayt's "40 percent living below the poverty line" from the rest of the population? The inarticulate "subaltern" to which he tries to give voice goes far beyond the 'ashwa'iyyat. His "poor" are the new middle class emerging under government of the precarious. Abu al-Ghayt's essay gropes toward an articulation of a precariat—the "flexible" labor force essential to globalized neoliberal states.

Some workers experience precarious labor as an exuberant independence, but the wider experience of precarity is exactly what the word denotes in everyday language—unsure, unstable, uncomfortable; and the longer it goes on the more it becomes all of them. In that sense it resembles protracted liminality, the "uncanny" state of being unable to anticipate the future. But precarity is structured; it is a deliberate effect of governance, not part of a managed transition or an unexpected crisis. Turner had a term for structured liminality: liminoid, "the quasi-liminal character of cultural performances in modern societies—theatre, concerts, exhibitions, television and film—which are usually produced by specialized groups or industries, and are not deeply integrated into the collective core of social experience" (Peterson 2015a, 169; and on the concept of the liminoid, Turner 1974). Precarity can be seen as liminoid, as "synthetic liminality," but in a different sense—as a kind of cage constituted by the limits of starvation and rebellion. The only kind of performance allowed within this liminoid space is the achievement of "market rationality" (Gershon 2011, 538), in which selves are managed "as if they were a business" (Gershon 2011, 539).

This makes for a crude description of Egyptian society. Techniques of cultivating the self can be part of the broader privatization and neoliberal policies of the Mubarak era, and yet entirely compatible with Islamic ethical projects (Mahmood 2011; Hirschkind 2006). Selves may also be reckoned relationally with respect to family members and other important figures in social networks, rather than conceived as an individualist project. Such constructions can function to instill patriarchal values; patriarchy itself requires a relational construction of the self with respect to senior male authority (Joseph 1994; Ghannam 2013, 87). In much of Egyptian society relationality itself operates in extremely complex ways, particularly in the economic sphere, which blends piety with a "future-oriented capitalism," and results in an ethos consisting of "the actually affective disposition to existence, self and relationality, which may or may not be part of an aspirational project of active self-making, and which may or may not be actively reflected on" (Schielke 2015, 127). Studies on Egyptian elites perhaps allow greater scope for the "active management of the self," emphasizing connectivity to the world outside, but also to Egypt as a national collectivity (de Koning 2009; Peterson 2011). Possibly greater income and transnational mobility enables people to experiment with actually living such alternatives. But it is a leap from contrasting different forms of connectivity implicated in constructions of the self to making broad claims about a "neoliberal subjectivity."

Another way of formulating neoliberalism focuses on an interface between laws and ideas on one hand, and the social action of individuals on the other:

> As in other parts of the globe, the idea of freedom of the individual in modern Egypt has merged with the idea of the free market, expressed in part in the Supreme Constitutional Court's reforms of the bureaucratic laws that were seen to be holding back private enterprise. . . . In the period of economic and political liberalization a plethora of NGOs has created an expanding space of "civil society": middle-class activists, with institutional funding from Euro-America and entry to Western networks, telling their fellow-citizens to claim their rights as free persons from their state and to produce more efficiently in a free economy. (Asad 2015, 201)

In Asad's formulation the question of neoliberalism as a totalizing subjectivity never arises. A "liberal incitement to individual autonomy" (Asad 2015, 203) affects people differentially. "People still belong to families and associations, and they claim they have friends" (Asad 2015, 203), which is a shorthand way to acknowledge the sort of connective constructions of the self mentioned above. These may be pressured by pervasive ideological constructions of individual autonomy as Asad suggests, though pressure should not amount to total domination.

But note that Asad also refers briefly to another related aspect of the neoliberal restructuring of society that bears emphasis, namely that to the extent to which non-Islamist political mobilization was organized in the revolution, a significant proportion of it had been incubated in formally constituted nongovernmental organizations (Asad 2015).

In practical terms foreign funding of movements such as April 6, and of human rights NGOs generally, became a stick with which the government was able to beat the revolution vigorously, a tactic that had long been part of the state's repertoire of repression (Pratt 2004; 2005). Nongovernmental organizations operate within the terms of neoliberalism, and some argue that the routing of opposition through such organization rather than through political parties limits rather than enables democracy in the Arab world (Pratt 2004; Langohr 2004). This does not in any way detract from the courage of NGO-connected activists who worked often at great personal risk. But it is difficult to completely disentangle the political confluence between human rights NGOs and opposition to the Mubarak regime and its successors from the "liberal incitement to individual autonomy" to which Asad alludes. In brief, a key non-Islamist site of resistance to the regime came from both the same class and subject position as the upper echelons of the regime. Moreover, the Muslim Brotherhood had been increasingly financed by private-sector businessmen such as Hasan Malik and Khayrat al-Shatir, and the organization's network of charities played a role in projecting its presence into social circles wider than its core membership. Charity is compatible with neoliberalism.[15] It consists of either the atomized actions of individuals, or of both private and quasiprivate (often religion-inspired) charitable organizations assuming social functions formerly performed by the state. The provision of "micro-credit," particularly to women, articulates with private and quasiprivate charity by shifting the burden of welfare onto individuals through a rhetoric of "empowerment" that rarely delivers on its promise (Ismail 2006, 87–92). Salwa Ismail describes the welfare system that evolved from the 1970s to the present as "a hybrid ethic of religious charity and modern philanthropy" (Ismail 2006, 74). In Egypt organized charity, including the activities of Islamic social institutions, must be registered with the Ministry of Social Affairs (Singerman 1996, 253–54). An Islamic "counterpublic" (Hirschkind 2006, 105–42) can therefore operate through charitable practices in concert with a state from which it seeks to demarcate itself.

One may question the usefulness of neoliberalism as a totalizing form of subjectivity, but there *is* something to be said about implicitly neoliberal practices in crucial political sites such as NGOs. The January 25 Revolution as both a revolution against neoliberalism and a neoliberal revolution are hard to tease apart. This was by no means an Egyptian paradox. One encountered it equally in the American Occupy Movement and in European protest votes for leftist politicians such as Alex Tsipras or Jeremy Corbyn. It is hard to stake an effective position outside of it. Neoliberalism is like quicksand: the harder one struggles to extricate oneself from it, the more one gets sucked down into it.

However, not all these qualifications on the notion of cultivating the self invalidate precarity as an effect of governance. The replacement of a welfare state (which can also accommodate multiple forms of subjectivity) by a space delimited through lower and upper thresholds, but set below the level of a privileged elite, is a process that may be linked to the cultivation of the self, but is not reducible to it. 'Ashwa'iyyat can be seen as a local synonym for liminal. In spatial terms 'ashwa'iyyat are on the discursive and sometimes literal margins; in the social imaginary they are the limen. But the word does not serve well as a synonym for "lower class." 'Ashwa'i is a condition, not just a space, and one that steadily expands, as the welfare state shrinks and the security state expands. In the final analysis one might say that "The Poor First" overlaps substantially with what used to be called middle class.

CHAPTER 7

Copts and Salafis

DUELING YOUTUBE VIDEOS ON
THE EDGE OF A PRECIPICE

"The army is from us."

—Dissident priest Philopateer Gamil, the night before the
Maspero Massacre ("Filubatir Gamil Yukhatit" 2011)

"The army is from us."

—Hasanayn ʿAbd al-Rahman, my Salafi washing machine
repairman, two weeks after the Maspero Massacre

IN THE AUTUMN OF 2011 the course of the revolution was still unclear, or
at least all the revolutionaries, both Islamist and non-Islamist, still thought
there was something to play for. This was the situation leading into the most
important period in the revolution, namely the last three months of 2011. By
that time the revolutionary forces—those that stayed mobilized or that remo-
bilized periodically throughout the year—had articulated a series of demands
that went far beyond the ubiquitous but vague "bread, freedom, and social
justice" slogan. They included the cleansing of institutions from Mubarakist
elements (demands made within these institutions and not just in public
squares), greater autonomy and political freedom within universities and al-
Azhar, independent labor unions, the cessation of military trials for civilians,
unambiguous civilian rule, and redress for those killed or injured by the security forces.

None of this had anything to do with an institutionally nurtured "democratic transition" that occupied the attention of political scientists;[1] none of it
was *acknowledged* by institutions or powerful public figures, who never devi-
ated from the line that the revolution was incoherent, and merely the product
of a few feckless youths. Hence chants at demonstrations of "down with military rule" were heard by March, but it was a series of massacres and street

battles beginning in October and lasting until early February 2012 that brought anti-SCAF sentiment much more openly into the mainstream than anyone could have dreamed, given the deeply institutionalized reverence for the military in Egyptian public culture. At that point the military had little choice but to push ahead with elections that it knew would result in a transfer of power to the Muslim Brotherhood.

Within the broad spectrum of the revolutionary forces, the process of calculating power resources (Turner 1988, 91) within a protracted state of liminality could, by October, be expressed as a simple polarization between Islamists and non-Islamists, both of them claiming the mantle of rationality in a contest against an opponent animated only by sheer political fantasy. The only problem was that neither of the revolutionary camps could really read the intentions of the SCAF. The bitter elections versus constitution argument had taken place ultimately in an echo chamber. The Supreme Council for the Armed Forces had not budged: elections it was.

Islamists, particularly the Muslim Brotherhood, initially thrived in electoral contests—and this had become apparent in the vote on constitutional amendments long before October. However, the Muslim Brotherhood were ultimately inept at building political alliances, and prone to misinterpret their electoral victories as a sign of much greater popularity than they actually enjoyed. There is no doubt that many non-Islamists voted for Muslim Brotherhood candidates in the earlier rounds of elections (the constitutional referendum in March 2011 and the parliamentary elections in early 2012) on grounds that they were assumed to be both less corrupt than the NDP had been, and more competent. The Muslim Brotherhood's long domination of university and professional syndicate elections buttressed this impression. No doubt the organization's provision of social services and charity also helped. But to non-Islamists the Muslim Brotherhood's social services were nothing more than electoral bribes—dismissed derisively as *sukkar wa zayt* (sugar and cooking oil given out both at holidays and on election days). Moreover, there were rumors that the elections themselves were far less "free and fair" than observers made them out to be, tainted by blatant campaigning from mosque pulpits, and manipulated in myriad ways short of the outright stuffing of ballot boxes that the NDP used to do. One technique of manipulation was supposedly to organize Ikhwan supporters to vote as early as possible and then have some members just stand in line endlessly, not moving, until everyone else got frustrated and went home. A journalist friend said that in her mother's home village the local Ikhwan knew exactly who would vote against them and simply intimidated their opponents from leaving their houses. Everything looked fine to observers at the village's polling place because suppression of the non-Ikhwan vote had happened elsewhere.

To non-Islamists the Muslim Brotherhood's weaknesses crystallized over the two and a half years after the fall of the Mubarak regime. The percentage of the vote in favor of people or issues supported by the organization declined in each successive election. It also became clear that electoral support for the Muslim Brotherhood was weakest in the big cities, where the largest number of well-educated voters lived. Voters in these parts of the country began to bristle at the fact that their fates could be decided by people they considered their inferiors living in places they thought of as backward and inconsequential. One may fairly criticize such attitudes as elitist, but they were nonetheless politically significant. Also, it became increasingly obvious that the Muslim Brotherhood could marshal impressive numbers at urban demonstrations, the only demonstrations that really counted in terms of national and international media impact, only by bussing in supporters from the countryside.[2] Almost imperceptibly a historically urban and middle-class movement had, according to some observers, become both "ruralized" and "Salafized."[3]

These ruralized and Salafized Islamists were front and center at a huge Islamist rally that I attended on July 29, 2011, just before the beginning of Ramadan. Non-Islamists derisively named it the Gum'at Kandahar (the Friday of Kandahar), in reference to the diacritica of Salafi jihadists—the sort of people who had gone to fight the Soviet Union in Afghanistan in the 1980s, and who now could be seen carrying al-Qa'ida banners in demonstrations. More precisely, Gum'at Kandahar was simply a derogatory label from an urban non-Islamist perspective for bearded men, all of whom were conflated into a noncivilized Islamist Other. The official name of the demonstration for those who participated in it was Gum'at Iradat al-Sha'b (the Friday of the People's Will).

Islamist participation in demonstrations up to this point tended to be brief and finite, partly as a strategy for staying in the good graces of the military while the Muslim Brotherhood negotiated with them for a leading role in the post-Mubarak era. This made a pointed contrast to the demonstrations organized by non-Islamist activists, which tended to be the starting points of long-running sit-ins that were in some degree annoying for those opposed to the revolution. Indeed, as time went by the non-Islamist political forces themselves began to debate the effectiveness of open-ended sit-ins that were both vulnerable when numbers decreased, and easy for enemies to infiltrate. Most Islamists, on the other hand, had simply been against the tactic of using sit-ins from the beginning.[4] Non-Islamists sometimes referred sarcastically to the Islamists' faux-polite tactic of holding brief demonstrations without any pretence of keeping up the pressure after the demonstration as "thaura thaura hatta al-'asr" (revolution, revolution until the afternoon prayer), a play on the often-chanted slogan "thaura thaura hatta al-nasr" (revolution, revolution until victory). But it was more than a tactical disagreement. Non-Islamists were furious when 'Isam al-'Eryan, a high-ranking member of the Muslim Brotherhood's Guidance Bureau and, at that time, vice chairman of the Freedom and Justice Party, gave a television interview just after the Friday of the

People's Will demonstration in which he strongly denounced sit-ins that had occupied the square in the weeks prior to the giant Islamist flexing of muscles on July 29, 2011:

> I have seen in Tahrir Square in the past two weeks faces that I've never seen before, and who I categorically do not know. And I do not see how they have had any role, not in expressing the revolution, or in participating in the events of the revolution throughout the eighteen days [that led to Mubarak's overthrow]. I saw some itinerant vendors usurping the square along with some others. I think that what happened today was against the wishes and will of the itinerant vendors who have tried to take over the square during the days and nights of Ramadan, particularly the nights, when they expect to make huge profits from people who will congregate in the square for tourism, or because they participated in the revolution—that's their right, but to turn Tahrir Square, which has become a global symbol and image for governments and presidents and ministers all over the world, into a theater just for a few itinerant peddlers? They can have someplace to sell their wares, but not Tahrir Square! This is something deviant! I believe that the step the political forces must take is to issue clear and decisive communiqués that there will be no sit-ins. And then if anything is to be done in Tahrir Square it must be by national consensus, and any return to Tahrir Square should be by general national agreement, which should specify the demands and goals of the revolution for which we can return to the square, and the time that we should remain in the square, and that we should then leave the square to return to its normal state. ("'Isam al-'Aryan" 2015)

This was uploaded onto YouTube on August 1, 2011, just after military police in concert with security forces had brutally dispersed what was left of the sit-in. Even if the continuous sit-in tactic had been in dispute among the non-Islamist political forces themselves, it was not for 'Eryan to speak for them, and it was beyond the pale to speak out in favor of government violence against the revolution. In 2013, when Muslim Brotherhood supporters were themselves waging long sit-ins in Raba'a al-'Adawiyya and Nahda Squares, the video resurfaced and was again angrily recirculated by non-Islamist activists who were infuriated when 'Eryan had undermined them in 2011.

The Friday of the People's Will rally, the "thaura hata al-'asr" event that preceded 'Eryan's infamous interview, was technically a Salafi event, as the Muslim Brotherhood had officially pulled out of it. But as long as nobody was carrying Muslim Brotherhood signs one could only guess who was Ikhwan and who was a Salafi. In other words, there was no foolproof way to ascertain with certainty whether all the protestors were in fact Salafis.[5] In 2011 the short duration of Islamist demonstrations was a duplicitous means to side with

SCAF and still pose as revolutionaries. Whether the protestors were all Salafis or a mix of Salafis and Ikhwan, the official purpose of the demonstration as articulated from the podium was to promote the implementation of shari'a, or of their strategy to side with the army and the police, in direct opposition to the non-Islamist political forces who were determined to oppose them.[6] Several of the speakers from the podium in the event said as much, and on one side of the square I found a poster that laid it all out with clarity:

> Egypt calls for help against oppression and tyranny that has prevailed throughout the ages since the abrogation of the merciful shari'a. O community of the Quran [*ummat al-Qur'an*], which has created you and made you equal and given you sustenance, it is this Quran that rules you and commands you and proscribes you. An urgent call to Imams of mosques—religious functionaries, preachers, religious associations, Muslim men and women: the people want!! The people want!! The people want!! . . . But *God in his glory* from atop his throne loves, *commands* and wants *implementation of shari'a!!* The one certain sure guarantee of escaping the dilemma we are in is the honorable and praiseworthy commanding of shari'a. No law [*qanun*], no constitution: Egypt will be ruled by the Quran. To the noble leadership, to the Military Council and the army, to youth of the revolution and hope of the nation [*umma*]: cooperate in reverence and piety, unity is power, for the sake of the merciful shari'a. Dearest Egypt: our slogan is politeness and respect for the army, the police, and all [political] currents. May God grant us success for the benefit of the nation and the servants of God and for the achievement of all of Egypt's goals that may please him.[7]

The poster was a local product, sponsored by an Islamic charity in the Cairene neighborhood of Shubra. But the "politeness and respect for the army" and "the police" that it advocated was also a practical accommodation to the non-Cairene origin of many of the people who participated in the Friday of the People's Will. Mobilizing so many people for a one-day event was an impressive logistical feat, but sustaining a presence in large enough numbers to make it difficult for the authorities to break it up would have been well-neigh impossible. Downtown Cairo on the morning of the Friday of the People's Will felt like an occupied country to those who normally lived in it, and for most of those who frequented it for leisure or work—though the latter category encompasses the full social spectrum of Egypt. The protestors themselves may have felt that they were claiming a share of the symbolic loadstone of the revolution that was rightly theirs. There were busses all over the area, and everywhere there was a mosque, there were anywhere from dozens to hundreds of mostly bearded men sitting outside on the pavement (because the inside space was full) waiting for the demonstration to begin after the noon prayer and sermon. The men were perfectly polite and peaceful. I took my son Jan to a bakery near

Tahrir Square for a croissant, and we passed by the throngs of protestors without incident. Later in the day when I was walking home from the demonstration I passed through a parking lot where dozens of busses were waiting to take their passengers back to the provinces. I overheard a burly bearded man in a white *galabiyya* walking in front of me toward a bus say to another man, "now the *'almaniyin* [secularists] will see who really runs the country!" That moment seemed surreally like a scene from a television drama written by non-Islamists—all it needed was an evil chortle tacked on to the overheard snippet of conversation.

But while the Friday of the People's Will, despite its open calls to cooperate with the military and security forces, was interpreted at the time as an intimidating Islamist muscle-flexing exercise, non-Islamists also seem to have noticed vulnerability along with power. Islamists were clearly not as strong in cities as they were in the provinces. In 2013, when Muhammad Morsy had taken the presidency and opposition to the Muslim Brotherhood was increasingly violent, the organization was forced to mobilize its provincial base again and again either to mount demonstrations (for example, in support of the president at the Presidential Palace), or to defend urban institutions such as the Muslim Brotherhood headquarters in the upscale Cairene neighborhood of Muqattam (eventually sacked and burned shortly before the fall of Morsy in 2013). The busses themselves became a liability. Many were attacked and burned, and provincial Muslim Brotherhood supporters were likely to find themselves stranded in the city.

If the Friday of the People's Will had been a Salafi rather than Muslim Brotherhood event as advertised, then it still leaves "Salafi" as a notoriously broad term. On one level they are simply followers of the *salaf*—the Prophet Muhammad and the first three generations of his followers, who formed an exemplary Islamic community for followers of the movement. The most prominent Islamic reformers of the late nineteenth and early twentieth centuries, such as Jamal al-Din al-Afghani, Rashid Rida, and Muhammad 'Abduh, were all influenced by Salafism in the broadest sense, as was the Muslim Brotherhood. In modern times Salafism has also sometimes became conflated with Wahhabism, the socially conservative movement founded in eighteenth-century Arabia by Muhammad Ibn 'Abd al-Wahhab that became allied politically with 'Abd al-'Aziz Ibn Sa'ud. Contemporary Egyptian Salafis usually refuse the conflation of their movement with Wahhabism.[8] In Egypt contemporary Salafism is both a theological position and a social movement, but there are many different strands of it, some more overtly involved with politics than others (Maguire 2016). Followers of Salafism became a wild card in Egyptian politics. Some Salafi leaders had collaborated with the Mubarak regime, either willingly or because they were forced to do so. In that context they functioned as bogeymen. The regime's message was "keep us in power, or these bearded puritans will ruin the country." After the revolution many Salafis at least tacitly supported the Muslim Brotherhood, while others turned against them. The term "Salafi" sometimes refers to the Da'wa Salafiyya (the "Salafi Call"), a product of the student political movements of the 1970s, conservative but not members of the Muslim Brotherhood. The political arm of the Da'wa Salafiyya after the revolution was the hastily formed and surprisingly effective Hizb al-Nur (the "Party of Light"). But the term "Salafi" covers a wide spectrum of generally conservative and scripturally literalist tendencies, which are, however, also more independent and even sometimes more flexible than the highly disciplined Muslim Brotherhood (Ahmed 2012).

One of the political magnets that attracted this largely conservative but independent social profile was the lawyer Hazem Salah Abu-Isma'il, a charismatic figure who had been a member of the Muslim Brotherhood, left the movement, and attracted a wide following as a new political option after the fall of the Mubarak regime. Abu-Isma'il was a frequent presence in Tahrir demonstrations and sit-ins, spoke revolutionary rhetoric that drew some grudging admiration from non-Islamists (and also from members of the Muslim Brotherhood), and was a consistent opponent of military rule. His followers were particularly enthusiastic, and when he threw his hat into the ring for the presidency in 2012 one could argue that he was the only truly charismatic candidate in the race. Unfortunately for his followers, Abu Isma'il's candidacy was nullified by the courts before the first round of voting, on grounds that his mother had taken American citizenship (the election law forbade candidates and their immediate families from having citizenship other than in Egypt). Abu-Isma'il's disqualification was based on a technicality that probably amounted to a political dirty trick.

I had no close contacts with either Muslim Brotherhood members or with Salafis. But I did have at least a casual recurrent Salafi interlocutor. His name was Hasanayn 'Abd al-Rahman, and he was my washing machine and air conditioner repairman. As both machines broke regularly, I had been calling on his expertise two or three times a year since 2008. Hasanayn was a large jolly man who liked to talk. His modus operandi was to come to my flat to diagnose the problem with his assistant, Khalid, a thin man with a hang-dog look, and decidedly not a good talker. Once the diagnosis was made Hasanayn would send Khalid out to buy some replacement part, and we would have an hour or two to have tea and talk while waiting for him to return. We became friends, though our occasions for socialization were always on some business pretext— our repair jobs of course, and once he learned of our interest in old things and in potentially purchasing property he tried to create new business links. His repair shop was in al-Munira, just south of downtown, but it turned out that he was born and raised in 'Abdin, the downtown-ish neighborhood where we lived and had purchased one of our flats, though his current residence was in a different central Cairene neighborhood. On one occasion he took me to see a couple of 'Abdin flats that he hoped we might become interested in buying.

Another time he came to my 'Abdin office flat and fixed the air conditioner, then took me to the street and bought me pickles and sausage—the best in 'Abdin in his opinion.

Before the revolution I had never thought of Hasanayn as a Salafi, though he displayed some of the diacritica, particularly a fairly long beard and a zabiba (literally a "raisin")—a thick callus on the forehead from presumably zealous praying, which is a distinctively Egyptian way to piously mark the (usually male) body. There was also some indication that he had made a conscious decision at some time in his life to change his cultural orientation. On one house call he brought me a couple of LP records of popular Western music (a Beatles album and one by Elvis Presley), telling me that he and his family no longer valued them. He had seen that we collected lots of old media, so he wanted to give the records to me. But beards and zabibas are not exclusive to Salafis, and for all I know he might have wanted to unload the records just to clear out his house, or did not want to bother acquiring a record player just to hear a few old American tunes. So I made few assumptions about his social and political positions. In the end it was the conversation I had with him after the fall of the Mubarak regime that crystallized his Salafism. I never asked what texts he read or what mosque he frequented, but on that occasion he simply self-identified as Salafi.

It was late October 2011, a couple of weeks after an incident known as the Maspero Massacre, in which the army—military police and security force, though most lethally the former—killed twenty-eight mostly Christian protestors. Maspero, named after a French Egyptologist, is a neighborhood north and a little bit west of Tahrir Square. Most of the area known as the "Maspero Triangle" lies between the industrial neighborhood of Sabtiyya on the north, the parallel boulevards of Ramsis Street and Gala' Street (the latter covered in an elevated highway called the October Bridge) from south to northeast, and the Nile Corniche on the west. The southern tip of the triangle abuts 'Abd al-Mun'im Riyad Square, which is essentially an adjunct of Tahrir Square. Most of the Maspero Triangle consists of the nineteenth-century industrial neighborhood of Bulaq Abu al-'Ila, which is slated for elite commercial and state development or for extinction, depending on how one feels about the current mostly lower-class residents. The corniche side of the area has long been highly developed with office towers, shopping malls, and state institutions. The most striking part of that strip of large buildings along the Nile is the Radio and Television Building, dating from 1959. It has a rounded high front facing the Nile, from which juts a square tower, atop of which is fixed a giant antenna. The iconic building and its quintessentially modern institution together are often referred to simply as "Maspero." In times of political tension it is assumed that the Radio and Television Building, the administrative nerve center of the state's media apparatus, would be a prime target for anyone wishing to overthrow the government. Consequently when the Republican Guard, an elite military unit under the direct control of the president, moved into Cairo on January 29, 2011, the first place its armored cars and tanks headed to was Maspero. And given Maspero's status as the headquarters of state media, it served as a focal point for protests once the early chaos of the revolution had settled into a more stable pattern.

On October 9 protestors marched from the mixed Coptic/Muslim neighborhood of Shubra on the north side of Cairo to Maspero. The march highlighted an incident that had occurred recently in the Upper Egyptian city of Edfu in Aswan Province, in which the construction of a church (actually in a village called Marinab rather than in Edfu itself) became a bone of contention between Salafists and Copts. This resulted in the Marinab Church being destroyed, after which the governor of Aswan denied that there had even been a church in the first place, describing the building that had been burned as a "guest house" that had been illegally transformed into a church (Tadros 2011b). This resulted in a sit-in at Maspero starting on October 4, and the large procession on October 9, organized by the Maspero Youth Union and the Free Copts, both of them lay groups independent of the Coptic Church (Tadros 2011b). The march was attacked en route, and when it reached Maspero it turned into a bloody fiasco. Military police assaulted the march using live ammunition and ran over protestors in heavily armored personnel carriers. Twenty-eight protestors, most of them Copts including one very prominent revolutionary activist named Mina Daniel, were killed, and around two hundred injured. In the aftermath several things became clear. One was that state media, probably under direct orders from SCAF, had played an atrocious role in the event, first by its one-sided reporting of the Aswan tensions and more blatantly during the massacre itself, when a television presenter named Rasha Magdi reporting on the event openly stoked sectarian tensions:

> Three soldiers from the army have been killed and thirty others wounded when Copts gathered in front of the Radio and Television Building opened fire on them. Eyewitnesses confirm that hundreds of Coptic protestors who have cut off the road in front of the building started pelting the army soldiers with rocks and Molotov cocktails. ("Al-Tilifizyun al-Misri" 2011)

As she spoke a banner at the bottom of the screen reiterated that "Coptic protestors are throwing stones and Molotovs at soldiers from the October Bridge and burning cars." It is almost impossible to overstate the shocking effect of such a broadcast. The official line on Coptic-Muslim tensions in Egypt had *always* been that there was no such thing, and that there was complete unity between the two constituents of the nation. At the same time the Mubarak regime had cynically produced the very same tensions that it claimed did not exist by posing as "a firewall against sectarianism" (Brownlee 2013, 11). Production of that discourse effectively put the Copts in the line of fire in the state's often repressive policies against Islamists. Moreover, it came against a backdrop of tolerating a steady expansion of Islamism in the public sphere (the carrot juxtaposed against the stick of harsh policing and imprisonment and torture of Islamists), while simultaneously refusing to update outdated laws from the Ottoman era that discriminated against Copts. This essentially prohibited them from freely practicing their religion by putting all authority to build churches or other religious institutions directly under the control of the ruler (the president in modern times), which had the effect of making church construction both stultifyingly bureaucratic, and also intrinsically sectarian because Christians were forced to get special permission from the president to pursue what should have been routine matters (Brownlee 2013).

It was probably inevitable that when Hasanayn came to fix my washing machine the dynamics of Coptic-Muslim sectarianism would form the backdrop of our conversation. Some commentators on the Maspero incident later argued that the sectarian angle was largely a product of foreign reporting, and that the real significance of the event should be framed as part of the military's campaign against the revolution, emphasizing the presence of Muslims (even Salafis) showing solidarity with Christians in both the demonstration and the funerals for those killed by the army's attack (Khazaleh 2011). This was half right. There surely was an agenda to use this event to further the ongoing fracturing of revolutionary forces. The half-wrong part is that what happened at Maspero did strongly fuel sectarian tensions. It was not just foreign media that emphasized the sectarian narrative.

Hasanayn arrived at my flat in late October to fix the washing machine and went through the usual ritual of sending Khalid out for spare parts. I made some tea. He did not need much prompting to start talking about the revolution. I told him that many people I knew were becoming depressed about it, not just because of what happened at Maspero, but because Maspero seemed to be part of an endless pattern of reversals to revolutionary aspirations. "No," he replied, "that's just the talk of the secularists. Islamists think it's going great. We're going to get everything we've always wanted." I was mildly surprised. Before the revolution he had never concealed his deep dissatisfaction with social and political conditions in Egypt, but this took the form of generalities. "All I want is for my children to be able to attend decent schools, and to be able to get decent medical care." Such complaints were almost generic in the years before the revolution, when there was a general feeling of being "suffocated" (makhnuq) under the weight of declining services, collapsing infrastructure, and growing precarity in employment. He had certainly never identified himself as an Islamist (islami, pl. islamiyun—a term he himself used on this occasion). Now he spoke with great confidence about the revolution and revealed that he had spent a lot of time in Tahrir Square during the most highly charged events.

I asked him about the upcoming parliamentary elections, over which there was bitter disagreement among the Egyptian political forces. Islamists and

SCAF wanted to push forward with the elections; the non-Islamist political forces favored writing a constitution first. It was a chicken-and-egg situation: who could be authorized to write a constitution if there had been no elections? But how could elections take place when there was no agreed-on constitutional framework for them? A surprising victory of Islamists in the Tunisian Constituent Assembly elections had been announced the day before, raising tensions even further. "Of course the Islamists will win here too," Hasanayn said matter-of-factly and with evident satisfaction. I asked which Islamists, assuming that there were significant cleavages between Salafis and the Muslim Brotherhood. "It will be some of both," he replied. "The differences aren't that great. We're happy to see the Muslim Brotherhood win. We can work with them. We want the same thing." He downplayed doctrinal and tactical differences between the two main blocs of Islam-inspired religious parties. "Look what happened in Tunisia. It will be the same here."

What, I asked, would Islamists do, either in Egypt or in Tunisia? "Apply shari'a of course," he replied flatly. In the fevered speculations of pundits and academic observers the intentions of Islamist parties, whose likely electoral dominance was emerging even more strongly than predicted, was still unclear. It was not a foregone conclusion that something as provocative as flat-out implementation of shari'a is what Islamists wanted, at least in the short term (Parker 2011). Political maturity was implicitly defined as the capacity to compromise tactically, and in the longer term to take a creative approach to the "Islamic reference" of politics such that a civil and democratic state founded on universalized Islamic ethics took precedence over an Islamic state founded narrowly on literal interpretations of law (T. Ramadan 2012, 102–7):

> Implementation of the shari'a ("the path of faithfulness to the higher goals of Islam") . . . does not mean enforcing prohibitions and imposing a strict, time-less penal code, as it is often understood by some literalist Islamists or as it is perceived in the West. . . . Far from being reduced to a disputed article in a constitution, reference to the shari'a must be placed in a much broader context. (T. Ramadan 2012, 113–14)

Hasanayn may have been the indirect recipient of such evolving political sophistication. On the other hand, he was no philosopher, and I am fairly sure more of a follower than a leader. We talked about distinctions between variants of Islamic parties, primarily the two emerging behemoths of the postrevolution period, the Muslim Brotherhood's Freedom and Justice Party, and the Salafi Nur Party. The latter was generally considered more openly oriented toward top-down imposition of shari'a than the Muslim Brotherhood, but Hasanayn stuck resolutely to his professed lack of concern with any distinctions between them on what he considered the most important issue, namely implementation of shari'a. When I asked him his preference in the presidential election that would eventually follow the looming parliamentary election, he replied without hesitation: Hazem Salah Abu Isma'il. Given Hasanayn's apparent disinterest in distinctions between the largest two formal blocs of Islamist parties, Abu Isma'il was a logical choice. His father, Salah Abu Isma'il, had been a Muslim Brotherhood member and one of their nominees in parliamentary elections before the revolution. Hence his son Hazem's affiliation was ambiguous. Hazem had himself been a judicial activist on behalf of Muslim Brotherhood members in prominent court cases. Even though Hazem Salah Abu Isma'il was more often labeled as a Salafist than as a Muslim Brotherhood member, after the coup in 2013 that brought 'Abd al-Fattah al-Sisi to power he was quickly jailed, whereas Nur Party politicians, who strongly supported the removal of Morsy, were allowed to remain free.

If, as Hasanayn believed, *tatbiq al-shari'a*—implementation of Islamic law in a narrow sense—was really a common agenda of the main Islamic political parties of that moment (October 2011, when the country was still reeling from the effects of the Maspero Massacre), then I wondered what it would mean for Egypt's place in the global order. How would an Islamic economic system, for example, articulate with international economics? Whatever limitations Hasanayn may have had as an ideologue or as a philosopher, on this issue he had a rather well elaborated response:

> Capitalism is about to cause the destruction of the European Union. Haven't you been following the news about the economic crisis? It's a disaster for Greece. They're going to kick it out of the union. Then the whole thing will collapse. Economics is more of a problem for them than it is for us. An Islamic economic system would work better than what they have now.

Maybe so, I replied. Collapse of the European Union seemed fairly far-fetched to me in October 2011, but much less so when I wrote these lines in 2015—Hasanayn certainly proved to be a better prognosticator of European politics than I was. But would such a collapse truly impoverish Europe? Would it not still be rich even without an economic union? And how would Islamic economics work on practice? How would taxes be raised? What would fund all the things revolutionaries say they want? If capitalism led to the January 25 Revolution, then what would Islamic economics do differently?

> No, Europe will not remain wealthier than us if the union collapses. Economic power buttresses political power. The demise of one will cause the demise of the other. But for us the important thing is that capitalism has failed. Socialism failed before that. Now it's time to try the Islamic way. In economics Islamists believe in the sanctity of private property. There won't be any problem with that—we can do all the business we want with Europe and get investment. And the state? The state will have greater resources than before. It won't need to tax, because

those who can afford to help will do so through *sadaqat* [charitable giving on a free-will basis] and *zakat* [a more formalized alms tax]. And the banks? They'll just have to learn to play by Islamic rules—no interest, the bank takes a share of profits in investments, and also a share of the risk.

I was impressed. For an appliance repairman this seemed like a fairly well elaborated political position. But I was still skeptical that a voluntaristic tax system could work and asked why people would consent to paying such taxes, and whether this would be an adequate means of funding a state faced with greater postrevolution demands. "It would. Because people would trust it," he said. "They'd be giving money to an ethical government [*hukuma akhlaqi-yya*]. They would pay with enthusiasm." I could neither agree nor disagree. It was a faith-based statement, and lacking the faith all I could say was that I could not imagine it working for me. It was rather like talking about politics to my brother in Nebraska—a strongly committed Christian fundamentalist who disagrees with me on just about everything social and political, and is impossible to argue with him because we simply lack any normative ground for discussion.[9] And so it was with Hasanayn too, though I found debating with him generally more productive than trying to talk politics with my brother. Or at least that was the case before the issue of Maspero came up.

Maspero was on everyone's mind. It was hanging in the air during Hasanayn's repair call. Finally he asked my opinion on the matter, and I responded as neutrally as possible, suggesting that the horror had been precipitated by an unknown element, a *taraf talit*, literally "third party," meaning a "hidden hand," someone working covertly to sow chaos on behalf of some malign agency such as the old regime (one or more elements of it, potentially working at cross-purposes, or alternatively, the security forces or even the military); or if the accusation was coming *from* a supporter of the old regime, then *taraf talit* meant shadowy "foreign" forces, or traitorous elements from within society. I half believed it. Although widely circulated videos of army vehicles wildly careening through crowds buttressed by detailed eyewitness accounts of the slaughter left no doubt about who did the killing at Maspero itself ("Maspero Testimonies" 2011), someone had already raised tensions long before the procession reached the Radio and Television Building by attacking the protestors en route. But Hasanayn surprised me by ignoring my gambit to meet him halfway on the field of conspiracy theorizing. It is easy to assent to a taraf talit proposition because one can just insert one's own enemy of political convenience: the old regime, or thugs in the pay of military intelligence for me; shadowy forces in the pay of foreign forces for you. And maybe neither of us really believes it, or only half believes it. At least it functions as a path toward discovering what one's interlocutor really thinks. But he would not play that game. "It was the Copts themselves who caused it," he said:

They went there trying to cause trouble. They're being misled by radical Coptic priests. Haven't you heard of Father Philopateer? He's a Coptic priest who calls for violence against the state. What the army did was in self-defense. The Copts went there armed, looking for trouble. They attacked first, and then the army defended itself.

Philopateer Gamil was a Coptic priest from a parish in Giza who had championed the cause of the burned-out Marinab Church, which was the latest in a series of similar incidents that had occurred with increased frequency in previous years (El Gergawy 2011). Although the Maspero sit-in and march had been organized by lay groups, Philopateer was the most prominent member of the clergy associated with the events. He was unquestionably a dissident priest, though not in the way that Hasanayn understood dissidence. On the night before the march to Maspero he gave a fiery speech to supporters, which was amplified by YouTube:

> We will conduct a march like none Egypt has seen before. And we will end our march inside of Maspero [the Radio and Television Building]. With us will be a large number of the respectable liberal parties, the April 6 Movement, and a large number of our brother Muslims. I want to tell you something very important: we can only claim our rights by our protesting with Muslims in Egypt. There are a small number of people who come from one country or another, who carry out Wahhabist agendas. But they're not the majority in Egypt. They're greedy for Egypt. The real Egyptian is the Muslim protestor and the Christian who is here in this country. Together tomorrow we will all demand our rights. Standing with our Muslim brothers we will demand our rights. Don't think for a moment that you are a minority. We are a *majority* in this country—not as Christians, but as protestors [*mu'tasimin*]. These are the real Copts. The minority in this country are those who are trying to return the country to the stage of backwardness. They're the minority. We're the majority in this country. ("Filubatir Gamil Yukhatit" 2011)

In making such statements Philopateer was taking on everyone. First, he was bucking the Coptic clerical hierarchy all the way up to Pope Shenouda, who had colluded with the Mubarak regime in tying the Copts to the regime essentially as hostages. The equation for Copts was "cling to the regime, or face a sectarian backlash," and the more they clung, the more real the backlash became. Secondly, he was throwing down the gauntlet to Islamists— "Wahhabists . . . trying to return the country to backwardness," while at the same time reaching out to non-Islamist Muslim allies. Thirdly, he was implicitly provoking SCAF. A sit-in at Maspero to protest the Marinab Church burning had *already* been broken up violently by military police a few days before, on October 6 (the massacre was on the ninth). The speech translated above took place at an event to honor a Coptic activist named Ra'if Anwar Fahim, who had been harshly beaten with clubs by the military police in that incident. The beating was available on a YouTube video, and this had seriously heightened tensions between Coptic revolutionary activists and the military. The preamble to his speech alludes to the beating:

> It is a disgrace on the Egyptian army that there should be people like this [who beat Fahim]. But we love the armed forces and the army, because that army comes from us. If you think about it, you have friends and relatives in the Egyptian army. . . . We love the armed forces and the Egyptian army, but this small group that was there at Maspero is a disgrace on the Egyptian army, and we have, today, and on Thursday, have [*sic*] begun legal proceedings against them. ("Filubatir Gamil Yukhatit" 2011)

Philopateer's speech was interpreted by some as a polemic, a general provocation against Muslims and against public order. One version of the YouTube video of his speech was labeled "Know who the principal terrorist thug provocateur of the Maspero events was" ("Ta'arrif 'ala" 2011). In that video his statement about loving the army was omitted. A fuller version of the speech was labeled "The terrorist priest Philopateer must be arrested for incitement." But the content of Philopateer's speech shows that his target was not Muslims in general, and that he was by no means trying to foment an undifferentiated sectarianism. He was pointing, rather, specifically at Salafis, and he had a reputation for being outspoken against them already. For example, in a talk show in May 2011 he had said, "the armed forces . . . were victorious over Israel. We are warning them now about a more dangerous enemy . . . because when we deal with Israel it unites us. But the enemy now, the Salafi leadership, is more dangerous, because they divide us against each other" ("Al-Anba' Filubatir" 2011).[10]

In a nutshell, Philopateer threatened SCAF not because he divided society along sectarian lines—that division had already been created throughout the decades of Mubarak's rule. The problem was that he threatened to unite Christian and Muslim revolutionary forces, to the exclusion of Islamists, Salafis in particular—precisely the group that most openly advocated polite cooperation with the military and security forces. Hence suspicions that the slaughter of Coptic protestors at Maspero was premeditated were not far-fetched, even if they were ultimately unprovable.[11] Also, a revolutionary alliance of lay Christians and non-Islamist Muslims threatened the Muslim Brotherhood perhaps the most among all the political forces, because the brotherhood had the most to lose from a widening conflict with SCAF. By this time parliamentary elections were just over the horizon. A large-scale uprising against SCAF could delay the elections, and that was the last thing the Muslim Brotherhood wanted. Hence if certain Salafi figures (but not necessarily Salafis in general) may have been spoiling for a fight with the revolutionary Copts, the Muslim Brotherhood had every reason to stay on the sidelines. At the same time, to remain passive in the face of SCAF's aggression would diminish their revolutionary credentials, which were already dismissed by most non-Islamist activists, but not by Islamist youth.[12]

Hasanayn saw all these dynamics strictly through the eyes of the most aggrieved Salafis.[13] When I told him that I had seen videos of the army's vehicles smashing through crowds running over people, targeting them even, he countered by bringing up a video of his own:

> I saw a video on YouTube where Copts were walking under Ahmad Hilmy [a bridge over the road the march took from Shubra to Maspero]. They had dynamite strapped to their bodies, and signs saying "shahid" [martyr]. That was no peaceful demonstration. Aside from the dynamite many of them were carrying weapons. They were going to attack the military.

I got out my laptop to try to find the video he had in mind. Later I read an eyewitness account that did in fact mention that at the front of the march "was a group of men in long white bibs, 'martyr upon demand' written on their chests" (Carr 2011). But this was a declaration *not* to use arms, not a call to use them, and obviously a far cry from men with dynamite strapped to their bodies. We tried a number of search terms, using Arabic script. *Masirat al-aqbat* (procession of Copts), *tahrid* (incitement) and Maspero, the same terms with Sabtiyya (the neighborhood next to the Ahmad Hilmy Bridge, which was the place Hasanayn remembered), all to no avail. Eventually Hasanayn remembered the site where he thought he had seen the video: none other than al-Marsad al-Islami li-Muqawamat al-Tansir (the Islamic Observer of Resistance against Christianization)—the same site that had posted Khalid Harbi's provocative rant about Sally Zahran discussed in chapter 4 ("Al-Marsad" 2011). On this site there was a long and predictably partisan video about Maspero, but no images of armed or dynamite-packing Copts. Failure to find his video had no effect on Hasanayn's convictions about what had happened. Nor would he countenance any doubts about the army's motives. "They really know how to sort out the country," he said. In his opinion ultimate security for *his* revolution lay in the notion that the Military Council's hands were tied by the lower-order officers and soldiers—the "will of the people" as he put it. "The army is from us," he said, using exactly the same words Philopateer had in the preamble to his speech on the night before the massacre—a sentiment anchored in Egypt's history of universal conscription (though in many ways conscripted manpower is distinct from the professional officer corps). He would not entertain my opinion that SCAF had its own agenda.

I saw Hasanayn only a couple of times after that, chance meetings, once in a café in 'Abdin that we both frequented. He bought me tea. But we did not talk about politics on those occasions. I was out of the country when Muhammad Morsy was removed from power by Sisi's coup and did not see Hasanayn after the Raba'a Massacre. In retrospect it is clear that our political conversation took place on the edge of a precipice, or perhaps Egypt was already over the precipice falling into an abyss. The Maspero events foreshadowed the worst violence of the revolution, and the revolution's ultimate defeat at the hands of SCAF: the Battle of Muhammad Mahmud Street, the Maglis al-Wuzara' incident, the Port Said Massacre, the march on the Ministry of Defense in al-'Abbasiyya, and eventually the conflagration of Raba'a al-'Adawiyya. The Battle of Muhammad Mahmud Street, about a month after my conversation with Hasanayn, was probably the decisive turning point in the revolution. It was the moment when chants of *yasqut hukm al-'askar* (down with military rule) resounded most widely among all the political forces. Muhammad Mahmud, a street leading off of Tahrir Square toward the hated Ministry of Interior, was the site of vicious battles against the security forces. It was set off initially in the context of a demonstration against "supraconstitutional principles" that sought to agree to immunity for the military from civilian oversight in advance of both elections and the writing of a constitution. Pitched battles between a coalition of youths and activists on one side, and the security forces on the other, forced SCAF to put its long-negotiated deal with the Muslim Brotherhood into effect by plowing ahead with elections in December and January despite the violence. Slaughter in Maspero was a preliminary skirmish to the larger Battle of Muhammad Mahmud Street. The sum total of these battles was a vital context for the political work that defeated the revolution, and brought 'Abd al-Fattah al-Sisi to power.

CHAPTER 8

Scripting a Massacre

Clearly the thing has some sort of muzzle, of a cannon or something.
—Television presenter Ahmad Musa (Musa 2013)

Almost overnight, many Egyptians panicked. Who were these strangers, they wondered?
—Hazem Kandil, *Inside the Brotherhood* (2014, 1–2)

Religion is sincere counsel. What's the problem if a Guide of a Muslim society guides others for the good of the community?
—Shaykh Rashid Rida to Hasan al-Banna in the television serial *al-Gama'a* (Yasin 2010)

The Ethnographic Present

The previous chapter left us in the midst of the decisive months in the revolution, from October 2011 to February 2012, a maelstrom of massacres and street battles. In retrospect this period looks almost like a revolution within the revolution. The Maspero Massacre in October 2011 served as a threshold into a new state of liminality that lasted until February 2012, but this time marked as an ordeal of communitas forged in tear gas rather than the utopia described by so many people in the early days of the revolution.[1]

My purpose in this chapter is to consider some of the discursive resources deployed in polarization. On one hand polarization was a product of revolutionary politics that intensified with each successive conflict: the Battle of Muhammad Mahmud Street, breakup of the Maglis al-Wuzara' sit-in, or the increasingly hopeless campaign against the Ministry of Interior after the Port Said Massacre in February 2012. These were battles between protestors and the security forces (including on some occasions the army). But each successive battle also sharpened the distinction between those who fought and those who did not—and the latter category increasingly meant the Muslim Brotherhood. After the big battles, particularly after the election of Morsy in June 2012, there were countless smaller skirmishes that took place not so much between protestors and the security forces as between the Muslim Brotherhood and civilian opponents of brotherhood rule. These skirmishes were less deeply inscribed in the revolutionary narrative than the cataclysmic events near Tahrir.[2] All these were experienced as visceral events by those who participated directly in them—thousands of people, but certainly not millions. The vast majority of Egyptians, millions rather than thousands—knew revolutionary events more through media—both mass and social—than through direct experience.

On the other hand, the contingencies of crisis also triggered a process of explanation—of "return and repetition" (Bryant 2016), to revisit a "traumatic past that here had been retained as a visceral experience" (Bryant 2016, 21), but effectively also to enable actors in such events to construct a bricolage of "facts," arguments, and justifications. In this sense past experiences were highly relevant as guides to future-oriented actions. Mass-mediated images substituted for direct experience as the polarization of the political field hardened in late 2011 and early 2012, and so they too were among the crucial formative elements of opinions that determined actions not yet taken.

Turner observed that when liminality remains protracted communitas subsides and people begin to divide themselves into factions, in which "one [faction] will proceed under the ostensible banner of rationality, while the other will manifest in its words and deeds the more romantic qualities of willing and feeling" (Turner 1988, 91). On its own the previous chapter runs a risk of typifying Islamists, as refracted through Hasanayn 'Abd al-Rahman, not so much as champions of romantic qualities as carrying a "banner of irrationality," or as simply "incoherent and even inhuman" subjects (Fadil and Fernando 2015, 82). This is not my intention, but I had to confront a problem specific to writing a book on the revolution: from the beginning of 2012 until the defeat of the revolution in the summer of 2013, extreme polarization became a fact of life. No account of the revolution can ignore it. Islamists—members of organized political movements that seek to solve modern problems by reference to Muslim texts (Halliday 2006)—were part of that polarization. Ultimately the two camps facing each other were composed of Islamists and other Muslims (including some Salafis) loyal or sympathetic to the Muslim Brotherhood on one side, and on the other side a coalition of non-Islamists (including many people who considered themselves pious Muslims) and Islamists (mainly Salafis) *un*-sympathetic to the Muslim Brotherhood. These two coalitions are often, misleadingly, labeled "Islamists versus secularists," or "Islamists versus liberals." But whatever the actual social complexity of the sides taken during the revolution, by the end of 2011 a new political dynamic was unmistakable and unavoidable. Its outcome was evident in the words and deeds of the polarized, not in more nuanced expressions of those able to remain outside it.

It is still a fact that I have not distilled a partisan "secularist" counterpart to Hasanayn 'Abd al-Rahman's point of view, or to the anti-Christian polemics of Khalid Harbi. None of my politically articulate friends and acquaintances were Muslim Brotherhood supporters, though they certainly were divided in their opinions on the revolution. If I had a self-consciously "secular" opposite number to Khalid Harbi it would have been a writer I knew, author of a memoir on the first eighteen days of the revolution, who embraced the coup in 2013 not as a "lesser evil," but with great enthusiasm. "I favor extermination" was this writer's flatly expressed commentary on the Rab'a sit-in. Extermination, that is, of the Muslim Brotherhood and their supporters.

But while many others of my circle were less chillingly vulgar in their pronouncements, I would not say that most of them were exempt from being swept up in the contagion of polarization. Nor would I characterize their views as more "rational" than Hasanayn 'Abd al-Rahman's. Indeed, Turner's notion of forming sides within the condition of protracted liminality as a division between those who "proceed under the *ostensible* banner of rationality" while others exhibit "the more romantic qualities of willing and feeling" (Turner 1988, 91; my emphasis) suggests he was well aware that rationality was a product of the winner's prerogative to write history, and not a quality to be understood literally.

My non-Islamist (though in some cases self-consciously pious) interlocutors usually spoke about the Muslim Brotherhood through a coherent discourse that crossed over their divided opinions about the revolution. For example, the Muslim Brotherhood were "not real Muslims," often expressed by the derogatory term *muta'aslimun* (Islamized)—meaning that they merely affected the appearance of Muslims without actually living or understanding the moral precepts of Islam. Or allegations that the Muslim Brotherhood were a cult that drew on sinister ideological sources, and which mesmerized followers into unquestioning obedience. It was building an army, starting with secret militias, for the purpose of imposing its doctrines on the population by force; it was indistinguishable from smaller more openly violent jihadist groups; it would persecute, exterminate, or expel all Christians; it was in thrall to foreigners, and was itself the spearhead of an international organization with no roots in Egypt; it was importing shipping container loads of cash for the purpose of surreptitiously and untraceably purchasing key sectors of the economy; it was killing masses of Egyptians in much greater numbers than the Mubarak regime ever had done. Such attitudes were a mixture of selective fact, fiction, outright lies, and paranoia, and they seemed to have been consistently normalized among a wide spectrum of the people I knew, ranging from pro-Mubarak and prosecurity lawyers, journalists (both pro- and antirevolution) working for large public-sector institutions, artists and intellectuals, and activists deeply involved in the revolution. In my experience the elements of the discursive case against the brotherhood were well articulated by the beginning of 2012. It became difficult to draw a line between straightforward analysis (for example, observations that the brotherhood was inept at forging alliances with non-Islamists) and a cloud of half-truths, exaggeration, or lies. Moreover, by that time some figures in the media were beginning to crystallize all the negative elements into a coherent frightening image (a subject for the next chapter). The task of crystallization was greatly eased by the widespread circulation of a *preexisting* discourse about the brotherhood.

The process of taking sides during a protracted and "uncanny" moment of liminality could not happen on a tabula rasa; it had to involve falling back on past experience, but experience reorganized into new configurations and for novel purposes appropriate to the present crisis. Questions inevitably arise about what past experiences were drawn on. My goal here is therefore to explore an earlier vision of the Muslim Brotherhood widely accessible to the non-Islamist public—a "secularist" or "enlightened" vision that put words in the mouths of the Muslim Brotherhood for the purpose of crystallizing a holistic image of the organization. In doing so I hope to provide a counterbalance to the apparent excesses of Hasanayn 'Abd al-Rahman (and behind him the polemical mass-mediated discourse of such figures as Khalid Harbi).

The vision in question is a television biopic series titled *al-Gama'a* (The society; Yasin 2010).[3] Its subject was the life of Hasan al-Banna, the founder of the Muslim Brotherhood. In some ways it would be more accurate to specify *al-Gama'a* as part of the revolutionary threshold than as a distant past. The serial was broadcast in Ramadan of 2010 (August 10 to September 9). Already by that time the crescendo of politics culminating in the revolution was building. *Al-Gama'a*, though broadcast in 2010, was a silent presence during the coup against Muhammad Morsy on July 3, 2013, and all that came after it.

Fast Forward

After the coup violence was in the air for some time before it broke with full fury on the broad avenue in front of the Rab'a al-'Adawiyya Mosque in the northeastern Cairene neighborhood of Madinat Nasr. On August 14, 2013, around a thousand supporters of the Muslim Brotherhood conducting a long-running sit-in at Rab'a were killed in one day when the Egyptian security forces advanced on them with deadly force.[4]

For weeks leading up to the assault on the sit-in the press and the television media were full of lurid tales about a buildup of "heavy weapons" in the area, which the brotherhood would use to inflict massive casualties on the security forces. Between the coup on July 3, 2013, and the massacre during the clearing of the Rab'a sit-in, the media—almost all of it non-Islamist once the pro-

Muslim Brotherhood television channels and newspapers had been closed down[5]—hammered away at the Muslim Brotherhood. The weapons narrative was one of the most prominent strands of the campaign.[6] Consider, for example, a segment broadcast on television during Ramadan of 2013 with the television presenter named Ahmad Musa, known for his high-pitched emotional outbursts, and for his slavish devotion to the Sisi regime. The upload date is July 29, about two weeks before the massacre:

> Let's look together at what's happening in Rabʻa al-ʻAdawiyya. [The camera cuts to six bearded men carrying a long, lumpy object wrapped in an Egyptian flag through the crowds in Rabʻa.] Of course as you see—show the scene again from the beginning Hisham [he addresses the cameraman], just the part where they're entering and the picture is clear, forget the rest, the first part, stop it there for me . . . because that shows clearly the thing they are carrying. It's not like they're, or course . . . like people think . . . people are surprised, they're looking . . . clearly the thing has some sort of muzzle, of a cannon or something. The main thing is that it's weapons. Go a bit further in the video . . . a little further . . . yes . . . do you see? That's the complete picture, and they're not carrying a body; it's an act. They're laughing; you can see how they're smiling, those killers who are carrying weapons. Do you see the smiles? And it's wrapped in the Egyptian flag. The Egyptian flag! Which is innocent of this bloodiness, innocent of these killers. And the criminals carrying it—it's a type of . . . I don't really understand military stuff; that takes a weapons expert. But clearly it's maybe a kind of mortar, maybe a portable cannon or something like that. Fast forward a bit Hisham; I want to see it from the rear . . . yes . . . if someone . . . see . . . yes, stop here. It's the part that's sticking out on the top. It's some sort of tube; I don't know, it needs some special assembly, but you can be sure that there are weapons in this area. (Musa 2013; see figure 8.1)

One can assess the authenticity of Ahmad Musa's cannon story by contrast to the numerous videos of Rabʻa and the breakup of the sit-in, in which there are no signs of the "heavy weapons" supposedly revealed in the video.[7] It was the worst one-day political slaughter in modern Egyptian history, and among the worst in the world. The notion that supporters of Muhammad Morsy in Rabʻa were defending themselves against the security forces with "heavy weapons," as Musa's video put it—meaning cannons, machine guns, mortars, at the very least military assault rifles—is not credible.

But in the summer of 2013, large segments of the non-Islamist public in Egypt seemed remarkably receptive to the sort of laughable propaganda that Ahmad Musa was peddling. The details appear not to have not mattered very much. If the "heavy weapons" story did not pan out, then one could always pivot smoothly to a different narrative, for example, that the Muslim

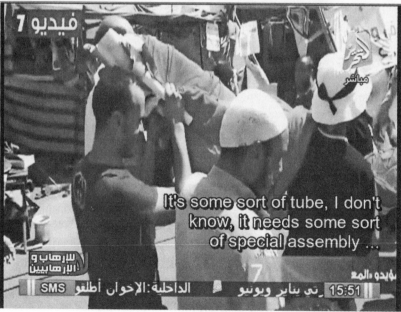

FIGURE 8.1. Stills from television presenter Ahmad Musa's broadcast about alleged weapons brought to the Rabʿa al-ʿAdawiyya sit-in by supporters of Muhammad Morsy. August 2013.

FIGURE 8.1. (*continued*)

Brotherhood was paying poor people from the countryside to stay at the Rabʻa sit-in, knowing that they would eventually be slaughtered, essentially using them as pawns or human shields. That story is also easily refuted. The majority of people killed in Rabʻa were from Cairo, and they fit a basically middle-class profile (Ketchley and Biggs 2015).

In fact, the court of non-Islamist public opinion had already issued its verdict by the time the massacre occurred: guilty. But how was the verdict reached? Some tried to explain the massacre and implicitly justify it as an outcome of the revolutionary politics that emerged in 2011. Hazem Kandil's book *Inside the Brotherhood* (2014), for example, claims that media coverage of the Rabʻa sit-in for forty days prior to the massacre was an eye-opener for the non-Islamist public:

> It was a rare opportunity to eavesdrop on this exceptionally discreet group. And what the people saw and heard was somewhat different from what they were used to from the normally polished Brothers: political competitors were religiously condemned; images of Prophet Muhammad's epic battles were conjured; biblical stories, from David and Moses to Armageddon, were invoked; claims that Archangel Gabriel prayed at the Islamist campsite were flaunted; and sacred visions were relayed on stage night after night. This was not the vocabulary Brothers typically employed in their public interactions. Almost overnight, many Egyptians panicked. Who were these strangers, they wondered? (Kandil 2014, 1–2)

It was not wrong to characterize the tone of many Rabʻa speeches as apocalyptic, though in doing so one might want to acknowledge the considerable violence against Muslim Brotherhood members that had already occurred.[8] But "what the public was used to" from the brotherhood was not necessarily polished and rational discourse simply because the "exceptional discretion" of the group was not entirely at *their* discretion. Before the revolution Muslim Brotherhood officials had little access to the mass-mediated public sphere on their own terms. There were brotherhood websites and bloggers, but the organization only published a newspaper that was distributed on the streets from October 28, 2011, until the coup on July 3, 2013. A Muslim Brotherhood satellite television channel, Misr 25, broadcast from September 2011 until the coup. It is true that after the fall of the Mubarak regime for the first time non-Islamist mainstream television was obliged to cover the words and deeds of the Muslim Brotherhood as politicians rather than members of an outlawed movement. However, coverage of Muslim Brotherhood officials in the mainstream non-Islamist media was heavily biased. At no time, including the year of Muhammad Morsy's rule, were the mainstream media, both print and television, restricted from criticizing or indeed polemicizing against the brotherhood or their figureheads. The appearance of brotherhood officials in the non-Islamist media was always heavily outweighed by criticism and invective. An exception was the pan-Arab al-Jazeera Satellite Network, which was broadly sympathetic to the Muslim Brotherhood—much more openly after the fall of the Mubarak regime according to its critics. In my experience al-Jazeera started the revolution with almost reflexive credibility across the prorevolution political spectrum as a relatively fact-based news source. By the time of the coup, and certainly well before the Rabʻa sit-in began, it was widely reviled by non-Islamists as a crude mouthpiece of the Muslim Brotherhood. Prior to the Rabʻa Massacre some of the non-Islamists I knew practically spat in disgust at the mention of al-Jazeera and referred to it derisively as "al-Khanzeera"—"the pig."

The notion that by July 2013 large sections of the non-Islamist public were shocked and panicked at the sight and sound of the Muslim Brotherhood officials and protestors in Rabʻa al-ʻAdawiyya implicitly assigns the role of rational arbiter to the non-Islamist public. In fact the appearance of "polished" Muslim Brotherhood representatives in the media alarmed the non-Islamist public long before the Rabʻa sit-in. Whatever panic the non-Islamist public may have felt at the sight and sound of brotherhood rhetoric in Rabʻa must therefore be prefaced with a different question than the "who were these strangers" query posed by Kandil: why should we assume that the non-Islamist public was able to form comparatively rational assessments of the history and character of Islamism? Rational or not, on what information were the assessments of non-Islamists based?

Rewind

Al-Gamaʻa was a twenty-eight-part series broadcast in the Ramadan that fell in 2010 (from August 10 to September 9). Dramatic serials broadcast in Ramadan, it should be emphasized, reach vast audiences, particularly high-profile series that are heavily promoted prior to the beginning of the month of fasting—and certainly *al-Gamaʻa* was among the most highly anticipated series of that year.[9]

The series depicted the life of Hasan al-Banna, the founder of the Muslim Brotherhood, from his childhood in the delta town of Mahmudiyya, beginning during the First World War when al-Banna was about ten years old, until just before his assassination in 1949. Of course the story of al-Banna's life was also the story of the Muslim Brotherhood itself. *Al-Gamaʻa* was a temporally complex series, touching on its present as a television serial, the history of its subject, and the future of Egypt. The contrast between a troubled present, a past that "explained" this present, and an implied future crisis established a crisis threshold.

A key scene serves as a fulcrum for the dramatic content of the entire series. *Al-Gamaʻa* unfolded through a juxtaposition of contemporary time and

the time of Hasan al-Banna. The contemporary story begins with the character of Ashraf, a *wakil al-niyaba*—public prosecutor responsible for investigating criminal cases on behalf of the state. Ashraf is asked to investigate a case
involving a demonstration by Muslim Brotherhood students at al-Azhar University who had been expelled because of their political activities. Some of the
students in the demonstration wore black balaclavas and performed martial
arts routines. This was interpreted by the authorities as militia activity, essentially a menacing flexing of muscles by the brotherhood. This was a real
incident from 2006 (Al-Buhairi 2006; "Milishiyat" 2012 [from 2006]). The
circumstances were of course contentious. The brotherhood claimed that the
"kung fu and karate routines," as they were called in the press, were an athletic
display, and that the ruling party was using it as a pretext to crack down on
the leadership. The state and the National Democratic Party insisted that the
display was essentially military, and that it was hugely alarming. The re-
creation of the "militia display" in *al-Gama'a* was a larger and more precise
than the original event (and accompanied by sinister nondiegetic background
music). But anyone who had seen the earlier video would recognize the refer-
ent instantly.

In *al-Gama'a*, when Ashraf begins his investigation he is shocked to discover that he knows one of the students being investigated in the militia
incident. The young man is from a family linked to Ashraf's own family. Astonishingly, nobody in the boy's family had any idea that he was a Muslim
Brotherhood member. Suddenly confronted with the unexpected complexity
of the case, Ashraf realizes that although the Muslim Brotherhood has been a
semipublic presence in society throughout his life, he knows next to nothing
about the organization. Ashraf tries to recuse himself from the investigation
on grounds of his personal connection to one of the suspects and his ignorance
of the organization to which he belongs. He represents the epitome of rational
judgment. But Ashraf's superior refuses his request for recusal. So Ashraf em-
barks on a quest for knowledge, his own personal mission to understand what
the Muslim Brotherhood really is and where it came from.

The quest leads to his fiancée, Shirin. Her grandfather 'Abdallah is a gruff
old retired judge. His career in the same field that Ashraf works in obviously
helps bind them together. But more importantly for the narrative, 'Abdallah
happens to have been a member of the Muslim Brotherhood in his youth.
Because of this he knows their history thoroughly. It is through 'Abdallah that
the serial develops its historical track. His narration of Hasan al-Banna's
story segues into a reenactment of al-Banna's life. Throughout about three-
quarters of the twenty-eight-part series the story alternates between the
modern and historical tracks, with the historical track gradually crowding out
the modern track.[10]

The contemporary story in *al-Gama'a* was heavily nostalgic, as was the
historical portrayal. One scene in particular, taken from the contemporary

track of the program, provides a crystal-clear articulation of nostalgia. It comes in episode 10, by which time relations between Ashraf's family and Shirin's family are heating up as the couple become more serious about their marriage plans. The cast of characters in this scene includes Ashraf, Ashraf's mother, Su'ad, an elegant middle-aged woman, Shirin, and her grandfather 'Abdallah. Up to this point in the series 'Abdallah has been telling Ashraf the story of the Muslim Brotherhood Shahrazad-style, a kind of endlessly unwinding narrative that provides pretexts for the television serial to go back in time and immerse the viewer in its depiction of al-Banna's social and historical milieu. At this point the two families are in the countryside, at 'Abdallah's 'izba—a family farm, located somewhere in the delta, not far from the events of Hasan al-Banna's youth. The two families have just finished dinner and decide to have watermelon for dessert. Ashraf and Shirin get up to fetch the melon. 'Abdallah and Su'ad then have a conversation about the past and the present. It appears that there is a bit of light romance developing between the old folks, maybe spurred on by the presumably impending marriage between the younger couple. As the conversation takes place Ashraf and Shirin stand in the doorway listening (see figure 8.2):

'ABDALLAH: [to Su'ad] Can I ask you a question?

SU'AD: Of course. At your service 'Abdallah Bey.

'ABDALLAH: I wonder if our time was better than it is for these kids now?

SU'AD: It seems to me that everyone lives in their own time.

'ABDALLAH: But our times were better. Remember when people's faces were smiling and laughing?

SU'AD: Remember when we were lighthearted?

'ABDALLAH: Remember when people used to love each other?

SU'AD: Remember when women could walk in the streets unafraid and self-assured, out walking their kids with their baby carriages in front of them?

'ABDALLAH: Remember when men and women could sit together at a football match?

SU'AD: Remember how people used to look at an Umm Kulthum concert?

SHIRIN: [watching and listening with Ashraf from the doorway] Why are they making us hate our own times?

SU'AD: Young lady, this is how it is supposed to be for all times.

'ABDALLAH: If I knew who ruined our lives and stole the joy from our hearts and minds, and if I were still serving as a judge, I would sentence him to death!

Everyone in the scene—and everyone watching—knew that the thief of joy was the subject of the serial, Hasan al-Banna. A judge in a television series of

FIGURE 8.2. The "death sentence" scene from the 2010 television series *al-Gama'a*.

course can't pronounce a real death sentence. But for many real people 'Abdal-lah's wish came true almost exactly three years later, when the security forces moved against the sit-in at Rab'a al-'Adawiyya.

The historical track in the series explains how Hasan al-Banna and his brotherhood became the thief of hearts, minds, and joy. A twenty-eight-part series with a budget of LE 50 million (said to be a record at the time) has the capacity to unfold numerous subplots. *Al-Gama'a* depicted al-Banna as a cyni-cal opportunist with boundless ambition. He uses and is used by both British intelligence and Saudi-backed Salafists, who are in effect crypto-Wahhabists. In the 1940s he turns the brotherhood's scouting wing (al-Gawwala—the rov-ers) into a paramilitary force ostensibly to join the fight against Zionists in Palestine, but by the last few of the twenty-eight episodes the best of the Gaw-wala are being directed by al-Banna's Tanzim Sirri (secret apparatus), an elite

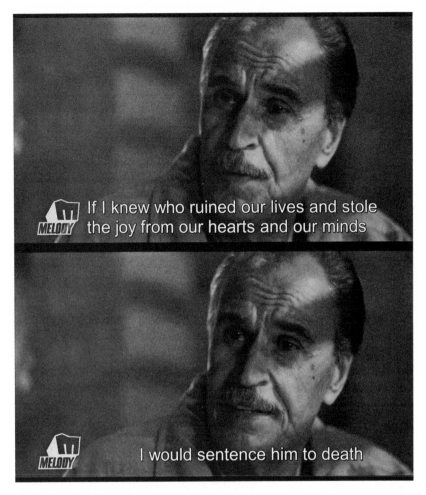

If I knew who ruined our lives and stole the joy from our hearts and our minds

I would sentence him to death

FIGURE 8.2. (*continued*)

cell within the larger organization, to sow terror within Egypt through political assassinations and indiscriminate attacks on the Egyptian Jewish community. By the end of the series al-Banna betrays his own followers by denying that he had issued orders to assassinate a judge who had ruled against the Muslim Brotherhood.

Much of this is quasihistorical. The Tanzim Sirri existed, and the Muslim Brotherhood was unquestionably a major player in the widespread political violence of the late 1940s. But the writer of the serial, Wahid Hamid, carefully wove a contextual background that always led to an image of the brotherhood as essentially schismogenetic—a departure from a previous state of normality, and one that was monstrous by the standards of that previous condition. The result was dehumanizing, but in the important sense that the humanity most worthy of "grievability" (Butler 2009) had to be part of the national community. Excommunication from the nation therefore amounted to a potential death sentence.

In Egyptian television serials writers are usually more celebrated as the authors of the work than directors, contrary to cinema in which the author function is more commonly assigned to the director. Wahid Hamid has been a prolific writer of scenarios for both television and cinema since the late 1960s ("Wahid Hamid" 2017). Many of his works are socially critical, but on the whole he worked quite comfortably with state institutions and is moreover known as a strong proponent of a hegemonic discourse of "enlightenment" (al-tanwir),[11] as an opponent of political Islam (Al-Dib 2012), and as having a particular affinity to the national security apparatus. When Hamid was awarded the state's prestigious and lucrative Nile Prize in 2012, film critic Yaqut Al-Dib nicely summed up the quasi-official view of Hamid's oeuvre:

> The great writer Wahid Hamid is one of those concerned with debating the issues of society and of people, and this is no exaggeration or flattery on our part. But this does not mean that his having achieved the highest cultural award in Egypt, the Nile Prize for the Arts, is a true valuation of the weight of this man. It is perhaps an official recognition of his efforts over half a century, but the real coronation that he himself seeks is the delivery of his message of enlightening enculturation [al-tathqifiyya al-tanwiriyya] to all who are concerned for the soil of this Egyptian land that encompasses civilizations, has witnessed kings and empires, and in which human history both particular and general inheres. (Al-Dib 2012)

The nostalgia evoked by the "death sentence" scene related above was redolent of Hamid's tanwir discourse. In this context—the broadcast of al-Gama'a in 2010—it was also a crucial element of excommunication, conveying a seductive image of society before a moment of schismogenesis, and even offering the possibility of a return to the earlier condition before its occurrence. In the historical track of the series nostalgia comes through in other ways. A reported budget of LE 50 million afforded the possibility of uncommonly meticulous attention to detail. No doubt a careful eye could pick out many errors in dress or appearance, but the overall effect was to plunge viewers into the world of interwar Egypt, where everything appeared more quaint than the joyless present, folkloric, and more like the glory days of colonial modernity, which are often extolled in contemporary neoliberal gentrification initiatives.

In the historical track of the serial the clearest articulation of nostalgia came in the handling of interwar-era Egyptian politicians, who were shown as mostly decent and well meaning.[12] The young King Faruq, only sixteen at the time of his accession in 1936, and a popular ruler in his early years, is depicted as mildly peevish and generally a step behind the older and more politically sophisticated prime ministers. But he is still a nationalist, and there are only hints of the extravagant lifestyle he fell into by the 1940s. Overall the series grants the government a certain *haybat al-daula*—a "gravity of the state," or "prestige," or one might even say "awesomeness of the state." The term was never explicitly mentioned in the series, but fortuitously (if one believes in coincidence), it became a key grievance in counterrevolutionary discourse a couple of years after *al-Gama'a* was broadcast. During the revolution the idea was that antiregime protestors were besmirching haybat al-daula, and this meant they were trying to destroy the state itself, which was considered completely unacceptable by the state's self-appointed "rightful owners." Restoration of haybat al-daula became a key rhetoric for undermining the legitimacy of the revolution. *Al-Gama'a* cemented a highly nostalgic image of haybat al-daula before it became an active political issue.

Hamid clearly had a soft spot for Wafdist leader Mustafa al-Nahhas, who got all the best politician lines. At one point al-Nahhas appears at a meeting of the Wafd leadership. Several of the others timidly express fears that al-Banna is going to tar them with the brush of being "against religion," which of course means against Islam. Al-Nahhas explodes and gives them an angry lesson in civil society:

> I totally reject dragging religion into matters that are not its concern, just as I reject putting any special religious authority over civil authority! Nobody is more careful than I am in honoring and respecting Islam, and nobody is more careful than we are to respect the rule of the constitution. As for the king's constitutional rule, this is of a national scope. It must pertain to all Egyptians, to the entire people. They should celebrate their king, Muslims, Christians, and Jews. Religion is for God, and the nation is for all men.[13]

Except for the reference to the king, it is a rather modern-sounding speech, particularly in its invocation of the priority of civil authority (*al-sulta al-madaniyya*) over religious authority. The politicians in the series generally come across as high-minded and implausibly comfortable with the idioms of contemporary politics. This depiction of the political leadership of the liberal era naturally links to both Hamid's larger tanwir discourse, and more specifically to the "who stole our joy" question raised in the modern track of the series. Al-Banna's "thief of joy" status contrasts with the serial's positive view of what historians often depict as a dysfunctional political system of interwar Egypt.[14] This dysfunctionality is, to be sure an oversimplification, but not as much as a vision of interwar politics as united struggle against colonial occupation, interrupted only by the disastrous nationalist discord introduced by the Muslim Brotherhood. The British are the main beneficiaries of this nationalist discord, and indeed the series shows them as the architects of it, and the Muslim Brotherhood as their primary instrument for achieving it.

In one scene a British intelligence officer notices al-Banna's rising prominence and determines to exploit him. At that point in the narrative the brotherhood is just getting started and has to confront the issue of funding. They do this by requiring members to give regular donations as a condition of their membership in the organization. It is a slow, steady, and organic method of funding, but the pace is too gradual to fulfill al-Banna's towering ambitions to build not just a national organization, but an international one. When the British get wind of this dynamic they arrange for the head of the Suez Canal Company, a Frenchman, to donate five hundred Egyptian pounds to al-Banna. Even though the Muslim Brotherhood's ostensible goal is to combat foreign influence in Egypt, al-Banna is not at all reluctant to take money from the Frenchman. In fact, he arrogantly tries to get him to give more, pointing out that the Suez Canal Company had given far more to build churches for foreign workers. The only thing that concerns al-Banna is that at the end of the meeting the canal company director tells him that the only condition of the donation is that al-Banna must publicly acknowledge the source of the funds. He does not actually do so, but the British arrange for it to be done by a mainstream preacher in a sermon. This sets up the following dialogue between the British intelligence agent and a subordinate, which reveals the contours of the game the British are playing:[15]

INTELLIGENCE OFFICIAL: Ah, John. Glad tidings, what?

SUBORDINATE: All as you expected, Sir.

OFFICIAL: Give me particulars. What precisely happened.

SUBORDINATE: The acceptance of cash caused quite a rift between the members and their leader. They are of the view that it would be a sin to build a mosque with funds from the enemy.

OFFICIAL: Just as I expected. You do recall my statement that Egyptians—Arabs as a whole in fact—will defend religion more fiercely than king and country?

SUBORDINATE: Yes, I recall it, Sir.

OFFICIAL: Good. Now let me tell you something of no small importance. When Muslims are united, they become a force to be reckoned with, not to say invincible. This is why we must always insure that they are divided, what? It is most fortunate that they are singularly obdurate when they are divided by matters of religion. This holy man, this group, will serve us well in creating that rift.

SUBORDINATE: At the very least they may distract them from us, and all the infernal call for independence and British evacuation. And of course fill their minds with religious matters.

OFFICIAL: This group will not remain religious for long. It must turn to politics. If it does not, politics will find it.

SUBORDINATE: I never imagined that £500 could cause such a rift.

OFFICIAL: If you wish to corrupt a holy man you may do one of two things: you may bestow power and position on him; or you may place a sum of money at his disposal.

SUBORDINATE: So when all is said and done, what do you suggest should be done with that holy man and that band of his?

OFFICIAL: Why nothing. Nothing at all. We shall act as though unaware of its existence.

SUBORDINATE: If I may say so, Sir, I'm hardly at ease regarding this group. I fear that they might constitute danger to us in the future.

OFFICIAL: Well, it is most natural that such a group, should it continue, may give us a spot of trouble. But in the end, should we lose to it, we stand to lose very little, and to gain considerably.

It cannot be doubted that the British were aware of the Muslim Brotherhood at least by the mid-1930s,[16] but the blatant manipulation of the movement depicted in the scene is entirely a product of Wahid Hamid's politicized poetic license. To be an Egyptian elite in the interwar era was to have a relation to the British Empire and to Britain as a local colonizing entity. "A relation" could encompass both resistance and accommodation. But no politician of any consequence could remain aloof from British influence. If one supposes that al-Banna actually took money from the colonizers, his real sin would have been presumptuousness: making deals with the hegemon was a closely guarded privilege of the elite.

By the time of Rab'a another justification for the Muslim Brotherhood's national excommunication was its alleged internationalism, particularly its links to transnational Islamist radicalism. This also was thoroughly embedded in anti-Islamist "tanwir" discourse prior to the revolution. Throughout *al-Gama'a* contacts with Saudi Arabia are mentioned very prominently. Al-Banna did in fact admire Saudi Arabia's alliance between the Al Saud family and Wahhabi ideology, as did other Islamic figures of his day (Krämer 2010, 80). In *al-Gama'a* al-Banna's admiration for the Saudis was refracted through his interaction with Shaykh Muhibb al-Din al-Khatib, who was himself a migrant from Syria, though his family was originally from Baghdad. He was the son of Abd al-Qadir al-Jilani, the founder of the Qadiriyya Sufi order. Al-Khatib was a Salafi, and a prolific publisher.[17] Throughout the series al-Banna often seeks his counsel. This is historically correct—al-Banna had many reasons to be friends with al-Khatib. But in *al-Gama'a* he functions primarily to highlight connections with austere and fanatical Saudi Islam, which, the series implies, is not part of Egypt's "native" understanding of religion. Al-Banna's meetings with al-Khatib are sometimes accompanied by ominous background music that leaves no ambiguity about their significance.

To make sure that the importance of al-Banna's connection to al-Khatib is crystal clear, the modern track of the series articulates it plainly. In the modern track of the series a conversation between Ashraf, the prosecutor, and 'Abdallah, the retired judge and lapsed Muslim Brotherhood member, 'Abdallah notes that "al-Banna was influenced by Shaykh Muhibb al-Din al-Khatib," and al-Khatib "wasn't just any shaykh." Building on his Syrian origin, Khatib was meant to be extremely clever at setting up secret and international organizations in the Arab countries. 'Abdallah stresses to Ashraf that al-Banna "learned a lot from him and developed what he learned." Ashraf asks 'Abdallah what he means exactly by al-Banna's having "developed" al-Khatib's expertise in setting up secret organizations. 'Abdallah responds:

> Don't forget in the West at that time there was fascism in Italy, Nazism in Germany, and communism in Russia. These were gigantic organizations. For sure Hasan al-Banna benefitted from these organizations. Islamic history is full of secret organizations. For sure Hasan al-Banna studied Shi'ism very carefully.

Hence the line runs from al-Khatib to fascism to Nazism, to communism, to Shi'ism, seamlessly and completely without evidence. Broadly speaking al-Khatib was well known to have been an advocate of anti-imperialist causes and, if anything, was a campaigner against Shi'ism rather than a crypto-Shi'i as 'Abdallah's grand conflation suggests. One is reminded of Ahmad Musa's certainty about the "heavy weapons" flooding into the Rab'a sit-in. Though he is no expert in weapons, Musa has no problem "recognizing" a cannon or a mortar when he sees a long object wrapped in cloth. And so it is in 'Abdallah's depiction of Khatib: he knows a Shi'i rabble-rouser when he sees one. Evidence is superfluous.

'Abdallah does not mention the Saudi connection in the passage above, but another scene does the job very bluntly. It begins with al-Banna arriving at al-Khatib's office to discuss the publication of a Muslim Brotherhood magazine. Still in a hallway, he hears an anguished voice, instantly recognizable as that of Rashid Rida, the famed Islamic reformer, known particularly for his writings on the idea of an Islamic state, and also al-Khatib's business partner.[18] After al-Banna calms him a bit, the reason for Rida's distress comes out:

> AL-KHATIB: Some communist and secularist scoundrels have started a mad campaign against him. They say the Shaykh is paid by the Saudis to spread Wahhabism in Egypt.
>
> AL-BANNA: [with ominous music playing and a devilish smile on his face] What do you think Shaykh Rashid?
>
> RIDA: My boy, I don't . . . I . . . I don't think anything.
>
> AL-BANNA: And so what, Master? So what then? It's the truth, and nobody can deny it. Don't the Saudis read your books, just as you buy books from Shaykh Muhibb? Then you advocate what you see in them and work hard doing it.

AL-KHATIB: You've become quite the legalist Shaykh Hasan.

RIDA: Bless you. You remind me of Imam al-Layth Ibn Sa'd when he got the Caliph Harun al-Rashid out of a jam.

AL-KHATIB: Shaykh Hasan now has the status of an Imam Shayh Rashid.

RIDA: I was confused, didn't know how to respond, to the point that I thought of saying that King 'Abd al-'Aziz is my friend. But if I had said that I'd have put myself in an even greater predicament. [He begins blubbering in tears.] May you always be well, Hasan.

AL-KHATIB: We all put our confidence in Shaykh Hasan.

RIDA: Tell me, Hasan, does your movement need anything?

AL-BANNA: Shaykh Rashid, we have many great ambitions.

RIDA: Yes. And there are more and greater responsibilities.

AL-BANNA: We're now expanding the society's base, and recruiting the best youth.

AL-KHATIB: The battle that the Society of Brothers has been waging against Christian missionaries has gained it much fame and sympathy from all Egyptians.

RIDA: No, no—fame and love and sympathy aren't what's important. It is enough to break and defeat the enemy.

AL-BANNA: Praise God, Shaykh Rida. We've disgraced them and their methods. We've exposed their incitements and made the ruler face the danger to religion.

RIDA: The Egyptian people's faith in Islam is deep, and their zeal for it intense. The people of Egypt—their feelings of nationalism are violent. I wish this society of yours would concern itself with matters of the nation, as it does with matters of religion.

AL-BANNA: But . . . this is politics, Shaykh Rashid!

RIDA: And so what? Religion is sincere counsel. What's the problem if a Guide of a Muslim society guides others for the good of the community?

Al-Banna's smirking face when Rida tells him he should be as concerned about the nation as he is about religion communicates the real point of the scene better than the words (see figure 8.3). Like so much of the historical track of the series, the dialogue has a distinctly contemporary feel. Lauzière (2010) notes that al-Khatib's publishing projects began as part of the Nahda's Islamic reformism (headlined by Muhammad 'Abuh and Rashid Rida), and that he did indeed also publish conservative and Wahhabi tracts, even to the point that he opened a branch of his publishing house in Mecca. But he (and Rashid) did so openly. Egypt did not yet recognize Saudi Arabia in the 1930s, but Rida's consternation at the revelation of his Saudi background is implausible. Saudi Arabia in the 1930s was nothing like the oil-rich kingdom that many contemporary

But ... this is politics Shaykh Rashid

FIGURE 8.3. Hasan al-Banna grinning devilishly at Rashid Rida's implication that mixing politics with religion is legitimate. From the television series *al-Gama'a*, 2010.

Egyptians look at with decidedly conflicted emotions—as a much-resented regional hegemon, as profligate vulgarians with less "culture" than the proud seven-thousand-year-old civilization of the Nile valley, or as the domineering holder of Egypt's national purse strings. The main domestic conflict with Saudi Arabia had to do with vestigial rivalries over a potentially reconstituted caliphate (Krämer 2010, 80).

A similar scene crystallizes the Muslim Brotherhood's alleged innate violence. This also comes to the audience through another of al-Banna's many contacts with foreign radicals, this time Shaykh Muhammad Sa'id al-'Urfi, a scholar from Deir al-Zur, the largest city in eastern Syria and in our times one of the epicenters of the Syrian Civil War. 'Urfi comes calling as a kind of Islamic radical consultant. The exact relation between him and the Muslim Brotherhood is never spelled out. Presumably one is meant to apply the Ahmad Musa rule: if you think it looks like a cannon, then insist on calling it a cannon. But substitute "Islamist radical" for "cannon." Al-'Urfi *was* in truth a kind of transnational Islamic radical—one of the leaders of the Syrian nationalist movement against France in the 1920s and 1930s, a participant in an international conference on Arab unity in Mecca in 1922. When al-Banna first mentions his name to his followers and explains where he is from, one of them expresses surprise that their leader is entertaining people from so far away. Al-Banna admonishes him: "The people of the Sham are our people, and the people of the Hijaz are our people. All Muslims are our people." Al-Banna and 'Urfi stroll about in a park, where 'Urfi offers advice. Faith, he says, is the most powerful weapon in life. But then he goes on with further advice that fits very well with al-Banna's cynical ambition. Al-Banna, he says, should specifically recruit young men with "imperfect faith." "If you know that fear of God resides in their hearts, and that they respect order, and that they are obedient, then you'll find that repentance will be forthcoming, and they'll be among the most sincere adherents to you and your *da'wa* [his mission, or call for followers]." But then he proceeds to tell al-Banna to be careful to avoid two types of people:

> The first type is the atheist who has no faith at all, no matter how much piety he might show on the outside. The second type is the truly pious man who does not respect the organization, and will not obey. Whoever will not adhere to the order you impose, and will not obey your commands—he is of no use to you or to the society. His presence will corrupt the society, will incite it with his piety and righteousness, and will divide it with disputes. They will therefore unsettle the straight rank and corrupt it. If people see one person outside the line they won't say "one person has left the line." Rather they'll say "the line is crooked." So beware, Hasan. All your works are contingent on this da'wa.[19]

Al-Banna's conversation with 'Urfi provides a succinct illustration of a point that opponents of the Muslim Brotherhood often make, namely that the organization is more concerned with the appearance of faith than it is with actual piety. Al-Banna drinks in Urfi's advice eagerly. Then he wants to do a kind of show-and-tell with his elder radical colleague. He takes him to see his militia training:

'URFI: [seeing a military encampment in the distance] What are the English doing outside their bases?

AL-BANNA: These tents have nothing to do with the English. These tents belong to the Gama'a. Gama'at al-Ikhwan al-Muslimin.

'URFI: What's the Gama'a's purpose out here in the desert Hasan?

[CUT TO SCENES OF SCOUTS IN COMBAT TRAINING IN A DESERT ENCAMPMENT.]

AL-BANNA: They're the Rovers' vanguard. Strength is a necessity. We won't be the oppressed on earth.

'URFI: You're preparing these youths to defend the Gama'a, Hasan?

AL-BANNA: God willing. But we have deeper and more comprehensive goals.

'URFI: Please explain more, Hasan.

AL-BANNA: The point isn't just to create an organized means of deterrence, trained as a military force, but rather for these youths to be observed by our trainers, and by me personally, so that we know which are the most zealous, the most sincere, the most obedient.

'URFI: You're choosing your men already, Hasan?

AL-BANNA: I'm choosing them. Choosing them and giving them

strong preparation. The da'wa can only be built on the shoulders of the strong.

'URFI: You're just the person for this, Hasan. Now I am very well reassured by you, and by your Gama'a.

The Rovers—Gawwala as al-Banna calls them—were the Muslim Brotherhood version of the Boy Scouts. The Muslim Brotherhood did use the Gawwala to recruit, train, and indoctrinate young men, and the organization did have a paramilitary function. However, so did the Wafd's, and the Young Egypt movement's scouting wings; all three movements saw the paramilitary nature of scouting as training for actual military use.[20] So did the international Boy Scouts movement. One might (or might not) see this as a perversion of the true purpose of scouting. But what cannot be doubted is that the brotherhood's Rovers were part of a broad "healthy spirit in a healthy body" movement that originated in Europe, and was global. Krämer writes that the Muslim Brotherhood version of scouting included specific kinds of indoctrination, such as "reference to the hero-warriors of the early Islamic period, prayer and night vigils" (Krämer 2010, 91). The brotherhood also employed Sufi practices of self-discipline and required members to study some of the writings of Hasan al-Banna. Later some of the Rovers were recruited to form small "battalions" (*kata'ib*), some of which fought in Palestine, others against the British, and probably also against the local Jewish community in 1948.

The point is not that the serial's interpretation of the brotherhood's Rovers was completely outlandish, but rather that it was cleverly, deliberately, and pointedly undercontextualized in order to mislead. We understand al-Banna's Rovers differently if we juxtapose them with the international scouting movement. Everywhere it was paramilitary; everywhere it was connected both to religion and to nation, pointedly *in that order*. The brotherhood's emphasis on "hero-warriors of the early Islamic period" was actually compatible with the franchised model of global scouting. A more recent Christian Arab scouting poster, for example, displays St. George slaying the dragon in its upper left corner ("Al-Wa'd al-Kashfi" 2017). St. George was the saint most venerated by the Crusaders, which could potentially make his prominence on an Arab Boy Scout poster seem aggressive.[21] But the symbolism is not out of line with the way scouting has worked everywhere and at all times since its creation in 1908. The Scouting oath, in both Arabic and English, states "On my honor I will do my best to do my duty to God and my Country." One widespread Arabic translation of the passage is more explicit about priorities than the original English: *U'id sharafi bi-an aqumu bi-wajibi nahwa Allah*, ***thumma*** *al-watan*; I pledge my honor to do my duty to God *and then* to my country" ("Al-Wa'd al-Kashfi" 2017; emphasis added).[22] But aside from such nuances, it is the same scouting oath I learned in the 1970s. God comes first in most versions of the *interna-*

tional scouting oath. There was no need for the brotherhood to impose putting God above nation in their Rover indoctrination. It was already there.

But connecting the Rovers to the actual phenomenon of scouting was the last thing Wahid Hamid wanted to do. His point rather was to connect the Rovers as a *militia* to the Muslim Brotherhood militia that was represented in the contemporary track of the series—the "kung fu" routines performed by brotherhood members in the march at al-Azhar University. It amounts to the visual equivalent of the conflation 'Abdallah, the retired judge made: Muhibb al-Din al-Khatib, to fascism, Nazism, communism, and Shi'ism. In this case it is the Rovers in the 1930s to the militia parading at al-Azhar University in 2006. And it was a short step further to television propagandist Ahmad Musa's unshakeable certainty that he was seeing a video of a cannon being carried into Rab'a al-'Adawiyya, making the protestors there fair game for anything the state security forces might do to them. It is easy to see how a dehistoricized public might have internalized the notion that violence is encoded in the DNA of the Muslim Brotherhood.

Conclusion: A Prefabricated Threshold

We return to a question posed earlier: why should we assume that the non-Islamist public was able to form comparatively rational assessments of the history and character of Islamism? In a liminal void sides were inevitably taken once communitas became a thing of memory rather than a visceral experience. But it should also be noted that the revolution created a series of thresholds, not just the initial threshold of the plunge into the void when the label "revolution" was applied to events on January 25, 2011. The Maspero Massacre was a threshold; the Battle of Muhammad Mahmud Street was too, and so were a number of other crisis events, including the Tamarrud demonstration against Muhammad Morsy in 2013 and the coup that followed shortly thereafter. But the "recognition . . . of a generalized social bond that has ceased to be and has simultaneously yet to be fragmented into a multiplicity of structural ties" (Turner 1977, 96) applied to more limited sets of actors in those later events. None of them involved the Muslim Brotherhood.

It is not entirely wrong to partially attribute the coup, the massacre, and the certainty of those who backed these actions to the notion that revolutionary politics left no alternative to violence, which manifested in the Rab'a Massacre. But it is entirely wrong to neglect the long-standing discursive apparatus of excommunicating the Muslim Brotherhood from the national community that was operational during the period of revolutionary liminality *and* before it. Resorting to such concepts as imitation and crisis in no way obviates the need to delve into the production, meaning and circulation of this discourse. If anything, the need to document and interpret the means of excommunication are heightened by our attention to the form of crisis: the creation or occurrence of a threshold in the present; a plunge into liminality (or an "uncanny present"), and then a reckoning. The reckoning can be interpreted through the concepts of communitas and a subsequent calculation of power resources, as the specter of polarization materializes. But the reckoning cannot be pulled out of thin air. "Return and repetition" (Bryant 2016), the marshalling of experience in the face of crisis, requires recourse to the past. *Al-Gamaʻa* powerfully focused attitudes about the Muslim Brotherhood in a high-profile narrative broadcast on the eve of the revolution. In the weeks leading to the Rabʻa Massacre it was at least as much implicated in the production of anti-Islamist propaganda as Ahmad Musa's "heavy weapons" claim. The experience of revolutionary politics over the previous two and a half years cannot be separated from the lies. The case against the brotherhood had been made; a verdict had been delivered: who stole our joy? The Muslim Brotherhood. Guilty! All the elements of excommunication had been tried, tested, and formulated into a coherent package before the revolution began.

It should not be imagined that *al-Gamaʻa* was an exceptional occurrence. On the contrary, the program was a kind of "seal of the prophets"—the last and most perfect revelation of a message. The oppositional "message" about the "true nature of the brotherhood" may be as old as the organization, but its most recent formulation dates from the tanwir campaign of the mid-1990s. Wahid Hamid had been on the ground floor of that campaign, and his own taboo-breaking efforts to dramatize the "true face of Islamism" had opened doors to many others.[23] One may assume that the actual Muslim Brotherhood of course has many flaws as a political party or social movement.[24] In power they may well have been horrible. But to say that many people were faced with no choice but to oppose the brotherhood is not the same as saying that it had to be opposed by any means necessary, including lies, exaggerations, and half-truths. "The differential distribution of grievability across populations has implications for why and when we feel politically consequential affective dispositions such as horror, guilt, righteous sadism, loss, and indifference" (Butler 2009, 24). Horror, guilt, and loss were conspicuously absent in the immediate aftermath of the Rabʻa Massacre. Also (in different social locations) in the aftermaths of the Maspero Massacre, the Battle of Muhammad Mahmud Street, the breakup of the Maglis al-Wuzaraʼ sit-in, and dozens of other less famous confrontations. The absence of grievability does not happen by accident. It is important to acknowledge and interrogate the frame that excluded and excommunicated the brotherhood, making intentional sadism and indifference on the part of their opponents so prominent in the final act of the revolutionary drama. But this is only a preview of that final act. The liminal void of the revolution still had many tricks to play.

CHAPTER 9

The Trickster in
Midan al-ʿAbbasiyya

[A middle-aged man on a talk-show set faces the camera intently] Beware: thirteen, thirteen, 2013 [he smacks his hand on the desk].... If you're alive ... thirteen, thirteen, 2013 [said very slowly and clearly], the Freemasons ... [he is suddenly distracted by a voice off camera] what do you want? ... Say it, don't be afraid ... what? [he recovers and addresses the camera again] I'm sorry, thirteen 2013, excuse me ... thirteen 2013 ... pay attention, there's no thirteenth month ... good ... the thirteenth day, on the thirteenth night, on the thirteenth party, in the year 2013. This is the greatest challenge—the greatest. The greatest. Before that there is, like ʿImad just told me in the earpiece, he said, there is a 12/12/2012, also there's some talk more or less, that they might make another attempt. But the date 12/12/12 for them, in the Masonic system, I mean, it isn't as big a deal for them [mayikhallihumsh yiwassalu tazkara bi-arbaʿin dular, literally "it doesn't make them deliver a forty-dollar ticket"] ... 13/13/2013, not the thirteenth month, not the thirteenth month, the thirteenth night. Hmm? The thirteenth night. In the year 2013, on the date of the thirteenth, that will begin from the night of Christmas. Hmm? From what night? Christmas. Do you get it?

—Taufiq ʿUkasha on "Masr al-Yaum," November 15,
2011 ("Taufiq ʿUkasha Yahdhar" 2011)

Kindly take the necessary steps toward having leaders at all levels instruct officers, junior officers, and soldiers on the necessity of watching the Faraʿayn Channel, as its programs can be described as impartial, objective, and as putting the interests of the nation above all other interests.

—Alleged leaked memo from Egyptian Air Force General
Yunis al-Sayyid al-Masry (Abdelazim 2012)

*I will hold the Muslim Brotherhood in particular responsible for my
security, and responsible for closing the Fara'ayn Channel. That's first.
Second, I hold the Military Council responsible for my security, from Field
Marshall Muhammad Husayn al-Tantawi down to the last member of the
Military Council, who is General 'Abd al-Fattah al-Sisi, the director of
military intelligence, and the Muslim Brotherhood's man in the armed
forces. And also everyone who is responsible within the Supreme Council
for the Armed Forces, I hold them responsible for my personal safety,
because they might kill me, and then it will be said that it was the Muslim
Brotherhood who killed him. And maybe the Muslim Brotherhood might
kill me, and it will be said that it was the Military Council that killed
him. No, what I want to say is that the two of them are together, because
they're partners, and they'll be partners in everything—partners in closing
the channel, partners in killing me, and partners in any problem that
might arise.*

—Taufiq 'Ukasha speaking on the Fara'ayn Channel the day
after Muhammad Morsy's victory in the presidential election
was announced ("'Ukasha Yatanaba'u bi-Tai'yin" 2012)

IN THE WAKE OF THE Mubarak regime's collapse it seemed to most observers that the initiative for restructuring society and the political system lay with the young prodemocracy activists who started the revolution. It soon became apparent that while the regime had fallen, opposition to the revolution was continuous.[1] Opponents of the increasingly fragmented revolutionary forces were seen as variously the old regime, a "deep state," opportunistic Islamist political parties, and SCAF. But it was never a foregone conclusion that political initiative was the prerogative of either mobilized activists or well-established Islamist social movements, or indeed even that the antirevolution forces consisted straightforwardly of the old regime or the military. As I have argued in previous chapters, revolutions do not just pry open the field of political contention. They can instead be seen as moments of protracted liminality in which new political agents can emerge, and in which all political agents are forced to act as bricoleurs, assembling new political formations from diverse cultural resources.

In this chapter we encounter Taufiq 'Ukasha, a talk-show host and minor parliamentarian in the ruling National Democratic Party (NDP) before the revolution, re-created in the protracted state of antistructure after the fall of the regime as a "media personality" and advocate for a cult of Egyptian militarism. He became a primary spokesman for the counterrevolution, and ultimately a political force in his own right. 'Ukasha was often seen during his moment in the political limelight as an appendage of SCAF. It seems likely that he was, but I do not think he can be reduced to a SCAF puppet. He showed a remarkable ability to emerge onto the political stage at a particular moment—

specifically, from near the end of 2011 until the rise of Sisi in the summer of 2013. But his political capacities depended crucially on a well-publicized "loose cannon" media persona. It was never likely that 'Ukasha would achieve meaningful power, but he does exemplify potentialities of revolutionary liminality not well captured by viewing a revolutionary situation as a theater in which contention occurs between established political actors.

'Ukasha emerged as a Trickster within the larger arc of the revolution. Before Thomassen's formulation of a politics of liminality (2012; 2014) the term "Trickster" had rarely been invoked in the context of politics. Tricksters are normally figures one encounters in studies of mythology, folklore, anthropology, or literary studies. The potential to be both creative and destructive lies at the heart of the Trickster, who is exquisitely ambivalent: potentially powerful, ridiculous, and dangerous (Radin 1956, ix). The term designates both a character and a type of narrative found across all modern cultures and in antiquity. The Greek god Dionysus is a Trickster figure, as is Hermes. Anansi, a west African spider-shaped folk character, is a Trickster. Juha and Nasreddin Hoja in the Middle East. Pan, Puck, and Bre'r Rabbit are Tricksters. In Norse mythology Loki is a Trickster. So is Rumpelstiltskin, the Pink Panther, the Joker, Dr. Who. Bart Simpson is a Trickster. It may also be that many authoritarian politicians are Tricksters. 'Ukasha, as we will see, was a little Trickster who paved the way for a much bigger and more dangerous one.

Taufiq 'Ukasha

Taufiq Yahya Ibrahim 'Ukasha was a minor politician from Daqahliyya Province northeast of Cairo in the delta. Before the revolution he was a television journalist. In the early 1990s he worked for state television, managing to become the presenter of a political program called *Parties and Parliament* (*Ahzab wa Barliman*), which was broadcast in the wee hours of the morning "graveyard shift." 'Ukasha was a failed candidate in the 2005 parliamentary elections for an NDP seat in the People's Assembly. In 2008 he established his own satellite television station, al-Fara'ayn (the Pharaohs), and began to recreate himself as an *i'lami* (pl. *i'lamiyin*)—nominally a media professional (in television working in front of or behind the camera), but most often used in the sense of a "media personality," a quasicelebrity located somewhere on a spectrum between news anchor and purveyor of "infotainment." This worked well enough to get him elected in the 2010 parliamentary elections in his hometown of Nabaruh in Daqahliyya. Those elections were blatantly rigged by the NDP and contributed greatly to the outrage that fed the January 25, 2011, Revolution. Consequently 'Ukasha's time "in government" was short. The parliament elected in November of 2010 was dissolved by SCAF on February 13, 2011, one day after Mubarak's abdication.

Before the revolution 'Ukasha's television station was a vanity project for furthering his frustrated political ambitions. After the revolution he often claimed to have been at odds with the NDP. The substance of his conflicts with the luminaries of the ruling party is vague, but it is true that the NDP dominance was so great that political contention over control of resources and patronage took place within the party rather than between parties.

Arab television boasts a wide range of talk shows. The hosts of these programs, like the Americans CNN reporter Anderson Cooper or right-wing commentator Glen Beck, or the British newscaster John Snow, achieve a measure of celebrity. However, similarities between Egyptian media personalities and foreign counterparts belie a distinctive political economy. Egyptian private channels before the revolution were owned by politically connected businessmen such as Ahmad Bahgat (the Dream channels) or Naguib Sawiris (OTV and OnTV), hence "private" did not mean completely free of regime control.[2] Nonetheless even before the revolution, the possibility of media personalities (most often talk-show hosts) establishing a following made them commodities with transferrable value. The existence of an increasing number of alternative platforms, even if they were not entirely independent of the regime, was important because it gave presenters themselves a degree of autonomy. Spectacle, controversy, and sometimes principled political criticism, even within the limits of Mubarak-era censorship, endowed media personalities with social capital convertible to both the fees they could command (a subject of intense gossip and gross exaggeration) and advertising fees that the stations could attract. Mubarak-era restrictions on licensing news channels enabled Egyptian i'lamiyin to become the public faces of political talk shows that skirted a ban on establishing straightforward news networks. On prerevolution satellite television Taufiq 'Ukasha, host of a political talk show titled *Misr al-Yaum* (*Egypt Today*), was a very small fish compared to such whales as Hala Sarhan, Mahmud Sa'd, or 'Amr Adib.

After the revolution new channels proliferated, as the ban on news reporting was relaxed, and political forces other than the regime and its cronies were able to establish a toehold in broadcast media. One might think that an expanded field of talk-show platforms might have made 'Ukasha an even smaller fish in a larger pond. However, he thrived in the increasingly chaotic postregime environment though a spectacular mix of virulent attacks on the revolution, unswerving allegiance to the military, and a drumbeat of conspiracy theories "proving" that the revolution was brought about by foreign agents who wanted to destroy Egypt. 'Ukasha presented this bouquet of themes in a folksy idiom obviously designed to appeal to a rural and lower-middle-class audience. Many people I spoke to were convinced that the overall package was successful within this very substantial niche, but *only* within that niche. It was also widely believed that 'Ukasha worked with the Military Intelligence Service and that he was, moreover, a prime suspect in organizing the infamous Battle of the Camel, in which the Mubarak regime attacked protestors in Tahrir Square on February 2 with irregular "thugs" and security personnel. Such allegations cannot be proved, but there is little doubt that 'Ukasha's political activities went beyond his television program.

The program's lavish praise for the military, police, and judiciary did not always extend to individuals. 'Ukasha forcefully supported Field Marshall Hussein Tantawi, the leader of SCAF, until the moment on June 24, 2012, that Morsy was announced as the winner of the presidential election. Thereafter he denounced Tantawi as "the heir to Field Marshall 'Abd al-Hakim 'Amr" (the military commander when Egypt was devastated by Israel in the June War of 1967). There were accusations that 'Ukasha incited lower-ranking officers to carry out a coup against the Military Council (R. Hasan 2012). Since the exact nature of 'Ukasha's relation to both SCAF and the deposed Mubarak regime was exquisitely murky, viewers had scope to interpret 'Ukasha's "falling out" with Tantawi as part of a devious strategy in which SCAF would depart in a fake coup that would bring younger officers to power, who would then forcibly remove the Muslim Brotherhood from power.

Spectacle

I first became aware of 'Ukasha at a counterrevolution demonstration in al-'Abbasiyya Square on December 23, 2011. Counterrevolution demonstrations had been announced throughout the year, generally to little effect. However, by November 2011 sizeable anti-Tahrir protests had occurred. These events were labeled by their organizers, most prominently 'Ukasha, as a "corrective revolution" (tashih al-thaura) rather than as a counterrevolution. The al-'Abbasiyya demonstration I attended was the only occasion in the two years after the fall of the regime in which I felt unsure about my safety vis-à-vis demonstrators (as opposed to the security forces) as a foreign observer. December 23 was a day of "dueling demonstrations." The al-'Abbasiyya happening was explicitly billed by 'Ukasha as an alternative to the Gum'at Radd al-Sharaf (the Friday of Restoring Honor) in Tahrir Square, in response to the army's attack on a sit-in in which soldiers had beaten and humiliated women in particular. Gum'at Radd al-Sharaf was part of a campaign to reassert the relevance of the non-Islamist revolutionary forces in the wake of Muslim Brotherhood domination of parliamentary elections, and a series of pitched battles with the security forces involving young men allied to the non-Islamist revolutionary forces. In response, 'Ukasha labeled his event Gum'at al-'Ubur—the "Friday of the Crossing"—to honor the armed forces by invoking their historic breaching of the Bar Lev Line in the October War of 1973.

Al-'Abbasiyya Square, a small and unpleasant place for a demonstration, was chosen for its proximity to the Ministry of Defense. With much of the square walled off to contain construction work on the Cairo Metro, al-'Abbasiyya Square could host perhaps a couple thousand people, a bit more if the peripheral areas were packed. Traffic flyovers—raised highways carrying noisy traffic—dominated the square. Many of those attending 'Ukasha's "corrective revolution" were members and families of the police and the military, both in plain clothes for this event. Speakers thundered against the United States, Israel, Europe, and Iran, all of whom were said to be in league with each other against Egypt. But local enemies were the focus of vilification. One speaker thundered that the political essayist and novelist Alaa Al Aswany

> announced the choice of [Mohamed] El Baradei as president of a government of national salvation, [and] and after an hour El Baradei accepted the position, and another hour after that France is warning Egypt to surrender power to a civilian government right away . . . surrender to El Baradei.

The crowd chanted *batil, batil, batil* ("invalid"—at a demonstration tantamount to yelling "bullshit").

The protestors at 'Ukasha's event featured few women, little class diversity, and not even much diversity in age. Middle-aged men dominated, unlike the more youthful and often more gender-mixed and class-mixed crowds in the heyday of the Tahrir demonstrations. Few of the al-'Abbasiyya crowd marked themselves Islamically, with a beard for men or a head or face covering for women.

The al-'Abbasiyya demonstration was made for television. State television mobile broadcast vans were parked nearby. Prorevolution channels were positively forbidden. Banners hung from the traffic flyovers displayed four prorevolution television presenters in nooses.[3] Text on the banners thundered that "the people want death (*i'dam*) for traitors and agents [of foreign interests]."[4] Later in the day news reached me that BBC reporters who tried to file a story from the al-'Abbasiyya demonstration were roughed up. The rude treatment of foreign journalists was ironic given that at one point the crowd had chanted "al-gazira fayn, ish-sha'b il-masry aho"—"where is al-Jazeera, here are the Egyptian people," as if there were a plot by the foreign media to underreport the "corrective revolution" rather than a determined effort by the crowd to prevent coverage. I took some pictures from a traffic flyover, and while walking down the off-ramp on my way back to the square, I paused by a knot of people crowded around an interview for the al-Hayat channel, considered by revolutionaries as a *fulul* (defeated remnants of the old regime) mouthpiece. The interview was just ending. I heard a man standing beside me say to a friend, "al-nas dool illi fi midan al-tahrir mish bani admin" (those people in Tahrir Square aren't human beings).

FIGURE 9.1. Tough-looking men carrying antirevolution posters on the
street leading into al-'Abbasiyya Square. From the Gum'at al-'Ubur (Friday
of the Crossing) demonstration on December 23, 2011. Author's photo.

The al-'Abbasiyya demonstration was hypercoherent. Handwritten signs
reiterated consistent themes, as if distributed by a committee. "The People and
the Police and the Army Are One Hand" was everywhere. On a banner suspended beside the images of prorevolution television personalities in nooses
one could see "the army, the police, and the judiciary."[5] A group of tough-
looking men standing near the entrance of the square sported additional ven-
omous antirevolution signage (see figure 9.1):

> There are still Egyptians who haven't gone into the [public] squares.
> Beware the return of the Egyptians. Egypt and the Egyptians are bigger
> than [foreign] agendas and funding.

> We demand the emptying of Tahrir Square immediately.

> Egypt above Tahrir. Corrective revolution.

Another man carried a sign saying:

> Friday of the Crossing [al-'ubur]. The people of Manufiyya[6] support
> and pledge our loyalty to the armed forces, the police, and the judges.
> No to destruction, no to foreign directives. We die, and long live Egypt.

The appearance of coherence was no illusion. All the signs were straight out of
'Ukasha's program.

FIGURE 9.2. Al-'Abbasiyya Square from the traffic flyovers above, on the day of Gum'at al-'Ubur. December 23, 2011. Author's photo.

State and state-allied television channels never filmed the al-'Abbasiyya demonstration from the traffic flyovers in wide-angle shots (see figure 9.2). A video montage of the demonstration in al-'Abbasiyya filmed from within the crowd and aired on 'Ukasha's channel gave an impression of a red-and-white sea boiling with frenzied flag-waving patriotism. One version of the video was put to the song "Sura" (Picture) by Nasser-era icon 'Abd al-Halim Hafiz:[7]

> A picture, a picture, a picture
> We all want a picture
> A picture of a joyous people
> Beneath the victorious flag
> Photograph us for posterity
> Gather closer together
> Whoever stays away from the midan
> Won't ever appear in the picture

Protestors in Tahrir used to play the same song on loudspeakers. In al-'Abbasiyya, combined with the angry rhetoric and the television coverage, it made for rather effective propaganda.

'Ukasha the Trickster

Understanding 'Ukasha as a Trickster requires taking a closer look at his primary stage, namely his television show. To call *Egypt Today* a "talk show" is misleading. Sometimes there were guests, and sometimes he took calls from off-air viewers. But usually 'Ukasha himself did the talking, for up to three straight hours, extolling the martial prowess of the Egyptian army, and fulminating against the forces that brought down the Mubarak regime, which he nominally condemned. Mubarak was nonetheless portrayed as having been brought down not by the Egyptian people, but by agents of foreign powers, most prominently the United States and Israel, but allied with a grand conspiracy encompassing the European Union, Iran, Hamas, Hizballah, South Sudan, Qatar, communists, the Muslim Brotherhood, the Youth of April 6 Movement, the Kifaya movement, Mohamed El Baradei's National Association for Change, Google, Facebook, the Masons, and the Jews. 'Ukasha's exhortation to attend the al-'Abbasiyya demonstration described above was broadcast on *Egypt Today* (see figure 9.3) two nights before the event:

> Egypt is in danger that nobody could have imagined. Foreign agendas and unfortunately [he snickers bitterly] Arab agendas. . . . Egypt: the oldest state in the world. The oldest state in the world! It has the oldest people in the world, the smartest people, the most powerful people. The "mustachioed elephant" [*il-fil abu-shanab*] wants to rule Egypt.[8] The mustachioed elephant thinks he can buy the people; he pays his money, but the Egyptian people can't be bought. I implore you in the name of Egypt to be present in al-'Abbasiyya Square on Friday after prayers. I've gotten lots of letters asking me to invite Shaykh Muhammad Hassan to come pray with us in al-'Abbasiyya.[9] So I'm inviting him, and to every person who loves Egypt, to be present in al-'Abbasiyya on a day that we're calling "the Friday of the Crossing" [*gum'at al-'ubur*].[10] THE CROSSING! EGYPT! THE GREAT . . . [his raised hand and his voice shake together] EGYPTIAN ARMY! . . . is being insulted. It's being insulted in satellite channels. First they say that the Military Council is one thing, and the army another. In the second stage, it's the whole Egyptian army. And they've pounded on the police forces, accusing them of vandalism [*kharaba*] and thuggery [*baltaga*] and lack of security spreading throughout the country. They say, "It's not enough; we have to finish off the army." The main thing is the army, because then there won't be any protection. A state without an army and without police and without a judicial authority and institutions is no state. Those leftist and communist effendis who don't believe in the existence of the divine being [*bi-wugud al-zaat al-ilahiyya*] are telling you "we want to burn it."

FIGURE 9.3. The station logo of Taufiq 'Ukasha's *Egypt Today* program on his al-Fara'ayn channel.

'Ukasha's style is repetitious, circular, pitched to the oral rhythms of illiterate or semiliterate viewers:

> Egypt calls for her sons' help! Will her sons stand [with her]?! I am as certain as my belief in God that on Friday they will be there by the millions; not by the thousands, and not a phony "*millioniyya*" [like those in Tahrir]. Millions, millions by God's will [*bi-izn-illah*] will go out on the "day of crossing," on the day of completing the corrective revolution, on the day that this nation [*umma*], with its people crosses to security [*illa al-aman*], to liberty, to building a civilization for the twenty-first century! An Egyptian civilization! That the Egyptian people will build! In the twenty-first century by God's will.

For many, 'Ukasha's address in al-'Abbasiyya was simply absurd. This is not surprising. A Trickster is meant to be laughed at. As Paul Radin's classic study of the Trickster put it:

> Laughter, humour and irony permeate everything Trickster does. The reaction of the audience in aboriginal societies to both him and his exploits is prevailingly one of laughter tempered by awe. There is no reason for believing this is secondary or a late development. Yet it is difficult to say whether the audience is laughing at him, at the tricks he plays on others, or at the implications his behaviour and activities have for them. (Radin 1956, x)

Accordingly, 'Ukasha has been the butt of much mockery. On his Pharaohs channel his occasional guests as well as a regular female sidekick named Hayat al-Dardiri, who sometimes prompted his lengthy monologues with brief questions, consistently referred to him adoringly as "Dr. 'Ukasha." 'Ukasha's bio on the website of a postrevolution political party he cofounded with the late Tal'at al-Sadat (Anwar al-Sadat's nephew)[11] claimed that he obtained a PhD in "media institution management" from Lakeford University in Bradenton, Florida ("Taufiq Yahya Ibrahim 'Ukasha" 2012). Numerous self-appointed internet investigators have pointed out that no such institution exists.[12] In 'Ukasha's campaign in the first postrevolution parliamentary election for a seat in a district of the delta province of Daqahliyya, his detractors claimed that he received only nine votes.

Video clips of 'Ukasha's most ridiculous statements are legion. In one he warns of a Masonic plot that will unfold on "13/13/13" (the thirteenth day of the thirteenth month of the year 2013). A technician speaks to 'Ukasha through an earpiece, alerting him to his mistake. 'Ukasha spends three minutes stumbling through a contorted explanation of how he meant "thirteen nights in the year 2013." Another heavily circulated 'Ukasha video asserts that Mohamed El Baradei, former director general of the International Atomic Energy Agency and a key figure in Egyptian revolutionary politics, should not be allowed to be president unless he knows whether a peasant woman fattens the male duck for the market, and how she does it; he should also know the price of a male goose in the Tuesday and Thursday local markets, and the price of cow manure.

For the liberal urban intelligentsia 'Ukasha's manner of speech was ridiculous. At the moment I was at the demonstration in Midan al-'Abbasiyya, across town in Midan al-Tahrir Rami 'Isam, known as the heavy-metal troubadour of the revolution, stood on a stage singing a song about "'Uksha"—a derogatory diminutive of "'Ukasha"—to a gleeful audience:

> Move your meaty face on the screen and cut the crap, 'Uksha
> Hey, broadcasting on your own dime, you king of the duck pen,
>   'Uksha
> Hey, really short dick [member] from among the dicks of the
>   committee, 'Uksha[13]
> In his hands the cow lays eggs and the rooster goes and makes cheese,
>   'Uksha
> Hey, boss of al-'Abbasiyya, which was disgraced by you 'Uksha
> He's a one-man case; put on your pants and hide your shame 'Uksha
> What drug are you on 'Ukasha? It's put you in a bad way
> Your bloat fills the screen, your double chin needs a porter ('Isam
>   2011)

'Ukasha's physicality also drew both attention and laughter (see figure 9.4). Tricksters are often grotesque figures. In Native American culture the Trickster

FIGURE 9.4. Facebook cartoons mocking Taufiq ʿUkasha. From 2011 and 2012.

FIGURE 9.4. (*continued*)

"possesses intestines wrapped around his body, and an equally long penis, like-wise wrapped around his body with his scrotum on top of it" (Radin 1956, x). Television could never accommodate such fantastical imagery, but grotesquery appropriate to the historical and social contingencies of 'Ukasha's medium comes across in his on-screen mannerisms. For example, in one show he played the politician in a kind of mafia don register, apologizing for coming late to a program because he had to deal with saboteurs from the Hizb al-Thaura Mus-tamirra (the "revolution continues," a postrevolution youth party), who stole his election campaign posters in the delta town of al-Mansura. Glowering at the camera, he speaks in a low threatening voice:

> I want to say to them: you're like my children, and you're new to elec-tions. . . . Don't do this thing again, because there are people who filmed you on their mobile phones, and we have the pictures, so if you do that again perhaps . . . someone will hang you by your legs on Kubri Talha. My words are clear.

Often accused (and frequently sued) for incitement to violence, in the next instant 'Ukasha would flash an impish grin, revealing his gapped front teeth and dimples. His hands were in constant motion as he spoke. He was remark-ably mobile for a television presenter. In one heavily parodied video he pauses in midsentence, pulls out a tissue, and loudly blows his nose on air,[14] typical of his exaggerated on-screen physicality. He and his cohost on *Egypt Today*, the voluptuous forty-something Hayat al-Dardiri, often went through long inter-ludes of faux emotional disclosure, expounding on the social difficulties caused by their uncompromising commitment to speaking truth, or the physical and financial toll taken by keeping the station operating in the face of the many plots against them.

But there was more to him than physical comedy. Grotesque as he may have been, 'Ukasha's Trickster was not free-floating or "unbound." One might think of him as a deformed latter-day effendi. The term "effendi" is anachronistic in contemporary Egypt, still used ironically but stripped of its specific sociological referents from earlier generations. In historical writing "effendi" is often a gloss for "middle class" from the late nineteenth century up to the seizure of power by the Free Officers in 1952. But it was a more complex term in the sense that it mediated between other social categories—upper and lower class, as the "middle class" gloss suggests, but also rural/urban, traditional/modern, and in some circumstances Egyptian/foreign.[15] The notion of Tricksters as mediators comes from Lévi-Strauss (1963, 224–27), who noted that in Native North American mythology Tricksters were usually assigned the form of ravens or coyotes.[16] If we translate Lévi-Strauss's structuralist "mythic thought" into poststructuralist terms—rejecting the essential quality of binary oppositions between identifiable things, and focusing instead on the underlying historical and epistemological assumptions of how systems of difference are constituted as systems of open variations—then we can see modern Egyptian mythic thought as simply a product of modern storytelling, or discourse if one wants to put it in Foucauldian terminology. Broadly speaking, in Egyptian mass-mediated popular culture—films, fictional writing, and later television seri-als—the most intensive narrative work almost always focuses on mediating figures, either the effendi or upper-class characters who mediate (often less positively) between the categories of Egyptian and foreign. This is where the resolution of problems raised in fictional plots occurs.[17]

To a considerable degree the mediational qualities of the term "effendi" were simply updated and labeled differently after it fell out of use after 1952. "Middle class" as an average income means almost nothing in Egypt, and pos-sibly the same point can be made about the use of the term anywhere. But as a formulation of social capitals, "being in the middle" still means reckoning one's position with respect to a series of historically inflected binaries: modern and traditional, university educated versus illiterate, a salaried employee (*mu-wazzaf*) versus day laborers or precariously employed in the informal economy, "secular" versus "pious," "properly pious" versus "Islamist," a suit-wearing man versus a galabiyya-wearing man. All these could be attached to different forms of expertise attached to the broad rubric of "middle class": the businessman, the media professional, the adept politician. 'Ukasha could and did insert him-self between all these binaries, playing the perverted effendi to his critics while attracting the ears and eyes of the less politically committed.

A Dangerous Man

I never attempted to interview 'Ukasha, as it seemed possibly dangerous to do so. Beginning in December he had begun to devote prodigious energy to de-nouncing American-funded democracy and human rights NGOs. The anti-NGO campaign resulted in the issuance of warrants for the arrest of forty-three of their personnel, including twenty Americans.[18] 'Ukasha's program had a field day with the NGO crisis, gleefully displaying document after docu-ment given to him by the military "proving" that American-funded NGOs were directing the revolution from the start. Some of the documents may have been authentic. For example, on his December 26 program 'Ukasha displayed a document allegedly taken in the NGO raids, from the Human Rights De-fenders Fund, an Israeli NGO that provided legal aid to Palestinians, and operated only in the West Bank, Gaza, and the Negev.[19] Following that he showed a form purporting to show Ahmed Maher (one of the founders of the revolutionary April 6 Movement) applying for a grant from them. Then he moved on to show documents pertaining to organizations that certainly were operating in Egypt. These include the National Endowment for Democracy and the Middle East Partnership Initiative, which 'Ukasha alleged were funded by the CIA. He paused over an NGO-funded training program in

Syracuse University. The documents stated that participants were supposed to be fluent in English. He sneered that the Egyptians on this program obviously lied about their English and stumbled elaborately over a labored mispronunciation of "Syracuse" in order to establish his own credentials as a non-English speaker (a tactic he employed constantly to burnish his nativist credentials, despite also claiming to have received a PhD in an American university). Then he went back to the original document by the Human Rights Defenders Fund, which was supposedly funded by the American Israel Public Affairs Committee (AIPAC), which he said "owns 75 percent of the one hundred largest companies in the United States." Hence the NGOs raided by the military in December were neatly tied to the CIA, AIPAC, Israel, and the April 6 Movement. "Bil-mustanadat!" (supported by documents), as 'Ukasha often proclaimed triumphantly.

My own circumstances precluded writing anything like a conventional ethnography on 'Ukasha, by which I mean a long-term study based in a bounded field site.[20] In 2012 one might have identified an " 'Ukasha site," for example in delta towns, where he was presumed to be influential; or a counter-'Ukasha society among Islamists, who loathed him; or a semiclandestine 'Ukasha-phile society among Mubarakist fulul. However, 'Ukasha's rise was extremely rapid. One might be fortunate to be in the right place at the right time, but on the whole 'Ukasha's moment(s) were likely to have ended too quickly to organize a conventional field site.

The constraints of my circumstances were not unusual, or necessarily crippling. Much anthropological writing is based on serendipitous experience or simply happens well outside the boundaries set by grant applications. A field site always "enables certain kinds of knowledge while blocking off others, authorizes some objects of study and methods of analysis while excluding others" (Gupta and Ferguson 1997, 4).[21] In my case circumstances dictated that I could not have a field site in depth, but my presence, in the context of 'Ukasha's growing ubiquity, still gave me a site in breadth.

I found that asking people directly about 'Ukasha elicited indexical responses, rather like asking about Gamal 'Abd al-Nasir, who is both a political icon and a social litmus test. "What do you think about 'Ukasha" indexed the revolution: for or against; Islamist or not Islamist. But if fieldwork requires one to be attentive to the "buzz of implication" in daily life (Dresch and James 2000, 9), the aside from 'Ukasha's polarizing indexicality, the buzz around him came through at varying volumes and social scales. As time went by I found I no longer had to solicit opinions on 'Ukasha.

The "buzz" about 'Ukasha was accompanied by a growing realization that he could be dangerous. 'Ukasha clearly had connections to military and security personnel, many of whom operated clandestinely. Foreign researchers (and in different ways Egyptian researchers as well) can hardly conduct research in a military or security forces milieu, with which an " 'Ukasha field site" might very well intersect. Moreover, the clandestine presence of the military and security forces steadily expanded. This was underlined for me when a close friend (a foreigner) decided that he wanted to support the protestors directly. He went to sit-ins and started talking to people he did not know, striking up surprisingly easy friendships with a couple of "activists" who described themselves as hard-core revolutionaries. My friend's new acquaintances used him as a means to gain entry to a location known as a gathering place for antiregime activists. Once they had joined the circle of conversation, the spies (instantly recognized as such by the activists) proceeded to loudly advocate using firearms against the military, trying unsuccessfully to draw others into supporting violence. Taking up arms against the military would have been suicidal and was not something real activists ever espoused.

In 'Ukasha's program, from late 2012 to the election of Muhammad Morsy in June 2012 (after which President Morsy swiftly took 'Ukasha off the air for several months), conspiracy against Egypt by the United States was a major theme. American policy toward Egypt deserves severe criticism, but 'Ukasha's rhetoric actually directed attention far away from important matters such as American pressure to enact economic liberalization agendas, or the securing of Israel's security through America's extremely close relationship with the Egyptian military. That was the last thing 'Ukasha wanted to draw attention to in 2011 and 2012. Consequently the gist of 'Ukasha's programs centered on dark allegations about the intentions of the United States, or American-Israel plans to divide Egypt into warring cantons, or the notion that the entire January 25 Revolution was organized at the tactical level by American spies in the country for the purpose of "destroying Egypt."

On some occasions such sentiments emerged as policy. Early in the revolution, long before 'Ukasha became prominent, the regime ratcheted up foreign conspiracy rhetoric to a deafening volume. Foreigners were rounded up by the army on my street. Cars found to be carrying foreigners were searched for evidence that the passengers were journalists, and many were detained.[22] This lasted only a few days, after which it appears that new orders were issued, and the detentions ceased.[23] Aside from official policy, 'Ukasha often made strenuous efforts to burnish his own credentials by aggressively calling for attention from prominent foreigners. On one occasion 'Ukasha got wind that the American op-ed columnist Thomas Friedman was in Cairo. He lavished a large portion of his January 15, 2012, show on Friedman, identifying him as the author of *The Clash of Civilizations* (presumably he meant *The World Is Flat*, or maybe *The Lexus and the Olive Tree*). 'Ukasha's monologue on Friedman is a good illustration of why one would not have wanted to draw his attention:

> The electronic media corrupts peoples and nations [*umam*] because its goal is that there should be a rupture between people, and that there should not be groups or leaders or cadres—this isn't me talking, not me

at all; it's Thomas L. Friedman, the American Jewish journalist who writes and participates in the forming of American political strategies, and who was trained by the Center for Strategic Studies of the Middle East, and he's in Egypt now. I say to him, to Thomas L. Friedman, who's in Egypt now, and I say to the Memri Center—the Center of Middle Eastern Media Studies—I say to them, I wish Ustaz ["professor"][24] Thomas L. Friedman would call me, as he's called some other people; I wish he'd call me, and I wish I could know his address and his phone number so that I could call him so that he might receive me in the US and we could fulfill our obligations, as I hosted him here in Egypt ten or eleven years ago. I affirm again . . . and I say to *al-akh al-fadil* ["the distinguished brother"—sarcastically]—and he is, by the way, a serious man; as a media man I have to respect him, regardless of his ideas, but he has to be respected; he's a professional, and also a political professional, and he's among the political journalists who I . . . don't respect, but follow, and pay attention to how he uses media to fashion policy and to fashion a regional and global order, and how they use journalism to forge the political strategies of the most powerful state in the world. That's clear, it's true; we have to make it clear to people. That's Thomas L. Friedman, American, of the Jewish religion, and who also has a strong relationship with AIPAC, the American Zionist organization, indeed, is one of their most important thinkers. That is what he does. It's no shame. We also have people involved in similar activities, like the revolutionary socialists, or the anarchists, and those people, you know; we also have people like that. Does that mean we'll throw them [away]? No. In the end they're Egyptians. Either we open a dialogue with them so that we can rebuild their ideas and refashion their thoughts, and open up a scientific dialogue, an objective one tied to documents, and evidence and support, or we just renounce them. My personal opinion? No, we shouldn't let them be. We have to open a dialogue with them; we have to talk with them. A group of their audience has to participate in the political thought and philosophy—pay attention, I'm going to say it now—the Egyptian political and social philosophy, and not an Arabization.

I am, of course, not a public figure and would not expect to get the same treatment. Friedman, of course, does indeed support US political and economic hegemony and certainly is a supporter of Israel and Zionism (see Fernández 2011). In the hands of an 'Ukasha he came wrapped in elaborate packages of conspiracy, mixed sometimes with fact and sometimes outright fantasy. But it was a quite wide-ranging stance, not at all restricted to only broadsides volleyed at the most prominent American targets. For example, here is 'Ukasha on the division of the Sudan into two countries in 2011 just before the outbreak of the revolution in Egypt: "This is the birth pangs of the second stage of the Sykes-Picot agreement, and of course at the same time serves the Masonic idea to establish a world government next to the Egyptian pyramids" (from his December 18, 2011, episode). Or on another occasion, his February 9, 2012, episode, he gave a rambling accusation of a Jewish plot to engineer a decline in the population of Germany:

> I'm saying this to the Jews. I'm saying, "brothers, don't lie to yourselves." You've now played with the demography of Germany as much as you can. You've received an order to make the Germans hate marriage, so that there's no children. But what's happening today in Germany? Since exactly five years ago? They're marrying like crazy [*al-zawaag zayy al-saruukh*—"marriage like a rocket"]. And having tons of kids. In Germany. Today. You're following me? If they [the Jews] had succeeded . . . if they had made Germans hate marriage, the population of Germany would stay the same, like France.

But one should also not forget that taking such loopy passages out of context understates 'Ukasha's effectiveness as a propagandist. His program could spin public opinion. For example, the country was rocked by images broadcast on December 18, 2011 (just before the al-'Abbasiyya demonstration described above), of soldiers dragging a female protestor on the ground, and exposing her body as one of them stomped on her exposed stomach. It became known as the "dragged woman" case (*al-fatat al-mashula*) or sometimes in English the case of the "blue bra" woman. The prorevolution newspaper *al-Tahrir* emblazoned the image on the paper's front page two days in a row. When I saw it on the second day I commented on it to the newspaper vendor on my street corner, and he replied sourly, "It's because they're really proud of it." We chatted about the incident, and I was taken aback by his rejection of what seemed a clear affront on the citizenry by the military. He thought the whole thing was fake. Perhaps not uncoincidentally, the moment the video of the woman being dragged and stomped went viral 'Ukasha's program had vigorously hammered against the credibility of the image, claiming that it had been staged by a *taraf talit* (hidden hand—literally "third party") to discredit the military.[25]

In the "dragged woman" case there was no direct link between my newspaper vendor and 'Ukasha. In another case 'Ukasha clearly put a fabricated narrative into circulation. This was a story in late April 2011 that the Islamist-dominated People's Assembly was debating a "law of intercourse" (*qanun al-mudaja'a*) making it legal for a man to have sex with a deceased wife for six hours after her death. The story spread widely and was picked up by the foreign press. Probably the origin of the story was a fatwa by an incendiary Moroccan shaykh named 'Abd al-Bari' al-Zamzami ("'Asifat Ghadab" 2012). The notion that the People's Assembly was debating adapting such a law was

attributed to an editorial in *al-Ahram* published on April 24 ('Abd al-Sami'
2012). But the source of the story was actually 'Ukasha, from his April 16
program:

> I'm really scared of this guy [Muhammad al-Katatni, the Muslim
> Brotherhood Speaker of the parliament] who's a member of the People's
> Assembly, who went to the parliament when the people elected him in
> order to tell you [about] "farewell intercourse" [*mudaga'at al-wida'*].
> Farewell intercourse. By God you're right. Can you imagine that I wasn't
> aware of that? I read about it in the foreign press, and I still didn't fol-
> low it. So I went back and checked and found that it was true. I mean,
> [there's] someone who considers that it's part of the parliament's busi-
> ness to allow, by law—you see?—to permit by law, to make a law, called
> "The Law of Farewell Sex." What does a "Law of Farewell Sex" mean? It
> means that when a wife dies it's the right of the husband to "be with
> her" as a husband for six hours after her soul has ascended to her cre-
> ator. Oh my God! These are the problems of the Islamic nation [*al-
> umma al-Islamiyya*]. These are the problems of Muslim men. [his
> voice rises; his face contorts] The problem of Muslim men is "farewell
> sex"! God is greater! I don't understand this.

Although both Arab and foreign papers carried the story, the lie was recognized within a few days. Even the British tabloid the *Daily Mail* eventually
published a recantation ("Egypt's 'Plans'" 2012). But very few of the many
articles and blog posts tracing the history of the story recognized that the liar
was actually 'Ukasha.[26]

Taufiq 'Ukasha, Seriously

As the previous examples show, there is more to 'Ukasha (or to a Trickster)
than laughter. A Trickster is productive, even if unintentionally. A Trickster
provokes "laughter tempered by awe," as Radin put it (1956, x). In a liminal
crisis the tipping point between laughter and awe is precisely where the Trickster becomes dangerous: "the perfect scene for different sorts of self-
proclaimed ceremony masters who claim to 'have seen the future,' but who in
reality establish their own position by perpetuating liminality and by empty-
ing the liminal moment from real creativity" (Thomassen 2012, 699).

It was easy to literally see the laughter because it left copious textual evidence on the internet. The people who were listening but not laughing left far
fewer traces. Outside virtual space, in the actual world, the prominence of
'Ukasha became palpable. From at least December 2011 comments on 'Ukasha
were constantly in my peripheral hearing—frustratingly so; I rarely caught the
full content of strangers' conversations in public spaces. It was always snatches
of "did you hear what 'Ukasha said," or "'Ukasha will go nuts when he hears

about this," said by passersby. Every time I mentioned to Egyptian friends (by and large secular and left-leaning) that I was interested in writing about ʿUkasha, they smiled, often assuring me in more serious tones that he was influential, specifically among the lower-middle-class and rural people that *Egypt Today* obviously targeted, and who ʿUkasha himself repeatedly said were his "silent majority" supporters. Some people who followed him probably would not admit it. One day when I was talking politics with my staunchly antirevolution landlord he started repeating ʿUkasha's talking points—leftists allied with Muslim Brothers trying to overthrow the state, and all of them pawns of outside forces. When I said "you sound just like ʿUkasha" he strenuously denied having watched his program.

I did meet a hard-core ʿUkasha fan—a wildcat taxi driver in an unmarked 1970s vintage Fiat, who picked me up in Fagala, where I was buying a toilet for one of our apartments just before Morsy was elected. He claimed to be a former air force plane mechanic, who subsequently worked in the civil aviation sector until he was laid off because they preferred hiring younger mechanics. The revolution, he said, had wrecked (*kharrabit*) the nation. That made me sit up and take notice, as *takhrib*—vandalism, wrecking—was one of ʿUkasha's most commonly voiced accusations against revolutionary activists. My driver then let it slip that ʿUkasha was indeed his favorite political commentator. "Why do you watch ʿUkasha," I asked? "Because he is the only man on television who tells the truth." I questioned ʿUkasha's veracity, suggesting that he was in politics for his own gain. "Why? He has no self-interest. Taufiq ʿUkasha isn't trying to make money or get a political position. I am certain that he has very close relations to SCAF—people in the military have told me this. But he acts only out of love for Egypt."

By the period leading up to the presidential elections (late spring 2012) ʿUkasha simply became the public face of an antirevolution and anti–Muslim Brotherhood coalition—separate constituencies but of numerical significance. Doubtless for some ʿUkasha was a strange bedfellow, but the degree to which he had stamped his name on a political position was nonetheless remarkable. In the tense days before the announcement of the winner of the presidential election hundreds of thousands of pro-Shafik protestors congregated in Madinat Nasr at the Minassa, the memorial where Sadat was killed by Islamists in 1981—obviously a highly significant location for an anti–Muslim Brotherhood demonstration. The immense numbers, albeit bolstered by bussing supporters in from the provinces (as the Muslim Brotherhood also had to do to achieve a respectable-looking demonstration), were considered to be ʿUkasha's achievement. At a rally in Tahrir Square the day before the announcement I heard Muhammad Beltagi, secretary of the Muslim Brotherhood's Freedom and Justice Party, whip up the crowd by telling them that "rumors have been put out by Shafkasha [an amalgam of Ahmad Shafiq and ʿUkasha] that April 6 [i.e., activists of the mostly secular April 6 Movement who had openly supported

Morsy's candidacy against Shafiq] has withdrawn from the square. This is a lie! They are still here with us!"

For me the most telling sign of 'Ukasha's prominence came a bit after the presidential race was settled. A group of three carpenters were working in one of my apartments. One mentioned that Omar Suleiman, a former chief of Egypt's General Intelligence Service and himself briefly a presidential candidate, had died. One of the others had not yet heard and was shocked. The third replied, "wi Mursy ta'ban kaman" ([Muhammad] Morsy is also sick). The first carpenter laughed and said, "wi hatshuf—Taufiq 'Ukasha bardu hayitla' ta'ban" (you'll see, Taufiq 'Ukasha will also turn out to be sick). It was not exactly a ringing endorsement for "Ukasha's politics; indeed, it was more an expression of skepticism toward politics generally. But it was incredible that 'Ukasha, practically unknown a year ago, had gotten into a conversation about candidates for the Egyptian presidency. The Trickster had managed to put himself in rarified company indeed. Surely the tipping point between laughter and awe had been passed.

Conclusion

Observing the rise of Taufiq 'Ukasha from the middle of 2011 to the middle of 2012 was a bit like watching the birth of Adolf Hitler or of Donald Trump: a Trickster seemingly coming from nowhere, suddenly no longer a laughing-stock; suddenly frighteningly real. As far as his own professed political ambitions went, 'Ukasha's little Hitler proved to have been stillborn. That was my assumption when I left Egypt in August 2012. It proved correct four years later, when 'Ukasha, a newly minted parliamentarian under Sisi, got himself expelled for making unauthorized contacts with, ironically, the Israeli ambassador ("Bil-Suwwar" 2016; "Isqat 'Adawiyyat 'Ukasha" 2016). But upon my departure in 2012 I thought he had crested in June, at the time of the near-election of Ahmad Shafiq.

But when I returned to Cairo for a brief visit six months later, in February 2013, I was not so sure. I found myself in an Egyptian Weimar. The cities were seething with anger at the Muslim Brotherhood. Violent clashes were occurring every day between supporters and opponents of the government, and the security forces appeared to have adopted a calculated paralysis. Prices were shooting up, employment was plummeting, and everyone knew the country was on the precipice of far worse economic pain. I heard nostalgia for the Mubarak era expressed openly by people who had been ambivalent or prorevolution for the first time since the beginning of 2011. Many were also calling openly for the army to return to power and oust the Muslim Brotherhood. In a week I spoke to as many people as I could. Moods were swinging from deep despair at *ikhwanat al-daula* (brotherhood-ization of the state) to giddy optimism that the "totalitarian project" of the Muslim Brotherhood, as Faruq al-

Masry, my university professor friend, described it to me, was in utter ruins and could never revive. The one thread that united every person I spoke to was rage against the United States for selling the country out to the Muslim Brotherhood. It sounded like an echo of German rage against the Versailles Treaty following World War I.

In a café I talked to some friends. One was a filmmaker working on a documentary about baltagiyya (thugs—hired muscle paid by political warlords).[27] Part of his task was to try to trace where the money came from, a very frustrating endeavor because the trail always seemed to just peter out before he could figure out the real source(s). 'Ukasha, as one of the potential sources for hiring baltagiyya, was a person of interest for him. When I explained my theory that 'Ukasha had peaked in Shafiq's failed campaign for the presidency he strongly disagreed. "Watch what happens in the next two or three months," he said, suggesting that 'Ukasha would be officially "brought in" to a governing apparatus for whatever organization he was working with, probably military intelligence.

Comparisons with Weimar and the rise of Hitler aside, the rise of Taufiq 'Ukasha powerfully instantiated revolution as liminal crisis. To some extent a sudden collapse of familiar sociopolitical anchors resembled what political scientists and sociologists call a "revolutionary situation," which "splits a regime into two or more blocs, each one controlling some significant segment of state power and/or territory, and receiving significant popular support" (Tilly 2006, 160). In this vein 'Ukasha could be seen as an appendage of one player among "contenders or coalitions of contenders advancing exclusive competing claims to control of the state or some segment of it" (Tilly 2006, 159). But was he? Such a view gives little scope for understanding him as an autonomous agent, and in the ominous atmosphere of Egypt in early 2013, one could not help wondering whether SCAF may have needed 'Ukasha more than he needed them.

As many scholars who conjure with in-between states have shown, liminality is culturally productive. Uncontained liminality is also dangerous. "In the liminal period we see naked, unaccommodated man, whose nonlogical character issues in various modes of behavior: destructive, creative, farcical, ironic, energetic, suffering, lecherous, submissive, defiant, but always unpredictable" (Turner 1968, 580). In a state of liminality so protracted that no end to it can be imposed or agreed on, beings at home in liminality flourish. 'Ukasha-as-Trickster was both a buffoon and a "culture-hero": a mythological being who "embodies all possibilities—the most positive and the most negative—and is paradox personified" (Babcock-Abrahms 1975, 148). Obviously such a description applied to 'Ukasha seems unspeakably grandiose, but the point is not so much his capacity to produce anything as it is the audacity of his self-presentation and his ability to move listeners, and possibly even turn them into followers. In 2011 I chuckled at 'Ukasha's exhortations on his December 21

Egypt Today program to turn out for his al-'Abbasiyya demonstration: "Millions, millions by God's will, will go out on the 'day of crossing,' . . . this nation, with its people crosses to security, to liberty, to building a civilization for the twenty-first century! An Egyptian civilization! That the Egyptian people will build! In the twenty-first century by God's will!" In fact only a few thousand police and their families turned out. But then a little more than a year later, in a Skype conversation with a journalist friend in Egypt, I was told, *"ya duktur,* people are listening to him. Not just farmers anymore. All kinds of people in the cities. Millions of them. The things he predicted are coming true!"

A bit later, when Sisi came to power, 'Ukasha styled himself *mufaggir al-thaura*—"the igniter of the revolution," by which he meant the demonstrations that initiated and confirmed Sisi's coup in the summer of 2013. In August of that year 'Ukasha's Pharaohs station broadcast a "report" claiming that throughout Egypt's history at all the most fateful moments alliances between two men had been formed to save Egypt: Moses and Harun (the biblical Aaron—Harun in the Quran, Salah al-Din al-Ayubi and 'Isa al-'Awwam,[28] al-Zahir Baybars and Sayf al-Din Qutuz,[29] 'Umar Makram and Muhammad 'Ali,[30] Sa'd Zaghlul and Makram 'Ubayd,[31] Nasser and Muhammad Naguib, and "the two men of this age" General 'Abd al-Fattah al-Sisi and *al-i'lami* Taufiq 'Ukasha ("Taqrir Qanat al-Maganin" 2013). As usual, opponents of 'Ukasha laughed. By 2016 the best-quality videos of the "report" that could be found online had been uploaded by his detractors and labeled as the "report of the station of the crazies" (*taqrir qanat al-maganin*). Despite 'Ukasha's election to parliament two years later, the incredible bombast of the "two men report" (a media production worthy of Donald Trump) was the beginning of the end for him, but not necessarily because the public was no longer heeding the call of the Trickster; rather because Sisi's brand of Tricksterism was far more potent and certainly could never share a stage with anyone else.

'Ukasha could not successfully will himself into being as a permanent political force. He had backers and allies with prosaic political agendas carried out in a field of political contention (as Hitler did, one remembers). But he did instantiate a process that may be common in revolutions and, intriguingly, other periods of extreme sociopolitical confusion, in which political Tricksters potentially gain real power. By a few years after the January 25 Revolution the entire world felt like the Weimar Republic in 1931. The triumph of "Brexit" in the United Kingdom and the capture of a major US political party by Donald Trump—a textbook Trickster if there ever was one—plus an ominous rise of right-wing political figures throughout Europe and much of the rest of the world (the Turkish Erdoğan immediately comes to mind) leaves one with a suspicion that what happened in Egypt was hastened by a revolutionary catalyst, but at the same time structured by global precarity. The notion of Trickster politics discussed here help us to bring a widespread, if locally nuanced, "age of the Trickster" into focus. Liminal crisis can be the result both of sudden rupture and of long-term structures. Absent an awareness of the reality and danger of liminality, we tend to have an ocular problem with both the rupture and the structure—we simply cannot see them, analytically speaking. The rise of the political Trickster is by no means exclusive of other factors such as the economic distress, political contention between formal organizations, ideology, or the organizational capacity of social movements. Neither do such factors, by themselves or in concert, explain the rise of an 'Ukasha very well. He is a denizen of the revolutionary void, and a void pregnant with both destructive and creative potential is what a revolution is. But in the Age of the Trickster, revolutionary liminality may also be "the new normal."

CHAPTER 10

A New Normal?

THE IRON FIST AND THE FALSE PROMISE

Khalluni aakul khara. Wi dilwa'ti yi'ulu lazim akammilluh?
They made me eat shit. And now they say I have to finish *it?*

—Reaction of a university professor to the notion that Muhammad
Morsy should have been allowed to finish his term in office

THE GENESIS OF THE SCHISM from which 'Abd al-Fattah al-Sisi emerged
came more with a whimper than with a bang.[1] The series of dramatic events
in 2013—a mass demonstration against the president, a coup, a series of massacres—seemed a continuation of the dramatic events of the previous two
years. Until the Rab'a Massacre in August, it was hard to put one's finger on a
single event that functioned as a door to the threshold between revolution and
a new normal. And yet the schism and the new normal beyond it had already
happened before the massacre.

At first I was reluctant to call what happened in the summer of 2013 a coup
d'état, partly because I initially did not believe that the revolution was really
over, and partly in response to the indignant policing of foreigners' comments
on those events by many Egyptian elites determined to cast Sisi's actions as a
necessary response to an existential threat posed by the Muslim Brotherhood.
Moreover, while I was taken aback by the rapid conversion of some academics
who had welcomed the revolution into apologists for a new military regime, I
agreed with them, to a degree, that the statements of American and European
politicians on Egyptian events could not be taken at face value. In this respect
I was ultimately right, though for the wrong reasons. The problem was not that
American and European officials were too willing to ignore the nuances of
Egyptian politics and jump on the coup bandwagon. It was rather that the
same governments, which initially tut-tutted about coups and democracy, very
quickly turned toward a nauseating normalization of an authoritarian regime.

All official talk of a coup was quickly swept under the rug, as Western governments embraced the Sisi regime.

But aside from the dynamics of high politics and elite apologetics, the events of 2013, culminating in the Rab'a Massacre, crystallized a truly schismogenetic moment in Egyptian politics and society. The character of social interaction, as well as the emotional and ethical practices of the postrevolution generation, were all altered by it. The Rab'a Massacre in particular constitutes a litmus test of political orientation as potent as the Nasser era had been for previous generations. One can justify the massacre and the ensuing cycle of violence it initiated, or one can condemn it. But nobody can have it both ways, and the opposed positions on it are mutually generative. This is not to say that Egyptians have necessarily come to terms with Rab'a and the political order it initiated. It cannot be openly talked about, written about, or mass mediated outside the private circulation of images and videos on the internet, and even these are increasingly blocked within Egypt by filtering protocols. But the violence of 2013 has nonetheless become part of a new political system. The system cannot persist without it.

Nonetheless, in Egypt during 2013 prior to Rab'a, aside from anti–Muslim Brotherhood propaganda, and political manipulation of the anti-Islamist opposition by the military and the old regime, the schismogenetic moment had not yet crystallized. Liminality was still the primary ground on which politics were practiced. An urge to oppose Mohammad Morsy was in fact widespread and genuine, and the fluidity of the months leading up to the massacre made it possible to express both opposition and support for the brotherhood. For non-Islamists there were valid reasons for considering whatever social contract might have existed between Morsy and the voters to have been abrogated by his and the brotherhood's actions during that one year. By the summer of 2013 it had, nonetheless, become quite difficult to disentangle the case against the Muslim Brotherhood that was speculative and fed by propaganda from that which was based on what the Muslim Brotherhood had actually done.

Some of the reasons for overthrowing Morsy were easy to dismiss. The notion that he was destroying the economy, for example. He simply was not in office long enough to have done very much for or against the economy, nor had he expressed any reservations against the free-market orthodoxy that his critics espoused. There was also great alarm at what Muslim Brotherhood rule would mean for freedom of expression. But while suspicion at Morsy's motives was not necessarily unjustified, it was still mainly speculative. The will to suppress freedom of expression may have been part of the collective ethos of the brotherhood, but the means to do so were never in Morsy's hands. And again, the damage Morsy did to freedom was a drop in the bucket compared to what Sisi did once he came to power. Certainly freedom to openly criticize the executive branch of government was never greater than in the Morsy year, whether or not this is what he intended.

Other objections to Muslim Brotherhood rule were more substantive, but still debatable. Faruq al-Masry, my university professor neighbor, expressed concern at an armed insurrection simmering in Sinai, described by anti-Islamists straightforwardly as "terrorism" connected to the Palestinian Hamas movement, and later to the Islamic State. Since Hamas was widely assumed to be an offshoot of the Muslim Brotherhood, Morsy's critics conflated the two organizations unreflectively, particularly after Sisi took power, though the narrative was already taking shape during the Morsy era. Muhammad al-Beltagi, a high-level Muslim Brotherhood figure, had poured oil on the fire of that rumor by declaring during the Raba'a sit-in after Morsy's overthrow that peace would come to Sinai only once Morsy was restored to the presidency. But there was no way to be certain that his statement was anything more than bravado.[2] No independent journalists were allowed to report from Sinai, hence whatever was known publicly was filtered through the security forces and military and hence patently unreliable. Not even the government was trying to claim that attacks in Sinai were targeting civilians, as one might expect when the label "terrorism" is applied. On the contrary, there were many rumors of heavy-handed Egyptian military tactics that resulted in civilian casualties. Moreover, the local population of north Sinai, where the violence was occurring, had economic grievances that might well have made them receptive to outside insurgency forces—Hamas, and then the so-called Islamic State once it emerged in the two years after Morsy's fall (Goldberg 2015).

Another constellation of propaganda-fed panic formed around rumors of *ikhwanat al-daula* (Muslim Brotherhood-ization of the state). The brotherhood and its supporters justified this as the rightful claiming of electoral spoils. Faruq and others I knew who were working in cultural institutions talked resentfully and cynically about ikhwanat al-daula as an existential threat. A man who worked for *Akhbar al-Adab*, a popular weekly literary magazine, told me that his new boss was not a member of the Muslim Brotherhood, but was *muta'akhwin* ("quasi-Ikhwan," essentially a sympathizer). "They want to 'brotherhood-ize' everything, but they don't have enough trained cadres. So they're appointing *mi'arrasin* [pimps]."[3] Ultimately Egypt was a highly centralized state in which a ruling party could hardly do anything *but* appoint its own trusted officials. A systematic decentralization of the state that would have facilitated sharing power outside whatever party held the presidency was not in the brotherhood's agenda, but neither was it in the agenda of any of the revolutionary forces.

This is not to say there were no real grievances against Morsy. According to Faruq, Morsy's constitutional declaration in November 2013, in which he took dictatorial powers for himself in order to ram through a Muslim Brotherhood–authored constitution, was a point of no return for him and for many others. Morsy restored powers to other branches of government after the constitution was passed, but if he could take dictatorial powers once, he could do it again.

The dangers seemed obvious. Protestors against Morsy's constitutional declaration established a sit-in at the Presidential Palace, quickly resulting in fighting between them and Muslim Brotherhood members. The police stood by passively, resulting in Muslim Brotherhood members on their own detaining and torturing some of the anti-Morsy protestors. This of course confirmed non-Islamists' alarm at the constitutional declaration. As Faruq put it, *that*— the torture carried out by Ikhwan members—even more than the constitution declaration itself, was the beginning of the end for Morsy.

In addition to the constitutional declaration and its aftermath, the other undeniable black mark against the Muslim Brotherhood was that it tolerated and fomented sectarianism. The rise of sectarianism in Egypt was a long-running dynamic, starting at least in the 1970s if not earlier (Abou-El-Fadl 2013; Sedra 2013). But there was no question that Morsy and the Muslim Brotherhood had made a bad situation worse. Morsy could officially disavow any support for violence against Copts, such as a shocking attack in April 2013 on the Coptic cathedral in al-'Abbasiyya at the conclusion of a funeral for Christians killed in an earlier sectarian attack in a northern Egyptian town (R. Abu al-'Aynayn 2013). Police stood by and did nothing, which could be taken as evidence that the president did not want them to intervene (something Morsy denied), or as evidence that the police were trying to undermine the president. But it was harder for Morsy to distance himself from a stadium rally in June 2013 attended by Sunni clerics, including Salafi allies of the Muslim Brotherhood. Morsy announced that Egypt would sever ties with Syria; some of the Salafis called for jihad against Shi'is, which meant, in those circumstances, calling for Egypt to intervene in the Syrian Civil War—a horrifying prospect to many Egyptians, particularly if the intervention was to be on what they regarded as the wrong side, namely jihadists fighting the Asad regime (Tadros 2013a). Subsequently four members of Egypt's very small Shi'i community were lynched. I had on several occasions been surprised by negative reactions of Egyptian interlocutors to any mention of Shi'ism, even though they had never met a Shi'i. Hence I took note when Hisham, from my pro-Mubarak Pyramids Road friends, posted a condemnation of the lynchings on his Facebook wall. A Morsy supporter might still have argued that the Muslim Brotherhood's record on sectarianism while in office was at least ambiguous— that he could have done more, but he did not actively *promote* sectarianism. Nonetheless the explosion of Islamist violence against Christians and churches following Morsy's removal from office definitively crushed any sense of ambiguity (Tadros 2013a; 2013b).

In the end the twin charges of first sectarianism, and then of abusing power through the constitutional declaration, stuck to Morsy like tar. On the basis of these two issues, if I had been an Egyptian citizen, I can hardly imagine myself *not* joining in protests against Muslim Brotherhood rule. These were among the most common reasons that people joined Tamarrud, a campaign to demand the rerunning of presidential elections immediately, notwithstanding the extremely dubious origins of the initiative, of which they were largely unaware.[4] It must still be remembered that Tamarrud was against Morsy and not necessarily for Sisi. Sisi would have to work harder to channel the anti-Morsy sentiment into a pro-him sentiment. In this respect the post-Morsy environment played right into his hands.

Back to Cairo

We returned to Oxford in August 2012, just after Morsy was elected, and came back the next summer. For the first time we were able to live in our now completely renovated apartment in Ma'ruf, not far from Tahrir Square. We were not present for the massive Tamarrud demonstration on June 30 that set the stage for the removal of Morsy on July 3. When we arrived in mid-July it was Ramadan—a somber affair according to friends, because of the depressed economy and political uncertainty. Nonetheless, most people I knew were happy at the apparent demise of the Muslim Brotherhood.

Tahrir was a place of cognitive dissonance. Nobody I knew who considered themselves prorevolution by the standards of the January 25 Revolution frequented Tahrir Square at that time. A friend who lived downtown warned me to stay away on grounds that whoever was there has nothing to do with his revolution. Nonetheless when I did go fairly large and peaceful crowds were present, attending the *iftar*s (fast-breaking meals) that were being laid out each night in the square. This was before the violent breakup of the sit-ins in Rab'a al-'Adawiyya and Nahda Squares. The full-scale criminalization of the Muslim Brotherhood had not yet been declared. Whoever it was in Tahrir, they had the full consent of the military and security forces, who were there in full uniform, including policemen, now treated as heroes. A "no-sexual-harassment" zone had been blocked off by traffic barriers in front of a stage.[5] In open areas on the margins of the square young men on motorcycles, the "cavalry" and ambulances of the pitched battles fought there a year and a half ago, performed wheelies. The scruffy few who were there were treated to performances of poetry read from the stage to the mostly empty space of the "no-harassment zone," and to the crowds standing outside the cordon protecting it. Songs were also played, not live when I was there, but over a powerful loudspeaker, which repeatedly blared a recording of an anti-Ikhwan song by Rami 'Isam. Standing in just about the same spot I had occupied about a year earlier, when I came to see Muhammad Morsy accept the presidency, I took in 'Isam's "al-Ka'in al-Ikhwani," which one could gloss as "The Ikhwan entity" ('Isam 2012):[6]

> An Ikhwan has no place in my midan
> We're the ones who made the revolution, how can he take my place

If we see an Ikhwan coming to us in the midan
His mother's night will be black, he'll go home angry
The Murshid . . . yuck![7]
Morsy . . . yuck![8]
And al-Shatir . . . yuck!
And al-Biltagi . . . yuck!
And al-'Aryan . . . yuck!
And Higazi . . . yuck!

To add to the dissonance, just after "al-Ka'in al-Ikhwani" concluded, a young man on the stage urged people to attend an iftar planned for the next night at Maspero to commemorate the birthday of Mina Daniel, the most prominent activist slaughtered there in October 2011 by the army. The Mina Daniel iftar was announced in exactly the same space where posters glorifying the new SCAF chief 'Abd al-Fattah al-Sisi were being sold, and a few days before vast crowds were to carry these same posters in the demonstration al-Sisi called for explicitly to receive what he called a mandate to suppress the Muslim Brotherhood.

The Maspero Massacre was in fact on many people's minds, because a large number of Islamist protestors had just been killed in fighting when the army broke up a sit-in at the Republican Guard headquarters, where Morsy's supporters believed he was being held just after his removal from office. Revived memories of the Maspero Massacre in that polarized atmosphere, however, were by no means indicative of *sympathy* for the victims of the Republican Guard incident. Indeed, everyone I talked to skated very lightly over what had happened, refusing to label it as an atrocity. On the contrary, Mariyam, a novelist who had been active in the protests against SCAF rule two years previously, was more inclined to view the Republican Guard killings with a large dose of schadenfreude. She joined us for a barbecue a few days after our initial arrival, and during the after-dinner conversation she angrily asserted that Islamists had been extremely unsympathetic to those killed in the Maspero Massacre, even to the point of accusing the activists who were killed at Maspero of provoking the attacks by their own thuggery.[9] The same basic lack of sympathy for the Muslim Brotherhood was common among most people I knew, both those I spoke to in person, and those whose comments I read on social media. Broadcast media, once the pro-Islamist stations had been shut down immediately after Morsy's downfall earlier that month, were openly and much more crudely hostile to the brotherhood.

Across town Islamists were chanting "yasqut hukm al-'askar" in Rab'a al-'Adawiyya Square, just as non-Islamists had from March 2011 to the election of Morsy in 2013. In Tahrir Square posters glorifying SCAF commander and Minister of Defense 'Abd al-Fattah al-Sisi as the presumptive heir to Nasser and Sadat were selling briskly, and elsewhere being given away, paid for by shadowy forces that nobody could quite identify. *Sisi qalb al-asad* (Sisi the lionhearted), or *Sisi qahir al-irhab* (Sisi, conqueror of terrorism) were superimposed over two standard variants of the SCAF commander, one a side shot of him in sunglasses and a jaunty beret, the other of him bare headed looking straight at the camera.

A few days later I visited Hamdi, my book dealer. His father-in-law, 'Amm Husayn, was there. He told me that these were being handed out in 'Ataba where he lived for free. We were sitting and smoking *shisha* (water pipes) in an alley in Bab al-Sha'riyya outside Hamdi's *makhzan*, a warren-like store room probably built originally as a workshop, now crammed with an unbelievable quantity of old magazines and books. 'Amm Husayn claimed to have gone to Rab'a. I was a little bit skeptical that he actually had. The political quasifriction between him and Hamdi was a long-running show, more like a rivalry between fans of different football teams than a true political dispute. But if the personal stakes were low, the difference in opinion was nonetheless real. Hamdi was among the most pro-Mubarak people I knew, and one of the most vehemently anti–Muslim Brotherhood. "The day Muhammad Morsy won the presidential election was the saddest day in my life," he had once told me.

Both Hamdi and 'Amm Husayn himself had patiently and slowly explained to me—apparently to make sure I or anyone else in earshot did not misunderstand an important point—that 'Amm Husayn was *like* a Muslim Brotherhood member, but not an *actual* Ikhwan. From what I had seen of 'Amm Husayn he was nothing like a Muslim Brotherhood member at all. He had worked in Europe at an earlier period in his life, but returned to Egypt, a slightly defeated man with sad and kindly eyes, but still proud of his adventure. He had poor health and no regular job and essentially worked for his son-in-law sorting magazines. 'Amm Husayn was not more obviously interested in piety than any other member of his generally observant family, and certainly not active in any social or political movement. And he played along with the bellicose but good-natured interrogations of American foreign policy that Hamdi put me through whenever I came by. But the delicate explanations of 'Amm Husayn's Muslim Brotherhood sympathies did flag up a sore point, albeit not one of existential importance in the context of their relationship. 'Amm Husayn expounded on the topic of the now-ubiquitous Sisi posters. "Those pictures of Sisi in dark glasses are being distributed because intelligent people can read the dishonesty in his eyes," he told me. I pointed out that in the other standard poster variant of al-Sisi's image, obviously from his youth, he wore no glasses. "But notice that they whitened his skin in that picture," 'Amm Husayn pointed out. He may have been right, or maybe it was just a bad printing job. "Someone is trying to make his image look better," he continued, "but the man can't be trusted. It's not right that he removed Morsy from office" (though I noticed that he carefully refrained from using the inflammatory word *inqilab*—coup). "Morsy was the first elected president in Egypt's history. We have to respect the election, if not the man."

In Tahrir, when I had been there a few days before that conversation, the posters were not being handed out for free. Sisi images, along with others showing dehumanizing images of the Ikhwan, were selling briskly. One of these featured sheep (*khirfan*, the non-Islamists' vicious put-down of members of the Muslim Brotherhood over the year of Morsy's rule—*al-khirfan al-muslimin* rather than *al-ikhwan al-muslimin*) with faces of prominent Muslim Brotherhood members being slaughtered. Another depicted the Muslim Brotherhood's leadership superimposed on the bodies of fat babies drinking from bottles of blood. Nearly identical images had been sold two years ago with the faces of Mubarak regime members.

The broad coalition that favored forcible removal of the Muslim Brotherhood from power, including many people like Hamdi's family who considered themselves pious Muslims, were unapologetic. The notion that Morsy should have been allowed to serve out his term and challenged only through elections was dismissed out of hand. Non-Islamists rejected Muslim Brotherhood and Salafi prowess in elections as the product of vote buying—*sukar wa zayt* (sugar and cooking oil—material support given by Islamists to buy support). Islamist rule was a *sunduqratiyya*, a "ballotocracy," every bit as phony as the fake elections run by Mubarak's National Democratic Party before the revolution. My neighbor Faruq summarized the political atmosphere among non-Islamists succinctly: "They made me eat shit [accede to Morsy's taking the presidency]. And now they say I have to *finish* it?"

The New Binary

Both the June 30 rebellion and the January 25 Revolution had united disparate political forces in fragile opposition to a regime. In 2013 the antiregime coalition was initially somewhat more durable precisely because the Islamists were absent from the spaces in which the non-Islamists congregated to perform their political rituals. Hence the major political rift between rival groups in the period leading up to Morsy's election was simply not there in the summer of 2013. Nonetheless at that point in this new phase of the revolution none of the hard decisions about what would happen next had occurred. While the chasm between Islamists and non-Islamists may have disappeared from the square, plenty of other fissures remained just below the surface, particularly tensions between those who had participated in the January 25 Revolution in 2011, and those who saw the June 30 rebellion in 2013 as vindication of the old regime. This would eventually be cast in the "coup versus revolution" debate, which to some degree simplistically marked the boundary between supporters of either Muhammad Morsy or 'Abd al-Fattah al-Sisi, or a transposed construct of the Muslim Brotherhood against "secular" Egyptians.

In reality of course not all supporters of Morsy were Muslim Brotherhood members or even Islamists, and motivations for supporting Sisi certainly did not exclude piety or grievances that went beyond opposition to the Muslim Brotherhood. But such a stark dividing line did serve to buttress the "war on terror" discourse that has shaped the post-Morsy era more powerfully than anything else. Morsy versus Sisi; Ikhwan versus non-Islamists; you're with us or against us. It was a simple binary code based on a terrifyingly repressive logic.

A joke circulating on Facebook two years later showed the enduring quality of the binary, though also a sense of its frustrating excessiveness. It took the form of a three-panel cartoon commenting on the celebrations that were to take place for the inauguration of the "new Suez Canal" that had been a central element in Sisi's legitimation strategy. Money for a substantial though not unprecedented upgrade to the canal had been raised by selling bonds to the public, and sold as a project to build a parallel channel (actually it was only along thirty-five kilometers of the canal's 193 kilometer length). The project was to be completed on a "miraculous" one-year schedule. As the completion date neared, on schedule, a national celebration was planned, did indeed take place on August 6, 2015, and was acknowledged by most observers to have been quite large and enthusiastic. In the lead-up to the appointed day anyone who criticized the project was dismissed as a Muslim Brotherhood member—and this of course served to dampen criticism from other quarters, as few non–brotherhood supporters wanted to be labeled as such.[10]

In this environment *ifrah*—"celebrate"—came across to critics of the regime as an unwelcome command. The cartoon showed an elegant woman sitting on a chaise longue at the beach. In the first frame a young man with a Sisi face crudely photoshopped onto his body grins broadly at the women. The caption says *Masr bi-tifrah*—"Egypt celebrates." In the next frame we see her unamused face looking back at her harasser. The caption is simply "no" (see figure 10.1). In the final frame the Sisi figure looks back at her, smile replaced by a slightly threatening look: *inti shaklik ikhwan 'ala fikra*—"by the way, you look like a Muslim Brother." The cartoon nicely captures both the durability of the "us versus them" discourse and its absurd oversimplification of reality—an oversimplification that was, in the real world, underpinned by violence.

In the summer of 2013 the us-versus-them binary was becoming immovable. Nobody could be sure whether or not this meant that the revolution was over, finally defeated, that someone had finally found a way to close the uncloseable liminal crisis. It is a problem that bedevils any attempt to define a revolution strictly by its success or failure to achieve a revolutionary outcome. By when must the outcome be settled? In a month? A year? A generation?

In those days—mid-July 2013, after the fall of Morsy but before the Rabʻa Massacre—Faruq, my neighbor, sat morosely at home in front of his television, watching news, cursing the Muslim Brotherhood not because he favored *ibada*—"extermination"—(though I heard that sentiment voiced by others),

FIGURE 10.1. Meme of 'Abd al-Fattah al-Sisi as a harasser on the
beach. When the woman rejects his attention he tells her she looks
like a member of the Muslim Brotherhood. August 2015.

and certainly not because he wanted the military to take power. It was because he saw the Muslim Brotherhood as having squandered the best chance Egyptians would have in his lifetime to institute a more fair and humane political system:

> Rejection of the Ikhwan was real; it wasn't whipped up by old regime money as some are saying. The country was slipping into civil war under Morsy. Morsy was through after June 30. If the military hadn't intervened Morsy would have fallen, but after a very long, protracted, and bloody conflict. I don't want military rule, but the military's intervention saved lives. Also, *khalli balak* [pay attention]: if the military hadn't intervened the conflict would have extended to *inside* the military, not at the level of the officer corps, but at the level of the conscripts. An intramilitary conflict would have been immensely violent. Soldiers all have access to weapons! This gives us a second chance. If we don't get it right this time we're lost. I don't care if the old regime comes back to some extent. *Fulul* isn't a useful term. The NDP was the only political option during the Mubarak era; not everyone in it was equally bad.

The problem, as many others were pointing out then and have since, was the brotherhood's political ineptitude. Faruq was delighted, thrilled even, that the Muslim Brotherhood had been dealt what he thought was a political death blow. He did not have high expectations of Sisi but very firmly believed him to be the lesser of two evils. "We'll end up with a Russian-style democracy. It's not what we wanted, but it's better than what we had. Sisi is our Putin. We will have elections that are mostly for show, but we can never go back to the way it was under Mubarak." He assumed there was still plenty of political drama to come. "The problem with Sisi is that he doesn't have a political body. He has no party affiliation. He can't rule without one." What would this political body consist of? Faruq's greatest fear was that it would be a kind of political Frankenstein's monster—Salafi parts fused together with the most reactionary elements of the old NDP. His better-case scenario, and the one he thought more likely, was that Sisi's body would leave out the Salafis: "a few will become jihadists, many will withdraw from politics altogether and go back to da'wa [religious outreach, or proselytization], and a small number will form a political party, but it will be a symbolic opposition party." Sisi's body would instead be formed by the more progressive (and less corrupt) elements of the old NDP fused with a few pieces of mainstream-ish revolutionary politicians. Faruq was not reckoning with the possibility that Sisi might turn out to be a Trickster president, closer in spirit to Taufiq 'Ukasha (who was probably Sisi's own operative when he was running military intelligence) than to the dull autocracy of Mubarak or the slightly more flamboyant but politically open (in Faruq's opinion) Putin.

Faruq typified a pragmatic "lesser of two evils" calculation and muted political optimism, plus frank pleasure in seeing the Muslim Brotherhood smashed. But he never relinquished his basic humanity. He was not advocating violence or producing apologetics for it. I heard variations of this less histrionic reading of the situation repeated often that summer, but only in private settings: an artist who cautioned that "they will come for us after they are through with the Ikhwan" (a prophetic stance); an academic from a provincial university, who contacted me through a staunchly pro-Mubarak family I knew, expressing careful support for a fledgling (but ultimately stillborn) "Third Midan" movement (not Tahrir and not Rab'a; not the military or the Ikhwan); Hamdi the bookseller's pro-Morsy-but-not-Ikhwan father in law, 'Amm Husayn, and his wife as well, who brought us some *mahshi* (vegetables stuffed with rice) and expressed horror at the violence: "We don't agree with them, but they are our neighbors and like our children. They shouldn't be slaughtered!" One certainly also encountered the hard-hearted and even the hypocritical: *ana ma' al-ibada*—"I am for extermination"—this said by a writer who had published a well-received memoir of the first eighteen days of the revolution in which she had described being beaten by thugs and security forces, and her joy at the downfall of the Mubarak regime. In the summer of 2013 she commented on the Rab'a debacle with an impeccably straight face: "Now we need to stand back and let the police and army do their jobs." Thus among those who favored Morsy's removal by the military one encountered everything on a spectrum from utterly callous to tenderly humane. At least among the people I knew, in July 2013, before Rab'a, a schismogenetic self-perpetuating cycle of escalating violence was not inevitable.

But significantly, one encountered nuance and variation only in private conversations. In all facets of public culture, the tone was unremittingly strident. Television stations, both public and private, all ran "Fighting Terrorism" banners across the bottom of the screen—in English no less, as if Egyptian television had purchased secondhand graphics left over from the United States' post-9/11 "War on Terror" campaign. For me the feeling of post-9/11 hysteria was suffocating. Still, a political process of sorts continued, particularly through efforts by Mohamed El Baradei to broker some sort of walking back from the slaughter that many already feared from the Rab'a sit-in, and also a new interim political solution that would stop well short of a full takeover by the military. El Baradei was a resonant figure with people like Faruq. Indeed, the first I ever heard of El Baradei's interventions into Egyptian politics was Faruq's admiring description of him in late 2010, just before the revolution began. El Baradei had backed the downfall of Morsy, but not a military coup. In mid-July there were rumors that he would be appointed prime minister, but then he instead agreed to serve as vice president with responsibility for foreign affairs. As such he continued attempts to broker some sort of solution to the political impasse. Then came 'Abd al-Fattah al-Sisi's call for a tafwid—a "mandate"—to "fight terrorism" by any and all means necessary.

The call came in a speech to the graduating class of the military academy on July 24, 2013. The conventional political calculation was that the intended audience for the huge demonstration that ensued on the twenty-sixth were foreign governments, who needed to be convinced that the coup d'état label was incorrect. It could have also been implicitly aimed at the lower ranks of the military itself. Outside a professional officer corps the Egyptian army relies on general conscription for manpower. After the assassination of Sadat in 1981 officers were carefully screened to exclude candidates with affiliations to the Muslim Brotherhood or other Islamist organizations. The conscript rank and file is not as carefully screened and more closely approximates the social diversity of the entire nation. Hence the army itself, particularly the conscripts, may have needed reassurance that the public backed the military in a coming confrontation with Islamists.

But aside from such "normal" political calculations, it was very likely the Tafwid demonstration on July 26 that cemented Sisi's political ascendency made this a schismogenetic moment. Horvath and Thomassen paraphrase Gregory Bateson's central concept: "what is it that 'goes wrong' in some societies, how does it happen, and how can the error survive, and even thrive, to the apparent 'satisfaction' of most members of that society?" (Horvath and Thomassen 2008, 19). Their answer is that protracted liminality multiplies both the opportunity for political Tricksters to gain prominence, but also the potential for such figures to be imitated and followed. It is certainly a suggestive formulation in the context of the still-liminal summer of 2013. The response to Sisi's call for a "mandate to fight terror" was enthusiastic and huge. Not having been present for the June 30 Tamarrud demonstration, I cannot say whether the Tafwid demonstration on July 26 was comparable. When we arrived in Cairo in the summer of 2013 our pro-Mubarak informants were repeating implausible claims that a third of the country turned out for Tamarrud (see Ketchley 2016 for a more realistic appraisal). But certainly nobody contests the fact that the turnout on June 30 was immense, and it was immense on the night of July 26 as well. A journalist from a very well off family invited me to join his family in their Tafwid March. "We're going from the Gezira Club into Zamalek," he said. Though I was tempted, I declined, as I had an iftar (fast-breaking meal during Ramadan) invitation from my friends in Pyramids Road—two lawyers 'Id and Hisham, both of them devoted supporters of the Mubarak regime, and now of Sisi. I took a microbus from the Giza Metro stop, and Hisham met me at the appointed street corner. He was very upbeat, immediately telling me how pleased he was at the removal of Morsy. *Nizilt fi al-tamarrud?* I asked him—"Did you march in Tamarrud?" Indeed he had, the only demonstration he had joined in his life. The dinner was at 'Id's massive but sparsely furnished flat and lasted late into the night, as iftars tend to do. Conversation was laced with conspiracy theories and slightly aggressive challenges to American hegemony. "Why does the United States support the Ikhwan?" asked 'Id. He answered his own question: "It's because they're in alliance with Israel, and they both want to destroy Egypt. They don't like Sisi because he stands up to the Ikhwan." Hisham chimed in: "Don't watch Al-Jazeera. It's the Ikhwan's own station. We hate it." I countered by trying to argue that the Arabic Al-Jazeera was a substantially independent entity, and that the English and Arabic sides of the network often didn't see eye to eye. He did not buy that line. "We call it 'al-khanzira' (the pig)," said Hisham. The Jazeera/khanzira joke turned out to be prescient populism. A few weeks later a belly dancer/actress/singer named Sama al-Masri released a peerlessly vulgar video mocking al-Jazeera (al-Masri 2013), calling it *al-khanzira* just as Hisham had. *Al-tisht 'al-li al-tisht 'al-li, ya khanzira 'umi istahammi 'ashan tindafi ya mi'affina* (the washtub told me "hey pig, get up and bathe so you can clean yourself, you piece of filth").[11]

I went home around eleven o'clock, assuming the crowds from the demonstration would be diminishing by then. Hisham said he wanted to go with me but backed out once we got to the street where I picked up the microbus heading to the Giza Metro station. Assuming that the Tahrir Metro stop would be either closed or utterly packed with people, I got off one stop early at the opera house. The crowds were still so immense that what would normally have been a fifteen-minute walk over the Qasr al-Nil Bridge (the main entry from the west to Tahrir Square) turned out to be a two-hour snail's slog, in which I had to detour over to the October Bridge about half a kilometer to the north. Adoration for the leader was everywhere and contagious, and at the same time threatening and ominous. It was like the dark 'Ukasha rally in Midan al-'Abbasiyya that I had attended a year and a half earlier; the undercurrent of violence was unmistakable. Many people were carrying Sisi signs, almost all of them mass produced—there was very little of the homegrown sign-making wit that had distinguished the January 25 Revolution. The military was symbolically present in the form of helicopters circling overhead. People from below were lighting them up with green laser pointers. Helicopters were dropping lightweight Egyptian flags down to the people below. The next day I posted a derisive comment about the state of the streets following the demonstration on Facebook and was instantly attacked by a pair of liberal academics at the American University in Cairo (who saw my message reposted by someone else).

After the demonstration we found that our television was on the fritz, and Zizo came by with a friend who worked installing satellite dishes to fix it. Zizo and his friend went up to the rooftop to make the necessary adjustments. When they came down Zizo brought four flags with him. Though Zizo had always been apolitical as far as I knew, he rolled a joint and we chatted a bit about politics. He had participated in the June 30 demonstrations—the only demonstration he marched in, just like Hisham. He inspected our collection of promilitary posters impassively, finally opining that one showing Sadat,

Nasser, and Sisi together was beautiful. He had never expressed very much opinion about the Muslim Brotherhood, though I recalled that when Morsy was elected he had been optimistic that he would prove to be a good man. But no longer. "You know, ya duktur, the Ikhwan were behind the Port Said massacre." He was referring to a horrific incident in February 2011, when seventy-three football Ultras from the Ahly team had been murdered in a stadium at an away game in Port Said, most likely (or so everyone assumed at the time) as revenge for the Ultras' courageous and effective battles with the security forces in the early days of the revolution. "How do you know?" I asked. "Because, ya duktur, I saw a video of Muslim Brotherhood members throwing a young man opposed to them off of a rooftop in Alexandria. It looked just like when people got thrown off of the top of the stadium seats in Port Said." I tried to diffuse this analogical reasoning by mildly observing that surely below the level of the leadership some member of the Muslim Brotherhood were bad, and some good, just like people everywhere. "Maybe so," he said. "Some are good, and others"—he stroked his chin to signify growing a beard—"aren't." In any case, their numbers are going down. They can't put lots of people in the street anymore."

Violence and Schism

The Raba'a Massacre came on August 14, after the 'Id al-Fitr (the holiday of breaking the fast at the end of Ramadan). Just over a thousand supporters of Muhammad Morsy, most of them Muslim Brotherhood members, were killed in one day. It was easily the worst day of violence in the revolution, and the largest one-day loss of life caused by state in the history of modern Egypt.

And so the revolution began to end, though not straightforwardly with a closing of the liminal crisis that had begun in 2011. It was more like a schismo-genetic establishment of a "new normal" that actually enshrined liminality at the center of society. For one thing, the massacre and eventual confirmation of Sisi as president did not result, as Faruq had assumed it would, in Sisi grafting his briefly charismatic head onto a hopefully fairly benign political body. Parliamentary elections were delayed until the end of 2015. When I went back to Cairo in mid-2015 for a very short trip I needed a haircut. It was 3 a.m. on the morning of my arrival, but I found a tiny barbershop open on the street below my office, which we continued to pay rent on even in our absence, as it still contained large quantities of books and magazines that we had no means to ship to Britain. In the middle of the haircut the barber, who had cut my hair several times before and who I had found previously to be quite prorevolution, suddenly said softly in my ear: "He's afraid to have a parliament." "Who?" I asked. "Sisi of course."

Maybe so. I ran that idea past a friend a day later, and he scoffed, saying that Sisi had just found he could rule the way he wanted to without one. Whatever the reason, by the summer of 2015 Sisi had made no attempt to attach himself to a party, or to any of the ever-shifting coalitions of half-formed parties that claimed to be putting themselves in position to contest elections that had not yet taken place. He had not even tried to establish something along the lines of Nasser's one-party Arab Socialist Union. The parliament that did eventually emerge in 2016 was predictably toothless, essentially a rubber stamp for the large number of presidential decrees Sisi had announced over the previous two years. I encountered a number of observers privately expressing surprise or dismay at Sisi's apparent lack of interest in politics, or more precisely, in "old-fashioned" politics centered on the sort of political machines that the Mubarak regime had run, or indeed in simply building the sort of political elite that Sadat had depended on—"state-nurtured capitalists on top, old ASU cadres and their rural allies in the middle, and state employees and workers . . . at the base" (Kandil 2012, 165). After two years Sisi, by contrast, seemed to be stuck somewhere between his military background, a public managed by spectacle, and a long line of elites from the private sector held at arm's length. But in this sense perhaps his apparent lack of interest in ordinary politics becomes intelligible. Even after a parliament at last took its seats in early 2016, he remained in-between: precisely where a Trickster flourishes.

What happened in the first two years of Sisi's rule was two pronged. One prong was violence: a body-less head ruling the country could never establish the sort of hegemony that Mubarak's NDP machine had engineered. In the absence of hegemony—domination exercised with the implicit consent of those under its sway—the Sisi regime had to use far more naked violence than the Mubarak regime had had to resort to. Some of the violence is well-known, such as the clearing of the sit-in at the Rab'a al-'Adawiyya Mosque in August 2013 (Human Rights Watch 2014), or the murder of Shayma' al-Sabbagh by security forces when she tried to lay a wreath for martyrs of the revolution on its fourth anniversary ("Egypt: Protestors Killed" 2015). But a great deal more violence was less widely mediated, including the suppression of intense and frequent efforts by supporters of the Muslim Brotherhood to mount demonstrations. Zizo was right when he said that the Sisi regime had, over time, degraded the brotherhood's ability to mobilize and confined their demonstrations to side streets, but demonstrations nonetheless continued. Another form of violence was the arrest and incarceration without charge and sometimes without even acknowledgement of anyone suspected of opposing the regime ("Egypt: Dozens" 2016). As of 2016 credible estimates of the number of incarcerated were as high as sixty thousand (Hammer 2017). The conditions of these out-of-sight prisons and torture centers, many of them run by the army, were appalling (Stevenson 2015). Extrajudicial killings were being carried out ("Egypt: Police" 2015), and mass death sentences based on the flimsiest of evidence were being handed down (Shahin 2015). Everyday violence carried out by the police was worse than before the revolution. The high level of violence showed no sign of abating. Nominally the violence was just a phase in which security forces asserted control in an effort to stabilize the country. On the other hand, while there may have been no functional hegemony—as long as Sisi ruled as a bodiless head—violence was nonetheless structured as a "permanent crisis" justified on grounds of security and stability. Constant exhortations to fight a "war on terror" were very effective given the incredible violence elsewhere in the region, particularly Syria and Iraq but also neighboring Libya. Under the circumstances it was easy to forget that Egypt did not have the social cleavages that resulted in civil wars elsewhere, hence there was no reason to think that Egypt would become like Syria, Iraq, or Libya. Moreover, fears of civil war in Egypt prior to Morsy's removal, a primary rationale for legitimizing Sisi's seizure of power, were being raised by political forces that had been *contributing* to that dynamic. Muslim Brotherhood and FJP headquarters all over the country had been attacked, looted, and burned in the months preceding Tamarrud. The police stood by and watched. After the fall of Morsy state-sponsored violence in Egypt made it impossible to tell where the boundary was between actual threats and violence provoked by the state itself. "War on terror" rhetoric defined who the attackers were (Islamists, all of them either members of the Muslim Brotherhood or inspired by and allied with the brotherhood) and made the military and security forces by default the protectors.

Thus a permanentization of the crisis began to emerge. For me it took an eerily familiar form: Egypt in the summer of 2013 felt like the United States (and to a large extent Britain) in 2001. Subsequently the strategy that crystallized in Egypt greatly resembled that of post-9/11 America. Egypt under Sisi employs a variant of the American doctrine of counterinsurgency that "produces its own defeat again and again, with no memory of prior losses, thus repeating the same fundamental mistakes" (Khalili 2013, 5). As in Khalili's analysis of American and Israeli asymmetric warfare, Egypt's "war on terror" is a mistake only in the sense that it destroys lives, and in the sense that its avowed goals are something else—"the urgency of a civilizing, or democratizing, or modernizing, or improving" (Khalili 2013, 4) in the American case. In the case of Sisi, violence was justified along very similar lines. Consider this passage from the speech he gave on the opening of an extension of the Suez Canal on August 6, 2015:

> I say to Egyptians that you . . . that Egyptian civilization . . . have presented, today . . . Egypt presents to humanity . . . a gift, maybe not a really big gift like in the days of the ancient Egyptians, but in one year they've exerted great efforts on behalf of the world and for Egypt . . . a gift for humanity, for development, for building, for restoration. I want to tell you something. Egypt didn't do this just within this past year, or the past two years to be precise, just this one project. No. History will record that Egypt has repelled and confronted the most dangerous ter-

rorist extremist thought that, if it had been established in this land, would have burned it. It was the Egyptians who repelled this thought. They opposed it in order to say to humanity "no." They presented the true tolerance of Islam and Muslims. They presented building and restoration and development and progress, not the killing, ruination, and destruction of humanity. ("Kalimat al-Ra'is" 2015)

The logic of everything Sisi had done in the previous two years was not at all to bring stability that would enable "development and progress." On the contrary, the massacre in Rab'a al-'Adawiyya and the subsequent enlargement of a huge network of savage prisons (underpinned by a perverted legalism, but only when it suited the state, much as in the American and Israeli cases that Khalili discusses) was guaranteed "to produce its own defeat" again and again, not in the sense that the army and security forces could actually lose an asymmetric war against Islamist insurgents. That never happened. But Sisi's American-style counterinsurgency tactics guaranteed defeat in the sense that the war could never be won because the opponent was large, amorphous, and constantly provoked. It was the counterinsurgency that produced the insurgency. The political logic was to use overwhelming force to respond to an attack; the use of force caused "blowback," or retaliation; the state would then inevitably use more force to respond to the retaliation; the cycle repeats endlessly. With a few adjustments, Sisi's tactics "continually slip[ed] between exemplary or performative forms of violence meant to intimidate and more 'humane' and developmental warfare intended to persuade" (Khalili 2013, 4). Substitute Sisi's constant references to "humanity" (*insaniyya* in his speech), and the same logic applies. In Khalili's American and Israeli cases that the enemy must be racialized. In Sisi's rhetoric Islamists were dehumanized and excommunicated from the nation. Just after the passage quoted above from Sisi's Suez Canal speech he continued as follows:

> The Egyptian people that built the new Suez Canal didn't do it in normal circumstances. They worked in very difficult circumstances—economically and structurally. The extremist elements and terrorist groups, which I call "people of evil" [*ahl al-sharr*] have tried to harm Egypt and the Egyptian people, and to obstruct their path and progress. What I want to say is that the work in Egypt didn't proceed under normal circumstances. No. These were circumstances of fighting terrorism, and these circumstances are still here. We are fighting it, and will continue to fight it. And we will defeat it, no doubt about it. ("Kalimat al-Ra'is" 2015)

Sisi's "people of evil" category was endlessly elastic. It could refer to the newly emerged "Islamic State" in Iraq and Syria and the Sinai Province group (Wilayat Sina') that had until recently been called Supporters of Jerusalem

(Ansar Bayt al-Maqdis). But Sisi and the media constantly conflated these with the Muslim Brotherhood, more as an assertion of power than on the basis of evidence.

One of George Bush's aides (probably Karl Rove) famously stated that in the contemporary world "the reality-based community" (scholars, journalists, anyone with an attachment to facts) would be reduced to merely post ex facto interpretations of "history's actors." "When we act, we create our own reality" (Suskind 2004). The reality that Sisi helped to create was that all Islamist groups were collapsed into one, and the Muslim Brotherhood—ahl al-sharr, the "people of evil," excommunicated from the Egyptian nation—were their foundational model. There is much dispute over the size of the Muslim Brotherhood's membership. The organization itself did not keep precise records for security purposes, and it is very hard to distinguish between fee-paying members and the social circles around them, which may be sympathizers without being technically members. Most scholars work with numbers somewhere between two hundred thousand and about 750 thousand, but some put the numbers in the millions (Kandil 2014, 76–77). Even if one assumes a fairly low number, say two hundred thousand, the membership is sufficiently large that a counterinsurgency strategy will generate an inexhaustible supply of potentially radicalize-able youth, just as the American occupation of Iraq created an endless chain of radicalization that greatly fed the creation of jihadist movements in the Syrian/Iraqi conflagration that was raging in the years following the revolution.

The adoption of a political strategy "guaranteed to reproduce its own defeat" through defining a permanent opponent who can never *defeat us*, but who can in turn be perpetually renewed through our own asymmetric violence, is a form of schismogenesis—the systematization of violence that might in "normal" conditions be seen as monstrous or simply impossible.[12] "Normal" of course is a highly contingent concept, in other words, dependent on complex social and historical circumstances. The point is simply that people will never consciously choose to enshrine violence in their concept of normality, hence the "permanentization" of violence requires explanation, as it can easily degenerate into a vicious circle that persists despite its destructive effects.[13] And sometimes it *does*. In postrevolution Egypt such relations could be seen in Sisi's frequently stated opposition of "Egyptian citizens" to "terrorists," or the comparable American or Israeli constructions of their permanent opponents— "terrorists" or "uncivilized" peoples—a rhetoric neatly mirrored by those who have been labeled as outside the scope of social recognition. "Each group will drive the other into excessive emphasis of the pattern, a process which if not restrained can only lead to more and more extreme rivalry and ultimately to hostility and the breakdown of the whole system" (Bateson 1935, 181). The vicious circle of postrevolution Egyptian politics has not in fact led to the breakdown of the whole system as Bateson imagined. To be sure, violence has been enshrined in the system in a new and more virulent way, but the potential for waging violent opposition is increasingly asymmetric. The relationship between the state's violence and those who might want to oppose it became increasingly complementary (the alternative form of schismogenesis in Bateson's original formation), in which the state's active prosecution of violence has been met by a passive response. "This schismogenesis, unless it is restrained, leads to a progressive unilateral distortion of personalities of the members of both groups, which results in mutual hostility between them and must [also] end in the breakdown of the system" (Bateson 1935, 181). Whether the differentiation of the Sisi era from its predecessor is symmetrical or complementary, violence has become part of the "ecology" of Egyptian politics (Bateson 1987). "A schismogenetic rhetoric may continue to develop for some time, even in the face of a changing society, because that rhetoric is both sustaining and destructive: its destructiveness sustains a certain kind of dynamic equilibrium" (Wardle 2001, 25).

Schismogenesis as a permanentization of violence is substantially a transposition of a political dynamic that has been well described in other terms. Samir Amin, for example, writes of "permanent war and the Americanization of the world" (2004). Or Laleh Khalili argues that violent illiberal counterinsurgency practices (asymmetric warfare and incarceration) are not aberrations from liberalism, but rather "vital components . . . in the longer-term production of the liberal order when a state expands its reach beyond its own borders" (Khalili 2013, 8). What is happening in this instance of schismogenesis is not fundamentally different. I invoke the concept because it resonates well with another aspect of Sisi's rule, namely his capacity to act as a Trickster. Schismogenesis permanentizes crisis, and Tricksters flourish in conditions of crisis.

The Neoliberal Music Man

Sisi as Trickster may seem odd, given the way he was portrayed in international media, essentially as a stern ruler who was an unfortunate necessity. But a closer inspection will show that the Trickster label suited him well. In June 2015 'Abd al-Fattah al-Sisi visited Germany as part of the steady process of Western governments normalizing his rule. The centerpiece of the meeting was economic; the engineering and technology giant Siemens had just signed an €8 billion deal to provide natural gas and wind power plants to Egypt. Back home the trip caused a minor stir for a different reason. Some twenty media personalities, a collection of movie stars past their primes and a few of the most vehemently proregime talk-show hosts, had formed a "popular delegation" to accompany the president in order to oppose the Muslim Brotherhood crowds that would presumably dog Sisi's visit. Everywhere he went they appeared cheering for him and waving Egyptian flags. It is hard to know what the German press made of this gaggle of aging media personalities. They do seem to have been noticed, or at least one of my Facebook friends (a critic of Sisi) posted a picture of a pile of German tabloids with Egyptian actors' faces on them. The Egyptian press covered the story of the actors' initiative positively and politely, and only slightly over the top in a few instances, such as a *Shuruq* headline that described it as "the largest popular delegation" (A. Faruq 2015). The text of the article clarified that it was "the largest since Sisi took power." Apparently some sort of confrontation between the delegation and Egyptians critical of Sisi did take place, though I could find no video of it. But I did locate a video of Ahmad Musa talking about this alleged fight. Musa was an 'Ukasha-clone talk-show host on the Sada al-Balad channel owned by Muhammad Abu 'Aynayn, a former NDP stalwart and one of the suspects in organizing the Battle of the Camel. Musa was particularly noteworthy for his on-air emotional outbursts, which he typically delivered in a high-pitched whine:

> Terrorist elements today engaged with the artists and the delegation from Egypt and attacked them. At first they introduced themselves, and "how do you do," and then started talking to them. And after that they started saying stupid stuff, that silly talk of theirs. And then a fight started, with insults and, you know . . . they're "real polite." They said some really strange stuff that has no relation to religion or with . . . and by the way, those people are criminals, and every day they confirm it. It's not just us who say it. The Germans could see it. What do they see? They see that they have a terrorist group living among them. All along they haven't known that they're terrorists. All the time they're saying "what's happening in your country?" Here you are, they're doing it here in your country. ("Ahmad Musa: 'Anasir Irhabiyya" 2015)

Islamist and independent websites critical of Sisi mocked the delegation mercilessly. The news website *Wara' al-Ahdath* ran an article asking pointed questions about who paid the delegation's bills (it was said to have been an independent initiative with no official link to the president), and quoting a number sour remarks about the "scandal" of the nation having been represented by "a bunch of dancers" (Muhammad 2015). But by far the most clever commentary came in a meme circulated on Facebook that tried to imagine: how *would* Sisi have explained his retinue of devoted media personalities to Angela Merkel? The prankster who created the meme makes Sisi sound like an empty-headed gossip columnist reveling in glory reflected by the stars. The names of the actors will be unfamiliar to most readers, but the tone is translatable (just substitute your favorite slightly overripe Hollywood stars to get feel for the joke; "Charley Sheen said to Debra Winger . . ."):

> [The actor] Adil Imam smokes some hashish and comes in saying 'I've smoked hashish Su'ad' . . . this Su'ad is the actress Yusra, and I've

brought her with me. And the slightly chubby one, that's Ilham Shahin. She once played the role of Lawahiz, the cousin of Sayyid, and this "cousin Sayyid" was played by *ustaz* al-'Alayli [another actor]. . . . I've brought him with me too. ("Al-Sisi al-Qatil" 2015)

Of course in reality Sisi at most played a role in the gaggle-of-aging-actors incident by agreeing to let it happen, and one can easily imagine a president being too busy to even care about such things. Nonetheless, spectacle was a substantial element of Sisi's rule, sometimes on a grand scale, and at other times on a weirdly personal level through long contrived televised chats with journalists—a tactic one could never have imagined in the case of Mubarak. In the case of the much-hyped meeting with Merkel, Sisi came across as the person who was tricked rather than as the Trickster. The delegation may have gone over well with confirmed supporters of the president, but it was laughter fodder for anyone not already in his camp. He was not 'Ukasha; surely he would have been better off not soiling the jealously accumulated "prestige of the state" (*haybat al-daula*) by inviting ridicule. But aside from this episode, Sisi was more often the joker than the punch line.

After permanentized violence, the second prong of Sisi's regime can only be described as political tricks, which are perfectly consistent with the violence underpinning his rule (Horvath and Thomassen 2008). We recall from chapter 8 that a Trickster may be thought of as "a vagrant who happens to stumble into the village, appearing out of the blue . . . an outsider who has no home and no existential commitments" (Thomassen 2012, 695). This might seem a poor fit for Sisi at first glance. He was nothing if not an institutional man. Sisi was said to have been Mubarak-era minister of defense Muhammad Husayn al-Tantawi's handpicked successor (Fayiq 2013). He had held several high-level positions but most importantly was head of military intelligence throughout the revolution. However, after the revolution he was a stranger wandering into civilian government from a military netherland. His lack of interest in politics perfectly suited his lack of experience in the nonmilitary state. Moreover, his new role as head of the nonmilitary state pulled him away from SCAF. By 2015 he faced minimal danger from a populace weary of upheaval, but possibly more danger from his military colleagues and business elites frustrated at the expansion of the military's sphere of influence in the economy and the relative neglect of conventional state pursuits such as support for exporters. Hence he remained very firmly in power but aloof from the sort of political machinery that had sustained the NDP. He remained in-between, in liminality—instantiated in the unending "war on terror" security void, which he actively cultivated, but also in economic precarity. The latter was not exclusively of his own making. Certainly it had been developing through the decades of neoliberal restructuring of the economy that, by design or intention, kept everyone but elites within the thresholds of absolute poverty on one hand, and rebellion on the other; and compelled to believe that the only way to attain the kind of se-curity afforded to elites was through personal self-improvement (Lorey 2015). But the postrevolution economy under Sisi certainly accelerated economic precarity, particularly through his emphasis on high-profile "megaprojects." Thomassen notes that "the trickster is not really interested in solving the lim-inal crisis: he simply pretends. In fact, being at home in liminality, or in home-lessness, his real interest often lies in perpetuating such conditions of confu-sion and ambivalence" (Thomassen 2012, 696). The pretending may or may not be conscious. Only those close to 'Abd al-Fattah al-Sisi could really be sure. But there is no doubt that his basic political orientation toward commanding violence while making grand political spectacles, building populism more than building coalitions, was apparent early on.

In the run-up to the election that confirmed his grip on power in June 2014 he had famously said in an interview that he would not specify a political or economic program, and that those who expected to see gains for "sectoral" (*fi'awi*) interests would be disappointed. "Mish 'adir adik"—"I cannot give you [anything]" ("Liqa' ma' 'Abd al-Fattah" 2014). He said it again more loudly to be sure he had been heard. And he indeed did not give anything of practical value. On the contrary, in many of his speeches he was an apostle of self-reliance, a perfect complement to a reinvigorated neoliberal system. Mean-while the decades-long decrepitude of national institutions continued un-abated: electricity generation was still in crisis; the tourism sector remained relatively moribund; the currency had been devalued causing steep inflation; and poverty and unemployment were very high. Given the long-term nature of all these problems—not to mention longer-term structural problems such as a looming shortage in the water supply and environmental degradation—Sisi had effectively inoculated himself politically by promising nothing. On the other hand, at the same time that he promised nothing in practical terms, he promised the sun, moon, and stars in political terms.

The public got its first inkling of Sisi's pretend politics soon after he came to power, and well before his position was ratified by election. In February 2014 a press conference was held, allegedly attended by both Prime Minister 'Adli Mansur and interim president (technically given that his rule had not yet been confirmed by a fake election) 'Abd al-Fattah al-Sisi,[14] in which an Egyptian military doctor named "General" Ibrahim 'Abd al-'Ati announced that he had invented a cure for the stubborn hepatitis C infection, which plagues Egypt more than any other country in the world. Moreover, the same device could cure AIDS. A caller on a talk show who was allegedly a doctor on 'Abd al-'Ati's "team" revealed that it could even cure cancer and diabetes. Famously 'Abd al-'Ati claimed that his device takes AIDS from the patient and feeds the pa-tient on AIDS: "I give it to him as a piece of *kufta* [roast lamb sausage cooked on a kebab skewer] to feed on." Thereafter 'Abd al-'Ati became known as the "kufta doctor." Another device called C-FAST invented by the same doctor and unveiled at the same press conference could supposedly detect the presence of any virus noninvasively, merely by pointing a kind of divining rod at the patient.

The inventions were quickly debunked. 'Abd al-'Ati turned out not to be a real general—his title of *liwa'* was strictly honorary, bestowed by the director of the military's Engineering Directorate because "he liked 'Abd al-'Ati's ideas" ("Man Yakun" 2014). 'Abd al-'Ati also turned out not to be a real doctor, but rather an herbalist ("Man Yakun" 2014). An attempt to patent his devices was ludicrously unsuccessful. The research backing the devices was published without a shred of peer review in a "predatory journal" that publishes anything for a fee.[15] The noninvasive C-FAST remote virus detection device that looked like a divining rod turned out to be less useful than a divining rod. It was identified as a fake bomb detector that had been sold in Iraq and very likely resulted in loss of life to people who believed it worked (Ohlheiser 2013; Spencer 2014). The "Complete Cure for AIDS" turned out to be a giant hoax, described in one article as "the greatest scam in Egyptian history" ("Man Yakun" 2014).

It may seem a cheap shot to pin the great kufta hoax on Sisi. He was not directly responsible; obviously the military's Engineering Directorate, which organized the press conference, had been taken in. Quite a few media personalities fell in line, both praising the invention and denouncing anyone who cast doubt on it,[16] but many heaped scorn on it, including Sisi's own science adviser 'Isam Higgi (S. Hasan et al. 2014). In a world of old-fashioned politics Sisi would have benefitted immensely from just walking away from the spectacle and saying as little as possible. Instead the military's Engineering Directorate upped the ante by announcing that treatment by the devices would begin for the public on June 30, 2014, the first anniversary of the Tamarrud demonstration that ultimately resulted in Sisi coming to power. June 30, 2014, came and went with little fanfare. A few Facebook postings asked sarcastically when the treatments would begin. The military finally made the scandal go away by announcing that further tests would have to be done, and once that happened the device would begin treatments at some vague future date. But by the time that happened new and bigger spectacles were in the works.

The kufta hoax was less an anomaly than a tone setter for everything Sisi has done outside the security sphere. Aside from the iron fist, Sisi employed a consistent strategy of using high-profile spectacles to divert attention from his actual exercise of power, including a steady imposition of presidential decrees that positioned the economy for new rounds of neoliberal reform that would intensify precarity, making the lives of poor and middling-income citizens much harder. The spectacles consisted of megaprojects that were almost as pretend as 'Abd al-'Ati's Complete Cure for AIDS. Many of these were repackaged projects from the Mubarak era.

One of these was the new Suez Canal, already mentioned above, justified economically for its capacity to more than double the income of the canal, from

$5 billion annually to $13.2 within eight years of completing the project. In fact, improvements to the canal were necessary simply to maintain Egypt's share of the shipping trade, because an ongoing expansion of the Panama Canal would likely take some of the business that had been using the Suez Canal if Egypt had done nothing (Shea 2015). Many experts warned that there was no economic reason to fast-track the project,[17] but economic logic was beside the point. Sisi turned an ordinary infrastructural improvement into a national spectacle by getting the public to finance it in the short term, through the sale of bonds.[18] Hamdi, my pro-Mubarak (and even more pro-Sisi) book dealer was one of the purchasers of these bonds, though he did not tell me how much he invested.[19] The government predicted in no uncertain terms that the project would pay for itself rapidly,[20] yet with Europe still suffering in 2015 from the cold grip of endless neoliberal austerity, the odds of European imports (and therefore demand for using the canal) rising dramatically seemed remote. The "new Suez Canal" was entirely political theater, yet it had real economic effects by reducing the capacity of the state to spend on other priorities such as energy, education, urban infrastructure, or health care.

Mish 'adir adik—"I have nothing to give you"—was what Sisi told the public. But he had plenty to give to his own political legitimization, and the genius of this particular trick was that he got the public to pay for it willingly, and then to celebrate the project as a miraculous national achievement. The canal expansion project was also a triumph of neoliberalism—a necessary investment in national infrastructure converted rhetorically into a private investment, but actually a greater drain on state resources than it would have been if the state had simply paid for the project by increasing the national debt in the first place. In the end the most important objective of the project was regime legitimation, and on that level it worked very well. Reservations about the quick economic payoff of the project were recognized from the beginning, and so too was its political nature. The canal expansion was an exercise in confidence and morale building—something worthwhile to Sisi's supporters even if the economic criticisms did turn out to have merit.

Other civilian megaprojects were on the horizon, though they were slow to get off the ground.[21] The biggest megaproject of all was a massive "administrative city" sold to the public as a "new capital city" to be built between the Red Sea port of Ayn Sukhna and "old" Cairo. This project was announced with great fanfare at a donor's conference in Sharm al-Shaykh in March 2015. It was also to be financed entirely by gulf capital and would result in a massive new supermodern and luxurious city built in seven years at a cost of $45 billion (Cairo Capital Partners 2015).[22] The payoff for the foreign financing of the project was to come from new investment laws that would liberalize and streamline investment, eliminate the right of Egyptians to mount legal challenges to projects (for example, challenging the noncompetitive basis on which land for housing projects was allocated to developers), and gut labor laws. As of the summer of

2015 the only outcome of the project was demonstrations by public-sector employees alarmed that a new Civil Servants Law decreed by Sisi as part of the
new laws made it extremely easy for managers to fire them.[23] By 2017 the
project was reported to be creeping along without gulf partners, probably with
considerable work being given to the military, but possibly also to Chinese
companies (Abougabal 2017). The gleaming futuristic but tree-lined avenues
envisioned on the State Information Services website ("New Administrative
Capital" 2017) were nothing but a mirage, though the project's potential to suck
more of the state's resources away from the actually inhabited parts of the
country remained strong.

Confidence is the essence of a con job. The situation was reminiscent of the
American film *The Music Man*—a classic Trickster tale. A traveling salesman
comes to the fictional town of River City, Iowa, intent on swindling them. He
pretends to be a band director and cons the citizens of the town into paying
him to create a boys' marching band. They have to pay for uniforms and instruments, but his intention is to collect their money and then leave town before
the band can actually be created, and since he is not actually a band director,
he has no hope of training the boys anyway. He seals the deal by inducing a
moral panic over the effects of a newly opened pool hall, which he says will
corrupt the youth: "Ya got trouble; trouble in River City" (one can hear Sisi in
his inauguration speech: "Ya got terrorists; terrorists in Umm al-Dunya"). In
the end he gets outed by a rival salesman (just as Sisi's canal inauguration
extravaganza was exposed by multiple experts) but has in the meantime fallen
in love with the town librarian and decides he wants to stay. The uniforms and
instruments arrive. The illusion of the "band" he was supposed to create and
train seems on the verge of being revealed to all, and it will result in him being
tarred and feathered. But miraculously, when the untrained ragtag River City
youth band starts playing, the townspeople do not hear the actual out-of-tune
notes. They hear what they want to hear: a magnificent precision band marching through town playing "Seventy-Six Trombones" in perfect synchrony
("Egypt presents to humanity . . . a gift . . . a gift for humanity, for development,
for building, for restoration."). The morale building was undeniable in both
cases, but for Egypt the stakes were infinitely higher than for the citizens of
River City. Sisi's *mish 'adir adik*—"I can't give you anything"—turned out to be
frighteningly selective. It did not, for example, apply to the brand new French
Rafale jets that zoomed overhead during the canal inauguration, wowing the
crowds.[24]

Conspiracy

Trickster politics also resonates very strongly with conspiracy theories. This
was a specialty of 'Ukasha, but no less so of Sisi. Sisi learned some of his paranoia directly from 'Ukasha, but 'Ukasha himself imported it surprisingly from

an American source. There is a classic essay about the United States called "The Paranoid Style in American Politics" by the historian Richard Hofstadter, originally published in 1964, shortly after Barry Goldwater won the Republican nomination for the presidency. The Goldwater candidacy was the pinnacle of that particular episode in paranoid American politics; it had emerged initially during the anticommunist hysteria of the McCarthy era. The hallmark of the paranoid style was a sense of betrayal on the part of the right wing of the political spectrum. The idea was that "the old American virtues have already been eaten away by cosmopolitans and intellectuals." It was not just that conspiracies sometimes happened, but that conspiracies were themselves *the motive force* in historical events (Hofstadter 2008 [1964], 29). Hofstadter's 1950s paranoids were deeply imbued with racism and xenophobia. The civil rights movement was a communist plot; communists were infiltrating the highest echelons of the American government. Hofstadter quotes Robert Welch, founder of the racist right-wing John Birch Society, making amazingly precise predictions of apocalypse: "Evidence is piling up on many sides and from many sources that October 1952 is the fatal month when Stalin will attack" (Hofstadter 2008 [1964], 30). Change a few details, and Welch morphs into Taufiq 'Ukasha predicting dark Masonic conspiracies to unfold on the thirteenth day of the thirteenth month of the year 2013 ("Taufiq 'Ukasha Yahdhar" 2011). Such discourse may indeed be paranoid, as Hofstadter says, but it is also the hallmark of a Trickster's pretend politics.

A stellar example of Egyptian paranoid politics was the prominence of the term "Fourth Generation Warfare." The idea has an American genealogy. On one level it refers simply to warfare by means other than the military—disinformation in media, funding civil society NGOs, even the simple spreading of rumors, all facilitated by a blurring of lines between war and politics, combatants and civilians. But more than that, Fourth Generation Warfare is a contemporary expression of Goldwater-style paranoid politics. As a term Fourth Generation Warfare is particularly associated with the self-styled military strategist and conservative polemicist William Lind and dates at least from the late 1980s (Lind et al. 1989).[25] Lind is a "paleoconservative" obsessed with the infiltration of American society by what he calls "cultural Marxists." Paleoconservatism is a particularly reactionary form of American conservatism. Its proponents pointedly reject globalist forms of neoliberalism (or neoconservatism in American parlance), and "tend to centre upon the racial and ethnic identity of the United States, the historical presence of an innate social order; and the cultural threats posed by the federal government and the welfare state" (Foley 2007, 318). Lind's own formulation of paleoconservatism is best expressed by a novel titled *Victoria*, published in Finland under the pseudonym Thomas Hobbes (Hobbes 2014).[26] *Victoria* describes the breakup of the United States caused by unsustainable "political correctness," culminating in the emergence of a Christian state in New England that enters into an alliance with the reconstituted Russian czar against the Muslim world. With the election of Donald Trump, Lind and paleoconservatism can perhaps no longer be described as marginal to American politics.[27]

The idea of Fourth Generation Warfare was introduced into Egyptian political discourse by 'Ukasha in 2011, and later repeated by numerous other television personalities and politicians. When he talked about my article about him on one of his programs it was specifically to make the claim that foreigners had gone to Egypt to study *his own* techniques of Fourth Generation Warfare ("Al-Halqa al-Kamila" 2015). Once others started stealing his idea, 'Ukasha later one-upped himself and started talking about something called "Fifth Generation Warfare." Take away the blanket accusation of cultural Marxism, and Lind's big idea is essentially just an elaboration of "the well-established fact that lies, propaganda, and deceit are among the most powerful weapons in conflict and war" (Bubandt 2009, 560). States have indeed used many indirect means to weaken or confuse their opponents throughout history. But in the context of paranoid politics the label "Fourth Generation Warfare" is the perfect term for a phony expert or an authoritarian government looking for rationales to arrest opponents. Fourth Generation Warfare is the cousin of "fake news": *anything* that one opposes politically can be seen as having been caused by it, and everyone accused of it is fair game to be suppressed by paranoid governments.

Sisi also adopted the term openly—a fact known and followed with interest by American paleoconservatives (Bloom 2016). The Egyptian public was treated to a session of Sisi talking about "Fourth Generation Warfare" in early February 2015, during one of his many long and faux-intimate media appearances, in which he was shown sitting in his office, in a chair in front of his desk rather than seated behind it. This particular speech by Sisi was broadcast to counteract damaging leaks of recorded phone conversations in which he derisively talked about his gulf patrons, characterizing their money as "rice" and laughing about how the military was fleecing them for their own ends. He introduced his talk by invoking "Fourth Generation Warfare" in order to claim that the leaked conversation was fabricated by someone stealing his voice from the "thousands of hours" of recorded speech that had been broadcast:

> I remind everyone who listens to me: Fourth Generation Warfare is a generation of the utmost importance that is being used in the entire region, and in Egypt. This generation is used in terrorism as an instrument; it's used in modern media; it's used in psychological warfare. It's a complete system that's used to bring an incredible result. Don't ask about something that was said "Was it said or not?" Ask "*Why* was it said?" What was its purpose? ("al-Sisi: Misr" 2015)

The utility of the concept is that it is an endlessly elastic idea that can be used as a pretext for using violence against all political opponents—violence born in a schismogenetic massacre, and subsequently systematized. The fact that nations, movements, organizations, and individuals do indeed have agendas makes conspiracy theorizing powerful in a liminal moment, when nobody is sure who to believe or who to follow.

Conclusion: Permanentized Liminality?

In "Trickster politics" the figure of the Trickster is connected to liminality, and revolution can be understood as a liminal crisis that causes an unpredictable transition, and potentially a transition to a "new normal" that nobody can anticipate. Taufiq 'Ukasha instantiated a Trickster politician. He was a counter-revolutionary propagandist, and possibly an operative of Egyptian military intelligence when it was run by 'Abd al-Fattah al-Sisi. And I have suggested that Sisi himself is a Trickster insofar as he comes into political office as an outsider, and rules as an outsider—capriciously, in an atmosphere of relentless conspiracy, by resorting to violence as a fundamental condition of governance, but also by means of substituting fantastic promises for political hegemony.

But if we widen the angle of our view from Egypt we are presented with a problem. Sisi is legible not just as a Trickster, but as a global actor in an "age of the Trickster." While we might argue about whether a given politician truly deserves to be described as a Trickster, the figure of the Trickster is universal. One can scarcely contest its existence. But what makes Tricksters *audible*, and how can they become the creators of something new, and something monstrous by previous standards? Trickster politicians are always there on the margins of the political field, but people do not always listen to them. The conventional wisdom in the United States was that Trump would be another Ross Perot, a hopeless third-party candidate tilting at windmills, no threat to be nominated by a major party, and at worst siphoning enough votes from one of them to throw the election to the other. Now the whole world seems to be sitting up and paying attention to one Trickster after another—Trump, Berlusconi, Zeman, Erdoğan, Boris Johnson, Nigel Farage, and I would say 'Abd al-Fattah al-Sisi. In Egypt a revolution inadvertently created optimum conditions for the emergence of Tricksters, as all the usual certainties of the political field were shaken. The emergence of Sisi was schismogenetic. Bateson insisted on the relevance of the concept to modern politics:

> a process whereby dictators are pushed towards a state which, in the eyes of the world, seems almost psychopathic. This is a complementary schismogenesis between the dictator on one hand, and his officials and people on the other. It illustrates very clearly how the megalomaniac or paranoid forces others to respond to his condition, and so is automatically pushed to more and more extreme maladjustment. (Bateson 1936, 186)

But Bateson's comforting "in the eyes of the world" assumed a perspective from a "rational" world onto the rise of a Hitler, the dictator he had in mind when he wrote that passage. The great tyrants of the twentieth century, Stalin and Hitler, bear more than a passing resemblance to the figure of the Trickster (Szakolczai 2009, 157). But now it seems that megalomania, paranoia, and psychopathic are the new normal. We are certainly not laughing. Why is Trump frighteningly audible to American voters? Why was Nigel Farage able to get British voters to buy into the fantasies of Brexit at a particular moment? Why was Taufiq 'Ukasha able to prepare the ground for the emergence of 'Abd al-Fattah al-Sisi?

But if the emergence of 'Ukasha and then Sisi happened in the context of revolutionary crisis, then we must still ask why so many Trickster politicians are suddenly audible elsewhere, in societies that have not had revolutions. We may speculate that a number of factors increase the audibility of Tricksters. Some of them are of long historical duration, and others more recent. In the *longue durée* category, one might consider that modernity provides a structured production of instability, insofar as that it prioritizes endless progress through what some have called "creative destruction" (Schumpeter 2006 [1943], 81–87). In a similar vein Marx famously argued that the point of modernity was that "all that is solid melts into air, all that is holy is profaned, and man is at last compelled to face with sober senses his real conditions of life, and his relations with his kind" (Marx and Engels 1975 [1848], 476). This is a perfect recipe for liminality, which some see as the core condition of modernity (Szakolczai 2000; Thomassen 2014). Consequently, the figure of the specifically political Trickster in modern societies may have a resonance not found in the universal form of the Trickster. But Marx's notion that modernity's (and capitalism's) "uninterrupted disturbance of all social conditions" would compel man "to face with sober senses his real conditions of life, and his relations with his kind" (Marx and Engels 1975 [1848], 476) was shortsighted. The ideology and culture of modern societies was long designed precisely to mitigate the unending liminality of modern capitalism conceived in this manner. Constructs of home and the good life are predisposed to stability. Even if we live in a world designed to constantly fall away in favor of endless change, we were still encouraged to believe that we could live within a safe normal. Lauren Berlant describes such constructs straightforwardly as "fantasy" (2011). Political transpositions of such fantasies abound. Brexiteers are told they can "take back control" by leaving the European Union; Donald Trump's slogan was "Make American Great Again," obviously to many of his followers coded language for "make America white again," but it also provides Trump supporters with plausible deniability: it means "make it safe; bring back what I consider normal, namely a secure job, a decent living, and a future for my children." And in Egypt Sisi's supporters tried very hard to make him the new Nasser; not the Nasser of war and defeat, but the Nasser of progress and national pride.

Capitalism, grounded in the "all that is solid melts into air" ethos that Marx formulated, was about unending revolutionizing of the means of production, which is another way of expressing permanent liminality. But capitalism also sutured itself ideologically to all that was wholesome, secure, and traditional— home and hearth; solid bourgeois values; even religion. This was hegemony in the most technical sense—a case in which "particularity assumes the represen- tation of an (impossible) universality entirely incommensurable with it" (Laclau 2000, 142–43), the solidity of bourgeois family values, often buttressed by religion, assuming a universality with a capitalism entirely incommensu- rable with such values because it is predicated on the permanent revolution- izing of the means of production. Nonetheless this hegemony has functioned in many places over long stretches for the past couple of centuries. Social con- ditions that could have been experienced as permanent liminality instead were understood by many as solid, conventional, and conservative. But now it does not seem to work so well. Why?

One reason is that capitalism has evolved into neoliberal ideology at odds with the hegemony of bourgeois solidity. Neoliberalism, particularly as it was instituted since the 1970s, differs from classical liberalism in that it reduces freedom to the economic sphere. This is how political theorist Wendy Brown describes it:

> [Neoliberalism] transmogrifies every human domain and endeavor, along with humans themselves, according to a specific image of the economic. All conduct is economic conduct; all spheres of existence are framed and measured by economic terms and metrics, even when those spheres are not directly monetized. In neoliberal reason and in domains governed by it, we are only and everywhere *homo oeconomicus*. (Brown 2015, 9–10)

"Homo oeconomicus" has to be governed intensely in order to be productive. This type of governance strips away older forms of capitalist hegemony, leav- ing people in liminality.

And so perhaps we can see the difference between liminality in the form of the ritual process, and the structured liminality of precarious neoliberalism. Liminal crisis conceived in the terms of the ritual process writ large is a mo- ment of political fluidity characteristic of all revolutionary events, perfect for the emergence of a Trickster, but also genuinely open to contingency and hence potentially grounds for the emergence of other political formations. Perma- nentized instability is a synthetic form of liminality that governments endeavor to keep within manageable limits, above the limit of starvation but below the limit of rebellion. The degree to which it is *deliberately* structured is debatable, but it is worth noting that instability is not at all out of place in a neoliberal order. "Crisis capitalism"—the opportunistic exploiting of capitalism to further the cause of refashioning human beings as *homo oeconomicus*, is one way of expressing that kind of instability. Contemporary capitalism welcomes crisis because it affords opportunities to impose policies that voters in a democratic system would never endorse (Klein 2008). Milton Friedman, one of the primary ideological architects of neoliberalism, famously stated that crisis breaks "the tyranny of the status quo—in private and especially governmental arrangements" (Friedman 2002, xii–xiv), and that the function of those committed to "freedom" as he understood it, was "to develop alternatives to existing policies, to keep them alive and available until the politically impossible becomes politically inevitable" (Friedman 2002, xiv). That statement has been often remembered by academics and elaborated (e.g., Hanieh 2013, 48–52). Thomassen also suggests that liminality is built into the contemporary economic system in myriad ways, ranging from the permanentization of the carnivalesque instantiated in popular culture to the breaching of the most psychologically permanent refuge, "the home," in the interest of converting it into an economic asset that can in effect become a chip in the great game of "casino capitalism" (Thomassen 2014, 218–25). He does not mention "crisis capitalism" specifically, but it is consistent with his general logic of liminality coming to "occupy a more and more central place within the space of modernity, a process which is currently accelerating to the point of absurdity" (Thomassen 2014, 11).

Roitman and others have also noted that while the status of both "crisis" and "normality" as objects of inquiry need not be taken for granted, narrations of crisis have become particularly salient in recent years (Roitman 2013, 3). Reinhart Koselleck, in his crisis-centered conception of history, expresses skepticism at the "imprecision" of contemporary crisis narrations, complaining that a concept that "once had the power to pose unavoidable, harsh and non-negotiable alternatives, has been transformed to fit the uncertainties of whatever might be favored at a given moment" (Koselleck 2006, 399). But it is exactly the compulsion of taking "harsh and non-negotiable" decisions in the political-economic sphere that drives "crisis capitalism"—the formulation of crisis to which I allude here. Both capitalism and Marxism historically sought to convert all forms of economic indeterminism into calculable risks (Roitman 2013, 72–73). Neoliberalism, by contrast, puts greater emphasis on indeterminacy than on risk, because "creative destruction" (Harvey 2005, 12) provides much greater opportunity for reengineering society in order to protect capital accumulation by elites than state-centric risk management.

The result is "government of the precarious" in which "precarious living and working conditions are currently normalized at a structural level and have thus become a fundamental governmental instrument" (Lorey 2015, 63). The spread and deliberate fixing of precarity as a "crisis condition within the ordinary" (Berlant 2011, 194) has been widely noted from many perspectives (Agamben 2005; Phillips 2002; Rancière 2006; Sennett 1998). A neoliberal system that reneges on general welfare and instead prioritizes its resources more narrowly on safeguarding the security of an elite was a root cause of Egypt's revolution.

The point of a "government of the precarious" is to balance "a maximum of precarization, which probably cannot be exactly calculated, with a minimum of safeguarding to ensure that the minimum is secured at this threshold" (Lorey 2015, 65).

In other words, certain constituent parts of society are kept below the threshold of revolution, and above the threshold of absolute poverty, thus potentially prone to buying into a system requiring belief in the capacity for individual self-improvement. The Age of the Trickster is also the Age of Cruel Optimism (Berlant 2011). This why 'Abd al-Fattah al-Sisi's rule has been marked by incredible violence; because in the wake of revolution he must zealously defend the threshold of rebellion. At the same time he offers nothing to the public but their own self-reliance. *Mish 'adir adik*—"I have nothing to give you," as he said in one of his more memorable speeches.

But the space between these thresholds—a space of synthetic liminality— may also be the Achilles heel of this political-economic formation, because it is precisely the social position at which a Trickster politician is maximally audible: Taufiq 'Ukasha spinning bizarre conspiracy theories; Sisi pitching ever grander megaprojects destined for abject failure; British voters captivated by Boris Johnson's unfulfillable Brexit promises; Donald Trump whipping crowds into a frenzy with promises to "make America great again" by building walls to keep Mexicans out and forbidding Muslims from coming in. Maintaining the thresholds of this structured precarity is, ironically, a quintessentially precarious task. The path of least resistance for the charmed circle of elites who enjoy the state's security umbrella now withheld from everyone else is to see governance as the perfect job for a Trickster, someone who is "at one and the same time creator and destroyer, giver and negator, he who dupes others and who is always duped himself" (Radin 1956, xxii). One wonders why elites should be exempt from the wreckage of Tricksters, or why they should necessarily be the beneficiaries of a Trickster's dubious gifts.

The January 25 Revolution was a brief explosion of truly open liminality, followed by a savage reassertion of permanentized precarity. Both were conducive to Trickster politics. Yet it must be said that Trickster tales often end in disaster. Can we imagine, for example, a Trump presidency coming to disaster? Or more precisely (given the rhetorical nature of my question), will there be enough of a schism from the condition we once considered normal for his megalomania and psychopathy to have become the new normal? It was no accident that the first head of state to congratulate Trump on his winning the presidency was Sisi, or that Sisi was one of the first leaders Trump contacted once he was in office. Prior to Trump, Western governments thought it expedient to interpret Sisi as an unfortunate but necessary bulwark against the chaos that the undisciplined freedom of the revolution had unleashed. In the Age of the Trickster, Trump can simply express his sincere admiration (as sincere as a Trickster can be) for a pioneer of the new authoritarianism.

Zizo's Suicide Letter

THE REVOLUTION STARTED SUFFERING REVERSES immediately after the Mubarak regime fell. At first the reverses were offset by political gains, but the setbacks never stopped. The decisive tipping point was probably the Battle of Muhammad Mahmud Street, when the military's prestige was never lower. Clearly Muhammad Husayn al-Tantawi, the minister of defense and SCAF's interim president after the Mubarak regime fell, was not up to the task of staying in office as I think the military had hoped. An alternative to direct SCAF rule had to be found, at least temporarily. At that point the bargain between SCAF and the Muslim Brotherhood, long in the works, was finalized. I remember a middle-aged quasiretired activist friend, then an unofficial adviser to many of the young revolutionaries, chuckling and cautioning me to look at this as a temporary agreement, and not an actual alliance. "It's not a matter of 'if' one side betrays the other. Just a matter of when. They can't possibly stay together. The entire officers' corps is structured to oppose the Ikhwan. They can never live with them." Of course history proved him right, and the ultimate winner of the revolution was the military.

Whenever the revolution faced the specter of defeat, as it did repeatedly after the Battle of Muhammad Mahmud—never giving up, but operating with less and less political capital as the Islamists swept up one election after another—I encountered a tendency in my interlocutors to look for a silver lining. The basic narrative was that the revolution may be losing now, but in the end the younger generation had changed. Things could never go back to the way they were before. Egyptians would no longer accept being ruled the way they had been under Mubarak. I remember a middle-aged writer—a friend of a friend—telling his version of this story at a dinner party:

> My daughter was in a minibus with some friends when the police pulled them over and said they wanted to conduct a search. Before the revolution they'd have been terrified and submissive. But now they stood up

to the police and told them off. A crowd gathered around and started to get angry. The police had to back down. I'm so proud of her. Our generation could never have done this, but they have. They can never go back to the way it was before.

Many academics produced their own versions of the "silver lining" narrative, which might be better characterized as a long view, which I hasten to emphasize might still turn out to be the right view. In my introduction I touched on the notion (not generic to all academic approaches to revolution) that a revolution has to be a "rapid, basic transformation of a society's state and class structures . . . accompanied and in part carried through by class-based revolts from below" (Skocpol 1979, 4). What does "rapid" mean? In this context, was the rise of Sisi really the end? Not necessarily if, indeed, "something had changed."

A good example of this line of thinking is an editorial written by Asef Bayat and published under the title "Revolution and Despair" on the fourth anniversary of the revolution. It nicely sums up the scholarly long view that questions the apparent snuffing out of the revolution by Sisi's regime (Bayat 2015). He notes that all revolutions are initially followed by "a deep disappointment and demoralization." Hegel's "Phenomenology of Spirit" expresses it in the context of the French Revolution. A number of Russian revolutionaries committed suicide upon the ascendance of Stalin. Iranian revolutionaries had their moment of despair when the Iran-Iraq War raged and facilitated the ascendance of Islamist hard-liners. Rosa Luxemburg describes revolution as "the only form of 'war' in which the ultimate victory can be prepared only by a series of defeats" (Luxemburg 2010, 265). Egypt's current state of despair was therefore normal and to be expected. But Bayat insisted that all was not as it appeared, and that despite the temporary setback, political consciousness had been permanently changed. Workers and youth had had a taste of "unfettered spaces of self-realization" (Bayat 2015); women, having experienced the political limelight, had responded with "one of the most genuine movements in the nation's recent history" (Bayat 2015). Students demanded accountability from the educational authorities. Following Gramsci, the reform of the state could take place from below, even in the face of neoliberal authoritarianism, through a newly "active citizenry." Despite the apparent return of "the old ways," "something is fundamentally different . . . when the old order faces new political subjects and novel subjectivities" (Bayat 2015).

It is impossible not to hope that he was right. So did many others who expressed that hope once reversals to revolutionary aspirations began piling up. Despite whatever happened in the short term, the genie of revived political consciousness was out of the bottle and could never be put back in, because "something had changed." Or so we hope.

Bayat's article was being reposted constantly on Facebook in May 2015. I do not remember why—it was in response to some particularly depressing incident that served to emphasize the abjectness of the revolution's condition. At the same time, while preparing to attend a conference on the theme of "the ends of revolution," I heard from Lucie about Zizo, the young man I used to know in Cairo who worked for us all the way to the end of our apartment renovations. He has already been woven into my narrative in some of the earlier chapters.

Zizo was no longer in Egypt. He had recently departed for Qatar. I was shocked because for him to do this would be like dying. His last act in Egypt was to make an uncharacteristically political gesture, which I will explain in a moment.

Zizo was a young man from the 'ashwa'iyyat, by the look of him a *walad sirsagi*—that derogatory term mentioned in Muhammad Abu al-Ghayt's "The Poor First" blog. In the imaginary of middle-class Egypt, 'ashwa'iyyat are regarded as tough neighborhoods, where youth are de facto suspects perhaps justifiably exposed to police brutality; unemployment is spectacularly high, available employment such as there is undignified, low paying, and insecure; and drug use is common (usually of hashish, but also of pharmaceuticals like Tramadol). Zizo was from such a neighborhood, Bulaq al-Dakrur. He had a college degree from a fly-by-night private university in hospitality management. His degree did him absolutely no good. Getting a well-remunerated job in Egypt for him was a virtual impossibility.

The term *sirsagi* is contemporary youth slang. Long ago the word referred to young men who scavenged cigarette butts; in the polite society of 2013 it evoked youth who wore lots of hair gel and harassed women in the street. Zizo had the contemporary sirsagi look but was the living embodiment of why such terms of appellation have to be understood in strictly situational contexts—in this case either as a joking term used among friends (like African Americans using the N-word among themselves, and only among themselves), or as a derogatory class or race label applied to someone else. In reality, like many youths from his social milieu, Zizo actually lived by a totally un-sirsagi-like seat-of-the-pants honor code that armored him against often iniquitous circumstances in the spheres of livelihood and dignity.

This code is often elaborated discursively in the genre of popular music known as *mahraganat*, which some people refer to occasionally as "electro-sha'bi" music. It features heavy drum tracks, complex sonic layering by means of synthesizers and sampling, and a youthful vocal aesthetic that aspires to be "in your face" or "from the street." Aside from live concerts, the main distribution channel for *mahragan* is YouTube. The music does not sound very much like American hip-hop, but the mahragan genre shares with hip-hop the same hard-life visual codes, and vivid attachment to place, specifically the 'ashwa'i neighborhoods from which the singers originate. The aesthetic is like NWA's "Straight Outta Compton" ("You are now about to witness the strength of street knowledge," as Dr. Dre says in the beginning of the song), but in the case of a mahragan, straight outta Amiriyya, or 'Ayn Shams—or Zizo's Bulaq al-Dakrur. Mahragan also shares with hip-hop a cross-class appeal and marketability. The first time I heard about the genre somebody had sent me a link to a video of a concert by DJ Haha in London. When I viewed it I found several of our own Oxford students in attendance and obviously enjoying the music, and they were definitely not straight outta Amiriyya.

Once I knew that mahragan existed I grew to like it and listened to it some-times while working. A line from a mahragan song titled "Nahnu Nuridha Hals"—"we want it debauched" (Salah and Mitwalli [i.e., Oka and Ortega] 2013)—always reminded me of Zizo, though I do not know if he in fact liked the song. The line was *kulluh bil-hubb, wil-'aql wil-usul*: "everything for love, reason, and principles." The point is that the social milieu the music evokes is meant to be precisely the opposite: youth of the 'ashwa'iyyat are meant to live in a world completely *devoid* of love, reason, and principle. The song is not about *being* debauched, but about the constant degradation of young men from this milieu. The invocation of reason, love, and principles in the song (and the genre to a degree) amounts to a defiant rejection of present circum-stances. The line comes amid vivid depictions of being forced to lie, cheat, and deceive in order to makes one's way in this harsh world. A longer sequence of the lines is: *ba'd (i) ma sabahit hayyatna kullaha ghish fil-ghish, kulluh bil-hubb, wil-'aql wil-usul, Urtega wi Hariqa wi Oka, ikhwat wi-ashab 'ala tul*; "after our lives became cheat upon cheat; everything for love and reason and principles; Ortega, Hariqa, and Oka; brothers and friends to the end." Ortega, Hariqa, and Oka are the singers. Mahragan music often features callouts to specific people and invocations of particular places, but here the point is to evoke the people you *don't* cheat, because that's how you survive in a world where you have to lie and be lied to. This is what I could not imagine Zizo abandoning—those very close "brother-like" friendships that sustained him when everything connected to employment, livelihood, and ultimately respect were rigged against him.

His move to Qatar was years in the making. From early 2011 to 2015 he worked for us on again and off again as a jack-of-all-trades in our motley col-lection of real estate, while also trying out various dead-end, low-paying, no-security jobs in the private sector. Unlike most of the members of the crews of semiskilled labor we employed in our apartment renovation ventures, Zizo remained unfailingly loyal to us. Sometimes he was downright heroic. At one point we were struggling with the water supply to our Ma'ruf apartment. Since we were on the top floor we got no water from the building's decrepit old "*motor*" (pump). We wanted to install our own pump with a parallel pipe—a solution practiced all over the city as one can see from walking around and inspecting the clusters of pumps patched together to get water to where it needed to go. The owner of our building tried to stop us, claiming that our pump would reduce the water flow to the entire building and then nobody would have water. We were in despair. There seemed to be no way we would ever be able to actually use our laboriously renovated apartment. Then one day the building's own pump needed repair. Zizo was on hand and started chatting with the owner's plumber. "Is there any reason we can't attach a second 'motor' next to this one?" he asked. "Of course not, *'adi*," he replied—"it's typical." Zizo took the plumber upstairs to repeat what he had said in front of the owner. After that we were finally able to install our pump, and the last barrier to making our apartment habitable was removed (and the water supply to the rest of the building was unaffected). Zizo was always there for us. He sometimes looked after our affairs when we were away and was always happy to work when we needed help. Over the course of four years he became more of a friend than a worker.

Zizo was twenty-something (late twenty-something by the time he moved to Qatar). On the surface he was resolutely apolitical, but very likely he was just reticent with us. We were his employers, albeit rather odd employers by the standards of all his other work experiences. His political impassivity with us did not mean that he was unaffected by the revolution. Many of his friends were drawn into battles with the security forces, in which the motivation for hitting back at the police and security forces was expressed as a masculine ritual rather than articulated as ideology (Ryzova; n.d.). He himself was sometimes an onlooker in these battles. He watched, he listened, and he certainly thought more about politics than he had at any other time in his life, even if he did not act. Zizo was the sort of person who ideologically committed revolutionaries hoped would be drawn into politics. If indeed Bayat's claim that "something had changed" as a result of the revolution was correct, perhaps it would be evident in people like Zizo.

I have no doubt that Zizo was greatly moved by the revolution. It was part of his daily life even more than ours. We took him with us on several occasions to some of the larger demonstrations and talked to him about politics, but politics never came naturally to him in conversations with us. There was always a wall of reserve that never quite broke. At the same time, he often knew what was going to happen before we did. Sometimes he would warn Lucie to stay away from demonstrations. As she related to me, he said "Ya Madam, don't go to Tahrir today. There will be lots of *ashbal* there." *Ashbal*—"lion cubs"— meant adolescent men in their mid-to-late teens, a "generation" that from his late-twenties perspective were dangerously out of control. During breaks in the work on our apartments he and the other workers in our crew sometimes talked about the new drugs that these even more youthful youth took, various "cocktails" of synthetic compounds that made them completely crazy, not like his generation, "old-timers" who knew how to keep their intake safe and moderate. But more importantly, his ashbal warning and other comments he made about ongoing events made it clear that he was very sensitive to what was happening, despite his apolitical, nonchalant demeanor.

Zizo's departure to Qatar was an act of despair. He had long resisted family pressure to go to the gulf—either to Qatar or to Oman, in both of which his family already had a beachhead. It was not that he disputed the logic of traveling to make some money in order to *yukawwin nafsuh*—to "establish himself" in order to get married. But he did not want to go to the gulf because he knew he would be treated poorly there. He would have to forego his hashish ritual because the gulf countries treat drug in fractions extremely harshly. Most importantly, he would have to separate himself from his friends who were like brothers to him in the grotesquely unfair world of unemployment and persecution by the police. If he had to go somewhere, what he really wanted was to go to Europe. On several occasions he halfheartedly pushed me to give him an invitation to Britain, where he would disappear and find a job, or to help set up a fake marriage in order to get a visa. The urge to migrate among young Egyptian men is often structured like this; one goes to the gulf to make money, whereas "those who also want freedom are more likely to want to go to Europe or, even better, North America, where they can live a life free of the constraints and oppression they experience in Egypt" (Schielke 2015, 158). But in the end he finally capitulated to his parents and agreed to go to the gulf. We were his only contacts in Europe—really just me, because he would not raise such issues very strongly with Lucie. My explanation that an American citizen cannot sponsor an Egyptian visa application to Britain seemed to be reluctantly accepted. The last time I saw Zizo in Cairo, in August 2013, he was waiting for the final arrangements for travel to Qatar to be made. It was a long wait. He did not go until April 2015.

His final act before departure was to post an exquisitely ambiguous political song on Facebook, the only even remotely self-generated political comment he ever made in a form accessible to me. It was a rap song by a YouTube star named Shady Surur, titled "Damm Rikhis"—"cheap blood." Surur had acquired some fifty million followers for his amateur videos, which was enough to get him noticed and interviewed on talk shows ("Awwal Liqa'" 2014). But all the other videos on Surur's YouTube channel were comic sketches poking light fun at social mores. "Damm Rikhis" was, by comparison, a scream of anguish. It was about being a young man caught between the fascism of the state and that of the Muslim Brotherhood, though it never uses the actual word "fascist." The song is not production of "deracinated, denatured martyrs 'of Egypt,' sans political ideology or even ideas" (Gilman 2015, 693), typical of commercial video clips. It is angry, bloody, and shocking. However, it takes aim at both the state and the Muslim Brotherhood, and possibly pulls its punches with respect to the army and security forces—depending on how one interprets the figure representing the state, who comes into the video narrative at the end.

The video starts with Surur walking in slow motion through a Cairo street, interspersed with martyr imagery, both stills and videos, from many of the revolution's most violent episodes. It conspicuously avoids glorified images of youth fighting the security forces in the iconic Battle of Muhammad Mahmud Street—the event that most deeply captured the attention of nonpolitical spectators of the revolution like Zizo. Most of the martyr imagery focuses on massacres committed by the army and security forces, including Raba'a al-'Adawiyya, Maspero, and Shayma' al-Sabbagh (an activist murdered on the fourth anniversary of the revolution when she tried to walk to Tahrir Square from downtown to lay a wreath in honor of the fallen). There are a few iconic images, and lots of anonymous martyrs. Surur also inserts a few images of security forces and military martyrs, presumably from Sinai where government forces were killed in large numbers. The inclusion of security and military victims is much less overt than the pop video clips that Gilman explores (Gilman 2015), but it undeniably introduces a note of political ambiguity. Here are some samples of the lyrics:

> From the start this wasn't supposed to be a song
> But finally I had to get it off my chest
> We're a generation that's seen all sorts of suffering
> I'm young, but depression's spread all through me
> My brothers and friends are dying all around me
> I've started to feel that it's my turn next
> Blood has become cheap, and nobody cares
> If I'm killed tomorrow nobody will notice
>
>   . . .
>
> I'm not someone with a stake in politics,
> I'm just someone whose life has been crushed, and I want it back
> Twelve years in school, and then four in college
> Then military service, and the only job I can find is as a
>   security guard in a company in al-'Abbasiyya
>
>   . . .
>
> People just want some bling, some say you can be a big talker,
> Others say you're with the military or with the Ikhwan
> It's all bullshit, but I don't care; I'm here to say just one thing:
> I'm pissed off, Egyptian blood has become cheap, worthless
> The youth are wasted, fucked up a long time ago, when you die
>   your picture goes black and you're forgotten

Then the singer's voice shifts into a higher more insistent register, more directly addressing an interlocutor than singing a song:

> Silence, and people are still dying; you're still fighting over whose words
>   are right and whose are wrong
> Come on, let's join together unconditionally, if we don't try to change
>   we're screwed

I wish Egypt could go back to the days of the Pharaohs
    Seventy-four Ahlawis died, and thirty-two Zamalakawis, army
        officers, pathetic security forces soldiers, and kids in Raba'a
Egyptian blood has turned into a worthless product: the kids who
    died in Tahrir, and
    the Presidential Palace, and Maspero, and the constitutional court
And children who died in their school buses: it's your fighting that's
    ruining
    the country

The video ends with interventions first from the Muslim Brotherhood, then from the state. The singer enters an empty room in a ruined building. A bearded Islamist in white galabiyya starts barking new lines at him:

Shut up, I don't want to hear your voice, or even the sound of your
    silence from the
Day you're born to the day you die, you agent of America, you Jew
I'm the one who holds the reins, you'll never get rid of me
You hear the sound of bullets? Smell the smell of gunpowder? You're a
    regime tool.
I didn't kill soldiers. I'm right. I'm on the straight path
And you're the biggest reason for the mess we're in

As the Ikhwan speaks the camera flashes back and forth between him and the singer, whose eyes widen in fear. Then the camera swivels over to a slick-looking man in a black business suit, who also addresses the singer:

Shut up you Ikhwani, you're totally wrong
A terrorist, you killed laughter in the youth
Spreading hatred everywhere
Stop lying to people
Get out of politics and leave them to your betters
You wrecked this country and killed its children
Listen, you won't get anything you want, get back to prison.

The regime man pulls a pistol, aims it, shoots; the Ikhwan does the same; the singer appears, eyes wide in shock, spattered with his own blood, slowly sinking to the ground. The Ikhwan and the regime man stroll over to inspect the body. The Ikhwan calmly addresses the man in the suit: "Isn't he a regime guy?" The regime man, hands casually thrust in his pockets, answers, "I thought he was an Ikhwan."

What do I make of the fact that the normally apolitical Zizo posted this song on Facebook before quitting the country and finally going to Qatar—which he had always equated to a kind of death sentence? Is this evidence of what Bayat, in the hopeful long-view scholarly perspective, describes as the birth of a new political consciousness that cannot be denied? Of "something fundamentally different . . . when the old order faces new political subjects and novel subjectivities" (Bayat 2015). To be honest I cannot say. From what I know of Zizo his posting of this song was deeply sad, like a symbolic suicide letter. The song is emblematic of a social position that many observers had hoped would become infused with political will. I find the politics of both the song and its Facebook posting by Zizo on the eve of his emigration from Egypt to the symbolic death of life in Qatar utterly ambiguous.

Put Zizo to the side for a moment. He claimed to be apolitical, at least in my company, and may well still do so. What about those who were not? The existence of the hoped-for subterranean progressive political consciousness spreading beneath everyday oppression is frustratingly intangible. To be sure, previously unpoliticized people who lost friends or witnessed death experienced the revolution as a life-changing event, whether or not it "succeeded" in political terms. Many youths who were already politicized on the eve of the January 25 Revolution remained politicized but were either broken or biding their time in a state of political hibernation—or out of the country if they had the means to leave. The notion that from beneath a state of malaise a transformed generation would emerge to demand its rights is seductive and comforting. But this is a generational proposition. In the short term militarism ran rampant. Aside from several people I knew who had witnessed friends killed and determined to remain committed to the revolution on their behalf, the most striking example I knew of those who unquestionably had their political consciousness transformed (not counting, of course, those who were already politically committed) were those who became much more belligerently supportive of the new regime than they had ever been during the Mubarak era: Hamdi the bookseller, 'Id and Hisham the lawyers, and most of their families. 'Id's son, a university student by the time I finished this book, was posting his own images of dead bodies on Facebook—military propaganda photos of alleged jihadists in Sinai, bloody, bloated, with torn limbs, conveniently laid out next to their weapons, and given triumphalist captions glorifying the army's ability to kill.

The defining feature of a liminal crisis is pure contingency. To put it differently, we can never be entirely sure what will emerge from the void. Sometimes it is monsters rather than the angels we hope for. I remain convinced that good things emerged along with the naked violence. It will take time for the good things to rise to the top, but rise they will, even if it turns out to be too late to save the world.

NOTES

Acknowledgments

1. The conferences included panels at the 2011 Middle East Studies Association (organized by Flagg Miller) and the 2011 American Anthropological Association organized (organized by Julia Elyachar, Farha Ghannam, and Jessica Winegar); "The Egyptian Revolution, One Year On: Causes, Characteristics and Fortunes" (at the University of Oxford, organized by Reem Abou-El-Fadl in 2012); "Icons, Popular Culture and the Making of Publics in the Middle East" (at the University of Copenhagen, organized by Sune Haugbolle in 2013); "The Revolutionary Public Sphere: Contention, Communication, and Culture in the Arab Uprisings" (at the University of Pennsylvania, organized by Marwan Kraidy in 2014); "Ends of Revolution: Ideology, History and Critique in the Aftermath of Uprisings" (at Roskilde University, organized by Sune Haugbolle in 2015); "The Scandal of Continuity, Festschrift for Paul Dresch" (at All Souls College, Oxford, organized by Andrew Shryock and Judith Scheele in 2015); "From Mobilization to Counter-revolution: The Arab Spring in Comparative Perspective" (at St Antony's College, Oxford, organized by Neil Ketchley in 2016); "Islam, Islamists, and the Media in a Changing Middle East" (at George Washington University, organized by Marc Lynch in 2016); the Tenth Nordic Conference on Middle Eastern Studies (a keynote address titled "Egypt in the Age of the Trickster," at the University of Southern Denmark in 2016); "Lineages of the People: Embedded and Transregional Histories of Contemporary Populism" (at the University of Göttingen, organized by Srirupa Roy, Paula Chakravartty, and Gianpaolo Baiocchi in 2017); a keynote address at "History and Society on TV in the Middle East" (at the University of Maryland, organized by Madeline Zilfi in 2017); participation in a plenary panel at "Mosaic of the Contemporary Arab World" (Jagiellonian University, Krakow, organized by Przemysław Turek, the Middle-East Student Academic Society, and the Institute of the Middle and Far East).

Chapter 1. Introduction: Revolution as Liminal Crisis

1. Some prominent examples of social scientific approaches to the causes of the January 25 Revolution are Abdelrahman (2015), Achcar (2013), Gunning and Baron (2014), Ketchley (2017), and Kurzman (2012).

2. The January 25 Revolution would not have happened without a decade of labor unrest (Beinin 2010; 2012; Abdelrahman 2015, 55–63; Alexander and Bassiouny 2014); or a tactical willingness for Islamist and leftist movements to coordinate their activities developing in the 2000s (Abdelrahman 2015, 98–101; Hirschkind 2011b); or the spectacularly corrupt 2010 election, in which the question of Mubarak's bequeathing power to his son loomed over everything (El-Ghobashy 2010); or the brutal murder of Khaled Said and the social media campaign to protest it (Herrera 2014, 47–101); or the increasingly harsh tactics used to control underemployed youth (Amar 2013; Ismail 2006); or the bombing of the Qadisayn Church in Alexandria (Tadros 2011a); or the successful revolution against the Ben Ali regime in Tunisia; or the spectacular political tone deafness of the Mubarak regime's decision to upgrade Police Day to the status of an official national holiday in 2009 at pre-

cisely the moment when police behavior had become an issue of public concern. All this together was an unrepeatable alchemy.

3. The exceptions to this silence on liminality were Mark Peterson (2015a; 2015b) and Bjørn Thomassen (2012). Thomassen invoked the Arab revolutions only in passing, but it was a crucial intervention for me.

4. For example, Nugent and Vincent's volume on anthropology and politics (arguably the primary focus of the entire discipline) focuses primarily on long-term social processes such as feminism, globalization, or militarization (Nugent and Vincent 2007; see also Thomassen 2008). A review of anthropological writing over the course of 2011 highlights revolution but similarly emphasizes disciplinary work on processes as opposed to events (Dole 2012). Thomassen (2012) discusses the history of anthropology's lack of engagement with political revolutions per se.

5. Some summaries of the state of the art in ritual studies are Kelly and Kaplan (1990); Bell (2009), and Grimes (2013). My focus here is on liminality, specifically in the context of major transformations. Liminality is also a property of ritual in the context of human action in general, and ritualization certainly can be employed to produce a sense of the mundane. Ritual practices, according to Catherine Bell, set certain practices off from general human activity but at the same time are thoroughly intertwined with social constructions of order through "strategies of differentiation through formalization and periodicity, the centrality of the body, the orchestration of schemes by which the body defines an environment and is defined in turn by it, ritual, mastery, and the negotiation of power to define and appropriate the hegemonic order" (Bell 2009, 220).

6. I mention this preemptively only because I have had the experience on several occasions of invoking Turner and having anthropologists snap back "functionalist" almost reflexively. It should be noted that Turner remained good to think with for quite a few anthropologists. See, for example, Lewis's book on the anthropology of performance, which uses Turner's ritual process as its starting point and connects it to a wide range of performance-related theory that supposedly supplanted Turner (Lewis 2013).

7. For an influential formulation of the functionalist criticism, see Ortner (1984, 131). See also Weber (1995, 530) and Caton (1999, 7).

8. Foucault instantiates the two poles of heterotopia as the brothel and the colony. The former mixed everything that should not be joined together in normal space. What he had in mind for the latter was particular kinds of utopic colonies—Puritans in North America, or Jesuit colonies in South America. Interestingly, in Egypt, Tahrir Square was remembered by revolutionaries as a utopia, and often denounced by skeptics and counterrevolutionaries as a brothel.

9. With regard to the distrust of totalizing phenomena, one notes that anthropological thinking about the nature of structure may have changed in the 1970s and 1980s, but this hardly meant that the discipline abandoned all interest in pattern or normativity. Bourdieu's *habitus*, for example, touted as a conceptually robust alternative to totalizing visions of structure or "system" (Ortner 1984, 148), was offered as an explanation of how normativity emerges not as a denial of its existence. Indeed, contemporary anthropological attention to marginality, liminality, hybridity, ethnicity, or borders, for example, would be impossible in the absence of social constructs of normativity, whether we label them structure, *habitus*, culture, a constantly shifting Deleuzian assemblage, or some other term. Doctrinaire adherence to nominalist philosophies, particularly those of Deleuze or Latour, both of them prominent in contemporary anthropology, presents the greatest obstacle to conceptualizing boundaries—of objects, categories, structures, or systems. Nominalism dissolves boundaries insofar as it "rejects the existence of abstract objects, of universals, or of both of them

altogether[,] . . . is in short a claim that only individuals exist, and is . . . a contrasting stance towards ontology which grants that in some way universals, abstractions, and categories can be said to have an existence beyond their mere crafting and use by human beings in ways that have performative social effects" (Bialecki 2012, 302). Without boundaries there can be no in-between. Hence a pure vision of social worlds consisting of "immanent fields that people, in all their ambiguity, invent and live by . . . fields of action and significance—leaking out on all sides" (Biehl and Locke 2010, 335) makes it difficult to conceptualize liminality. Engagements with nominalist philosophies therefore often make compromises in order to acknowledge various forms of collective abstraction, for example, through "piecemeal appropriation of certain concepts for the remaking of middle-range theorizing that informs contemporary research projects" (Marcus and Saka 2010, 103). But such compromises are not made "if pushed too far, if insisted upon too literally—if it becomes anything more than an allusion—[rather, the Deleuzian] assemblage rapidly becomes a dead metaphor in one's work" (Marcus and Saka 2010, 106). The position taken in this book is practical. Nothing can be liminal or marginal in the absence of socially consensual categories, and "normal" is a kind of metacategory, even if a complex multiplicity of realities lurks below its surface. One may choose to understand structure in nominalist terms (with all the problems for conceptualizing liminality that such a position implies), but such understandings are about something else—philosophical arguments and debates about ontology. In the end liminality is as phenomenologically real as the multiple experiences of individuals. Kelly and Kaplan had already noted the affinity of Turner's ritual process with alternative theorizations of border zones such as Bakhtin's carnival, but it should be noted that in the context of revolution Turner's insistence on liminality as a component of transition is rather more suggestive than the carnivalesque as a setting for subversion. My topic in this book is not "celebratory attitudes toward pluralities of the modern" (Thomassen 2014, 9) that can easily be incorporated into a neoliberal order. It is rather the potentially dangerous quality (demonstrably so in the case of the January 25 Revolution) of liminality in a social and political transition.

10. Crampton (2013) catalogs and dissects Foucault's writing on space, territory, and geography. He gives significant emphasis to heterotopia, noting that "Of Other Spaces," a four-thousand-word essay delivered at an architecture conference, generated a vast secondary literature (Crampton 2013, 386). But he addressed the concept directly, and also very briefly, on only two other occasions (Crampton 2013, 385).

11. The concept of a "revolutionary situation" was first articulated by Trotsky as the moment of fluidity when "the economic and social premises of a revolution produce a break in the mentality of society and its different classes" (Trotsky 1931). It is a key concept for sociologists interested in the dynamics of political contention (McAdam, Tarrow, and Tilly 2001; Tilly 2006). Contingency in sociological writing on revolution assimilates readily to agency, as opposed to structure (see Selbin 1997 on agency in revolution theory; Wickham-Crowley 1997 on structure). Debates over the relative importance of agency and structure in the social sciences have a very long history (see Bourdieu 1977 and Giddens 1984 for prominent interventions). Foran's edited volume (1997), in which Wickham-Crowley's and Selbin's chapters appear, similarly divides the field into structural analyses opposed (not always absolutely) to those predicated on culture and agency.

12. See, for example, Jeffrey Paige's much more recent definition of revolution: "rapid and fundamental transformation in the categories of social life and consciousness, the metaphysical assumptions on which these categories are based, and the power relations in which they are expressed as a result of widespread popular acceptance of a utopian alterna-

tive to the current social order" (Paige 2003, 24). But aside from the immense complexities of such constructs as "state and class structures," and a lack of attention to such matters as ideology, ethnicity, and religious bases for mobilization (Goldstone 2001, 140), there is an obvious problem with the temporal dimension of revolution in such terms. What constitutes "rapid"? A year? A decade? A generation? By the strictest standards of defining "rapidity" (say two years) even such classic cases as the French and Bolshevik Revolutions seem dubious. More recent "fourth-generation" scholarship on revolution is more analytically flexible. Scholars of revolution have criticized earlier approaches as Eurocentric and put greater insistence on the importance of culture and ideology (Goldstone 2001). Most importantly, the strand of "contentious politics" within the field of recent revolution scholarship attempts to understand the relation of revolutions and social movements. The point is that the dynamics of political protest are tied to political, social, and economic contexts (Tilly 2006; 2008).

13. See, for example, Marshall Sahlins's analysis of Captain Cook's impact on the Hawaiian Islands in the eighteenth century (Sahlins 1985), or Veena Das's ethnography of trauma framed by "critical events" in Indian history (Das 1996). Niehaus faults them for focusing on events that were both historical and in the public sphere, "removed from the daily happenings that we encounter during fieldwork" (Niehaus 2013, 653). He prefers in his own ethnography to frame events by the scale of his informants' lives and perceptions. Steven Caton's *Yemen Chronicles* (2005) follows the same strategy. It is partly an ethnography of an event—his experience of being abducted in 1979 during his doctoral fieldwork in the context of a conflict between a local sanctuary and a tribal group. The event is in some ways connected to larger postroyalist politics following a civil war, but on the whole it sticks closely to the relations between the anthropologist and his informants. The book makes no pretence to being an ethnography structured by a large or cataclysmic event in the public sphere.

14. Shah and Pettigrew (2009) provide an excellent survey of anthropological work on revolutionary societies. They note a general lack of field-level data, and also that most anthropological work is done "post-conflict, when the guns are silent" (Shah and Pettigrew, 230). Anthropologists have also written about revolutions not just "when the guns are silent," but in a longer historical view (Friedrich 1977; Scott 2014). It should be emphasized that the point being made here is about the study of revolutions as events, and not about politics more widely. Anthropology is extremely attentive to politics, the political implications of everyday practices, and the exercise of power in societies.

15. Thomassen makes the same point (2012, 679–83), arguing that anthropologists have a tradition of writing about rebellion and protest movements, but the focus is on context and background rather than on revolution itself (Thomassen 2012, 681). What Caton calls an "anthropology of events" (1999) has potential relevance to the study of revolution—a point he himself made as a discussant at an American Anthropological Association panel on the Arab revolutions in 2011. But Caton also notes that "anthropology of events" literature is limited (1999, 6–9).

16. On social movements, see Edelman (2001) and Nash (2004). Social movement literature articulates with "public anthropology," which is a major current in contemporary anthropology (Checker, Vine, and Wali 2010). Anthropologists were attentive to Islamist social movements in Egypt and their relation to secularism (see Starrett 2010 for a critical review of this literature), and there is no doubt that Islamist movements crucially illuminate aspects of Egypt's revolution. Also on secularism: Agrama (2012); Asad (2003; 2011); Cannell (2010); Connolly (2011); Hirschkind (2006; 2011a). Liberalism as an anthropological

subject is often tied to discussions of secularism and (in the Middle East) to Islam. Mahmood (2011) places all three in a single analytical frame. Liberalism is also often prefaced with "neo," and while the distinction between liberalism and neoliberalism is sometimes debated, it should be noted that the literature on neoliberalism in anthropology is very substantial. Discipline-centered reviews of the topic include Ganti (2014) and Gledhill (2007).

17. Lucie is a historian of the modern Middle East. In addition to her historical work (Ryzova 2014; n.d.), she has written about the revolution (Ryzova 2011; 2015; n.d.).

18. My description of downtown in the paragraphs below draws heavily from Ryzova (2015; n.d.).

19. The demographics of neighborhoods on the periphery of downtown—al-'Ataba, parts of 'Abdin, Taufiqiyya, Faggala, parts of Lazoughly, and Bulaq—changed greatly from the 1950s to the present. Areas that had been intensely overpopulated in the 1950s and 1960s, before the explosion of 'ashwa'iyyat (informal housing) in more distant peripheral areas of Greater Cairo, were less populated by the 2000s. In the interim decades there was a steady replacement of overburdened housing with informal or semiformal workshops in such trades as carpentry, furniture making, metalworking, car repair, or eyeglass lens grinding. In addition to this demographic shift in the neighborhoods bordering downtown, in the decade before the revolution there was a massive expansion of informal itinerant peddlers selling all sorts of small consumer goods on sidewalks. Semipermanent markets for such trade developed in 'Ataba and Bulaq, but in the years leading up to the revolution downtown sidewalks were increasingly choked by informal commerce. After the fall of the Mubarak regime, once the police stopped policing and the formal economy went into a steep decline, informal peddlers took over virtually the entirety of downtown's sidewalks. One of the markers of "reaggregation" (Turner 1977, 166) engineered by 'Abd al-Fattah al-Sisi, once his seizure of power was ratified by a rigged election in 2014, was to forcibly remove all the informal trade from downtown. This was very popular with formal-sector merchants in the area and with middle-class Cairenes generally. It also had the effect of drying up the "swamps" where activists were able to blend in with a general state of anarchy.

20. There are many other ways that performance and performativity can be deployed in anthropological analyses. My concern is with the more limited instances of performance linked to the staging of politics in public. For a summary of the wider evolution of performance and performativity in anthropology, see Lewis (2013, 11–20).

21. This is a generic problem in the analysis of events (such as the revolution) and context (what passed for "normal" prior to the revolution) in any setting (Morris 2007, 361–67).

22. For a summary of the wider evolution of performance and performativity in anthropology, see Lewis (2013, 11–20).

23. 'Ukasha talked about the article once to discredit it on grounds that the translator was a member of the Muslim Brotherhood ("Ukasha fi Aqwa Ta'liq" 2015). I do not know if this was true or not. On the second occasion he attempted to use the article as validation. He had just been elected to the first postcoup parliament and was encountering quite a bit of criticism in the media. In his program he argued that foreigners were fascinated by his use of "Fourth Generation Warfare" tactics. His cohost held up a copy of the newspaper with the "Glenn Beck of Egypt" headline (Barakat 2015—all about my article) and mentioned that "Oxford University" had sent someone specifically to study him ("Al-Halqa al-Kamila" 2015).

Prelude. My Eighteen Days

1. This is not his real name. The names and personal details of my interlocutors have been changed to preserve their anonymity.

2. If I had been stopped by soldiers and asked for identification, I could not have provided it. The day before the revolution began I had been informed by ARCE that my residence visa was ready, and asked to drop off my passport so that someone could take it to the government office where the stamp would be put into it. After the revolution began nobody could get to ARCE because the office was located very close to Tahrir. That remained the case for most of the eighteen days. I did have a photocopy of my passport and took to carrying some utility bills with my name on them in order to show that I was in Cairo before the revolution began. I do not know if those documents would have helped if I had been stopped and questioned.

Chapter 2. The Material Frame

1. Protestors often called for milyoniyya marches, and this often meant specifically in Tahrir Square. The upper limit of numbers in a Tahrir protest were more like two hundred thousand, if one also included many of the large avenues leading up to the square. It is difficult to factor in the element of time. Large demonstrations continually cycled crowds through the square sometimes for hours, so if there were two hundred thousand at peak moments, the total number who moved through the space through a day would have been more by some indeterminable amount. But the bottom line is that "million-man march" is not a phrase to be taken literally. Ketchley suggests that the peak mobilization for the very largest demonstrations, such as the June 30, 2013, Tamarrud march (and possibly also some of the large mobilizations early in the revolution), was around a million throughout the entire country (Ketchley 2017, 103–4).

2. The "neo" in neoliberalism relates to its demotion of freedoms prominent in late Victorian liberalism, social democracy, Keynesian economics, or mid-twentieth-century welfare states. All of them were concerned with "the optimal expression and development of the individual" (Freeden 1986, 257), but in some balance with communal interests that states had a responsibility to regulate. Neoliberalism, by contrast, elevated the rights of property owners above all else. Its emergence in an era of unprecedented globalization made it aggressively expansionist. "The turn to neoliberalism reflected the accumulation needs of capital in an era of internationalization, i.e., capital with accumulation spaces increasingly spread across a global level" (Hanieh 2013, 14).

3. "Market rationality is an achieved state" (Gershon 2011, 538) and "can be constituted and kept alive only by dint of political interventions" (Lemke 2001, 193). One can make a distinction between a "roll-back" phase of neoliberalism that began in the 1970s, animated by a laissez-faire spirit and aiming primarily to reduce the size and influence of social democratic or welfare-state governments, and a "roll-out" phase marked by the creation of institutional "hardware" designed to regulate the imposition of free markets (Peck and Tickell 2002, 389–90).

4. To get a sense of the range of anthropological approaches to both defining neoliberalism and articulating its effects, see Collier (2012), Hilgers (2010), Ong (2006), and Wacquant (2012).

5. In premodern Europe, cemeteries were located in the centers of cities. But in the nineteenth century they were moved to the margins, because modern notions of death defined it as a kind of illness that had to be separated from the healthy living population, and also because individualized bourgeois society required more expansive private places

to commemorate the bodies of their loved ones, in the context of rising doubts about the immortality of their souls (Foucault 1986, 25).

6. Lefebvre is also known for having written on heterotopia, but his formulation of it departed from Foucault's. For Lefebvre an urban place ("isotopy") was intrinsically multi-functional (Lefebvre 2003, 128), whereas a heterotopy was a rather vaguely defined "other place"—marginal places of trade such as fairgrounds or caravanseries in premodern cities, places excluded from the "political city" (Lefebvre 2003, 9), but less easy to situate in modern cities that extend their political control to the countryside. Others have interpreted Lefebvre's heterotopias as rooted in "a sense of political and historical deviance from norms" (Smith 2003, xii), or as simply "liminal social spaces of possibility where 'something differ-ent' is not only possible, but foundational for the defining of revolutionary trajectories" (Harvey 2012, xvii). That is perhaps closer to the multifunctional nature of Tahrir Square, which however comes into view only if one views it as an alternating (rather than intrinsi-cally alternative) functionality.

7. A subsidiary agenda in this chapter is simply to deepen the spatial orientation of the reader. Many of the places, streets, and institutions introduced here will feature in the re-mainder of the book, and they are of course unfamiliar to anyone who has not lived in Cairo. A "walk-through" at this juncture will make it easier to follow quite a bit of my subsequent narrative.

8. Before the 1880s the site of Midan al-Tahrir had been swampy. It was filled in during the 1860s by the Khedive Said and first became the site of an army barracks.. Prior to the 1952 handover of the area from the British to newly independent Egypt, demonstrations were more likely to focus on Midan Abdin, about a ten-minute walk to the east, in front of Abdin Palace, which was then the main seat of the government. I will not discuss the politi-cal history of Midan al-Tahrir here. Elshahed (2011) discusses the politics of urban planning as applied to Midan al-Tahrir, noting that extravagant and even utopian dreams for turning the largest open space in the city, once the British evacuated, into a cultural, institutional, and political center of Cairo, had always fallen well short of their ambitions.

9. While value of sit-ins was a point of contention among the revolutionary forces, there were always some groups who insisted on remaining. When the tents disappeared from the saniyya it was inevitably because some combination of the security forces, the military, and hired muscle (baltagiyya) tore them down. Merchants in the area allegedly frustrated at the loss of business due to the sit-ins were said to have paid for at least some of the baltagiyya.

10. Sims's figures (from 1998) are a bit older than Monroe's (from 2013). But the basic balance between automotive mobility and other forms of motorized mobility in Cairo have not changed greatly.

11. More prosaically, tariff policy over the two decades prior to the revolution steadily liberalized automobile assembly and importation, thereby lowering the purchase price of private automobiles (KPMG 2005, 34 part 2). Laws governing the importation of automo-biles were liberalized in 1991 and 1993 (KPMG 2005, 36 part 2), and Egypt's participation in the Barcelona Process (signed in 2004) requires that "the customs duties on motor ve-hicles designed for the transport of persons will be reduced by 10 % each year from January 1, 2010 to January 1, 2019" (KPMG 2005, 35 part 2). Frighteningly (given the current state of congestion in Cairo's streets), "the Egyptian car market remains . . . small and underde-veloped by international comparison in terms of the level of vehicles for such a large popula-tion" (KPMG 2005, 29 part 1).

On a different front, policy favored road construction over public transportation (Sims 2010, 248–49; Ragab and Fouad 2009, 12). Banks began providing consumer loans for automobile purchase, and policy think tanks encouraged the Egyptian Central Bank to push harder on this front (KPMG 2005, 42 part 2). Sims cites a survey estimating that at prerevolution rates of purchase, private automobile ownership would double every thirteen years (2010, 236), and with a favorable climate (no snow, hence no corrosive salt on the streets) plus a massive cottage industry for fixing and restoring broken-down vehicles, it is safe to assume that the life of every vehicle in the country will be very long.

12. Sims cites one estimate that 36 percent of all daily journeys in Cairo were made on foot in the year 2000—up from 25 percent in 1970 (Sims 2010, 228).

13. This project was expedited after Sisi came to power and finished early in 2015. It was part of a high-priority campaign by the state to cleanse downtown of its quasibohemian character that had helped incubate the revolution by facilitating "order" and privatization. In an interview on the opening of the Garage Mustafa Sa'id, the governor of Cairo Province, put particular emphasis on the security elements of the new garage, including twenty-four-hour camera surveillance of Tahrir Square (Sa'd 2015).

14. The Metro is one of the legitimate Mubarak-era *ingazat* (achievements—a term that had been repeated ad nauseam in Mubarak's election slogans). The streets above were clogged with the cars of the lucky 11 percent, not just the ones moving at any given time, but particularly the ones parked in every open space, making movement on sidewalks all but impossible, thereby forcing most pedestrian traffic into the streets, and causing some to avoid *being* a pedestrian at all costs. Of course busses and other forms of collective transport were also part of the congestion, but they carried far more people relative to the space they took up and did not contribute to the narrowing of public thoroughfares through parking. Below the streets, the Metro, operational only since the late 1980s, already carried some 25 percent of Cairenes' daily vehicular trips within the city by the time just before the revolution (Sims 2010, 244). Cars, despite their overwhelming dominance everywhere above ground, account for about 20 percent (Sims 2010, 235). The economics of the Metro are complex. When one of my students at Oxford began researching the Metro for a thesis, she encountered conflicting statements about how heavily each Metro ride was subsidized (thanks to Miriam Berger for her insights on this matter). There is no question that the Metro moves vast numbers of people, but it is unclear whether the price for doing this is high or low. The bottom line is that while Tahrir Square was favored by the best transportation network in the city its diversity still amounted to a kind of transportation apartheid with the private automobile at the top and pedestrians at the bottom.

15. AlSayyad does not say whether the plan was to relocate the Cairo governorate from its current location on Abdin Square to the building on Midan al-Tahrir, or if there were plans to create a municipality as a new institution. Sims (2010, 251–56) lays out the basic structure of Egyptian governance. The city of Greater Cairo is divided among three governorates: Cairo, Giza, and Qalyubiyya. Governors are appointed by the president. Below the level of the governorates, there are some forty *ahya* (local districts), and nine *marakiz* (centers) in the peripheral areas that are technically rural, but actually informal parts of Greater Cairo. According to Sims, the governorates are politically and economically weak in relation to the central government. The ahya have elected representatives who are supposed to represent communities in their respective governing structures, but in fact functioned to distribute authority downward from the NDP, which totally dominated the local elections, as it did the national ones.

16. By the end of 2015 the burned-out NDP building had finally been demolished, and the land allocated to the adjacent Egyptian Museum.

17. It is something of a misnomer to call New Cairo (the general label for a collection of subdevelopments) a "suburb." Sims estimates that the total area of the new towns under construction around Cairo (both to the east where AUC is located and to "new Giza" and

its associated satellite towns on the west) is 2.2 times the built-up area of the existing city (Sims 2010, 201). A great deal of desert land outside the government's master plan for New Cairo has also been allocated (Sims 2010, 201). These immense new developments are planned to have a population of twelve million (Sims 2010, 187), but their population was only around eight hundred thousand (extrapolating from the numbers given by Sims [2010, 171]), which is about 5 percent of the total.

18. Public investment pays for roads, sewers, water, street lighting, public spaces, landscaping, and treatment plants (Sims 2010, 171). Sims notes that hard figures on public expenditure are hard to come by. He cites an outdated (covering the years 1997–2001) Egyptian government publication that stated the total percentage spent on the new towns as 22 percent of all public investment in housing (Sims 2010, 293–94). But this, he says, was probably a low estimate by the standards of the 2010s.

19. I know this from having spoken to a representative of the Ismaelia Group, and my own observations are amply buttressed by Lucie Ryzova, who interacted with Ismaelia Group representatives far more extensively than I did. Jon Argaman explores the dynamics of downtown redevelopment schemes systematically, observing that by the year before the revolution Ismaelia was trying to sell its downtown property, and government redevelopment initiatives had stalled for lack of funds (Argaman 2014, 77).

20. These included a skyscraper housing the Ministry of Foreign Affairs and several vast upper-end commercial tower developments.

21. The building, or actually complex of buildings, is the Nile City Corporate Complex, headquarters of the Orascom business group, which is headed by the Sawiris family, which collectively is the wealthiest family in Egypt.

22. I learned about the ways of walking in Bulaq when a real estate agent tried to sell me a flat there. The location, he said, was "in Taufiqiyya," a neighborhood on the downtown side of Ramsis Street. This was an estate agent's lie (like "cozy" to describe an impossibly cramped apartment). It was actually smack in the middle of Bulaq, across the street from a Carmelite monastery. It was not an uninteresting property though, at least by night, when I first saw it, hence I went back in the daytime to explore the area and imagine what living there would be like. The apartment in daylight turned out to have serious structural problems, but my interest had already evaporated from the walk, which proved beyond a shadow of a doubt that Bulaq was deliberately cut off and clearly slated for extinction. Ghannam (2002, 31) indicates that this has been the state's policy since the Sadat era.

23. By 2018 the government had finally achieved its goal of completely demolishing at least the southern part of Bulaq (the Maspero Triangle).

24. US aid to Egypt from 1979 to 2010 averaged $2.2 billion per year (Sharp 2010, 4). The aid was both economic and military, but after 1998 the balance tipped sharply to the military side. The 2013–14 level was about $1.2 billion per year ("Egypt, Military Budget" 2015), which at that time was about a quarter of the total Egyptian defense budget. Most of the aid was in the form of Foreign Military Financing (FMF)—US loans to purchase US military equipment (US Department of State 2015). Nominally the United States intends to phase out aid to Egypt, but the two countries have not been able to agree on a mechanism for this process (Sharp 2010, 5).

Chapter 3. The Martyrological Frame

1. This chapter was originally written for a workshop titled "Icons, Popular Culture and the Making of Publics in the Middle East," at the Royal Danish Academy of Sciences and Letters, April 18–20, 2013, organized by Sune Haugbolle. A later version of the paper was published in a volume edited by Reem Abou-El-Fadl (Armbrust 2015).

2. A number of philosophers make use of related concepts to refer to the demarcation of a set of practices, mechanisms, or objects that can be used by some agency of power (Agamben 2009; Butler 2009; Foucault 1980; Heidegger 1977).

3. On poetry, see Colla (2011); and on music, Swedenburg (2011). El-Ghobashy (2011) discusses the tactics and strategy of mobilizing protests during the revolution. An early advocate of the role of Twitter in the revolution was *Tweets from Tahrir* (Nunns and Idle 2011); later assessments of the role played in the revolution by information technology were more nuanced (e.g., Aouragh and Alexander 2011). Karima Khalil's *Messages from Tahrir* (2011) best visually captures the improvisational energy of the early phase of the revolution. A volume edited by Mehrez (2011) helps greatly to flesh out the context of Khalil's visual record of Tahrir signage.

4. The use of death-in-the cause to legitimize or sacralize state power is common, though "martyrdom" is not always the term of art. The United States, for example, has a very extensive history of wars, frontier conflicts during over a century of continual territorial expansion, and troop mobilization for the purpose of both domestic and foreign military engagements. American death-in-the-cause narratives range from Nathan Hale and the Alamo, to the Tomb of the Unknown Soldier and Arlington Cemetery. Those killed in the 9/11 attack on the United States in effect form the basis of a very powerful martyr complex (see Simpson 2006). Israel is another example of a nation-state in which martyr commemoration is crucial. There is also the so-called Masada complex—a contemporary rereading of an ancient mass suicide of Jewish rebels against Rome that has been thoroughly worked into the contemporary nationalist imaginary (Zerubavel 1994). Of course the Holocaust is absolutely central to Israeli nationalism. The full name of Israel's national Holocaust museum, Yad Vashem, is the Holocaust Martyrs' and Heroes' Remembrance Authority (http://www.yadvashem.org.il/). On the use of Yad Vashem, Masada, and archaeology in constructing Israeli nationalism as an implicit erasure of Palestinian nationalism, see Swedenburg (1995, 43–55).

5. On the politics of mobilizational martyrdom, see Khalili (2009) and Allen (2006) on Palestinian martyr culture in Lebanon and the Occupied Territories respectively; and on Lebanon, Deeb (2006), Haugbolle (2010), and Volk (2010). Martyrdom is of course also central to Shi'i social and political tradition outside the Arab world (e.g., Varzi 2006, to cite one example of an interpretation of how martyr discourses are embedded in Iranian everyday life.

6. The most permanent icons are religious precisely because the boundary between our world and the divine exerts a universal fascination for all human beings. And the issue of how to mediate (or *whether* to mediate) between the world and divinity exists in all religions. Icons are a Christian expression of the problem of mediation.

7. Egyptian revolutionary graffiti became the subject of countless articles and several books (e.g., Boraie 2012; Gröndahl 2013; Hilmi 2013; Maslamani 2013; B. Hamdy and Stone 2014). Mona Abaza, who wrote more (and more perceptively) on the phenomenon than anyone else (e.g., 2012a; 2012b; 2013; 2015; 2017), analyzes how revolutionary graffiti articulated with prerevolution graffiti and street art practices, and how revolution street art between 2011 and 2013 worked together with events, political initiatives, and other forms of artistic expression (literary, street installations, dance, music). She also chronicles the commercialization of revolutionary graffiti, which became iconic globally, but with distinctly ambivalent results. The spectacular art works that bloomed particularly on Muhammad Mahmud Street (the site of violent battles between protestors and the security forces in late 2011 and early 2012) became "low-hanging fruit" for foreign journalists eager to publish a literally eye-catching story about the revolution, but who had no means to relate

them to either history, the larger semiotic context, or the flow of events and personalities (Abaza 2015; 2017).

8. Commemoration of the 1967 June War was assimilated to the War of Attrition (the Harb al-Istinzaf) that took place up to 1970, when Nasser died and Sadat elected to concentrate on rebuilding the army rather than on maintaining pressure on Israeli military installations on the side of the Suez Canal that they controlled. Egyptian military performance in this series of feints and thrusts was relatively credible compared to its abject defeat in June 1967.

9. Louis (1984) details a diplomatic history of British-Egyptian relations in the late 1940s. See also Morewood (2008). Al-Hifnawi (1953) relates the diplomatic history from the Egyptian perspective. Thornhill (2006) details the fighting between British forces and Egyptian guerillas in the Suez Canal zone from 1946 to 1952 (not a war formally, but a substantial warlike conflict in Egyptian popular culture) through mainly British archival sources. Abdel Nasser (1994) examines the conflict through both British and Egyptian sources, concentrating on the 1945–52 period in half the book.

10. The British, plagued by the rising tide of armed insurrection against their presence in the canal zone, attempted to disarm Isma'iliyya's main police headquarters, including auxiliary forces quartered temporarily in the Bureau Sanitaire, formerly a group of hospital buildings (Thornhill 2006, 57). When given an ultimatum to withdraw to barracks outside the city, the police refused, probably on orders from the Wafdist government in Cairo. British soldiers, backed by heavy armor and air power, attacked. At least fifty of the policemen were killed, and many injured, against four British soldiers killed and ten wounded. The British were, however, taken aback by the determination of the Egyptians to resist and considered the event a watershed moment in rethinking their Egyptian policy (Thornhill 2006, 57–59).

11. There are many theories (some of them falling into the "conspiracy" category) about who started the fires. Nationalists firmly believe that it was done by British agents. The Muslim Brotherhood believes it was agents in the pay of the Free Officers. Nasserists say it was the Muslim Brotherhood. Nancy Reynolds catalogues the debate over who was responsible for the fire, without taking a position on who the guilty party actually was (Reynolds 2012, 181–82, 298–99). The question of who was actually responsible is, likewise, not relevant here.

12. Their faces published in the print edition of *al-Masry al-Youm* (but not in the online version of the article) were culled from Facebook pages: Mustafa al-Sawi, Karim Banuna, Sayf Allah Mustafa, Muhammad Mahrus, Sally Zahran, Islam Muhammad 'Abd al-Qadir Bakir, Ahmad Basiouny, Ahmad Ihab, Islam Ra'fat, Muhammad 'Imad Husayn, 'Amru Gharib, Husayn Taha, and Muhammad 'Abd al-Mun'im Husayn ("Shuhada' 25 Yanayir" 2011).

13. The Umm Sabir of 1951 was the *second* Egyptian martyr by that name. The first was a woman killed in the 1919 Revolution and commemorated in 1949 in a painting by the artist Gazbiyya Sirri ("Gazbiyya Sirri" 2013). According to the *al-Masry al-Youm* profile of her, she was known as "the icon of the 1919 Revolution" (Gazbiyya Sirri" 2013).

14. The history of Mudiriyyat al-Tahrir (located in Beheira governorate on the western side of the Nile delta) encapsulates elements of the political-economic dynamics that led to the January 25 Revolution over a sixty-year history. Mudiriyyat al-Tahrir was a centerpiece of huge land reclamation projects advocated by the Nasser regime starting in 1952. The scale and ambition of Mudiriyyat al-Tahrir was huge (Margold 1957). By 1980 Alan Richards was characterizing Mudiriyyat al-Tahrir as disappointingly plagued by higher-than-expected costs, rising salinity, and low production (Richards 1980, 9). However, Al-Dihi (2010) and Nawwar (2010) suggest that Mudiryyat al-Tahrir's fruit produce eventually

became a strong export business in the Mubarak era. Nawwar's article in particular compares Nasser's public-sector Mudiriyyat al-Tahrir project favorably to the Mubarak-era "public-private" Toshka venture in the western desert parallel to the Nile valley. In general Mubarak-era economic policies were indeed catastrophic for agricultural labor and detrimental to national food security, and agricultural exports benefited only a small group of well-placed entrepreneurs at the expense of increasing poverty (Bush 2007). By contrast Springborg (1979) focuses not on the often-contested economic realities of Mudiriyyat al-Tahrir, but instead on the capacity of the project to generate political patronage. In this respect it was extremely valuable and was fought over between factions close to or relatively distanced from the ruling officers, and between partisans of Russian-style collectivism and private enterprise.

15. The name of the station had reportedly been changed back to "Mubarak" by May 2014 ("Al-Metro Yu'id' 2014).

16. Another was Salih Harb Pasha, the head of the Association of Muslim Youth (Jam'iyyat al-Shuban al-Muslimin). Al-Banna had been one of the founders of the Shuban al-Muslimin. After the Muslim Brotherhood was banned in 1948 al-Banna had sought the intercession of the Shuban al-Muslimin to arrange meetings with government officials in an effort to have the brotherhood reinstated. It was after one of these meetings in 1949 that al-Banna was shot by two or three anonymous men, "mukhbirin" (government informers) according to the Muslim Brotherhood's wiki site ("Qissat Ightiyal Hasan al-Banna" 2014).

17. Abdalla's history of student activism referred euphemistically to "extra-parliamentary forces" (1985, 86–98; his one reference to the Muslim Brotherhood by name comes on p. 90). Erlich, by contrast, depicts the Muslim Brotherhood as important in student politics from the mid-1930s until the accession of the Free Officers. However, he casts doubt on the commitment of Muslim Brotherhood student members, suggesting that students were attracted more to the movement's call to action than to its ethos of discipline and obedience to the Murshid (Erlich 1989, 151). Hence in Erlich's estimation "Muslim Brotherhood members" might well have also been members of the Communist Party or other "extra-parliamentary groups," to use Abdalla's expression. This is worth keeping in mind when reading the Ikhwan-wiki site's version of history, which invariably puts the Muslim Brotherhood at the center of everything and characterizes the student martyrs of 1952 straightforwardly as committed members.

18. The most famous site of unofficial revolutionary commemoration was Muhammad Mahmud Street just adjacent to Tahrir Square. Murals here generally focused on specific individuals. Graffiti, often produced through quickly applied stencils of specific individuals or other iconic images, spread through many other parts of the city throughout 2011 and 2012.

19. Mina Daniel was an activist and member of several youth political organizations, killed by the military in the Maspero Massacre (an attack on mostly Coptic protestors who had marched to the state Radio and Television Building to demand protection of minority rights) in October 2011. 'Imad Effat was a prorevolution Azharite scholar and a senior official at the Dar al-Ifta', the government agency responsible for issuing Islamic legal opinions. He was killed by a military sniper in December 2011 at a sit-in at the Cabinet Office (*majlis al-wuzara*') protesting the appointment of the Mubarak-era politician Kamal Ganzuri to the position of prime minister. Gaber "Jika" Salah (Gabir Salah Gabir) was a member of the April 6 youth movement, killed by the security forces in December 2012 in a demonstration commemorating the Battle of Muhammad Mahmud Street that had taken place a year earlier (a long-running fight with the security forces following a demonstration against "constitutional principles" that would have locked concessions to the military into any future constitution).

20. There is only one other statue in Tahrir Square, also a recent addition to the area. Its subject is 'Umar Makram, an Azharite who rallied forces against the French invasion of Egypt in 1798. He was later instrumental in the rise of Muhammad 'Ali, though Muhammad 'Ali subsequently became wary of potential opposition to his own rule and sent Makram into exile. Both statues—'Abd al-Mun'im Riyad at the north end of Tahrir Square, and 'Umar Makram on the south near the mosque named after him (which is used for state funerals)—were the work of sculptor Faruq Ibrahim ('Ashari 2010).

21. Before his death in the October War al-Rifa'i led commando raids behind Israeli lines in the Sinai after the defeat of 1967. His commando team was named Magmu'at 39 Qital (the 39 battles group), after the number of raids they carried out in Sinai during the Israeli occupation. One of his raids was to retaliate for the killing of 'Abd al-Mun'im Riyad by destroying the Israeli position that fired the fatal barrage ("Al-Shahid Ibrahim" 2010). One can find quite a bit of popular commentary on al-Rifa'i's life and career (e.g., 'Isa 2010; Ghitani 2010; Foda 2011).

22. Decline in the military's prestige was not absolute, but the reemergence of SCAF's dominance in 2013, when 'Abd al-Fattah al-Sisi deposed Muhammad Morsy, created a false sense that the military's popularity was universal among non-Islamists. Harsh control imposed over the broadcast and print media together with crackdowns on all forms of political opposition—Islamist and non-Islamist—suppressed criticism of the military. This did not mean that the hegemony of the old regime had been restored. On the contrary, al-Sisi ruled through much greater exertions of violence than the Mubarak regime had done. But the more violence was required to silence criticism, the more likely it was that criticism would eventually reemerge.

Chapter 4. The Disputed Grievability of Sally Zahran

1. Parts of this chapter were published earlier (Armbrust 2012a; 2012b).

2. Al Aswany is a prolific writer of essays and novels. He is most famous internationally for *The Yacoubian Building* (Al Aswany 2007), a story about social class and political corruption refracted through the residents of a downtown Cairene apartment building.

3. Both the political agency of women and the political status of Christians would become fracture points that counterrevolutionary forces would exploit. Chapter 8 discusses the sectarian politics of the revolution through the lens of a massacre of mainly Christian protestors in October.

4. Isra' 'Abd al-Fattah was a cofounder of the April 6 movement ('Azzam 2008; Shapiro 2009). Mona Seif is a human rights activist who founded, with her brother, a blog aggregator called Manalaa (http://en.wikipedia.org/wiki/Mona_Seif), which was important in documenting abuses of the Mubarak regime. There are numerous other well-known female activists, many of whom were imprisoned when 'Abd al-Fattah al-Sisi came to power. Massry first became prominent in the mid-2000s as a member of the Kefaya movement, an initiative to put an end to the apparent inevitability of Mubarak extending his seemingly endless rule by handing power down to his son (Ali 2014). Naber (2011) discusses the general prominence of female activists in the organizing of the revolution and its early days.

5. Examples of such incidents include attacks on women's marches on International Women's Day (March 8) in both 2011 and 2012; the notorious "virginity tests" (mentioned above) conducted on orders from SCAF member 'Abd al-Fattah al-Sisi in March 2011; the lawsuit against the virginity tests carried out by Samira Ibrahim and its painful verdict in 2012 (Seikaly 2013); the case of the "nude blogger" Aliaa Magdy in November 2011 (El Said 2015, 114–21; Kraidy 2016); and the "blue bra" incident in December 2011, already mentioned above. After that, sexual violence against women in protest spaces became common,

and there was no doubt that it was a tactic intentionally employed by the counterrevolution to further split the revolutionary political forces.

6. It was later reported that an official from the Ministry of Culture had removed Basiouny's name from Egypt's Biennale exhibition catalog ("Al-Shahid Basiuni Yufaggir" 2011). The official in question denied that he had done so (Awad 2011). Dina Ramadan explores the politics of exhibiting his work in state-sponsored exhibitions after his death (D. Ramadan 2015).

7. The *al-Masry al-Youm* feature did not mention al-Sawi's membership in the Muslim Brotherhood. But brotherhood websites did. See "Ta'bin al-Shahid" (2011).

8. A subu' is a ceremony performed on the seventh day after a birth.

9. Most prominent in "Sabah al-Khayr" is visceral imagery of fertility; the pain of menstruation and childbirth are prominent, and the poem is propelled by evocations of women's child-bearing capacities. Women (Egypt) produce youth, and a corrupt state, which is never directly named in the poem, destroys them—but never their spirit, which is continually reborn *ma damit Masr wallada*—as long as Egypt remains fertile. The Citadel, a Mamluk-era fortification, was used in modern times—until 1983—as a prison; specifically, a place for political prisoners. Nigm himself had been a prisoner in the Citadel in the late 1960s, and again in 1973 when he wrote "Sabah al-Khayr."

10. Some samples: Mikhaeel (2011); "Hadhihi . . . Basmatik" 2011; 'Abdallah (2011); "Sally Zahran" 2011; Fayed (2011); Ibn Saba'in (2011). Authorship of these poems is not always clear, as some are posted on forums in a way that makes it hard to determine if the poster was also the author. Posters on such forums also sometimes use pseudonyms.

11. See "NASA to Honor" (2011) and "NASA Takrum al-Shahida . . . Illa al-Marikh" (2011). In both cases the headlines are deceptive; the content of the English version states that Zahran's name was to be put "on a microship [*sic*]." The day before these articles appeared the Arabic edition had actually run an article displaying a mock-up of a "certificate of participation" for Sally Zahran's name to go to Mars on a microchip ("Rihla Illa al-Marikh" 2011).

12. As reported in *Bikya Masr* ("NASA to Name" 2011); MSN News ("NASA Rocket" 2011); and Fatakat Forum ("NASA Takrum . . . Zahran" 2011). These are samples; the story was reported on thousands of sites, forums, blogs, and Facebook postings.

13. Some claimed that her mother was in fact the person behind the hijab campaign ("Walidat al-Shahida" 2011). But no Facebook posting, blog, or discussion forum entry that I could find claimed to have been authored by a member of Ms. Zahran's family. Indeed, the only public statement by a family member actually contradicted the hijab narrative. The last line of the article quoted Zahran's brother Karim saying, "On the contradictions in the pictures published in the press and on the internet with or without the hijab Karim said, 'my sister removed the *hijab* two years ago, and this is the secret of the pictures of her not wearing it'" ("Shaqiq Sally Zahran" 2011). However, such confident attributions of Ms. Zahran's mother as the author of the hijab campaign tend to come from the most provocative sources. "Walidat al-Shahida" (2011) was published on a Salafi website dedicated to combating "Christian proselytizing" in Egypt.

14. "Sandmonkey" blogged anonymously from 2005, attracting a wide following for his opinions, which often went against conventional wisdom. During the January 25 Revolution he revealed himself as Mahmoud Salem, a business development manager ("Rantings" 2011).

15. The tweets sent to me by my student also appear on the Storify page of a Washington human rights lawyer named Kimberly Curtis. This is what I am quoting here; I was not following Sandmonkey's tweets at the time they were sent, and thus far the Twitter medium has no archiving capacity.

16. Examples of false narratives: "Laysat Sally" 2011; "Sally Zahran min" 2011. Both center on "sightings" of Zahran after she had died. A demonstrably authentic video was "Cairo Complaints" (2011). This documents her participation in a "complaints choir"—the brainchild of a Finnish artist who did workshops at a private downtown gallery in 2010 ("Complaints Choirs" 2011).

17. *Baladna bil-Masry* ("Our country in Egyptian" [Arabic]) was one of the most prominent talk shows on Egyptian television, broadcast Monday through Thursday evenings on the private station OnTv, owned by the Coptic Christian businessman Naguib Sawiris.

18. There were some odd aspects to the OnTv broadcast. It introduced her as a third-year university student (she was actually twenty-three years old and had been living in downtown Cairo for some time working for a film production company). The OnTv narrator also claimed to have been surprised by learning the true story of her death, even though the fact that she died in Sohag was known by February 7, the day after the *al-Masry al-Youm* pictures were published. *Al-Masry al-Youm* itself had published this bit of information, and *al-Ahram* had subsequently begun a nasty finger-pointing campaign in an effort to discredit their rival's professionalism. This was in the public record and accessible from any computer screen long before the OnTv interview was broadcast.

19. The Women's Day incident was one theater in the sectarian struggle, or at least this was how *al-Masry al-Youm* reported the incident on March 9—as a clash between a Salafi march demanding the release of Camilia Shehata and the women's march ("Masira Salafiyya" 2011). The day before (March 8—the same day as the march) the English version of *al-Masry al-Youm* focused directly on the Women's Day debacle and made no suggestion of Salafi involvement (Mohsen 2011).

20. The website on which it was published, al-Hiwar al-Mutamaddin (http://www .ahewar.org/debat/nr.asp), "civil discourse," advocates a leftist and secular orientation.

21. A Sohag University online student newspaper echoed Tal'at's speculation about police pressure to change the story of Ms. Zahran's death ("Itlaq Ism Ibnat" 2011). There were also many allegations that individuals from the Ministry of Interior or figures aligned with the old regime attempted to bribe or threaten families of martyrs in order to make them drop charges against the security forces (e.g., H. Fahmy 2011).

22. Representations of "Egypt as a woman" (Baron 2005) have been in circulation for at least a century.

23. Qusur (sing. Qasr) al-Thaqafa were a network of state-funded institutions tasked with "enculturing" (*tathqif*) the masses. See Winegar (2009) for more on culture palaces and Mubarak-era cultural policy.

24. The event at which protestors had been killed was on April 8 was titled Gum'at al-Muhakima wal-Tathir (the Friday of Judgment and Purification—not to be confused with the Friday of Purification in February mentioned at the beginning of this chapter). It was an important event, though not directly relevant to my narrative. A group of uniformed army officers had attended and spoken out in favor of the government acceding to revolutionary demands, thereby raising tensions between the army and the protestors to a new level.

25. In political terms it was not just Islamists that my friend and many other artists were reckoning with, but also the state, which had maintained a cultural presence in neighborhoods through a network of "culture palaces" even as the Muslim Brotherhood's influence was growing. But once the Mubarak regime had fallen, its cultural apparatus was subjected to intense discussions about how to "de-Mubarakize" culture. This was one of the impulses behind the larger and more prominent monthly al-Fann Midan (art is a public square) festival (Darwish 2011), and also behind independent events such as the one my friend organized. Anxieties of non-Islamist intellectuals about their isolation from "the people" are old. A famous expression of such anxieties was a 1970s poem by Nagib Surur

(who was criticizing his own milieu) titled "Brutukulat Hukama' Rish"—Protocols of the Elders of Riche (Surur 1993).

26. The references are to actress Su'ad Husni and the businessman Marwan Ashraf. The former was a legend of the Egyptian screen, particularly in the 1960s, when she starred in many highly regarded films. The latter was married to the daughter of Gamal 'Abd al-Nasir. Both died officially from suicide, jumping from balconies while resident in London. Many considered the deaths suspicious and suspected foul play; Marwan was suspected by some to have been a double agent who worked with the Israelis.

27. It should be note that Harbi had already achieved a degree of local prominence before the revolution by campaigning against Christians in the "Camilia Shehata affair." The wife of a priest in Upper Egypt either converted to Islam and was then held against her will by the Coptic Church, or a disgruntled wife who simply left her husband was then abducted, possibly by the church, which acknowledges that it is holding her "under its protection" (Howeidy 2010).

28. I anonymized him as "Citizen X" because I was unable to contact him to ask why his Sally Zahran memorial was taken down. When it first went up he initially accepted my Facebook friend request but later defriended me. It may have been that he saw the political winds shifting. The translator of the original version of this chapter (Armbrust 2012b) wryly commented that "he must be getting married" (i.e., his fiancée might object to his fascination with another woman). When X's Sally Zahran page was up it had no restrictions placed on it, hence it was accessible to anyone. The bottom line is that the page is gone, and unless Muwatin X reconstitutes it himself or publishes it the old-fashioned way (which I thought initially must have been the reason he took it off the internet), it will stay gone.

29. He lists Dunqul's in a "sources" section of his Sally Zahran memorial page, though there is no citation appended to the passage itself. However, the poem is well known. It is likely that the point is for X to put himself in the rarified company of intellectuals who do not need the citation to know the provenance of the lines. I am not such a person; I discovered the author's name by Googling the first line of the poem.

30. He refers first to Dunqul's "Kalmimat Spartakus al-Akhira"—the last words of Spartacus (Dunqul 1986a)—and then to modern Islamic thinker Muhammad al-Ghazali, alluding to "a critical moment in which falsehood was at the peak of its power, and truth in its greatest distress." X give no exact reference to the Ghazali passage, but it appears on numerous revolutionary websites in several Arab countries. The Arabic passage (for anyone who might wish to pursue the matter) is reproduced in full in the Arabic version of this chapter (Armbrust 2012b).

31. I met survivors of revolutionary martyrs through my partner Lucie Ryzova. See Ryzova (n.d.).

Chapter 5. Martyr Milestones

1. Winegar (2011) documents and analyzes the cleanup campaign in Tahrir Square. Schielke discusses similar initiatives in a Delta town (2015, 198–201).

2. In politics Gramsci probably had in mind something along the lines of a distinction between direct attempts to overthrow a government in an open rebellion or revolution, and the infiltration of civil society (Schwarzmantel 2015, 205–6). He saw civil society not as distinct from the state, but as the part of the state devoted to securing consent of the subordinate classes, as opposed to the state's coercive apparatus, hence his focus was on "the educational system, the Church, the press and more generally what we would now call the mass media, and the complex of voluntary associations which form the network of the sphere between individuals and the state" (Schwarzmantel 2015, 202–3).

3. For a detailed analysis of comparable debates about reforming the Egyptian media in the postrevolution, see Sakr (2013).

4. On this point I must credit Miriam Berger, who learned about this aspect of the microbus trade in the course of her excellent research for a thesis on the Cairo Metro.

5. Readers will already have encountered such poetry in chapters 4 and 6. For an excellent analysis of the role of poetry in the revolution, both of this type and with respect to contemporary poetry, see Schielke (2016).

6. The role of the Ultras in the revolution—specifically for the Ahli and Zamalek teams, which have the largest national following—is very complex. In some circumstances "Ultras" was a label used by middle-class activists to sanitize social groups with whom they were in tactical alliance (Ryzova 2011; n.d.); in other words, lower-class young men who would normally be kept at arm's length, or suspected of committing sexual harassment in the streets. But the Ultras were actually socially diverse and not always politically united. For an excellent analysis of the Ultras both in the context of Egyptian football (soccer) and revolutionary politics, see Carl Rommel's *Revolution, Play and Feeling* (2015). Ryzova (n.d.) provides by far the best analysis of both the significance of violence in the revolution and the importance of the Battle of Muhammad Mahmud.

7. The terms "precarity" (from which "precariat" is derived) and *'ashwa'iyyat* are class descriptors—allusions to "lower class"—but not in a straightforward way. I will elaborate on them in the next chapter, which focuses on the significance of class in the revolution.

Chapter 6. The Poor First

1. He mentioned this in a television interview three years later, when he won the Samir Kassir Prize for Freedom of the Press ("Liqa' ma' al-Katib" 2014).

2. The images are largely gone from the web, but someone transferred them (but not Abu al-Ghayt's full text) to a Facebook page: http://tinyurl.com/hhed65b. Abu al-Ghayt's original text (minus images) is still on his blog page (Abu al-Ghayt 2011a).

3. See "Al-Safha al-Rasmiyya lil-Sirsagiyya" (2016) for a "definition" of the sirsagiyya. It was originally the "about" section of a Facebook group called the National Campaign against Sirsagiyya . . . the Bloody Fist (*al-hamla al-qaumiyya didda al-sirsagiyya . . . al-qubda al-damiyya*). The "National Campaign" page still existed in 2016, but the "about" section has migrated several times to other pages.

4. Sha'ban and Sabah may or may not have been real. They were (purportedly) a young couple of obviously lower-class background who posed for a photo together, he with a wispy moustache and wearing "cool" sunglasses; she in a neon-pink hijab and sweater. The photo circulated widely on blogs and Facebook (e.g., https://25janaer.blogspot.co.uk/2012/04/blog-post_8630.html). The reactions Abu-al-Ghayt referred to seem to have passed into the ether by the time I looked them up. The photo was there, but usually with little comment. Sometimes those who posted the picture elaborated slightly: "Greater than Qays wa Layla," or "Love down to the marrow" (*hatta al-nukha'*). It seems to have been considered funny merely for the humble youths' pretension at anything as great as love.

5. From the poem "'an al-Sumud" ("On Steadfastness"). I have used Barbara Parmenter's translation (Parmenter 1994, 78). Darwish, who died in 2008, was a leading Palestinian resistance poet, and a major poet of the Arab world generally.

6. Abu al-Ghayt's blog post is meant as a polemic, but aside from its polemical purpose it should be noted that the class dimension of the revolution had not gone unnoticed by academics. On this see Salwa Ismail's analysis of revolutionary violence in lower-class and informal neighborhoods of both Cairo and Damascus (Ismail 2014).

7. *Sis* sometimes appears as synonymous to *sirsagi* on websites devoted to defining the

term *sirsagi*. But Abu al-Ghayt's interlocutor clearly indicates that *sis* (or *wilad sis* in linguistic constructs) means "cowardly" or "weak"—whereas *sirsagi* is being used as an unwarranted (in Abu al-Ghayt's opinion) class derogation of lower-class youth.

8. The lines are from "Brutukulat Hukama' Rish"—Protocols of the Elders of Riche
(Surur 1993). The translation here is by Marwa Farag. Surur was a leftist writer active in
the 1960s and 1970s. "Brutukulat" was written in the 1970s and criticizes elite leftist intellectuals who used to frequent the downtown Café Riche.

9. More precisely, the text says "mu'tasimi mukhayyimat madinat al-salam" (the protestors of the tents of Madinat al-Salam). In June 2011 some of the residents of the 'ashwa'i
neighborhood of Madinat al-Salam on the eastern edge of Greater Cairo had established a
sit-in at the Radio and Television Building, often referred to simply as "Maspero" (the name
of the Radio and Television Building's neighborhood). The aim of the protest was to force
the government to make good on promises it had been made to provide them with decent
housing (residents of Duwaiqa, an 'ashwa'i neighborhood located beneath a cliff, that had
suffered a catastrophic rockslide in 2008). The Madinat al-Salam protest lasted for weeks,
hence the erection of tents to shield the protestors from the sun and give them a resting
place. The front of the Radio and Television Building is on the Nile Corniche, which is a
major traffic artery. There was considerable friction with drivers who were exasperated at
having their progress impeded by a rag-tag group of lower-class protestors (see "Tajaddud
al-Ihtikakat" 2011). Maspero was a secondary protest site throughout the revolution, and
the site of a horrific massacre, which will be discussed in chapter 7.

10. "Matalib fi'awiyya"—group, or sectoral demands. A key rhetoric for dismissing the
explosion of small protests that took place after the fall of the regime was to characterize
them as unwarranted "special interests."

11. Sims shows how the state responded to population expanses from the late 1940s up
to the 1967 June War (2010, 45–52). The war and the subsequent wartime economy (lasting
until the late 1970s) caused the state to divert resources away from such priorities as housing toward the war effort. Once the wartime economy ended, pent-up demand for housing
had increased greatly, but the economically liberalized state under Sadat was no longer
willing to assume the burden of satisfying this demand.

12. The construction of housing in 'ashwa'iyyat is sometimes flawed, but not markedly
more so than in the formal sector, and moreover 'ashwa'i buildings are often inhabited by
their owners, who certainly have no intention of having their houses collapse on their heads
(Sims 2010, 100). It is indisputable that 'ashwa'i housing is poorly provided for in terms of
its connections to utility and transportation grids. Connections to the formal city inevitably
came later, once the neighborhoods became faits accompli, but obviously roads, sewers, and
electrical lines function better when they are planned for and established before housing is
built, as opposed to being added on through myriad acts of political *fahlawa* (cleverness,
or "street smarts") on the part of residents, a process well described in Salwa Ismail's study
of how the state articulates with informal Cairene neighborhoods (Ismail 2006). The same
goes for policing, which tended to be more punitive than constructive everywhere, but
particularly in 'ashwa'iyyat, and government services, not to mention health care and education. All these urban institutions exist in 'ashwa'iyyat, but inevitably in a kind of "catch-
up" mode. The gap between the needs of residents in 'ashwa'iyyat and the state's ability to
"catch up" was often filled by charity, and charitable organizations were often religious or
Islamist.

13. The term emerged initially in the early 2000s as a platform for Western European
"post-socialist" political movements advocating on behalf of casualized workers (Tarì and
Vanni 2005). It was subsequently elaborated by academics in various ways, ranging from

moral philosophy (Butler 2004; Butler and Athanasiou 2013) to the articulation of a general existential state connected with capitalism (Mahmud 2015; Neilson and Rossiter 2008) or with neoliberalism specifically (Lazzarato 2004; Palmer 2014; Standing 2011).

14. "Al-Fuqara' Awwalan Ya Wilad al-Kalb" (Abu al-Ghayt 2011a) first appeared on June 17, 2011; Isa's article ('Isa 2011) on July 4. As a journalist 'Isa often played the role of the gadfly, occasionally annoying both the Mubarak regime and that of Sisi. He was nonetheless a quintessential insider, and very promilitary (see 'Isa 2010).

15. Mona Atia maps the geography of Islamic charities in Egypt and shows the tight intertwining of neoliberalism and quasiprivate charity (Atia 2013).

Chapter 7. Copts and Salafis: Dueling YouTube Videos on the Edge of a Precipice

1. An emphasis on "democratic transition" tends to structure the work of political scientists and political sociologists. This is evident in quick reactions to the revolution (Miller et al. 2012), and also in works with wider perspective (Ketchley 2017).

2. Neil Ketchley and Michael Biggs argue the protestors at Raba'a al-'Adawiyya in the summer of 2013 were *not* from a rural and lower-class background, as many critics of the Muslim Brotherhood claimed (Ketchley and Biggs 2015)—an important point in light of non-Islamist claims that the Raba'a protestors were paid and duped by the Muslim Brotherhood leadership. But the issue of who was at Raba'a is different from that of who was at the many short-term demonstrations mounted throughout the two years of the revolution. Certainly at the one-day Friday of the People's Will demonstration at the end of July 2011 downtown was full of busses dropping off and picking up protestors who came from some distance (see below). And in the weeks leading up to the coup in 2013, when brotherhood offices were being attacked throughout the country at the same time that the organization was forced to mobilize its membership to mount frequent demonstrations, there were many reports of antibrotherhood forces attacking the organization's transportation infrastructure.

3. Tamam 2012, 71–93; 95–135; Kandil 2014, 31–33. The notion of ruralization probably deserves more critical scrutiny. The assumption is that a historically urban organization has been taken over by people in rural areas, bringing their "rural" lifestyles and worldviews with them. It may be more accurate to say that the Muslim Brotherhood has always, since its creation in the 1920s, appealed to people who represent the first generations in their families to achieve high levels of education (secondary or university). In the 1920s such a demographic occurred mainly in the major urban centers. In the 1990s and 2000s it was located on the peri-urban (often 'ashwa'i) fringes of both the major cities and rapidly expanding provincial cities such as Port Said, Suez, Mahalla al-Kubra, Mansura, or Asyut. In other words, "rural" may mean shopkeepers or schoolteachers with relatively high levels of educational attainment for their families, living on the fringes of provincial cities with populations between half a million and two million. The social position of these "rural" new members of the organization was not so dramatically different than that of recently educated (and possibly newly arrived from rural areas) Egyptians who joined the Muslim Brotherhood in the interwar era when the organization first flourished.

4. One notable exception was a long-running sit-in outside the American embassy organized by Salafis, protesting the imprisonment in the United States of 'Umar 'Abd al-Rahman, the blind Gama'a Islamiyya leader convicted of being one of the masterminds of the 1993 World Trade Center bombing (not to be confused with the 2001 bombing that brought the World Trade Center towers down). The 'Umar 'Abd al-Rahman protest started

in mid-2011 and was left undisturbed by the authorities until the end of 2012, when it came under attack from unknown assailants.

5. Broadly speaking there are diacritica (visual marks that differentiate) that reveal Salafi versus Muslim Brotherhood affiliation. Salafis often have longer beards (Muslim Brotherhood members cut theirs shorter); Salafis might wear robes or trousers above the ankle, in the tradition of the Prophet as they see it. By the "eye test" I would have said that more of the protestors at this event were Muslim Brothers. But the diacritica do not constitute an enforced uniform. Individuals may display some but not all of them or may simply turn out to be not what the diacritica indicate. Also, it was a brutally hot day, and many of the participants in the demonstration were coming from far away. They may have put practical comfort above sartorial concerns.

6. One should be cautious about projecting the official message of the event instantiated in speeches onto the very large audience. There was no way to gauge the depth or intensity of feeling about the messages being voiced by the speakers. I do not assume that all members of the Muslim Brotherhood or the Salafi parties and organizations were confident that the military was really on their side, or even that it was a good idea to publicly court SCAF as the speakers and many of the signs and banners were doing.

7. My translation is from a text preserved in a personal photograph.

8. Egyptian Salafism had connections to both modernist reformism and Wahhabism. Intellectual currents of Salafism began to tip toward Wahhabism in the 1920s, in response to anticolonialist currents and the demise of the caliphate. But its intellectual proponents nonetheless retained many links to modernist currents. The essential quality of Salafism as an intellectual construct was ambiguity, and labels applied to it by outsiders always played a role in defining its nature in the public sphere (Lauzière 2010).

9. "Every time we contrast [normative] secularism and religion, we implicitly make a choice of sides between the two, and our implicit choice arises from our own positions within local, national, regional, and global systems of social organization and discourse" (Starrett 2010, 648).

10. The show was hosted by a presenter named Mu'tazz Matar on the Sharq Channel. He was a staunch critic of military rule, and the channel itself was assumed to have been funded by the Muslim Brotherhood. After Morsy's fall the channel continued to broadcast for some time from Istanbul (Khayal 2015). As for Philopateer, he had begun to defy the Coptic clerical hierarchy long before the revolution, for example, by defying Pope Shenouda to support Ayman Nur's presidential bid against Hosny Mubarak in 2005 (Koptikjihad 2005).

11. Suspicion that the Maspero Massacre was premeditated and counterrevolutionary was voiced immediately after the incident (El Husseini 2011).

12. Philopateer maintained his anti-SCAF stance after the removal of Morsy from office. As of January 2015 he had emigrated to Canada, where he continued to criticize SCAF, and by extension Sisi, and to insist that the Muslim Brotherhood had nothing to do with the Maspero Massacre, despite frequent insinuations that they were the taraf talit that caused the debacle by using firearms against the army (Girgis 2015). The accusation that firearms were used by mysterious elements who joined the demonstration as it reached Maspero, justifying the military's use of force, were made from the first moment of the incident by "security expert" (and former army officer) Samih Sayf al-Yazal ("Taghtiyyat Ahdath Masbiru" 2011). There are no credible eyewitness reports buttressing that claim, and there are many eyewitness accounts that claim the soldiers began firing without provocation (e.g., Saad 2011; El-Mohendes 2011).

13. This would undoubtedly mean a substantial majority of Salafis. Philopateer (perhaps disingenuously) targeted "certain of the Salafi leadership" in his speeches ("al-Anba'

Filubatir" 2011), presumably knowing that such statements would be taken as generally anti-Salafi. From the other side, the Salafi Call, one of the largest Salafi groups in the country and the parent organization of the Hizb al-Nur, issued a statement that condemned the violence as foreign instigated—the same position as the Military Council—while also strongly condemning anyone active in the Marinab issue that sparked the Maspero events. The statement stopped short of attacking Christians as a community but was at the same time not even remotely conciliatory (Hatim 2011).

Chapter 8. Scripting a Massacre

1. "Egyptians have become addicted to tear gas" was a long-running joke during the revolution, as Samuli Schielke recounted in his ethnography of youth during revolutionary times (2015, xx). "There is a sensual and spiritual quality to protests and clashes that attracts and transforms people. Getting exposed to tear gas without being defeated by it is part of the formative experience of protestors for whom demonstrations, sit-ins, and clashes are among the most beautiful and meaningful moments of their life" (Schielke 2015, xx). The "tear gas ordeal" of course was part of the early phase of the revolution as well as the street battle phase described here. But the extremely heavy use of tear gas in the street battles was distinctive, and more deeply inscribed into memories of the battles than into the initial "victorious" phase of the revolution. On a slightly different note, rituals that subject initiands to severe trials and ordeals are common (Turner 1977, 169).

2. The largest of these "skirmishes" was a substantial conflict in December 2012 outside the Presidential Palace in November of the year-long rule of Muhammad Morsy. Non-Islamists remember that incident as an alarming deployment of the Muslim Brotherhood's own "forces" against non-Islamist opponents. The Muslim Brotherhood saw it as evidence that it had to depend on itself to protect its members and property, as the security forces clearly would not help them. The smaller skirmishes were attacks on Muslim Brotherhood or Freedom and Justice Party (the MB's political arm) properties and headquarters throughout the country during the first six months of 2013. The brotherhood claimed that these attacks were organized and funded. Non-Islamists characterized the attacks as spontaneous local-level opposition to Muslim Brotherhood rule.

3. *Gama'a* literally means "group." But at least since Richard Mitchell's classic book on the brotherhood *Gama'at al-Ikhwan an-Muslimin*, it has usually been glossed in English as "the Society of the Muslim Brothers" (R. Mitchell 1993 [1969]).

4. The "Rab'a Massacre" incorporated casualties from both the Rab'a al-'Adawiyya site and a smaller sit-in at Nahda Square in Giza.

5. The notable exception to the blackout on pro–Muslim Brotherhood media was al-Jazeera Mubashir—a live feed station that continued to receive video postings throughout the sit-in. It was often accused of producing "fake news" by, for example, using old videos of mass demonstrations to claim that there were ongoing demonstrations during the period of the sit-in.

6. The other most prominent fictions told in the non-Islamist press were that non-Islamist visitors to the sit-ins (at Rab'a and Nahda Squares) were at risk of being captured and tortured, and that the Muslim Brotherhood was storing a grisly cache of corpses underneath the speakers' podium.

7. Two examples are "Fadd I'tisam" (2013) and "Ahdath Magzarat" (2013). Some of the available videos are edited more than others to exaggerate the violence of the security forces' assault on the sit-in, but the violence itself is well documented (Human Rights Watch 2014). The Egyptian Ministry of Interior said that forty-three of the dead were members of the security forces (Nadi 2013). The independent Wikithawra group put the number of security

forces casualties at eight ("Taqrir Shamil" 2013). There are no credible casualty estimates that suggest anything other than a massacre. The official line on the breakup of Rab'a was that Muslim Brotherhood snipers began firing both on demonstrators who were attempting to flee from the encroaching security forces, and on the security forces, and that prior to the gunfire from the protestors, the only weapons used by the security forces were tear gas and water cannons (S. Faruq and Kamal 2013).

8. The violence in Rab'a had been preceded by a massacre of around fifty Muslim Brotherhood supporters on July 8 at the Republican Guard headquarters when members of the brotherhood protested the presumed incarceration of Morsy at that site. The army claimed that the protestors were armed and initiated the violence.

9. J. Khalil and Kraidy discuss the history of Ramadan broadcasting in Arab television industries (2009). Buccianti (2016) explores the interface of television broadcasting and online dissemination. Abu-Lughod (2004) provides an ethnographic account of television watching in Egypt set before the advent of satellite broadcasting. On *al-Gama'a*, see "Haqa'iq" (2017) for a critical perspective on the serial from a Muslim Brotherhood perspective. The serial was reported to have been fairly popular—the second most watched series of that Ramadan (S. Hasanayn 2010).

10. There was supposed to have been a second season of the serial following immediately after the first, which presumably would have resumed the modern track. Part 2 was to cover up to the execution of Sayyid Qutb in 1966. The years of revolution interrupted the shooting of part 2. It was finally produced and broadcast in 2017.

11. Tanwir discourse in Egypt dates from the nineteenth-century cultural and literary *nahda* (awakening or renaissance). But Hamid's evocation of tanwir particularly in his anti-Islamist work was also directly connected to Mubarak-era initiatives to specifically combat Islamism through a renewed commitment to tanwir specifically, in a neoliberal framework. For more on this, see Abaza (2010) and Armbrust (1996).

12. Perhaps this does not include Ali Mahir (prime minister in 1936 and again in 1939–40). He is shown as being Hasan al-Banna's preferred prime minister. Also Sirri Pasha, an old man who served as prime minister during World War II, is shown as being weak in the face of British pressure.

13. The speech occurs in episode 17.

14. Marsot (1978) gives the classic formulation of dysfunctional interwar Egyptian politics. See Maghraoui (2006) for a more recent analysis of liberalism in Egyptian interwar politics, which highlights the contradictions between liberal ideals and colonial conquest.

15. The conversation takes place in episode 12, and the establishing of the British intelligence officer's plot to compromise al-Banna through the French donation takes place in the previous episode.

16. Gudrun Krämer's biography of Hasan al-Banna quotes a British intelligence official as saying, "I consider that the 'Moslem Brethren Society' will in the course of time be in a position to produce a reckless and heedless generation who will not abstain from selling their lives cheap and whose best wish would be to die as martyrs for the sake of God and their country" (2010, 82). The same official is quoted as saying that "while [the Muslim Brotherhood] was 'growing in strength,' he believed, it was 'not at present in any way dangerous.'" That was in 1936. The scene in *al-Gama'a* in which the British intelligence officer reveals his cunning plan to sow dissension in the otherwise unified ranks of Egyptian nationalists was meant to be in 1927 or so, just as the Muslim Brotherhood was getting started.

17. His Salafiyya Bookstore (al-Maktab al-Salafiyya), founded in 1909, and also its later and more famous descendent, the Salafiyya Press and Bookstore (al-Matba'a al-Salafiyya wa-Maktab), were important conduits of both modernist/reformist and conservative Islamic thought (Lauzière 2010).

18. There is no reason to think that al-Banna was particularly close to Rida, or at least

this is the opinion of Gudrun Krämer in her biography of al-Banna. The Muslim Brotherhood was founded in 1927; Rida died in 1935 while returning from the Hajj. Krämer speculates that Rida was too important and well established to have bothered much with a young upstart like al-Banna (2010, 44).

19. Krämer quotes a somewhat similar passage by al-ʿUrfi (2010, 63). But the gist of the passage is much less cynical than the Wahid Hamid's script—essentially an exhortation to accept new members to the society who were imperfect in their faith, because "the Islamic call is like a hospital with a doctor who offers treatment, and a patient who seeks such treatment. Do not close the door in their face" (2010, 44).

20. For more on scouting in Egypt during the interwar era, see Jacob (2011).

21. This is although the Crusader association is only one aspect of the St. George legend. St. George is both much older than Islam and has also been incorporated in various ways into Islamic tradition (Haddad 1969).

22. Some translations use the more neutral formulation of "Allah wal-Watan" (God and country), but often the more subtly prioritized formulation putting God over country is repeated (e.g., "Mansoura Scout" 2017; "Al-Waʿd wa Qanun" 2017). The original formulation in 1908 used the formula "God and the King" but was adapted to international contexts as the movement grew, but in most cases God remains part of the formulation.

23. Hamid's taboo-breaking anti-Islamist film was al-Irhab wal-Kabab (ʿArafa 1992). In television, he was the scenarist in 1994 for al-ʿAʾila (ʿAbd al-Hafiz 1994). The latter was an element in the launching of a state-sponsored campaign against Islamists that was steeped in the tanwir rhetoric of the Mubarak regime in the early 1990s. For more on the larger campaign, see Armbrust (1998); and on al-ʿAʾila (and its place in the anti-Islamist discourse of the mid-1990s), see Abu-Lughod (2004, 165–79).

24. There are many well-researched books on the brotherhood that do not shy away from discussing the political flaws of the movement or its social contradictions. See, for example, Kandil (2014) and Wickham (2013).

Chapter 9. The Trickster in Midan al-ʿAbbasiyya

1. This chapter is adapted from "The Trickster in the January 25th Revolution" (Armbrust 2013).

2. On the political economy of Arab media generally, see Sakr (2007); and on postrevolution journalism (substantially television journalism), see Sakr (2013).

3. These were ʿUkasha's more prominent prorevolution talk-show "colleagues": Yousry Fuda and Reem Magid, presenters of talk shows on OnTv (Akhir Kalam and Baladna bil-Masry respectively), Hala Sarhan (Nas Book on Rotana Misriyya and many other shows before the revolution), and Mona al-Shazly (al-ʿAshira Masaʾan on the Dream 2 channel).

4. Iʿdam imagery was common in Tahrir Square but always focused on high-level political figures. Lesser figures in media and government were "named and shamed" in various regime black lists, but such individuals were never subjected to the sort of incitement to violence that the al-ʿAbbasiyya demonstration encouraged for media figures.

5. The judiciary, or rigal al-qadaʾ (men of the law) as ʿUkasha often called them, were subservient to the president (despite attempts to promote judicial independence in the 1990s; see Moustafa 2007).

6. Manufiyya is Hosny Mubarak's home province. The NDP machine was (and remained) particularly strong there.

7. Many recordings of the song can be found online. The words are by Salah Jahin, poet laureate of Nasser. It was first performed on July 23, 1966, the fourteenth anniversary of the Free Officers revolution.

8. *Al-fil abu al-shanab* is Qatar, specifically the emir of Qatar, Shaykh Jasim Bin Hamid Al Thani. One of 'Ukasha's consistent political lines was to allege a strong alliance between Israel, the rulers of Qatar, and the Muslim Brotherhood.

9. Muhammad Ibrahim Hassan is a Salafi preacher with a degree in mass communications from Cairo University. He is, like 'Ukasha, legible as a Trickster. According to Hassan's online bio, he completed Islamic graduate studies (*dirasat 'ulya*) in an unnamed institution, after which he became an Imam in Saudi Arabia for a time ("Ta'arrif bi" 2012). He is from a village in Daqhiliyya Province, near 'Ukasha's hometown. Hassan is the owner and star of the conservative Rahma satellite channel (Field and Hamam 2009) and was accused of having helped organize the "Battle of the Camel" that took place on February 2, 2011 ("'Hassan' Yanfa Tawarrutahu fi 'Mauqa'at al-Gamal'" 2012).

10. 'Ubur (crossing) invokes the breaching of the Bar Lev Line when the Egyptian army crossed into the Sinai at the beginning of the October War in 1973. The successful attack against an "impregnable" Israeli position was the Egyptian army's finest hour. Films and photographs of it regularly circulate on national holidays.

11. 'Ukasha later resigned from the party, and his bio was removed. However, it was preserved on the Internet Archive's "wayback machine" (see http://archive.org/index.php; search by the URL listed in my bibliography under "Taufiq Yahya Ibrahim 'Ukasha" 2012).

12. Indeed, it is not even clear that he earned a bachelor's degree. 'Ukasha's bio was vague on this point, merely stating that he received a "bachelor's degree in social work" (*bakalurius khidma ijtima'iyya*) but without specifying what institution granted the degree ("Taufiq Yahya Ibrahim 'Ukasha" 2012). Many blogs and internet forum comments claim that he actually earned a diploma from some sort of vocational institution rather than a university.

13. I am assuming a sexual double entendre, and hence glossing *'udu* as "dick" (penis). The literal meaning is "member," reiterated in *min a'da' al-lagna*—"from among the members of the committee." I take "committee" to be a slightly indirect allusion to the SCAF (though the "council" in SCAF is a *maglis*).

14. See "al-Ughniyya al-Rasmiyya" (2011), a montage of 'Ukasha's antics (to the urban intelligentsia). The nose blowing comes near the end.

15. Ryzova (2014) unpacks the historical and social specificity of the effendi in the interwar era, showing the considerable conceptual limits of simply conflating "effendi" with "middle class." In her analysis the effendi is precisely a mediating figure in a passage, or transition, to modernity—a formulation that fits very well with understanding Egyptian history through a wide-scale conception of the ritual process. Her final chapter casts effendis in the last generation before the rise of Nasser as "Prometheus Effendi"—the bringer of the flame of knowledge to an Egypt in need of "reform." Hence the Nasserist project was in many ways a fulfillment of effendi ambitions. And Prometheus, it should be noted, is often understood as a Trickster.

16. "Mythical thought always progresses from the awareness of oppositions toward their resolution . . . two opposite terms with no intermediary always tend to be replaced by two equivalent terms which admit of a third one as a mediator" (Lévi-Strauss 1963, 224). To do this he composes a series of related polarized terms: life/death; agriculture/warfare; herbivorous animals/beasts of prey. Each set of terms demands a mediator, and mediators must be ambiguous equivocal figures, creatures that straddle the boundary between categories. Ravens and coyotes mediate between herbivorous animals and beasts of prey because "carrion-eating animals are like beasts of prey (they eat animal food), but they are also like food-plant producers (they do not kill what they eat)" (Lévi-Strauss 1963, 224). Since each new term becomes an element of a system, new mediators are continually formed, but the form of the basic structure remains the same.

17. For an analysis of several Egyptian films along these lines, see Armbrust (1996, 94–115; 2008).

18. See Khalid Fahmy (2012) for a good critical summary of the crisis.

19. This is what their website said in mid-2012 (http://hrd.org.il/). In 2013 that URL was a dead link, but there was a Facebook page for an Israeli wing of the organization: https://www.facebook.com/HumanRightsDefendersFund, which appears to have been affiliated with a US State Department initiative (http://www.state.gov/j/drl/p/c46943.htm; http://www.state.gov/j/drl/p/c46943.htm).

20. My use of the term "conventional" implies no criticism of those who have done long-term media ethnography in Egypt or elsewhere (e.g., Hirschkind 2006; Abu-Lughod 2004). However, in a purely practical sense 'Ukasha was, in 2012, a rather fast-moving target. In practice one had to approach him from wherever one happened to be.

21. Even the need to worry about grant applications is variable. Egyptian anthropologists obviously have a different relation to them than non-Egyptians, but this is true of foreigners as well. Compare Mark Peterson's *Connected in Cairo* (2011), based on five years of teaching at the American University in Cairo, with Lisa Wynn's ARCE-funded *Pyramids and Nightclubs* (2007), an ethnography of tourism (2007). Both meticulously describe the circumstances of their fieldwork. Peterson never had to consider questions of governmental permission; Wynn ties herself in knots explaining how she stayed within the terms imposed by Egypt's Ministries of Interior and Education but in practice ventures far from what was formally permitted. Ultimately it was disciplinary ethics that guided both researchers, far more than formal limits imposed by Egypt's government. Such complications are typical.

22. I assume that the foreigners I saw detained were harassed and intimidated, possibly in some cases sent home. We were never detained, probably because a couple with a child did not fit the profile the soldiers were told to look for.

23. Later, after the rise of Sisi in 2013, a much broader and less orchestrated xenophobia set in. It helped set the context in 2016 for the murder of one foreign researcher, Guilio Regini, an Italian doctoral student affiliated with Cambridge University. But the rise of postrevolution xenophobia was not directly responsible for Regini's death—he was almost certainly killed by some branch of the security services. Khaled Fahmy (2016) summarized the case and what it implied for academic freedom in Egypt. Aside from the Regini case, the dangers to Euro-American foreigners in general remained small at all times; dangers to researchers and journalists were somewhat higher, but still very limited compared to the risks experienced by even mildly critical Egyptians.

24. Not "professor" in a literal sense; the word is often used as a general honorific. But depending on context (and definitely in this context), it can also have a slightly ironic sense—a vaguely mocking honorific.

25. It was not 'Ukasha who attacked the "dragged woman" video, but his cohost, Hayat al-Dardiri. Undermining the "dragged woman's" morality was perhaps more effectively carried out by a woman.

26. Two examples of the many stories tracing the genealogy of the Egyptian lie (as opposed to the original Moroccan source) to 'Abd al-Sami' are Hägglund and Carlshamre (2012) and Musaji (2012). The only blog that mentions 'Ukasha as the ultimate source is Egyptian Chronicles (http://egyptianchronicles.blogspot.co.uk/), and I am fairly certain that this source learned about 'Ukasha's role in the event from my own posting on Facebook.

27. He estimated that there were as many as half a million of them operating throughout the country by that time. It was an undercover film, to some degree based on "fieldwork" among his subjects. He was not expecting the film to be shown for at least five years, or not, at any rate, before it could be shown without putting himself in danger.

28. 'Isa al-'Awwam was a military commander who fought with Salah al-Din (Saladin).

29. Baybars and Qutuz were thirteenth-century Mamluk rulers of Egypt who fought both the Crusaders and the Mongols.

30. Muhammad 'Ali was the Mamluk ruler at the time of the Napoleonic invasion of Egypt in 1798, and subsequently credited as founder of the modern Egyptian state. 'Umar Makram was an Azharite scholar at the same time who rallied local Egyptian resistance to the French.

31. Sa'd Zaghlul: the Egyptian politician most credited as leader of the nationalist struggle against British rule following World War I. Makram 'Ubayd: a senior Coptic politician during the interwar era in the Wafd Party founded by Zaghlul.

Chapter 10. A New Normal? The Iron Fist and the False Promise

1. Parts of this chapter were adapted from a paper written for a conference titled "Ends of Revolution: Ideology, History and Critique in the Aftermath of Uprisings," organized by Sune Haugbolle, Roskilde University, Denmark, sponsored by the Secular Ideology in the Middle East research group, May 28–29, 2015.

2. Al-Beltagi's statement was widely reported in the press (e.g., Tharwat 2014). A video of the statement itself was uploaded on July 8 ("Tasrihat" 2013). Al-Beltagi later said that he was misunderstood, and that the point of his Sinai statement was simply that unrest in all the provinces would end once Morsy was reinstituted in the presidency ("Al-Fidyu" 2013).

3. "Pimp" is a literal translation of *mi'arras*, sometimes simply *ars*. The semantic range of the word extends to any person or act that displays a lack of scruples. Often "sycophantic" is a better gloss than "pimp." After Sisi came to power the revolutionary singer Rami 'Isam made a bitter video clip about the term, "'Ahd al-'Ars" (Age of the pimp). There are at least two video montages that go with the song. The official montage ('Isam 2014a) directly confronts the military. Another widely circulated video montage of the song ('Isam 2014b) puts 'Isam's bitterly anticoup song over the video track of "Bushrat Khayr" (Glad tidings, Jasmi 2014), which was the unofficial anthem of the coup.

4. Neil Ketchley's research leaves no doubt that Tamarrud was an "elite-led" protest masterminded by the military from the very beginning (Ketchley 2016). But the extent of the military's involvement at the time was not necessarily well known, and it must be accepted that many people joined the march not to call for a military coup, but to protest Morsy.

5. Conspicuous efforts had been made to suppress sexual violence against women that had plagued the area over the past year. Many observers believed that at least a proportion of these incidents, ranging from groping to gang rape, had been organized by opponents of the revolution, possibly the Muslim Brotherhood itself, which across town in their own demonstration were hurling derisive taunts about rapes in Tahrir Square.

6. *Al-Ka'in al-Ikhwani Malush Makan fi Midani*—"An Ikhwan Has No Place in My Midan." *Ikhwan* is a plural but is sometimes used informally as a singular, as in the well-known blog "Ana Ikhwan"—I am a Muslim Brother (http://ana-ikhwan.blogspot.co.uk/). Also, I glossed *al-ka'in al-Ikhwani* as simply "an Ikhwan" to preserve the rhyme of *Ikhwan* and *midan*. But it should be noted that this understates the song's derisiveness. Literally it would be "the Ikhwan-entity," patterned on the phrase *al-ka'in al-sahyuni* (the Zionist entity), which was, and in some quarters still is, used informally as a way of referring to Israel without naming it and thereby implicitly acknowledging its legitimacy.

7. The Murshid: Supreme Guide of the Muslim Brotherhood Muhammad Badiʿ. The others named after him were prominent Muslim Brotherhood officials well known to the public.

8. The word used in the song is "The Morsy," I assume a put-down. The only person I knew who used that construct consistently in writing (always firmly and often sarcastically opposed to Morsy) was Wael ʿAbd al-Fattah (e.g., ʿAbd al-Fattah 2013).

9. The public position of the Muslim Brotherhood on the Maspero Massacre was that the violence had been provoked by provocateurs and not the army, and that there was no proof that soldiers had fired on the protestors or crushed them with armored cars as many eyewitnesses and videos had claimed ("Al-Murshid al-ʿAmm" 2011). Other Islamists gave more inflammatory statements on Maspero. See, for example, an editorial by Khalid Harbi, an anti-Christian polemicist with no clear affiliation to either the Muslim Brotherhood or to organized Salafi parties (Harbi 2011). Harbi did indeed call the Maspero protestors thugs and accused them of being part of a Christian/Zionist/liberal plot to undermine security and postpone the upcoming elections.

10. There was a great deal in the canal project that could be criticized, and some of these criticisms were made, both immediately after the canal project was announced ("al-Tahadiyyat" 2014), and closer to the opening ("Qanat al-Suways Tuuu" 2015). Kaldas (2015) gives a balanced appraisal of the potential benefits of the canal project as well as the flaws in the Sisi regime's claims about its transformative effects. See also "Argus" (2015).

11. The song went after the Muslim Brotherhood a bit, but mostly it attacked Qatar and Sheikha Mozah, the high-profile second wife of the ruler of Qatar at the time (shortly there-after succeeded by his son Tamim Ibn Hamad). The first line, al-tisht ʿqal-li . . . ʾumi ista-hammi comes from a song performed in the film Tharthara foq al-Nil. In that narrative—a critique of the failure of the intelligentsia based on a Naguib Mahfouz novel—the song is meant to signify the moral and professional degradation of one of the characters in the story. The Sama al-Masri video goes a few vulgar steps further than the film, first by show-ing the dancer/singer with her legs spread wide as she washes clothes (presumably a mili-tary uniform) in the tub, then by depicting an obviously perturbed Sheikha Mozah using a look-alike model dressed unmistakably like the ruler's wife (and shortly thereafter as Ta-mim's mother, once the younger Tamim took the reins of power from his father, Hamad). "Baltagiyya," A Sama al-Masri song from the Morsy year, had earned her a certain grudging respect from the left-oriented (as opposed to Hisham's proregime conservatism) non-Islamist intelligentsia. Maha El-Said saw "Baltagiyya" as an expression of resistance to the Muslim Brotherhood's misogyny (El Said 2015). "Al-Khanzira" glorifies the military, which El-Said characterizes as also a "misogynistic" system (El Said 2015, 110). In my opinion mockery or vilification of Islamists (if not necessarily the Muslim Brotherhood identified by name) has been permitted since at least the mid-1990s. What stood out about "Baltagi-yya" was less the mockery than the fact that it was produced during the year of Muslim Brotherhood rule. The song should therefore be seen not as an act of resistance, but as an index of the Muslim Brotherhood's weakness in controlling the media and cultural fields even when it was nominally in power.

12. Bateson's terms for describing the ethical implications of schismogenesis were ethos ("emotional tonality"), and eidos (cognitive communality—essentially "thought") (Horvath and Thomassen 2008, 11). A more contemporary formulation of Bateson's concepts is "af-fect," which combines embodied emotions with cognition (Clough and Halley 2007).

13. For Bateson socially routinized violence was structured through "a process of dif-ferentiation in the norms of individual behaviour resulting from cumulative interaction between individuals" (Bateson 1936, 175). It happens in one of two ways: either as sym-metrical or complementary schismogenesis (Bateson 1936, 176–77). As Thomassen notes,

"schismogenesis could become part of any communication system of 'communication rela-tionship' where individuals or groups interact" (2014, 106).

14. Their presence at the news conference is mentioned in "Man Yakun" (2014). The most commonly circulated and complete video of the press conference ("Al-Mu'tamar al-Suhufi" 2014) does not show them (in the video 'Abd al-'Ati comes in at 46:30). A report on the incident ("Taqrir Qanat al-Sharq" 2014) apparently shows Mansur and Sisi in the audi-ence, but it may well have been spliced in from a different event.

15. The patent application can be viewed at "WO/2011/116782" (2011). An entirely nega-tive preliminary report on the patentability of the device can also be found online ("Inter-national Preliminary" 2010). For a full debunking of the devices, see Yahia (2014).

16. Some of the many examples are Mazhar Shahin ("Maskharat Mazhar" 2014); Sabrin ("Shahid Radd Fi'l" 2014); Mustafa Bakri attacking 'Isam Higgi ("Mustafa Bakri Yuhagim" 2014); and Ahmad Musa attacking 'Isam Higgi ("Ahmad Musa 'an" 2014).

17. As mentioned above, criticism was silenced by intimidation or ridicule. But the ex-perts warning against the benefits of expediting the project were ultimately vindicated. By 2017 canal revenues had declined substantially every year since the construction of the much ballyhooed project in 2014 (Samir 2017).

18. The bond was issued to raise LE 64 billion (about $8 billion). The purchaser got 12 percent annual interest over five years. A LE 64 billion loan would ultimately cost the state LE 102 billion—around $13 billion at mid-2015 exchange rates. Since the loan from the public was paid to the state in Egyptian pounds, the repayment cost might diminish, as-suming that Egyptian currency would be further devalued over the five-year repayment period, and assuming that none of the bonds collected in Egyptian currency had to be converted to foreign currency to pay for some aspects of the project.

19. The problem is that the public was not actually buying the canal as an asset; these were investment bonds, not stocks. It was a short-term loan from the public to the state at rather high interest rates (an LE 64 billion loan to be repaid to the tune of LE 102 billion in five years).

20. Basic parameters of the project included projected "returns and outcome": "In-crease the Suez Canal revenues from $5.3 billion at present to $13.226 billion in 2023; an increase equal to 259% that shall positively contribute to Egypt national income of hard currencies" ("New Suez Canal" 2015). A widely published estimate of the amount global trade would have to increase annually in order to achieve that result was 9 percent (Maslin 2015). That sort of annual increase in global trade in the short term was predicted by no-body. The United Nations was predicting a 4.7 percent increase in 2014, and 5 percent for 2016 (United Nations 2015, 33).

21. There was, for example, a "million unit" "low-income" housing scheme called ("'Arabtek'" 2014), though "low income" did not mean the poor (Golia 2015). Actual hous-ing conditions were always substantially different from government or marketing rhetoric. In April 2015 an excellent article in the newspaper al-Masry al-Youm researched the avail-ability of finished housing in Cairo on a budget of LE 200 thousand—equivalent to 166 months of salary at the minimum wage. At the end of a long, frustrating search the author found that the only place such accommodation could be purchased was in the informal areas of the city (M. Abu al-'Aynayn 2015). Unfortunately the million-unit housing scheme was not going to help in the short term. By August 2015 even the slavishly proregime news-paper al-Yaum al-Sabi' acknowledged that there was as of yet no financing for the project, and "phase 3"—to build a mere fifty thousand units—was yet to begin (A. Hasan 2015).

22. Like the million unit housing project, it was part of a Mubarak-era scheme first publicized in 2007 (El-Hefnawi 2010), and massively discredited by urbanist scholars (Tar-bush 2012; Sims 2010, 88–89).

23. The basic features of the law are sketched out by Ayman Nour (2015). On the demonstrations, see Al-Sayyid et al. (2015).

24. The purchase of the Rafales came in a $5.9 billion package that also included a navel frigate. The purchase was financed by loans from Gulf Arab states and the French government (Shapir and Guzansky 2015). Additional military purchases were often rumored, as Egypt sought to both upgrade aging equipment, and diversify its sources ("All Over Again" 2016). Aside from actual defense needs, diversification away from the United States as a weapons supplier was highly popular, hence investments in guns were also a good investment in political legitimacy, even if they reduced the state's resources available for butter rather than for guns.

25. A more recent summary of the concept can be found in Lind's *4th Generation Warfare Handbook* (Lind 2016). Although Lind's initial "out-of-the-box" article was coauthored with military officers and published in the *Marine Corps Gazette*, Lind never served in the military or taught at a military academy. For a critical refutation of the Fourth Generation War concept from within the US military, see Echevarria (2005). The Strategic Studies Institute is part of the US Army War College, at which 'Abd al-Fattah al-Sisi was a student in 2006, hence one should not assume that Sisi's promotion of Fourth Generation Warfare (as will be explained below) reflects institutionalized US military thinking.

26. Lind's publisher, Castalia House, specializes in science fiction and political polemics, both authored by ultraconservative (mostly self-consciously conservative Christian) writers. Lind's work is featured in both categories.

27. Lind and Trump have met, to the alarm of liberal columnists, and to the amusement of Lind's ideological fellow travelers, who note the resonance of Lind's writing with Trump's campaign, but doubt whether Trump has actually imbibed Lind's "philosophy" (see Bloom 2016). For a liberal analysis of the Trump-Lind connection that is less coy about the ideological correspondences between the two, see Rosenberg (2016).

REFERENCES

Abaza, Mona. 2010. "The Trafficking with *Tanwir* (Enlightenment)." *Comparative Studies of South Asia, Africa and the Middle East* 30 (1): 32–46.

———. 2011. "Cairo's Downtown Imagined: Dubaisation or Nostalgia?" *Urban Studies* 48 (6): 1075–87.

———. 2012a. "An Emerging Memorial Space? In Praise of Mohammed Mahmud Street." *Jadaliyya*, March 10. http://www.jadaliyya.com/pages/index/4625/an-emerging -memorial-space-in-praise-of-mohammed-m, accessed August 22, 2017.

———. 2012b. "The Revolution's Barometer." *Jadaliyya*, June 12. http://www.jadaliyya.com /pages/index/5978/the-revolutions-barometer-, accessed August 22, 2017.

———. 2013. "Mourning, Narratives and Interactions with the Martyrs through Cairo's Graf- fiti." *E-International Relations*, October 7. http://www.e-ir.info/2013/10/07/mourning -narratives-and-interactions-with-the-martyrs-through-cairos-graffiti/, accessed Au- gust 22, 2017.

———. 2015. "Graffiti and the Reshaping of the Public Space in Cairo: Tensions between Political Struggles and Commercialization." In Eva Youkhana and Larissa Förster, eds., *Grafficity: Visual Practices and Contestations in Urban Space*. Paderborn: Wilhelm Fink Verlag, 267–94.

———. 2017. "Repetitive Repertoires: How Writing about Cairene Graffiti Has Turned into a Serial Monotony." In Konstantinos Avramidis and Myrto Tsilimpounidi, eds., *Graffiti and Street Art: Reading, Writing and Representing the City*. London: Routledge, 177–94.

'Abd al-Fattah, Wa'il. 2013. "Jabhat Inqadh al-Mursy." *Masress* (originally in *al-Tahrir*, March 13). http://www.masress.com/tahrirnews/326384, accessed August 13, 2016.

'Abd al-Hafiz, Isma'il. 1994. *Al-'A'ila*. Cairo: Qita' al-Intaj lil-Tilifizyun al-Misri (TV serial).

Abdalla, Ahmed. 1985. *The Student Movement and National Politics in Egypt*. London: I. B. Tauris.

'Abdallah, Bilal. 2011. "Ismaha Sally." http://www.youtube.com/watch?v=myTQbAQC1Ow, accessed June 2, 2011.

'Abd al-Sami', 'Amru. 2012. "Wa I'lama!" Al-Ahram (originally February 24). http://digital .ahram.org.eg/articles.aspx?Serial=878317&eid=11335, accessed April 1, 2013.

Abdelazim, Hazem. 2012. "Ja'ani al-Bayan al-Tali." Facebook wall photos of Abdelazim Hazem. https://www.facebook.com/photo.php?fbid=10151091309960447&set=a .10150283835485447.500464.784000446&type=1&theater, accessed March 4, 2012.

Abdel Nasser, Hoda Gamal. 1994. *Britain and the Egyptian Nationalist Movement, 1935– 1952*. Reading, UK: Ithaca.

Abdelrahman, Maha. 2015. *Egypt's Long Revolution: Protest Movements and Uprisings*. London: Routledge.

Abou-El-Fadl, Reem. 2013. "Sectarianism and Counter-revolution in Egypt: Not a Family Affair." *Jadaliyya*, July 2. http://www.jadaliyya.com/pages/index/12581/sectarianism -and-counter-revolution-in-egypt_not-a, accessed June 11, 2014.

Abouelnaga, Shereen. 2015. "Reconstructing Gender in Post-revolution Egypt." In Maha El Said, Lena Maeri, and Nicola Pratt, eds., *Rethinking Gender in Revolutions and Resis- tance: Lessons from the Arab World*. London: Zed Books, 35–58.

Abougabal, Hossam. 2017. "Chinese Return Could Be Bad for Egyptian Investors." *Middle East Business Intelligence*, June 4. https://www.meed.com/sectors/construction/chinese -return-could-be-bad-for-egyptian-firms/5016321.article, accessed July 23, 2017.

Abu al-'Aynayn, Muhammad. 2015. "Rihlat al-Bahth 'an Shaqqa: 200 Alf Ginayh la Takfi illa al-Sakan fi al-'Ashwa'iyyat." *Al-Masry al-Youm*, April 12. http://www.almasryalyoum .com/news/details/704540, accessed July 2, 2016.

Abu al-'Aynayn, Rania Hasan. 2013. "Ba'da Tashiyi' Juthamayn Dahaya al-Khusus al-Katadra'iyya Tata'arrada lil-Hugum li-Awwal Marra." *Masress* (originally in *Shumus*, April 8). http://www.masress.com/shomos/15115, accessed August 13, 2016.

Abu al-Ghayt, Muhammad. 2011a. "Al-Fuqara' Awwalan Ya Wilad al-Kalb." *Gedarea.* http:// gedarea.blogspot.com.eg/2011/06/normal-o-false-false-false.html accessed December 27, 2011; images and an abbreviated text preserved at https://www.facebook.com/notes /226210847408011/, accessed December 27, 2011.

———. 2011b. "'Indma Yasbuh al-Shudhudh al-Ginsi Halalan." *Gedarea.* http://gedarea .blogspot.co.uk/2011/06/blog-post_4438.html, accessed August 20, 2011.

Abu-Lughod, Lila. 1998. *Remaking Women: Feminism and Modernity in the Middle East.* Princeton, NJ: Princeton University Press.

———. 2004. *Dramas of Nationhood: The Politics of Television in Egypt.* Chicago: University of Chicago Press.

Achcar, Gilbert. 2013. *The People Want: A Radical Exploration of the Arab Uprising.* Berkeley: University of California Press.

Adham, Khaled. 2005. "Globalization, Neoliberalism, and New Spaces of Capital in Cairo." *Traditional Dwellings and Settlements Review* 17 (1): 19–32.

"Adieu Riad." 1969. *Images*, March 15–21, 1.

Agamben, Giorgio. 2005. *State of Exception.* Translated by Kevin Attell. Chicago: University of Chicago Press.

———. 2009. *What Is an Apparatus? and Other Essays.* Stanford, CA: Stanford University Press.

Agrama, Hussein. 2012. *Questioning Secularism: Islam, Sovereignty and the Rule of Law in Egypt.* Chicago: University of Chicago Press.

Agulhon, Maurice. 1981. *Marianne into Battle: Republican Imagery and Symbolism in France, 1789–1880.* New York: Cambridge University Press.

"Ahdath Magzarat Rab'a al-'Adawiyya." 2013. YouTube video. https://www.youtube.com/watch ?v=CQxnC_hwnE4, accessed August 9, 2017.

"Ahmad Musa: 'Anasir Irhabiyya I'tadat 'ala Wafd al-Fananiyin fi Almanya." 2015. YouTube video. https://www.youtube.com/watch?v=pi3W4RNs_Hg, accessed August 13, 2016.

"Ahmad Musa 'an 'Isam Higgi." 2014. YouTube video. https://www.youtube.com/watch?v= vNTk6VE4Ewg, accessed August 13, 2016.

Ahmed, Yasmine Moataz. 2012. "Who Do Egypt's Villagers Vote For and Why?" *Egypt Independent*, April 10. https://www.egyptindependent.com/who-do-egypts-villagers-vote -and-why/, accessed October 30, 2018.

"Al-Anba' Filubatir Yetahim al-Salafiyin wa Yaqul Innuhum 'Adu Akhtar min Isra'il wa Yatahada al-Maglis al-'Askari." 2011. YouTube video uploaded on May 9. https://www .youtube.com/watch?v=Iz5a94ICLc8, accessed January 24, 2016.

Al Aswany, Alaa. 2007. *The Yacoubian Building.* London: Harper Perennial.

Al-Buhairi, Ahmad. 2006. "Milishiyat 'Ikhwaniyya' Tasta'rad Maharat Qitaliyya Dakhil Jami'at al-Azhar." *Al-Masry al-Youm*, November 12. http://today.almasryalyoum.com /article2.aspx?ArticleID=40525, accessed August 12, 2017.

Al-Dib, Yaqut. 2012. "Wahid Hamid: Ga'izat al-Nil Takhtar Man Yahmiluha." *Masress* (originally in *al-Qahira*, July 17). http://www.masress.com/alkahera/4227, accessed August 14, 2017.

Al-Dihi, Nash'at. 2010. "Umm Sabir wa Karabij al-Ra'simaliyya." *Ruz al-Yusuf online*, no. 419. http://www.rosaonline.net/Daily/News.asp?id=46220, accessed June 16, 2011.

Alexander, Anne, and Moustafa Bassiouny. 2014. *Bread, Freedom and Social Justice: Workers and the Egyptian Revolution*. London: Zed.

"Al-Fidyu Alladhi Akhfaha al-'Ilam al-Masri wa Alladhi Yabra'u Muhammad al-Beltagi." 2013. YouTube video. August 31. https://www.youtube.com/watch?v=c3Roc4_myjk, accessed August 13, 2016.

Al-Halqa al-Kamila li-Birnamig 'Masr al-Yaum.' 2015. https://www.youtube.com/watch?v=3f_RgE3cU44, accessed December 19, 2016.

Al-Hifnawi, Mustafa. 1953. *Qanat al-Suways wa Mushkilatuha al-Mu'asira, al-Juz' al-Thani: Al-Niza' al-Masri al-Biritani*. Cairo: Dar Akhbar al-Yaum.

Ali, Amro. 2014. "Run Mahienour Run." *Mada Masr*, June 22. https://madamasr.com/en/2014/06/22/opinion/u/run-mahienour-run/, accessed October 26, 2018.

Al Ismaelia. 2015. Home page of Al Ismaelia for Real Estate Development. http://al-ismaelia.com/, accessed December 24, 2015.

Allen, Lori. 2006. "The Polyvalent Politics of Martyr Commemorations in the Palestinian Intifada." *History and Memory* 18 (2): 107–38.

"All Over Again: Egypt Looks beyond the USA for New Arms." 2016. *Defense Industry Daily*. http://www.defenseindustrydaily.com/all-over-again-egypt-looks-beyond-the-usa-for-new-arms-019091/, accessed August 14, 2016.

"Al-Marsad al-Islami li-Muqawamat al-Tansir." 2011. Anti-Christian Salafi website. http://tanseerel.com/main/, accessed January 24, 2016.

Al-Masri, Sama. 2013. "Sama al-Masri Tughanni li-Qanat al-Jazira al-Khanzira." YouTube video. https://www.youtube.com/watch?v=233ou31aF6U, accessed August 13, 2016.

"Al-Metro Yu'id Ism 'Mubarak' 'ala Mahattat 'Shuhada.'" 2014. *Wikalat Anba' ONA*. http://onaeg.com/?p=1658843, accessed July 23, 2014.

"Al-Murshid al-'Amm lil-Ikhwan: Al-Fulul Sabab Ahdath Masbiru." 2011. *Qissat al-Islam*, October 13. http://tinyurl.com/zq2uy7n, accessed August 20, 2016.

"Al-Mu'tamar al-Suhufi lil-Quwwat al-Musallaha lil-'Ilaj 'an Jihaz al-Kashf 'an al-Fayrusat." 2014. YouTube video. https://www.youtube.com/watch?v=_2Y7t7tQ56E, accessed August 13, 2016.

"Al-Safha al-Rasmiyya lil-Sirsagiyya." 2016. Facebook group. http://tinyurl.com/javemjw, accessed July 26, 2016.

Al-Sayyid, Muhammad, Hisham 'Abd al-Galil, and 'Amru Haggag. 2015. "Salalim Niqabat al-Suhufiyin 'Muqallab Zibala' ba'da Muzahirat Qanun al-Khidma al-Madaniyya." *Al-Yaum al-Sabi'*. http://tinyurl.com/pn9rhok, accessed August 14, 2016.

AlSayyad, Nezar. 2011. "A History of Tahrir Square." Harvard University Press blog. http://harvardpress.typepad.com/hup_publicity/2011/04/a-history-of-tahrir-square.html, accessed December 25, 2011.

"Al-Shahid Basiuni Yufajjir Jadalan Haula al-Musharika al-Misriyya fi Biyaniyal Finsiya." 2011. *Al-Ahram*, June 13. http://gate.ahram.org.eg/News/81822.aspx, accessed August 20, 2016.

"Al-Shahid Ibrahim al-Rifa'i." 2010. YouTube video. http://www.youtube.com/watch?v=BhuSSi55pA4, accessed May 30, 2010.

"al-Shahid 'Umar Shahin. 2014. *Wikipedia al-Ikhwan al-Muslimin*. http://www.ikhwanwiki.com/index.php?title=%D8%B9%D9%85%D8%B1_%D8%B4%D8%A7%D9%87%D9%8A%D9%8,6, accessed July 23, 2014.

Al-Sharif, 'Ala.' 2012. *Al-Almani*. Cairo: Art Template (film).

"Al-Sisi al-Qatil wal-Nazi wal-Fashi fi Almanya." 2015. *Shabakat al-Marsad al-Ikhbariyya*, June 4. http://marsadpress.net/?p=23142, accessed August 13, 2016.

"al-Sisi: Misr Tuwajih Akhtar Anwa' al-Hurub min al-Jil al-Rabi'." 2015. YouTube video. February 22. https://www.youtube.com/watch?v=QnPgyXES93M, accessed January 8, 2017.

"Al-Sisi wa 'Ukasha Inqadhu Misr min Thaurat 25 Yanayir?" 2013. YouTube video recording of a broadcast from the al-Fara'ayn network. https://www.youtube.com/watch?v=U_yWIcnAT9w, accessed May 6, 2018.

Al-Subki, Karim. 2013. *Qalb al-Asad*. Cairo: al-Subki Film (film).

"al-Tahadiyyat Allati Wajahat al-Ra'is al-Sisi fi al-100 Yaum al-Ula fi Hukmihi." 2014. *OnTv* YouTube video. https://www.youtube.com/watch?v=px6fGIjT7yY, accessed August 13, 2016.

"Al-Taharrush al-Jama'i bi-Masirat al-Mar'a fi Midan al-Tahrir." 2011. http://www.youtube.com/watch?v=oCXgZZ-Rwlo, accessed July 26, 2011.

"Al-Tilifizyun al-Misri wa Tahrid al-Misriyyin Dhidda al-Aqbat." 2011. YouTube video uploaded on October 10. https://www.youtube.com/watch?v=E7mo8JJdxao, accessed January 24, 2016.

"al-Ughniyya al-Rasmiyya lil-Duktur Taufiq 'Ukasha—Ana Fil." 2011. http://www.youtube.com/watch?v=-2y_PBpZDYc, accessed July 22, 2012.

"Al-Wa'd al-Kashfi." 2017. *Kashfiyyatna* (International Catholic Conference of Scouting, Arabic branch). http://www.cicsjo.org/images/ind/Scout.jpg, accessed August 13, 2017.

"Al-Wa'd wa Qanun al-Kashafa." 2017. *Al-Saha al-Kashfiyya*. https://tinyurl.com/ybyof9h2, accessed August 14, 2017.

Amar, Paul. 2013. *The Security Archipelago: Human-Security States, Sexuality Politics, and the End of Neoliberalism*. Durham, NC: Duke University Press.

Amin, Samir. 2004. *The Liberal Virus: Permanent War and the Americanization of the World*. New York: Monthly Review Press.

Anderson, Benedict. 2006. *Imagined Communities: Reflections on the Origin and Spread of Nationalism*. London: Verso.

Aouragh, Miriyam, and A. Alexander. 2011. "The Egyptian Experience: Sense and Nonsense of the Internet Revolution." *International Journal of Communication* (online) 5: 0. http://ijoc.org/ojs/index.php/ijoc/article/view/1191/610, accessed July 25, 2014.

"'Arabtek' Satibni Milyun Wihda Sakaniyya li-Dhawi al-Dakhl al-Mahdud fi Misr." 2014. *Al-Hayat*, March 1. http://tinyurl.com/nnvnfs2, accessed August 14, 2016.

'Arafa, Sharif. 1992. *Al-Irhab wa-l-Kabab*. Cairo: 'Isam Imam (film).

Argaman, Jonathan. 2014. *A City on the Edge: Aspiration, Anxiety Management, and the Politics of Urban Planning in Cairo*. PhD diss., University of Pennsylvania.

"Argus: Bigger Suez Canal Does Not Guarantee Increased Traffic." 2015. *World Maritime News*, July 31. http://worldmaritimenews.com/archives/168082/argus-bigger-suez-canal-does-not-guarantee-increased-traffic/, accessed July 13, 2016.

Armbrust, Walter. 1996. *Mass Culture and Modernism in Egypt*. Cambridge: Cambridge University Press.

———. 1998. "Islamists in Egyptian Cinema." *American Anthropologist* 104 (3): 922–30.

———. 2008. "Long Live Love: Patriarchy in the Time of Muhammad Abd al-Wahhab." *History Compass* 6: 251–81. http://www.blackwell-compass.com/subject/history/.

———. 2012a. "The Ambivalence of Martyrs and the Counter-revolution." *Cultural Anthropology: Journal of the Society for Cultural Anthropology*, online "Hot Spots" section. http://www.culanth.org/fieldsights/213-the-ambivalence-of-martyrs-and-the-counter-revolution, accessed October 26, 2018.

————. 2012b. "Sally Zahran: Ikunat al-Thaura." *Fusul*, no. 80: 84–12 (in Arabic, translated by Walid Sami Salim).

————. 2013. "The Trickster in the January 25th Revolution." *Comparative Studies in Society and History* 55 (4): 834–64.

————. 2015. "The Iconic State: Martyrologies and Performance Frames in the 25 January Revolution." In Reem Abou-El-Fadl, ed., *Revolutionary Egypt: Connecting Domestic and International Struggles*. London: Routledge, 83–111.

————. 2017. "Trickster Defeats the Revolution: Egypt as the Vanguard of the New Authoritarianism." *Middle East Critique* 26 (3): 221–39.

Asad, Talal. 2003. *Formations of the Secular: Christianity, Islam, Modernity*. Stanford, CA: Stanford University Press.

————. 2011. "Thinking about the Secular Body, Pain, and Liberal Politics." *Cultural Anthropology* 26 (4): 657–75.

————. 2015. "Thinking about Tradition, Religion, and Politics in Egypt Today." *Critical Inquiry* 42 (1): 166–214.

'Ashari, Nagwa. 2010. "Al-Haraka al-Tashkiliyya Tufqad Ithnayn min Kubariha." *Al-Ahram*, July 1. http://digital.ahram.org.eg/articles.aspx?Serial=191113&eid=834, accessed May 30, 2013.

"'Asifat Ghadab min Fatwa Maghrabiyya Tubih lil-Rajil Jama' Zaujitihi al-Mayyita." 2012. MBC.net. http://tinyurl.com/d9u2toc (originally posted on February 21, 2012), accessed April 1, 2013.

Atia, Mona. 2013. *Building a House in Heaven: Pious Neoliberalism and Islamic Charity in Egypt*. Minneapolis: University of Minnesota Press.

Augé, Marc. 2009. *Non-places: An Introduction to Super-modernity*. Translated by John Howe. London: Verso.

Awad, Muhammad. 2011. "Niqabat al-Tashkiliyin: Sanudafi'u 'an al-Shahid Ahmad Basiyuni fi Mishkilat Biyanyal Finisia." *Al-Yaum al-Sabi*, July 14. http://tinyurl.com/jcru8kn, accessed August 20, 2016.

"Awwal Liqa' Tilifizyuni ma' al-Mauhub Shadi Surur." 2014. YouTube video. https://www.youtube.com/watch?v=H6xRyLXk9-0, accessed August 14, 2016.

"Awwal Shahid al-Jami'a." 1952. *Al-Musawwar* 1423 (January 19): 1.

'Azzam, Muhammad. 2008. "Isra' 'Abd al-Fattah: 'Fatat al-Fays Buk' Allati Qadat al-Da'wa lil-Idrab." *Al-Masry al-Youm*, April 9. http://www.almasry-alyoum.com/article2.aspx?ArticleID=100602, accessed July 27, 2011.

Babcock-Abrahms, Barbara. 1975. "A Tolerated Margin of Mess: The Trickster and His Tales Reconsidered." *Journal of the Folklore Institute* 11 (3): 147–86.

Badawi, Muhammad. 2007. "Ahmad Fu'ad Nigm." In Hamdi al-Sakkut, ed., *Qamus al-Adab al-'Arabi al-Hadith*. Cairo: Dar al-Shuruq, 63–64.

"Baladna Bil-Masri: Ziyara li-Ahl al-Shahida Sally Zahran." 2011. http://www.youtube.com/watch?v=QqvSohh4bWk, accessed March 6, 2011.

Barakat, Y. 2015. "Taufiq 'Ukasha, Glin Bek Misr." *Al-Mugaz*, November 9. http://www.elmogaz.com/node/244630, accessed December 1, 2016.

Baron, Beth. 2005. *Egypt as a Woman: Nationalism, Gender, and Politics*. Berkeley: University of California Press.

Bateson, Gregory. 1935. "Culture Contact and Schismogenesis." *Man* 35 (199): 178–83.

————. 1936. *Naven: A Survey of the Problems Suggested by a Composite Picture of the Culture of a New Guinea Tribe Drawn from Three Points of View*. Cambridge: Cambridge University Press.

————. 1987 [1972]. *Steps to an Ecology of Mind: Collected Essays in Anthropology, Psychiatry, Evolution, and Epistemology*. Northvale, NJ: Aronson.

Bauman, Richard, and Charles Briggs. 1990. "Poetics and Performance as Critical Perspectives on Language and Social Life." *Annual Review of Anthropology* 19: 59–88.

"Bayan Raqm 3 lil-Maglis al-A'la lil-Quwwat al-Musallaha." 2011. YouTube video. https://www.youtube.com/watch?v=nSEEMeGs5hk, accessed August 7, 2016.

Bayat, Asef. 2015. "Revolution and Despair." *Mada Masr*, January 25. http://www.madamasr.com/opinion/revolution-and-despair, accessed August 14, 2016.

Beinin, Joel. 2010. *Justice for All: The Struggle for Worker Rights in Egypt*. Washington, DC: Solidarity Center

———. 2012. "Egyptian Workers and January 25th: A Social Movement in Historical Context." *Social Research: An International Quarterly* 79 (2): 323–48.

Bell, Catherine. 2009. *Ritual Theory, Ritual Practice*. Oxford: University of Oxford Press.

Berlant, Lauren. 2011. *Cruel Optimism*. Durham, NC: Duke University Press.

Berman, Marshall. 1988. *All That Is Solid Melts into Air: The Experience of Modernity*. New York: Penguin.

Bialecki, Jon. 2012. "Virtual Christianity in an Age of Nominalist Anthropology." *Anthropological Theory* 12 (3): 295–319.

Biehl, João, and Peter Locke. 2010. "Deleuze and the Anthropology of Becoming." *Current Anthropology* 51 (3): 317–51.

"Bil-Suwwar . . . 'Ukasha bil-Gazma.'" 2016. *Al-Yaum al-Sabi'* online. http://tinyurl.com/zbm7kw5, accessed August 4, 2016.

Bloom, Jordan. 2016. William Lind's Way of War. *American Conservative*, October 17, 2016. http://www.theamericanconservative.com/articles/william-linds-way-of-war/, accessed January 8, 2017.

Bonilla, Yarimar. 2011. "The Past Is Made by Walking: Labour Activism and Historical Production in Postcolonial Guadaloupe." *Cultural Anthropology* 26 (3): 313–39.

Boraie, Sherif, ed. 2012. *Wall Talk: Graffiti of the Egyptian Revolution*. Cairo: Zeitouna.

Bourdieu, Pierre. 1977. *Outline of a Theory of Practice*. Cambridge: Cambridge University Press.

Brenner, Neil, Jamie Peck, and Nik Theodore. 2010. "Variegated Neoliberalization: Geographies, Modalities, Pathways." *Global Networks* 10 (2): 182–222.

Brown, Wendy. 2005. *Edgework: Critical Essays on Knowledge and Politics*. Princeton, NJ: Princeton University Press.

———. 2015. *Undoing the Demos: Neoliberalism's Stealth Revolution*. New York: Zone Books.

Brownlee, Jason. 2013. "Violence against Copts in Egypt." Washington, DC: Carnegie Endowment for International Peace. http://carnegieendowment.org/2013/11/14/violence-against-copts-in-egypt-pub-53606, accessed August 14, 2016.

Bryant, Rebecca. 2016. "On Critical Times: Return, Repetition, and the Uncanny Present." *History and Anthropology* 27 (1): 19–31.

Bubandt, Nils. 2009. "From the Enemy's Point of View: Violence, Empathy, and the Ethnography of Fakes." *Cultural Anthropology* 24 (3): 553–88.

Buccianti, Alexandra. 2016. "Arab Storytelling in the Digital Age: From Musalsalāt to Web Drama?" In Malte Hagener, Vinzenz Hediger, and Alena Strohmaier, eds., *The State of Post-cinema: Tracing the Moving Image in the Age of Digital Dissemination*. Basingstoke, UK: Palgrave Macmillan, 49–70.

Bush, Ray. 2007. "Politics, Power and Poverty: Twenty Years of Agricultural Reform and Market Liberalisation in Egypt." *Third World Quarterly* 28 (3): 1599–615.

Butler, Judith. 1997. *Excitable Speech: A Politics of the Performative*. New York: Routledge.

———. 1999. *Gender Trouble: Feminism and the Subversion of Identity*. New York: Routledge.

———. 2004. *Precarious Life: The Powers of Mourning and Violence*. London: Verso.

———. 2009. *Frames of War: When Is a Life Grievable?* London: Verso.

Butler, Judith, and Athena Athanasiou. 2013. *Dispossession: The Performative in the Political*. Cambridge, UK: Polity.

Cairo Capital Partners. 2015. "A City Shaped by the Future." Developers' website promoting a new capital city project. http://thecapitalcairo.com/about.html, accessed August 14, 2016.

"Cairo Complaints Choir on Dream TV." 2011. http://thechoirproject.webs.com/apps/videos /videos/show/11100818-cairo-complaints-choir-on-dream-tv, accessed March 6, 2011.

Cannell, Fenella. 2010. "The Anthropology of Secularism." *Annual Review of Anthropology* 39: 85–100.

Carr, Sarah. 2011. "A Firsthand Account: Marching from Shubra to Deaths at Maspero." *Egypt Independent*, October 10. http://www.egyptindependent.com/news/firsthand -account-marching-shubra-deaths-maspero, accessed January 24, 2016.

Caton, Steven. 1999. "Anger Be Now Thy Song: The Anthropology of an Event." Princeton, NJ: Institute for Advanced Study Occasional Papers no. 5. http://www.sss.ias.edu/files /papers/paperfive.pdf, accessed April 3, 2012.

———. 2005. *Yemen Chronicles: An Anthropology of War and Mediation*. New York: Hill and Wang.

Checker, Melissa, David Vine, and Alaka Wali. 2010. "From the Public Anthropology Review Editors: A Sea Change in Anthropology? Public Anthropology Reviews." *American Anthropologist*, n.s., 112 (1): 5–6.

Clough, Patricia, and Jean Halley, eds. 2007. *The Affective Turn: Theorizing the Social*. Durham, NC: Duke University Press.

Colla, Elliott. 2011. "The Poetry of Revolt." *Jadaliyya*, January 31. http://www.jadaliyya.com /pages/index/506/the-poetry-of-revolt, accessed July 16, 2014.

Collier, Stephen. 2012. "Neoliberalism as a Big Leviathan, or . . . ? A Response to Wacquant and Hilgers." *Social Anthropology* 20 (2): 186–95.

"Complaints Choirs Worldwide." 2011. http://www.complaintschoir.org/history.html, accessed March 6, 2011.

Connolly, William. 2011. "Some Theses on Secularism." *Cultural Anthropology* 26 (4): 648–56.

Crampton, Jeremy. 2013. "Space, Territory, Geography." In Christopher Falzon, Timothy O'Leary, and Jana Sawicki, eds., *A Companion to Foucault*. Oxford: Wiley-Blackwell, 385–99.

Darwish, Hani. 2011. "'al-Fann Midan': Tajriba Fanniyya bi-Alwan al-Thaura al-Misriyya." *Qantara*, April 4. http://ar.qantara.de/content/lthwr-lmsry-wlhrk-lfny-lfn-mydntjrb -fny-blwn-lthwr-lmsry, accessed August 22, 2014.

Das, Veena. 1996. *Critical Events: An Anthropological Perspective on Contemporary India*. Delhi: Oxford University Press.

Deeb, Lara. 2006. *An Enchanted Modern: Gender and Public Piety in Shi'i Lebanon*. Princeton, NJ: Princeton University Press.

de Koning, Anouk. 2009. *Global Dreams: Class, Gender and Public Space in Cosmopolitan Cairo*. Cairo: American University in Cairo Press.

Denis, Eric. 2006. "Cairo as Neo-liberal Capital? From Walled City to Gated Communities." In Diane Singerman and Paul Amar, eds., *Cairo Cosmopolitan: Politics, Culture and Urban Space in the New Middle East*. Cairo: American University in Cairo Press, 47–72.

Dole, Christopher. 2012. "Revolution, Occupation, and Love: The 2011 Year in Cultural Anthropology." *American Anthropologist* 114 (2): 227–39.

Donham, Donald. 1999. *Marxist Modern: An Ethnographic History of the Ethiopian Revolution*. Berkeley: University of California Press.

Dresch, Paul, and Wendy James. 2000. "Fieldwork and the Passage of Time." In Paul Dresch and Wendy James, eds., *Anthropologists in a Wider World: Essays on Field Research*. Oxford: Berghahn, 1–25.

Dunqul, Amal. 1986a. "Kalimat Spartakus al-Akhira." In *Amal Dunqol: Al-A'mal al-Shi'riyya al-Kamila*. Cairo: Madbuli, 111–16.

———. 1986b. "La Tusalih." In *Amal Dunqol: Al-A'mal al-Shi'riyya al-Kamila*. Cairo: Madbuli, 324–36.

———. 1986c. "Maqtal al-Qamar." In *Amal Dunqol: Al-A'mal al-Shi'riyya al-Kamila*. Cairo: Madbuli, 68–71.

Echevarria, Antulio, II. 2005. *Fourth-Generation Warfare and Other Myths*. Carelisle Barracks, PA: Strategic Studies Institute.

Edelman, Marc. 2001. "Social Movements: Changing Paradigms and Forms of Politics." *Annual Review of Anthropology* 30: 285–317.

El Gergawy, Sherry. 2011. "Trigger for Copts' Anger: El-Marinab Church as a Model." *Al-Ahram Online*, October 11. http://english.ahram.org.eg/NewsContent/1/64/23839/Egypt/Politics-/Trigger-for-Copts-anger-Chronicles-of-a-church-bur.aspx, accessed January 24, 2016.

El-Ghobashy, Mona. 2010. "The Liquidation of Egypt's Illiberal Experiment." *Middle East Reports and Information Project*, December 29. http://www.merip.org/mero/mero122910, accessed October 13, 2012.

———. 2011. "The Praxis of the Egyptian Revolution." *Middle East Research and Information Project* 41 (258) (Spring): 2–13. http://www.merip.org/mer/mer258/praxis-egyptian-revolution, accessed July 16, 2014.

El-Hefnawi, Ayman. 2010. "Cairo Vision 2050: The Strategic Urban Development Plan of Greater Cairo Region." Presentation, World Urban Forum 5, Rio de Janeiro, Brazil, March 2010. http://www.urbangateway.org/system/files/documents/urbangateway/8635_42944_AymanEl-hefnawi.pdf, accessed on August 14, 2015.

El Husseini, Momen. 2011. "The 'Maspero Crime': Accounts against the Counter-revolution's Power, Media, and Religion." *Jadaliyya*, October 31. http://www.jadaliyya.com/pages/index/3022/the-maspero-crime_accounts-against-the-counter-rev, accessed January 24, 2016.

El-Mohendes, Amal. 2011. "Amal El-Mohendes's Testimony." *Maspero Testimonies*. https://masperotestimonies.wordpress.com/maspero-testimonies/amal-elmohandes-testimony-en/, accessed January 24, 2016.

El Said, Maha. 2015. "She Resists: Body Politics between Radical and Subaltern." In Maha El Said, Lena Maeri, and Nicola Pratt, eds., *Rethinking Gender in Revolutions and Resistance: Lessons from the Arab World*. London: Zed Books, 109–34.

El Said, Maha, Lena Maeri, and Nicola Pratt. 2015. "Rethinking Gender in Revolutions and Resistance in the Arab World." In Maha El Said, Lena Maeri, and Nicola Pratt, eds., *Rethinking Gender in Revolutions and Resistance: Lessons from the Arab World*. London: Zed Books, 1–34.

Elshahed, Mohamed. 2011. "Tahrir Square: A Collection of Fragments." *Architects' Newspaper*, March 9. https://archpaper.com/2011/03/tahrir-square-a-collection-of-fragments/, accessed August 25, 2018.

El-Shakry, Omnia. 2007. *The Great Social Laboratory: Subjects of Knowledge in Colonial and Postcolonial Egypt*. Stanford, CA: Stanford University Press.

Elyachar, Julia. 2011. "The Political Economy of Movement and Gesture in Cairo." *Journal of the Royal Anthropological Institute* 17 (1): 82–99.

"Egypt: Dozens Detained Secretly." 2016. *Human Rights Watch*, July 20. https://www.hrw
.org/news/2015/07/20/egypt-dozens-detained-secretly, accessed August 13, 2016.

"Egypt, Military Budget." 2015. GlobalSecurity.org. http://www.globalsecurity.org/military
/world/egypt/budget.htm, accessed December 27, 2015.

"Egypt: Police Account of Deadly Raid in Question." 2015. *Human Rights Watch*, July 31.
https://www.hrw.org/news/2015/07/31/egypt-police-account-deadly-raid-question,
accessed August 13, 2016.

"Egypt: Protestors Killed Marking Revolution." 2015. *Human Rights Watch*, January 26.
https://www.hrw.org/news/2015/01/26/egypt-protesters-killed-marking-revolution,
accessed August 13, 2016.

"Egypt's 'Plans for Farewell Intercourse Law So Husbands Can Have Sex with Dead Wives'
Branded Completely False." 2012. *Daily Mail* (posted originally on May 29 to correct a
story posted on April 26). http://www.dailymail.co.uk/news/article-2135434/Egypts
-plans-farewell-intercourse-law-husbands-sex-DEAD-wives-branded-completely-false
.html, accessed April 1, 2013.

Erlich, Haggai. 1989. *Students and University in 20th Century Egyptian Politics*. London:
Frank Cass.

"Fadd I'tisam Rab'a al-'Adawiyya." 2013. YouTube video. https://www.youtube.com/watch
?v=AIZbK30eBDc, accessed August 9, 2017.

Fadil, Nadia, and Mayanthi Fernando. 2015. "Rediscovering the 'Everyday' Muslim: Notes
on an Anthropological Divide." *Hau: Journal of Ethnographic Theory* 5 (2): 59–88.

Fahmy, Heba. 2011. "Martyrs' Families Frustrated with Slow Trials, Say Offered Money to
Drop Charges." *Daily News Egypt*, June 6. http://www.thedailynewsegypt.com/crime
-a-accidents/martyrs-families-frustrated-with-slow-trials-say-offered-money-to-drop
-charges.html, accessed August 3, 2011.

Fahmy, Khalid. 2012. "The Truth about Fayza." *Egypt Independent*, February 26. http://
www.egyptindependent.com/opinion/truth-about-fayza, accessed January 20, 2013.

Fahmy, Khaled. 2016. "Giulio and the Tragic Loss of Academic Freedom." *Mada Masr*. http://
www.madamasr.com/opinion/politics/giulio-and-tragic-loss-academic-freedom, accessed August 4, 2016.

"Fallen Faces of the Uprising." 2011. *Al-Masry al-Youm English*. http://www.almasryalYaum
.com/en/node/311971, accessed June 2, 2011.

Faruq, Ahmad. 2015. "20 Fananan Yurafiquna al-Sisi fi Ziyaratuh li-Almanya Dimna Wafd
Sha'bi." *Al-Shuruq*, June 1. http://www.shorouknews.com/news/view.aspx?cdate=
01062015&id=c400e8ef-b56d-4e27-a813-98be420fcb6c, accessed August 13, 2016.

Faruq, Isma'il. 2012. *'Abduh al-Mauta*. Cairo: Ahmad al-Subki (film).

Faruq, Samiya, and Muhammad Kamal. 2013. "Baha' al-Sharif, Qa'id 'Amaliyyat Fadd Rab'a
li-al-Wafd: Al-Ghaz wa-l-Mayah al-Asilah al-Wahid al-Mustakhdam fi Fadd al-I'tisam."
Masress (originally in *al-Wafd*, August 19). http://www.masress.com/alwafd/528080,
accessed August 9, 2017.

Fayed, Mervat Muhammad. 2011. "Sally: 'Arus al-Thaura al-Bayda.'" http://vb.naqaae.eg
/showthread.php?824-%D3%C7%E1%ED-quot-%DA%D1%E6%D3-%C7%E1%CB
%E6%D1%C9-%C7%E1%C8%ED%D6%C7%C1-quot, accessed June 2, 2011.

Fayiq, Ahmad. 2013. "Al-Sisi: Al-Milaff al-Sirri li-Akhtar Rajul fi Misr." *Al-Fagr*, May 14.
http://www.elfagr.org/341757, accessed August 13, 2016.

Fernández, Belén. 2011. *The Imperial Messenger: Thomas Friedman at Work*. London: Verso.

Field, Nathan, and Ahmad Hamam. 2009. "Salafi Satellite TV in Egypt." *Arab Media and
Society* 8. http://www.arabmediasociety.com/?article=712, accessed April 27, 2012.

"Filubatir Gamil Yukhatit li-Ahdath Masbiru." 2011. YouTube video uploaded on October
13. https://www.youtube.com/watch?v=VXJ4CmoHtBU, accessed January 24, 2016.

Foda, Yusri. 2011. "Al-Shahid Ibrahim al-Rifaʿi wa Magmuʿat 39 Qital." Episode of the talk show *Akhir Kalam* on YouTube. http://www.youtube.com/watch?v=hfP1x8NA6jg accessed May 30, 2013.

Foley, Michael. 2007. *American Credo: The Place of Ideas in American Politics.* Oxford: Oxford University Press.

Foran, John, ed. 1997. *Theorizing Revolutions.* New York: Routledge.

Foucault, Michel. 1966. *The Order of Things: An Archaeology of the Human Sciences.* New York: Pantheon.

——. 1979. *Discipline and Punish: The Birth of the Prison.* Harmondsworth, UK: Penguin.

——. 1980. *Power/Knowledge: Selected Interviews and Other Writings, 1972–1977.* New York: Pantheon.

——. 1986. "Of Other Spaces." *Diacritics* Translated by David Miskowiec. 16 (1): 22–27.

——. 2005 [1970]. *The Order of Things: An Archaeology of the Human Sciences.* London: Routledge.

Freeden, Michael. 1986. *The New Liberalism: An Ideology of Social Reform.* Oxford: Oxford University Press.

Friedman, Milton. 2002. *Capitalism and Freedom: Fortieth Anniversary Edition.* Chicago: University of Chicago Press.

Friedrich, Paul. 1977. *Agrarian Revolt in a Mexican Village.* Chicago: University of Chicago Press.

Ganti, Tejaswini. 2014. "Neoliberalism." *Annual Review of Anthropology* 43: 89–104.

"Gazbiyya Sirri: Al-Rasm bi-Risha Maghmusa fi Magri al-Nil." 2013. *Al-Masry al-Youm* profile. http://www.almasryalyoum.com/node/1582176, accessed May 30, 2013.

Gershon, Ilana. 2011. "Neoliberal Agency." *Current Anthropology* 52 (4): 537–55.

Ghannam, Farha. 2002. *Remaking the Modern: Space, Relocation and the Politics of Identity in a Global Cairo.* Berkeley: University of California Press.

——. 2013. *Live and Die Like a Man: Gender Dynamics in Urban Egypt.* Stanford, CA: Stanford University Press.

Ghitani, Gamal. 2010. *Al-Rifaʿi.* Cairo: Dar al-Shuruq.

Ghosh, Brishnupriya. 2011. *Global Icons: Apertures to the Popular.* Durham, NC: Duke University Press.

Giddens, Anthony. 1984. *The Constitution of Society: Outline of the Theory of Structuration.* Cambridge, UK: Polity.

Gilbert, Jeremy. 2013. "What Kind of Thing Is Neoliberalism?" *New Formations* 80/81: 7–22.

Gilman, Daniel. 2011. "'Martyr-Pop': Made in Egypt." *Norient.* http://norient.com/video /martyrpop/, accessed July 16, 2014.

——. 2015. "The Martyr Pop Moment: Depoliticizing Martyrdom." *Ethnos* 80 (5): 692–709.

Girgis, ʿAdil. 2015. "Al-Qass Filubatir . . . 'Sharir al-Kanisa.'" *Ruz al-Yusuf,* January 24. http:// www.rosa-magazine.com/News/12494/, accessed January 24, 2016.

Gitlin, Todd. 1980. *The Whole World Is Watching: Mass Media in the Making and Unmaking of the New Left.* Berkeley: University of California Press.

Gledhill, John. 2007. "Neoliberalism." In David Nugent and Joan Vincent, eds., *Companion to the Anthropology of Politics.* Oxford: Blackwell, 332–48.

Goldberg, Ellis. 2015. "Sinai: War in a Distant Province." *Jadaliyya,* July 30. http:// www.jadaliyya.com/pages/index/22303/sinai_war-in-a-distant-province, accessed August 13, 2016.

Goldstone, Jack. 2001. "Toward a Fourth Generation of Revolutionary Theory." *Annual Review of Political Science* 4: 139–87.

Golia, Maria. 2015. "Egypt's Need for Low-Income Housing." *Middle East Institute*, January 15. http://www.mei.edu/content/article/egypt%E2%80%99s-need-low-income -housing, accessed August 14, 2016.

Gramsci, Antonio. 2000. *The Gramsci Reader*. Edited by David Forgacs. New York: New York University Press.

Grimes, Ronald. 2013. *The Craft of Ritual Studies*. Oxford: Oxford University Press.

Gröndahl, Mia. 2013. *Revolution Graffiti: Street Art of the New Egypt*. Cairo: American University in Cairo Press.

"Gum'at al-Ghadab wa Maqtal al-Shahid Tariq." 2011. YouTube video. https://www.youtube .com/watch?v=LxgI1XnloSQ, accessed July 26, 2016.

"'Gum'at al-Tathir' fi Midan al-Tahrir." 2011. http://www.almasryalYaum.com/en/node /330170, accessed May 28, 2011.

Gunning, Jeroen, and Ilan Zvi Baron. 2014. *Why Occupy a Square? People, Protests and Movements in the Egyptian Revolution*. New York: Oxford University Press.

Gupta, Akil, and James Ferguson. 1997. "Discipline and Practice: 'The Field' as Site, Method, and Location in Anthropology." In Akil Gupta and James Ferguson, eds., *Anthropological Locations: Boundaries and Grounds of a Field Science*. Berkeley: University of California Press, 1–46.

Haddad, H. S. 1969. "'Georgic' Cults and Saints of the Levant." *Numen* 16 (1): 21–39.

"Hadhihi . . . Basmatik: Illa al-Shahida Sally Zahran." 2011. http://www.mrasina.com /Details.aspx?Badge=6497&Type=1, accessed June 2, 2011.

Hägglund, Helena, and Sam Carlshamre. 2012. "Necrophilia Law: How Western Media Savors Islamophobia." *Egypt Independent*, May 9. http://www.egyptindependent.com /opinion/necrophilia-law-how-western-media-savors-islamophobia, accessed April 1, 2013.

Halliday, Fred. 2006. "The Left and the Jihad." *Open Democracy*. https://www.opendemocracy .net/globalization/left_jihad_3886.jsp, accessed August 10, 2017.

Hamdy, Basma, and Don Stone. 2014. *Walls of Freedom: Street Art of the Egyptian Revolution*. Berlin: From Here to Fame.

Hamdy, Miriam. 2011. "Martyr Ahmed Basiouny Remembered at the Venice Biennale." Daily News. http://www.thedailynewsegypt.com/art/martyr-ahmed-basiouny-remembered -at-the-venice-biennale.html, accessed May 31, 2011.

Hammer, Joshua. 2017. "How Egypt's Activists Became 'Generation Jail.'" *New York Times*, March 14. https://www.nytimes.com/2017/03/14/magazine/how-egypts-activists -became-generation-jail.html, accessed August 24, 2017.

Hanieh, Adam. 2013. *Lineages of Revolt: Issues of Contemporary Capitalism in the Middle East*. Chicago: Haymarket Books.

"Haqa'iq Musalsal al-Gama'a." 2017. *Ikhwan Wiki*. https://tinyurl.com/ybyjzhaj, accessed August 10, 2017.

Harbi, Khalid. 2011. "'Indima Fadahithum Sally Zahran" al-Marsad al-Islami li-Muqawamat al-Tansir. February 23. http://www.tanseerel.com/main/articles.aspx?selected_article _no=18587, accessed June 23, 2011.

Harvey, David. 2005. *A Brief History of Neoliberalism*. Oxford: Oxford University Press.

———. 2012. *Rebel Cities: From the Right to the City to the Urban Revolution*. London: Verso.

Hasan, Ahmad. 2015. "Ra'is Qita' al-Tashayyud bal-Iskan: 'Adam Tawafir al-Tamwil bi-Sabab Ta'akhkhur Tanfidh al-Marhala al-Thalitha min Mashru' al-Milyun Wihda." *Al-Yaum al-Sabi'*, August 1. http://tinyurl.com/pmlu3wc, accessed August 14, 2016.

Hasan, Radwa. 2012. "'Ukasha Yuharrid Zubat al-Gaysh Ghayr Mubashir 'ala al-Inqilab 'ala al-Maglis al-'Askari." *Musta'gil News*, July 22. http://www.mesta3gelnews.com/post .php?id=2162, accessed June 24, 2013.

Hasan, Samah, Salwa al-Zughbi, Muhammad Magdi, and Muhammad Shanah. 2014. "Tas-rihat 'Isam Higgi lil-Watan haula Ikhtira' al-Jaysh." *Al-Watan*, February 26. http://www .elwatannews.com/news/details/426081, accessed August 13, 2016.

Hasanayn, Magdy. 1975. *Al-Sahra' . . . al-Thaura wa al-Tharwa: Qissat Mudiriyyat al-Tahrir*. Cairo: al-Hay'a al-Masriyya al-'Amma lil-Kitab.

Hasanayn, Sabry. 2010. "Al-Rabihun wal-Khasirun fi Marathun Drama Ramadan." *Ilaf*, September 9. http://elaph.com/Web/arts/2010/9/595386.html, accessed August 10, 2017.

"'Hassan' Yanfa Tawarrutahu fi 'Mauqa'at al-Gamal.'" 2012. *Al-Masry al-Youm*, February 27. http://www.almasryalyoum.com/node/682646, accessed April 27, 2012.

Hatim, 'Ali. 2011. "Bayan min al-Da'wa al-Salafiyya bi-Sha'n Ahdath Masbiru." YouTube video uploaded on October 13. https://www.youtube.com/watch?v=mxoUk-Wrp5E, accessed January 24, 2016.

Haugbolle, Sune. 2010. *War and Memory in Lebanon*. Cambridge: Cambridge University Press.

Heidegger, Martin. 1977. *On the Question of Technology and Other Essays*. New York: Garland.

Herrera, Linda. 2014. *Revolution in the Age of Social Media: Egyptian Popular Insurrection and the Internet*. London: Verso.

Hilgers, Matieu. 2010. "The Three Anthropological Approaches to Neoliberalism." *International Social Science Journal* 61 (202): 351–64.

Hilmi, Heba. 2013. *Guwayya Shahid: Fann Shari' al-Thaura al-Misriyya*. Cairo: Dar al-'Ayn lil-Nashr.

Hirschkind, Charles. 2006. *The Ethical Soundscape: Cassette Sermons and Islamic Counter-publics*. New York: Columbia University Press.

———. 2011a. "Is There a Secular Body? *Cultural Anthropology* 26 (4): 633–47.

———. 2011b. "The Road to Tahrir." *Immanent Frame*, February 9. http://blogs.ssrc.org/tif /2011/02/09/the-road-to-tahrir/ (based on an article Hirschkind had published in 2012).

Hobart, Angela, and Bruce Kapferer. 2005. "Introduction: The Aesthetics of Symbolic Con-struction and Experience." In Angela Hobart and Bruce Kapferer, eds., *Aesthetics in Performance: Formations of Symbolic Construction and Experience*. New York: Berghahn Books, 1–22.

Hobbes, Thomas [William Lind]. 2014. *Victoria: A Novel of 4th Generation War*. Kouvola, Finland: Castalia House.

Hofstadter, Richard. 2008 [1964]. *The Paranoid Style in American Politics and Other Es-says*. New York: Random House.

Horvath, Agnes, and Bjørn Thomassen. 2008. "Mimetic Errors in Liminal Schismogenesis: On the Political Anthropology of the Trickster." *International Political Anthropology* 1 (1): 3–24.

Howeidy, Amira. 2010. "The Camilia Conundrum." *Al-Ahram Weekly* 1014 (September 2–8). http://weekly.ahram.org.eg/2010/1014/eg8.htm, accessed June 23, 2011.

Human Rights Watch. 2014. *All According to Plan: The Rab'a Massacre and Mass Killings of Protestors in Egypt*. New York: Human Rights Watch.

Ibn Saba'in. 2011. "Sally Zahran La Turid an Tamut." http://flowersletters.elaphblog.com /posts.aspx?U=3596&A=75804, accessed June 2, 2011.

"Ihda' li-Shuhada' Ultras Ahli." 2015. https://www.youtube.com/watch?v=_aBBuM5tP88, accessed December 22, 2015.

"Ihtifal Jami'at al-Qahira bi-Dhikrat Istashhad 'Umar Shahin wa Ahmad al-Manisi wa Adil Ghanim." 2011. https://tinyurl.com/y92srkx5, accessed June 19, 2011.

"Inqadhu al-Ahya' min Usrat Umm Sabir." 1953. *Al-Ithnayn* 1006 (September 21): 30–31.

"International Preliminary Report on Patentability." 2010. *World Intellectual Property Organization.* https://patentscope.wipo.int/search/docservicepdf_pct/id00000018626118/IPRP1/WO2011116782.pdf, accessed August 13, 2016.

'Isa, Ibrahim. 2010. "Amir al-Shuhada' Ibrahim al-Rifa'i. YouTube video of a *Baladna bil-Masri* program in three parts. http://www.youtube.com/watch?v=-umn7HlvPjo; http://www.youtube.com/watch?v=mKer-aqXdtc; and http://www.youtube.com/watch?v=1W7SBeohuOk, accessed May 30, 2013.

———. 2011. "Al-Hurriyya Ahamm min al-Fuqara'." *Masress* (originally in *al-Dustur al-Asli,* July 4). http://www.masress.com/dostor/47116, accessed August 28, 2014.

'Isam, Rami. 2011. "Ughniyya Ya 'Uksha Ihda' li-Taufiq 'Ukasha min Midan al-Tahrir." YouTube video. https://www.youtube.com/watch?v=4aIFMviAUuc, accessed August 2, 2016.

———. 2012. "Al-Ka'in al-Ikhwani." YouTube video. https://www.youtube.com/watch?feature=player_embedded&v=aIAkzSkePyc, accessed August 13, 2016.

———. 2014a. "'Ahd al-'Ars" (official video montage). YouTube video. https://www.youtube.com/watch?v=zc7R3iN1nJE, accessed August 13, 2016.

———. 2014b. "'Ahd al-'Ars" ("Bushrat Khayr" video montage). YouTube video. https://www.youtube.com/watch?v=znNAzIHlcjI, accessed August 13, 2016.

"'Isam al-'Aryan Ad'u al-Saltatat illa Fadd I'tisam al-Tahrir bil-Quwwa." 2015 [2011]. YouTube video. https://www.youtube.com/watch?v=CEMkvTE4518.

Ismail, Salwa. 2006. *Political Life in Cairo's New Quarters: Encountering the Everyday State.* Minneapolis: University of Minnesota Press.

———. 2014. "Urban Subalterns in the Arab Revolutions: Cairo and Damascus in Comparative Perspective." *Comparative Studies in Society and History* 55 (4): 865–94.

"Isqat 'Adawiyyat 'Ukasha." 2016. *Al-Masry al-Youm* online. http://www.almasryalyoum.com/news/details/902885, accessed August 4, 2016.

"I'tiqal Shaqiqat Khalid Harbi al-Hamil li-Ijbarihi 'ala Taslim Nafsihi." 2010. Hulanda bil-'Arabi. http://www.hollanda.info/forums-salafi-arrest-of-his-brother-khaled-wars-pregnant-to-force-him-to-surrender-himself1205112/, accessed July 11, 2011.

"Itlaq Ism Ibnat Jami'at Sohag Sally Zahran 'ala Safinat Fada.'" 2001. Tulab Sohag. http://www.tolabsohag.com/new/index.php?option=com_content&view=article&id=1598:2011-04-25-11-18-36&catid=294:2011-04-04-17-54-09&Itemid=545, accessed August 3, 2011.

Jacob, Wilson. 2011. *Working Out Egypt: Effendi Masculinity and Subject Formation in Colonial Modernity, 1870–1940.* Durham NC: Duke University Press.

Jasmi, Husayn. 2014. "Bushrat Khayr." YouTube video. https://www.youtube.com/watch?v=QUBvVTNRp4Q, accessed August 13, 2016.

Joseph, Suad. 1994. "Brother/Sister Relationships: Connectivity, Love, and Power in the Reproduction of Patriarchy in Lebanon." *American Ethnologist* 21 (1): 50–73.

Kaldas, Timothy. 2015. "Neither a Gift to the World or a Money Pit." *Tahrir Institute for Middle East Policy,* July 8. http://timep.org/commentary/neither-a-gift-to-the-world-nor-a-money-pit/, accessed August 13, 2016.

"Kalimat al-Ra'is 'Abd al-Fattah al-Sisi fi Iftitah Qanat al-Suways al-Jadida." 2015. YouTube video. https://www.youtube.com/watch?v=oiBDwbILBGQ, accessed August 13, 2016.

"Kalimat al-Sha'ir Ahmad Fu'ad Nigm 'an al-Thaura." 2011. http://www.youtube.com/watch?v=6ln7g-ajuuk, accessed June 2, 2011 (posted on YouTube on February 1, 2011).

Kandil, Hazem. 2012. *Soldiers, Spies, and Statesmen: Egypt's Road to Revolt.* London: Verso.

Kandil, Hazem. 2014. *Inside the Brotherhood*. Cambridge, UK: Polity.

Kelly, John, and Martha Kaplan. 1990. "History, Structure, and Ritual." *Annual Review of Anthropology* 19: 119–50.

Ketchley, Neil. 2014. " 'The Army and the People Are One Hand!': Fraternization and the 25th January Egyptian Revolution." *Comparative Studies in Society and History* 56 (1): 155–86.

———. 2016. "Elite-Led Protest and Authoritarian State Capture in Egypt." *Project on Middle Eastern Political Science*. http://pomeps.org/2016/05/26/elite-led-protest-and -authoritarian-state-capture-in-egypt/, accessed August 13, 2016.

———. 2017. *Egypt in a Time of Revolution: Contentious Politics and the Arab Spring*. Cambridge: Cambridge University Press.

Ketchley, Neil, and Michael Biggs. 2015. "Who Actually Died in Egypt's Rabaa Massacre?" *Washington Post*, August 14. http://www.washingtonpost.com/blogs/monkey-cage/wp /2015/08/14/counting-the-dead-of-egypts-tiananmen/, accessed August 19, 2015.

Khalid, Khalid Muhammad. 1974 [1950]). *Min Huna Nabda'*. Beirut: Dar al-Kitab al-'Arabi.

Khalil, Joe, and Marwan Kraidy. 2009. "Ramadan: Drama, Comedy, and Religious Shows in the Arab Sweeps." In Joe Khalil and Marwan Krady, *Arab Television Industries*. London: BFI, 99–122.

Khalil, Karima, ed. 2011. *Messages from Tahrir*. Cairo: American University in Cairo Press.

Khalil, Omnia. 2015. "The People of the City: Unraveling the How in Ramlet Bulaq." *International Journal of Sociology* 45 (3): 206–22.

Khalili, Laleh. 2009. *Heroes and Martyrs of Palestine: The Politics of National Commemoration*. Cambridge: Cambridge University Press.

———. 2013. *Time in the Shadows: Confinement in Counterinsurgencies*. Stanford, CA: Stanford University Press.

Khayal, Muhammad. 2015. "Qanat al-Sharq Yuwaqqif Baththaha . . . wa al-Gazira Tismah 100 min 'Amiliha bi-ha." *Al-Shuruq*, August 1. http://www.shorouknews.com/news/view .aspx?cdate=01082015&id=0e0cfac0-0d9d-4916-a61e-a17aff235e16, accessed January 24, 2016.

Khazaleh, Lorenz. 2011. "The Cairo Massacre and How to Invent 'Religious Conflicts.' " *Antropologi.inf: Social Cultural Anthropology in the News* blog. October 12. http://www .antropologi.info/blog/anthropology/2011/cairo-clashes, accessed January 24, 2016.

"Khinaqat Ahmad Shafiq wa 'Ala' al-Aswani . . ." 2011. http://www.youtube.com/watch?v= ywVvT8MwuPs, accessed May 28, 2011.

"Khitab al-Liwa' Muhsin al-Fangari." 2011. YouTube video of an official communiqué. https://www.youtube.com/watch?v=pHx3Q_ihd1A, accessed August 7, 2016.

Klein, Naomi. 2008. *The Shock Doctrine: The Rise of Disaster Capitalism*. London: Penguin.

Koptikjihad. 2005. "He's Done It Again!" *The Rantings of a Liberal Egyptian* (blog post from August 14). http://koptikjihad.blogspot.co.uk/2005/08/hes-done-it-again.html, accessed January 24, 2016.

Koselleck, Reinhart. 2006. "Crisis." Translated by Michaela Richter. *Journal of the History of Ideas* 67 (2): 357–400.

KPMG (Klynveld Main Goerdeler and Peat Marwick international auditors). 2005. "Strategic Study to Upgrade Egypt's Automotive Sector." Report commissioned by the Industrial Modernisation Centre, Egypt. http://www.imc-egypt.org/index.php/en/studies /finish/56-executive-summery/5-automotive-sector-development-strategy, accessed December 25, 2015.

Kraidy, Marwan. 2016. *The Naked Blogger of Cairo: Creative Insurgency in the Arab World*. Cambridge, MA: Harvard University Press.

Krämer, Gudrun. 2010. *Hasan al-Banna*. London: Oneworld.

Kuppinger, Petra. 2004. "Exclusive Greenery: New Gated Communities in Cairo." *City and Society* 16 (2): 35–62.

Kurzman, Charles. 2012. "The Arab Spring Uncoiled." *Mobilization: An International Journal* 17 (4): 377–90.

Laclau, Ernesto. 2000. "Power and Social Communication." *Ethical Perspectives* 7 (2–3): 139–45.

Langohr, Vickie. 2004. "Too Much Civil Society, Too Little Politics: Egypt and Liberalizing Arab Regimes." *Comparative Politics* 36 (2): 181–204.

Latour, Bruno. 2002. "What Is Iconoclash? Or Is There a World beyond the Image Wars?" In Peter Weibel and Bruno Latour, eds., *Iconoclash: Beyond the Image Wars in Science, Religion and Art*, Cambridge, Mass: MIT Press, 14–37.

———. 2005. *Reassembling the Social: An Introduction to Actor-Network Theory*. Oxford: Oxford University Press.

Lauzière, Henri. 2010. "The Construction of Salafiyya: Reconsidering Salafism from the Perspective of Conceptual History." *International Journal of Middle Eastern Studies* 42 (3): 369–89.

"Laysat Sally Zahran." 2011. http://www.youtube.com/watch?v=9C_qzzH_LW8, accessed June 2, 2011.

Lazzarato, Maurizio. 2004. "The Political Form of Coordination." *Transversal*. http://transversal.at/transversal/0707/lazzarato/en, accessed July 16, 2016.

Lefebvre, Henri. 2003. *The Urban Revolution*. Translated by Robert Bononno. Minneapolis: University of Minnesota Press.

Lemke, Thomas. 2001. "'The Birth of Bio-politics': Michel Foucault's Lecture at the Collège de France on Neoliberal Governmentality." *Economy and Society* 30 (2): 190–210.

Lévi-Strauss, Claude. 1963. *Structural Anthropology*. Translated by Claire Jacobson and Brooke Grundfest Schoepf. New York: Basic Books.

Lewis, J. Lowell. 2013. *The Anthropology of Cultural Performance*. New York: Palgrave Macmillan.

Lind, William. 2016. *4th Generation Warfare Handbook*. Kouvola, Finland: Castalia House.

Lind, William, Keith Nightengale, John Schmitt, Joseph Sutton, and Gary Wilson. 1989. "The Changing Face of War: Into the Fourth Generation." *Marine Corps Gazette*, October, 22–26.

"Liqa' ma' 'Abd al-Fattah al-Sisi ma' Ibrahim 'Isa wa Lamis al-Hadidi." 2014. YouTube video. https://www.youtube.com/watch?v=tKO4bouQPS4, accessed August 13, 2016.

"Liqa' ma' al-Katib al-Suhufi Muhammad Abu al-Ghayt al-Ha'iz 'ala Ja'izat Samir Qasir li-Hurriyyat al-Sihafa." 2014. AlHayah TV Network. https://www.youtube.com/watch?v=ubalmx6CnDk, accessed July 27, 2016.

Lorey, Isabell. 2015. *State of Insecurity: Government of the Precarious*. London: Verso.

Louis, William Roger. 1984. "Egypt: British 'Evacuation' and the 'Unity of the Nile Valley.'" In *The British Empire in the Middle East, 1945–1951: Arab Nationalism, the United States, and Postwar Imperialism*. Oxford: Clarendon, 226–64.

Luxemburg, Rosa. 2010. *Socialism or Barbarism: The Selected Writings of Rosa Luxemburg*. Edited by Paul Le Blanc and Helen Scott. London: Pluto.

Maghraoui, Abdesalam. 2006. *Liberalism without Democracy: Nationhood and Citizenship in Egypt, 1922–1936*. Durham, NC: Duke University Press.

Maguire, Thomas. 2016. "The Politics of Sheikh Awesome: Quietism in Transnational Media." *Project on Middle Eastern Politics* blog. https://pomeps.org/2017/01/24/the

-politics-of-sheikh-awesome-quietism-in-transnational-media/, accessed August 24, 2017.

Mahfouz, Asma.' 2011. "Akhir Kalima Qabla 25 Yanayir." http://www.youtube.com/watch ?v=A8lYkrgKZWg, accessed July 27, 2011.

Mahmood, Saba. 2011. *The Politics of Piety: The Islamic Revival and the Feminist Subject.* Princeton, NJ: Princeton University Press.

Mahmud, Tayyab. 2015. "Precarious Existence and Capitalism: A Permanent State of Exception." *Southwestern Law Review* 44 (2): 699–726.

Makdisi, Saree. 1997. "Laying Claim to Beirut: Urban Narrative and Spatial Identity in the Age of Solidere." *Critical Inquiry* 23 (3): 660–705.

Malkki, Lisa. 1997. "News and Culture: Transitory Phenomena and the Fieldwork Tradition." In Akil Gupta and James Ferguson, eds., *Anthropological Locations: Boundaries and Grounds of a Field Science.* Berkeley: University of California Press, 86–101.

Mangilier, Patrice. 2013. "The Order of Things." In Christopher Falzon, Timothy O'Leary, and Jana Sawicki, eds., *A Companion to Foucault.* Oxford: Wiley-Blackwell, 104–21.

"Mansoura Scout." 2017. *'Ashira Kulliyat al-Tugara Jami'at al-Mansura.* http://tegascout .ba7r.org/t169-topic, accessed August 14, 2017.

"Man Yakun al-Liwa' 'Abd al-'Ati Mukhtara' Jihaz ''Ilaj' al-Aydz." 2014. *Radio Sawa*, February 27. http://www.radiosawa.com/a/244588.html, accessed August 13, 2016.

Marcus, George, and Erkan Saka. 2010. "Assemblage." *Theory, Culture and Society* 23 (2–3): 101–9.

Margold, Stella. 1957. "Agrarian Land Reform in Egypt." *American Journal of Economics and Sociology* 17 (1): 9–19.

Mar'i, Muhammad. 2011. "Hal Qatala Rusas al-Gaysh Shab?" *Thaurat 25 Yanayir* (Mar'i's blog). http://ehaborabi5.blogspot.co.uk/2011/04/blog-post_6354.html, accessed August 7, 2016.

Markaz al-I'lam al-Amni. 2009. "Al-Ra'is Husni Mubarak: 'Id al-Shurta Min Kull 'Am Agaza Rasmiyya.' " http://www.moiegypt.gov.eg/Arabic/Departments+Sites/Media+and+ public+Relation/News/ns040220091.htm, accessed June 20, 2011.

Marsot, Afaf Lutfi. 1978. *Egypt's Liberal Experiment: 1922–1936.* Berkeley: University of California Press.

Marx, Karl, and Friedrich Engels. 1975 [1848]. "Manifesto of the Communist Party." In Karl Marx and Friedrich Engels, *The Marx-Engels Reader*, edited by Robert C. Tucker. New York: W. W. Norton, 469–500.

"Masira Salafiyya wa Ukhra Nisa'iyya fi al-Tahrir wa Mushaddat bayn al-Mu'tasimin wa al-Mutalibin bi-Ikhla' al-Midan." 2011. *Al-Masry al-Youm*, March 9. http://www.almasry -alyoum.com/article2.aspx?ArticleID=289946, accessed July 26, 2011.

"Maskharat Mazhar Shahin." 2014. YouTube video. https://www.youtube.com/watch?v= arCQd_oXRwU, accessed August 13, 2016.

Maslamani, Maliha. 2013. *Graffiti of the Egyptian Revolution.* Doha: Arab Center for Research and Policy.

Maslin, Jared. 2015. "Egypt Hails $8bn Suez Canal Expansion as Gift to World at Lavish Ceremony." *Guardian*, August 6. https://www.theguardian.com/world/2015/aug/06 /egypt-suez-canal-expansion, accessed August 14, 2016.

"Maspero Testimonies." 2011. Archive of eyewitness accounts of the Maspero Massacre. https://masperotestimonies.wordpress.com/, accessed January 24, 2016.

McAdam, Douglas, Sidney Tarrow, and Charles Tilly. 2001. *Dynamics of Contention.* Cambridge: Cambridge University Press.

Mehrez, Samia, ed. 2011. *Translating Egypt's Revolution: The Language of Tahrir.* Cairo: American University in Cairo Press.

Mikhaeel, Ragy. 2011. "Ana Insan: Qasida Illa Ruh 'Salma Zahran' Shahidat Thaurat 25 Yanayir." *Al-Hiwar al-Mutamaddun*, no. 3411 (June 29). http://www.ahewar.org/debat /show.art.asp?aid=265187, accessed July 18, 2011.

"Milishiyat al-Ikhwan fi al-Azhar." 2012 [from 2006]. YouTube video. https://www.youtube .com/watch?v=VMPpGR-Pc3k, accessed August 12, 2017.

Miller, Laurel, Jeffrey Martini, F. Stephen Larrabee, Angel Rabasa, Stephanie Pezard, Julie Taylor, and Tewodaj Mengistu. 2012. "The Regime Transition in Egypt and Emerging Challenges." In Laurel Miller et al., *Democratization in the Arab World: Prospects and Lessons from Around the Globe*. Santa Monica, CA: Rand, 79–105.

"Misr Tushayyi' Shuhada' al-Jami'a al-Arba'a." 1952. *Al-Musawwar* 1423 (January 18): 12–13.

Mitchell, Richard. 1993 [1969]. *The Society of the Muslim Brothers*. Oxford: Oxford University Press.

Mitchell, Timothy. 2002. *Rule of Experts: Egypt, Techno-politics, Modernity*. Berkeley: University of California Press.

Mittermaier, Amira. 2015. "Death and Martyrdom in the Arab Uprisings: An Introduction." *Ethnos* 80 (5): 583–604.

Mohsen, Ali Abdel. 2011. "Women Suffer Assault and Derision at Tahrir March." *Egypt Independent* 8 (March 8). http://www.egyptindependent.com//news/women-suffer -assault-and-derision-tahrir-march, accessed January 8, 2016.

"Mona wa Hilmi fi Film 'an Thaurat 25 Yanayir." 2011. *Masress* (originally in *al-Wafd*, February 22). http://www.masress.com/alwafd/18300, accessed August 20, 2016.

Monroe, Kristin. 2013. *The Insecure City: Space, Power and Mobility in Beirut*. New Brunswick, NJ: Rutgers University Press.

Morewood, Steve. 2008. "Prelude to the Suez Crisis: The Rise and Fall of British Dominance over the Suez Canal, 1869–1956." In Simon Smith, ed., *Reassessing Suez 1956: New Perspectives on the Crisis and Its Aftermath*. Aldershot: Ashgate, 13–34.

Morris, Rosalind. 1995. "All Made Up: Performance Theory and the New Anthropology of Sex and Gender." *Annual Review of Anthropology* 24, 567–92.

———. 2007. "Legacies of Derrida: ~~Anthropology~~." *Annual Review of Anthropology* 36: 355–89.

Moustafa, Tamir. 2007. *The Struggle for Constitutional Power: Law, Politics, and Economic Development in Egypt*. Cambridge: Cambridge University Press.

Muhammad, Dina. 2015. "Hal Tu'awwid 'Rihlat al-Fananiyin' Ziyadat Mu'aradi al-Sisi?" *Wara al-Ahdath*, June 1. http://tinyurl.com/oyvak2p, accessed August 13, 2016.

Musa, Ahmad. 2013. "Asliha Thaqila fi Rab'a al-'Adawiyya." *Yaum al-Sabi'* video. https:// www.youtube.com/watch?v=cfA9qWK8eS8, accessed August 9, 2017.

Musaji, Sheila. 2012. "About That Necrophilia Law." *American Muslim*, April 27. http:// theamericanmuslim.org/tam.php/features/articles/about-that-egyptian-necrophilia -law/0019097, accessed April 1, 2013.

"Mustafa Bakri Yuhagim 'Isam Higgi." 2014. YouTube video. https://www.youtube.com /watch?v=EdfhVz6UaXg, accessed August 13, 2016.

Muwatin X (pseudonym). 2011. *Al-Sirr Wara' Sally Zahran . . . au al-Shahida al-Kamila*. http://www.facebook.com/notes/NAMEDELETED/-secret-beyond-sally-zahran -a-perfect-mar/204546449558827. Name deleted to preserve author's anonymity.

Naber, Nadine. 2011. "Imperial Feminism, Islamophobia, and the Egyptian Revolution." *Jadaliyya*, February 11. http://www.jadaliyya.com/pages/index/616/imperial-feminism -islamophobia-and-the-egyptian-revolution, accessed July 26, 2011.

Nadi, Mu'tazz. 2013. "Wazir al-Dakhiliyya: 43 Min Rigal al-Shurta Istashidu fi Fadd I'tisamay

Rab'a wa Nahda." *Al-Masry al-Youm*, August 14. http://www.almasryalyoum.com/news/details/249032, accessed August 9, 2017.

"NASA Rocket to Bear Name of Egyptian Woman Killed in Protests." 2011. *MSN News*. http://news.in.msn.com/international/article.aspx?cp-documentid=4908012, accessed June 2, 2011.

"NASA Takrum al-Shahida Sally Zahran." 2011. *Fatakat Forum*. http://forums.fatakat.com/thread1241347, accessed June 2, 2011.

"NASA Takrum al-Shahida 'Sally Zahran' Wa Tada'u Ismaha 'ala Markaba Muttagiha Illa al-Marikh." 2011. *Al-Masry al-Youm*, February 10. http://www.almasry-alYaum.com/article2.aspx?ArticleID=287499, accessed June 2, 2011.

"NASA to Honor Tahrir Square Martyr by Putting Name on Spacecraft." 2011. *Al-Masry al-Youm*, February 10. http://www.almasryalyoum.com/en/node/314995, accessed June 2, 2011.

"NASA to Name Space Ship after Egyptian Martyr." 2011. *Bikya Masr*. http://bikyamasr.com/wordpress/?p=26661, accessed June 2, 2011.

Nash, June, ed. 2004. *Social Movements: An Anthropological Reader*. Oxford: Blackwell.

Nawwar, Ibrahim. 2010. "Li-Man Nahrithu al-Ard . . . wa Li-Man Tathmuru al-Huqul?" Reprinted by Hizb al-Gubha al-Dimuqratiyya. http://www.democraticfront.org/index.php?option=com_content&view=article&id=61:2010-03-20-10-39-16&catid=38:2010-02-24-17-48-21&Itemid=82, accessed June 16, 2011.

Neilson, Brett, and Ned Rossiter. 2008. "Precarity as a Political Concept; or, Fordism as Exception." *Theory, Culture and Society* 25 (7–8): 51–72.

"New Administrative Capital." 2017. *State Information Service*. http://www.sis.gov.eg/section/352/5238?lang=en-us, accessed July 23, 2017.

"New Suez Canal." 2015. *Suez Canal Authority*. http://www.suezcanal.gov.eg/sc.aspx?show=69, accessed August 13, 2016.

Niehaus, Isak. 2013. "Confronting Uncertainty: Anthropology and Zones of the Extraordinary." *American Ethnologist* 40 (4): 651–60.

Nigm, Ahmad Fu'ad. 2005 [1973]. "Sabah al-Khayr." In *Ahmad Fu'ad Nigm: A-A'mal al-Shi'riyya al-Kamila*. Cairo: Dar Merit, 312–14.

Noshokaty, Shady. 2011. "Ahmed Basiony: At the Frontline of the Arts and Revolution." *Nafas Art Magazine*. http://universes-in-universe.org/eng/nafas/articles/2011/ahmed_basiony, accessed May 31, 2011.

Nour, Ayman. 2015. "Egypt Fighting Corruption: A New Law on Civil Service." *Al-Tamimi and Partners*. http://www.tamimi.com/en/magazine/law-update/section-11/junejuly/egypt-fighting-corruption-a-new-law-on-civil-service.html, accessed August 14, 2016.

Nugent, David, and Joan Vincent, eds. 2007. *A Companion to the Anthropology of Politics*. Oxford: Blackwell.

Nunns, Alex, and Nadia Idle, eds. 2011. *Tweets from Tahrir: Egypt's Revolution as It Unfolded in the Words of the People Who Made It*. London: OR Books.

Ohlheiser, Abby. 2013. "The Con Man Who Sold *Incredibly* Fake Bomb Detectors to the Iraqi Government." *Slate*, May 2. http://www.slate.com/blogs/the_slatest/2013/05/02/ade651_fake_bomb_detector_lands_jim_mccormick_10_year_prison_sentence.html, accessed August 13, 2016.

Ong, Aihwa. 2006. "Introduction: Neoliberalism as Exception, Exception to Neoliberalism." In A. Ong, *Neoliberalism as Exception: Mutations in Citizenship and Sovereignty*. Durham, NC: Duke University Press, 1–30.

Ortner, Sherry. 1984. "Theory in Anthropology since the Sixties." *Comparative Studies in Society and History* 26 (1): 126–66.

————. 2011. "On Neoliberalism." *Anthropology of This Century* 1 (May). http://aotcpress .com/articles/neoliberalism/, accessed December 25, 2015.

Paige, Jeffery. 2003. "Finding the Revolutionary in the Revolution: Social Science Concepts and the Future of Revolution." In John Foran, ed., *The Future of Revolutions: Rethinking Radical Change in the Age of Globalization*. London: Zed Books, 19–29.

Palmer, Bryan. 2014. "Reconsideration of Class: Precariousness as Proletarianization." In Leo Panitch, Greg Albo, and Vivek Chibber, eds., *Socialist Register* 50: 40–62.

Parker, Emily. 2011. "Tunisia's Election Results and the Question of Minorities." *Jadaliyya*, November 28. http://www.jadaliyya.com/pages/index/3310/tunisias-election-results -and-the-question-of-mino%20;%20http://www.jadaliyya.com/pages/index/3154 /freedom-and-justice-party, accessed January 24, 2016.

Parmenter, Barbara. 1994. *Giving Voice to Stones: Place and Identity in Palestinian Literature*. Austin: University of Texas Press.

Peck, Jamie, and Adam Tickell. 2002. "Neoliberalizing Space." *Antipode* 34 (3): 380–404.

Peterson, Mark. 2011. *Connected in Cairo: Growing Up Cosmopolitan in the Modern Middle East*. Bloomington: Indiana University Press.

————. 2015a. "In Search of Antistructure: The Meaning of Tahrir Square in Egypt's Ongoing Social Drama." In Ágnes Horváth, Bjørn Thomassen, and Harald Wydra, eds., *Breaking Boundaries: Varieties of Liminality*. New York: Berghan Books, 164–82.

————. 2015b. "Re-envisioning Tahrir: The Changing Meanings of Tahrir Square in Egypt's Ongoing Revolution." In Reem Abou-El-Fadl, ed., *Revolutionary Egypt: Connecting Domestic and International Struggles*. London: Routledge, 64–82.

Phillips, Adam. 2002. *Equals*. New York: Basic Books.

Postill, John. 2010. "Introduction: Theorising Media and Practice." In Birgit Bräuchler and John Postill, eds., *Theorising Media and Practice*. New York: Berghan, 1–34.

Pratt, Nicola. 2004. "Bringing Politics Back In: Examining the Link between Globalization and Democratization." *Review of International Political Economy* 11 (2): 311–36.

————. 2005. "Identity, Culture and Democratization: The Case of Egypt." *New Political Science* 27 (1): 73–90.

"Qanat al-Suways Tuuu." 2015. YouTube video. https://www.youtube.com/watch?v= a3R1Z15sjls, accessed August 13, 2016.

"Qissat Ightiyal Hasan al-Banna." 2014. *Wikipedia al-Ikhwan al-Muslimin* (drawn from the memoirs of 'Umar Tilmisani). http://tinyurl.com/ngesjcq, accessed July 23, 2014.

Radin, Paul. 1956. *The Trickster: A Study in American Indian Mythology; With a Commentary by Karl Kerényi and Carl G. Jung*. New York: Philosophical Library.

Ragab, Adla, and Hisham Fouad. 2009. "Roads and Highways in Egypt: Reform for Enhancing Efficiency." ECES Working Papers 152. Cairo: Egyptian Center for Economic Studies.

Ramadan, Dina. 2015. "From Artist to Martyr: On Commemorating Ahmed Basiony." *Nika: Journal of Contemporary African Art* 36: 76–86.

Ramadan, Tariq. 2012. *Islam and the Arab Awakening*. Oxford: Oxford University Press.

Rancière, Jacques. 2006. *Hatred of Democracy*. Translated by Steve Corcoran. London: Verso.

"Rantings of a Sandmonkey." 2011. *Egypt Today*, April 1. http://wwww.egypttoday.com/news /display/article/artId:216, accessed June 6, 2011.

Reynolds, Nancy. 2012. *A City Consumed: Urban Commerce, the Cairo Fire, and the Politics of Decolonization in Egypt*. Stanford, CA: Stanford University Press.

Richards, Alan. 1980. "Egypt's Agriculture in Trouble." *MERIP Reports* 84 (January): 3–13.

"Rihla Illa al-Marikh bi-Ism al-Shahida Sally Zahran." 2011. *Al-Masry al-Youm*, February 9. http://www.almasryalYaum.com/node/314550, accessed June 2, 2011.

Roitman, Janet. 2013. *Anti-crisis*. Durham, NC: Duke University Press.

Rommel, Carl. 2015. *Revolution, Play and Feeling: Assembling Emotionality, National Subjectivity and Football in Cairo, 1990–2013*. PhD diss., School of Oriental and African Studies.

———. 2016. "Troublesome Thugs or Respectable Rebels? Class, Martyrdom and Cairo's Revolutionary Ultras." *Middle East—Topics and Arguments* 6: 33–42. http://meta -journal.net/article/view/3788, accessed August 22, 2017.

Rosenberg, Paul. 2016. "Donald Trump's Weaponized Platform: A Project Three Decades in the Making." *Salon*, July 16. http://www.salon.com/2016/07/16/donald_trumps _weaponized_platform_a_project_three_decades_in_the_making/, accessed January 8, 2017.

Ryzova, Lucie. 2011. "Teargas, Hairgel and Tramadol: The Battle of Muhammad Mahmud Street." *Jadaliyya*, November 28. http://www.jadaliyya.com/pages/index/3312/the -battle-of-muhammad-mahmud-street_teargas-hair-, accessed August 12, 2016.

———. 2014. *The Age of the Efendiyya: Passages to Modernity in National-Colonial Egypt*. Oxford: Oxford University Press.

———. 2015. "Strolling in Enemy Territory: Downtown Cairo, Its Publics, and Urban Heterotopias." In Nadia van Maltzahn and Monique Bellan, eds., *Divercities: Competing Narratives and Urban Practices in Beirut, Cairo and Tehran*. Beirut: Orient Institut. http://www.perspectivia.net/publikationen/orient-institut-studies/3-2015/ryzova _strolling, accessed December 23, 2015.

———. n.d. (forthcoming). "The Battle of Muhammad Mahmoud Street in Cairo: Poetics and Politics of Urban Violence in Revolutionary Time. Past and Present."

Saad, Bishoy. 2011. "Bishoy Saad's Testimony." *Maspero Testimonies* https://maspero testimonies.wordpress.com/maspero-testimonies/bishoo-saad-testimony-en/, accessed January 24, 2016.

Sabea, Hanan. 2013. "A 'Time Out of Time': Tahrir, the Political and the Imaginary in the Context of the January 25th Revolution in Egypt." Hot Spots, *Cultural Anthropology* website, May 9. https://culanth.org/fieldsights/211-a-time-out-of-time-tahrir-the -political-and-the-imaginary-in-the-context-of-the-january-25th-revolution-in-egypt, accessed August 22, 2017.

Sa'd, Yasin. 2015. "Iftitah Garage al-Tahrir 25 Yanair, wa-Sanimna' al-Wuquf fi Midanuhu." *Al-Masry al-Youm*, January 20. http://www.almasryalyoum.com/news/details/635491, accessed December 26, 2015.

Sahlins, Marshall. 1985. *Islands of History*. Chicago: University of Chicago Press.

Said, Edward. 1978. *Orientalism*. London: Routledge and Keegan Paul.

Sakr, Naomi. 2007. *Arab Television Today*. London: I. B. Tauris.

———. 2013. *Transformations in Egyptian Journalism*. London: I. B. Tauris.

Salah, Muhammad (Oka), and Ahmad Mitwalli (Ortega). 2013. "Nahnu Nuridha Hals." YouTube video. https://www.youtube.com/watch?v=ktmXunDvoZo, accessed August 14, 2016.

"Sally Zahran." 2011. http://www.saihat.org/vb/showthread.php?t=166867, accessed June 2, 2011.

"Sally Zahran: Jeanne d'Arc al-Thaura al-Misriyya" (photo of painting by Ahmad al-Tuni). 2011. http://law4-all.net/vb/showthread.php?t=1603, accessed June 2, 2011.

"Sally Zahran min Ahad Asdiqa'iha." 2011. http://www.youtube.com/watch?v=E7SSJQ1jDvo, accessed June 6, 2011.

Samir, Mohamed. 2017. "Suez Canal Revenues Decline in Wake of Sluggish Global Trade." *Daily News Egypt*, July 23. https://dailynewsegypt.com/2017/02/22/suez-canal -revenues-decline-wake-sluggish-global-trade/, accessed July 23, 2017.

"@Sandmonkey's Thoughts on Egypt after the Revolution." 2011. Retrieved from Kimberly Curtis's Stories. March 2. http://storify.com/curtiskj/rant, accessed June 6, 2011.

Schechner, Richard. 1988 [1977]. *Performance Theory*. New York: Routledge.

Schielke, Samuli. 2015. *Egypt in the Future Tense: Hope, Frustration and Ambivalence before and after 2011*. Bloomington: Indiana University Press.

———. 2016. "Can Poetry Change the World? Reading Amal Dunqul in Egypt in 2011." In Karin van Nieukerk, Mark Levine, and Martin Stokes, eds., *Islam and Popular Culture*. Austin: University of Texas Press, 122–48.

Schumpeter, Joseph. 2006 [1943]. *Capitalism, Socialism and Democracy*. London: Routledge.

Schwarzmantel, John. 2015. *The Routledge Guide to Gramsci's Prison Notebooks*. New York: Routledge.

Scott, David. 2014. *Omens of Adversity: Tragedy, Time, Memory, Justice*. Durham, NC: Duke University Press.

Sedra, Paul. 2013. "The 'Sectarianization' of Egyptian Society." *Open Democracy*, August 22. https://www.opendemocracy.net/paul-sedra/%E2%80%98sectarianization%E2%80%80%99-of-egyptian-society, accessed August 13, 2016.

Seikaly, Sherene. 2013. "The Meaning of Revolution: On Samira Ibrahim." *Jadaliyya*, January 28. http://www.jadaliyya.com/pages/index/9814/the-meaning-of-revolution_on -samira-ibrahim, accessed August 22, 2017.

Selbin, Eric. 1997. "Revolution in the Real World: Bringing Agency Back In." In John Foran, ed., *Theorizing Revolutions*. London: Routledge, 118–32.

Sennett, Richard. 1998. *Corrosion of Character: Personal Consequences of Work in the New Capitalism*. New York: Norton, 1998.

Shah, Alpa, and Judith Pettigrew. 2009. "Windows into a Revolution: Ethnographies of Maoism in South Asia." *Dialectical Anthropology* 33 (3/4): 225–51.

"Shahid 'Ayan 'ala Qatl Ahad Zubat al-Gaysh al-Mu'tasmin Fajr 9 Abril." 2011. YouTube video. https://www.youtube.com/watch?v=Si-aVPyjEjU, accessed August 7, 2011.

"Shahid Radd Fi'l Sabrin 'ala Ikhtira' al-Jaysh." 2014. YouTube video. https://www.youtube .com/watch?v=J5svgb5aD2g, accessed August 13, 2016.

Shahin, Emad al-Din. 2015. "Sentenced to Death in Egypt." *Atlantic*, May 19. http://www .theatlantic.com/international/archive/2015/05/death-sentence-egypt-emad-shahin /393590/, accessed August 13, 2016.

Shapir, Yiftah, and Yoel Guzansky. 2015. "A Bridge over the Mediterranean: The French-Egyptian Arms Deal." *Institute for National Security Insight* 673 (March 12). http:// www.inss.org.il/publication/a-bridge-over-the-mediterranean-the-french-egyptian -arms-deal/, accessed October 26, 2018.

Shapiro, Samantha. 2009. "Revolution Facebook-Style." *New York Times*, January 22. http:// www.nytimes.com/2009/01/25/magazine/25bloggers-t.html?pagewanted=all accessed on July 27, 2011.

"Shaqiq Sally Zahran Yakshif Haqiqat al-Fabrika al-Suhufiyya l-Suwar al-Shuhada.'" 2011. *Al-Ahram*, February 27. http://digital.ahram.org.eg/articles.aspx?Serial=438444&eid= 6055, accessed June 2, 2011.

Sharp, Jeremy. 2010. "US Foreign Assistance to the Middle East: Historical Background, Recent Trends, and the FY2011." Washington, DC: Congressional Research Service.

Shayne, Julie. 2004. *The Revolution Question: Feminisms in El Salvador, Chile and Cuba*. New Brunswick, NJ: Rutgers University Press.

Shea, Daniel. 2015. "The New Suez Canal: Racing against Time." *Onboard Online*, January 28. https://www.onboardonline.com/industry-article-index/shipping/the-new-suez -canal-racing-against-time/, accessed August 13, 2016.

Shouse, Eric. 2005. "Feeling, Emotion, Affect." *M/C Journal* 8. http://journal.media-culture .org.au/0512/03-shouse.php, accessed August 22, 2017.

"Shuhada' 25 Yanair." 2011. *Al-Masry al-Youm* 2429: 9 (print edition); online edition at http://today.almasryalyoum.com/article2.aspx?ArticleID=287608, accessed July 10, 2011.

Simpson, David. 2006. *9/11: The Culture of Commemoration*. Chicago: University of Chicago Press.

Sims, David. 2010. *Understanding Cairo: Logic of a City Out of Control*. Cairo: American University in Cairo Press.

———. 2014. *Egypt's Desert Dreams: Development or Disaster?* Cairo: American University in Cairo Press.

Singerman, Diane. 1996. *Avenues of Participation: Family, Politics and Networks in Urban Cairo*. Princeton, NJ: Princeton University Press.

Skocpol, Theda. 1979. *States and Social Revolutions: A Comparative Analysis of France, Russia and China*. Cambridge, MA: Harvard University Press.

Smith, Neil. 2003. Foreword. In Henri Lefebvre, *The Urban Revolution*, translated by Robert Bononno. Minneapolis: University of Minnesota Press, vii–xxiii.

Spencer, Richard. 2014. "Egypt Army Embarrassment after It 'Cures' AIDS." *Telegraph*, February 27. http://www.telegraph.co.uk/news/worldnews/africaandindianocean/egypt /10665410/Egypt-army-embarrassment-after-it-cures-Aids.html, accessed August 13, 2016.

Spivak, Gayatri. 1988. "Can the Subaltern Speak?" In Cary Nelson and Lawrence Grossberg, eds., *Marxism and the Interpretation of Culture*. Urbana: University of Illinois Press, 271–313.

Springborg, Robert. 1979. "Patrimonialism and Policy Making in Egypt: Nasser and Sadat and the Tenure Policy for Reclaimed Lands." *Middle Eastern Studies* 15 (1): 49–69.

Standing, Guy. 2011. *The Precariat: The New Dangerous Class*. London: Bloomsbury Academic.

Starrett, Gregory. 2010. "The Varieties of Secular Experience." *Comparative Studies in Society and History* 52 (3): 626–51.

Stevenson, Tom. 2015. "Sisi's Way." *London Review of Books* 37 (4). http://www.lrb.co.uk/v37 /n04/tom-stevenson/sisis-way, accessed August 13, 2016.

Surur, Nagib. 1993. "Brutukulat Hukama' Rish." In Nagib Surur, *Al-A'mal al-Kamila*. Cairo: al-Hay'a al-Misriyya al-'Amma lil-Kitab, 261–327.

Suskind, David. 2004. "Faith, Certainty and the Presidency of George W. Bush." *New York Times*, October 17. http://www.nytimes.com/2004/10/17/magazine/faith-certainty-and -the-presidency-of-george-w-bush.html?_r=0, accessed August 13, 2016.

Swedenburg, Ted. 1995. *Memories of Revolt: The 1936–39 Rebellion and the Palestinian National Past*. Minneapolis: University of Minnesota Press.

———. 2011. "Troubadors of Revolt." *Middle East Research and Information Project* 41 (258): 18–19.

Szakolczai, Arpad. 2000. *Historical Reflexive Sociology*. London: Routledge.

———. 2009. "Liminality and Experience: Structuring Transitory Situations and Transformative Events." *International Political Anthropology* 2 (1): 141–72.

"Ta'arrif 'ala al-Muharrid al-Ra'isi li-Ahdath Masbiru al-Irhabi al-Baltagi Filubatir." 2011. YouTube video. https://www.youtube.com/watch?v=U3_-bfKLoCg, accessed January 24, 2016.

"Ta'arrif bi-Fadilat al-Shaykh Muhammad Hassan." 2012. http://www.mohamedhassan.org /ta3reef%20belshiekh.htm, accessed April 27, 2012.

"Ta'bin al-Shahid Mustafa al-Sawi." 2011. *Ikhwan Online.* http://www.ikhwanonline.com /new/Article.aspx?ArtID=79417&SecID=270, accessed May 31, 2011.

Tadros, Mariz. 2011a. "A State of Sectarian Denial." *Middle East Report,* January 11. http:// www.merip.org/mero/mero011111, accessed December 24, 2015.

———. 2011b. "Egypt's Bloody Sunday." *Middle East Report,* October 13. http://www.merip .org/mero/mero101311, accessed January 24, 2016.

———. 2013a. "Ripping Bodies Apart: The Brotherhood's Sectarian Policy in Practice." *Open Democracy,* June 26. https://www.opendemocracy.net/5050/mariz-tadros/ripping -bodies-apart-brotherhood%E2%80%99s-sectarian-policy-in-practice, accessed August 13, 2013.

———. 2013b. "The Backlash after the Demise: The Brothers and the Copts." *Religious Freedom Project (Berkeley Center),* August 12. https://berkleycenter.georgetown .edu/essays/the-backlash-after-the-demise-the-brothers-and-the-copts, accessed August 13, 2016.

"Taghtiyyat Ahdath Masbiru." 2011. YouTube video uploaded on October 9. https://www .youtube.com/watch?v=NCXD1UwoMkU, accessed January 24, 2016.

"Tajaddud al-Ihtikakat Sabah al-Yaum bayn Mu'tasimi al-Salam wa Ashab Sayarat Imama Masbiru." 2011. *Manqul.* http://www.manqol.com/topic/?t=82841, accessed July 27, 2016.

Tal'at, Umniyya. 2011. "Shahidat Yanayir wa Ghumud Qissat Sally Zahran." *Al-Hiwar al-Mutamaddin.* http://www.ahewar.org/debat/show.art.asp?aid=248299, accessed July 27, 2011.

Tamam, Hosam. 2012. *Al-Ikhwan al-Muslimun: Sanawat ma Qabl al-Thaura.* Cairo: Dar al-Shuruq.

"Taqrir Qanat al-Maganin al-Fara'ayn al-Rajulan." 2013. YouTube video. https://www .youtube.com/watch?v=DUzLzmTDMWM, accessed August 5, 2016.

"Taqrir Qanat al-Sharq 'an Liwa' 'Suba' al-Kufta.'" 2014. YouTube video. https://www .youtube.com/watch?v=4b1TdbyNwKY, accessed August 13, 2016.

"Taqrir Shamil: Hasr Dahaya Fadd I'tsam Rab'aa Tafsiliyan." 2013. *Wikithaura.* http:// wikithawra.wordpress.com/2013/09/03/rabiadisperal14aug/, accessed June 11, 2014.

Tarbush, Nadia. 2012. "Cairo 2050: Urban Dream or Modernist Delusion?" *Journal of International Affairs* 65 (2) (Spring/Summer): 171–86.

Tarì, Marcello, and Ilaria Vanni. 2005. "On the Life and Deeds of San Precario, Patron Saint of Precarious Workers and Lives." *Fibreculture Journal* 5. http://five.fibreculturejournal .org/fcj-023-on-the-life-and-deeds-of-san-precario-patron-saint-of-precarious-workers -and-lives/, accessed July 19, 2016.

"Tasfiq Had li-Sonallah Ibrahim." 2003. *Muhawarat al-Masriyin.* http://www.egyptiantalks .org/invb/?showtopic=8075, accessed December 27, 2015.

"Tasrihat wa Tahdidat al-Beltagi 'an al-'Amaliyyat fi Sina.'" 2013. YouTube video. July 8. https://www.youtube.com/watch?v=kMkLwliHowg, accessed August 13, 2016.

"Taufiq 'Ukasha Yahdhar min 13-13-2013." 2011. YouTube video. https://www.youtube.com /watch?v=8YfVtNxMzTo, accessed August 2, 2016.

"Taufiq Yahya Ibrahim 'Ukasha." 2012. Bio of 'Ukasha on the Hizb Misr al-Qaumi website. http://egypt-national.com/news/index.php?option=com_content&view=article&id=15 %3A2011-05-22-19-12-39&catid=2%3A2010-12-09-22-47-00&Itemid=4, accessed April 26, 2012.

Tharwat, Muhammad. 2014. "Irhab Sina' . . . Tahdid al-Beltagi wa Sadhajat Mursi." *Al-Wafd* online, September 2. http://tinyurl.com/pud9y4v, accessed August 13, 2016.

Thomassen, Bjørn. 2008. "What Kind of Political Anthropology?" *International Political Anthropology* 1 (2): 263–74.

Thomassen, Bjørn. 2012. "Notes toward an Anthropology of Political Revolutions." *Comparative Studies in Society and History* 54 (3): 679–706.

———. 2014. *Liminality and the Modern: Living through the In-between*. London: Routledge.

Thornhill, Michael. 2006. *Road to Suez: The Battle of the Canal Zone*. Stroud, UK: Sutton.

Tilly, Charles. 2006. *Regimes and Repertoires*. Chicago: University of Chicago Press.

———. 2008. *Contentious Performances*. Cambridge: Cambridge University Press.

Trotsky, Leon. 1931. "What Is a Revolutionary Situation?" *Militant* 4 (36). https://www.marxists.org/archive/trotsky/1931/11/revsit.htm, accessed July 13, 2017.

Turner, Victor. 1968. "Myth and Symbol." In David Sills, ed., *International Encyclopedia of the Social Sciences*, vol. 10. New York: Macmillan, 576–82.

———. 1974. "Liminal to Liminoid in Play, Flow, and Ritual: An Essay in Comparative Symbology." *Rice University Studies* 60 (3): 53–92.

———. 1977. *The Ritual Process: Structure and Anti-structure*. Ithaca, NY: Cornell University Press.

———. 1980. "Dramas and Stories about Them." *Critical Inquiry* 7 (1): 141–68.

———. 1988. *The Anthropology of Performance*. New York: PAJ.

———. 1996 [1957]. *Schism and Continuity in an African Society: A Study of Ndembu Ritual*. London: Bloomsbury.

"Ukasha fi Aqwa Ta'liq 'ala Kitab Hawi al-." 2015. YouTube video. https://www.youtube.com/watch?v=Ks14_d9Lb8E, accessed January 7, 2017.

"'Ukasha Yatanaba'u bi-Tai'yin 'Abd al-Fattah al-Sisi Ragil al-Ikhwan fi al-Gaysh." 2012. YouTube video. https://www.youtube.com/watch?v=CYrJRWveQTw, accessed August 2, 2016.

"Umm Sabir." 1953. *Al-Ithnayn* 1006: 1.

"Umm Sabir, Shahidat al-Tughyan." 1951. *Al-Ithnayn* 910 (November 19): 1.

"Umm Sabir . . . Wa Madha Niktab 'ala Qabriha?" 1951. *Al-Ihtnayn* 910 (November 19): 2.

"Umniyya Tal'at." 2011. Good Reads. http://www.goodreads.com/author/show/3314165, accessed August 2, 2011.

United Nations. 2015. *World Economic Situation and Prospects, 2015*. New York: UN Department of Economic and Social Affairs.

US Department of State. 2015. "Foreign Military Training and DoD Engagement Activities of Interest, 2012–2013." http://www.state.gov/t/pm/rls/rpt/fmtrpt/2013/, accessed December 27, 2015.

"Usrat al-Shahida Sally Zahran Tunshur Sura Jadida Liha bil-Hijab 'ala Facebook." 2011. *Al-Masry al-Youm*, February 20. http://www.almasryalYaum.com/node/324871, accessed June 2, 2011.

van Gennep, Arnold. 2004 [1909]. *The Rites of Passage*. Translated by Monika Vizedom and Gabrielle Caffee. London: Routledge.

Varzi, Roxanne. 2006. *Warring Souls: Youth, Media and Martyrdom in Post-Revolution Iran*. Durham, NC: Duke University Press.

Verdery, Katherine. 1999. *The Political Lives of Dead Bodies: Reburial and Postsocialist Change*. New York: Columbia University Press.

Volk, Lucia. 2010. *Memorials and Martyrs in Modern Lebanon*. Bloomington: Indiana University Press.

Wacquant, Loic. 2012. "Three Steps towards a Historical Anthropology of Actually Existing Neoliberalism." *Social Anthropology* 20 (1): 66–79.

Wagner, Armin. 2012–13. *International Fuel Prices 2012/13*. Bonn: Deutsche Gesellschaft für Internationale Zusammenarbeit (GIZ).

"Wahid Hamid." 2017. *Elcinema.* http://www.elcinema.com/person/1087034/, accessed August 14, 2017.

"Walidat al-Shahida Sally Zahran Tunashid al-Iʻlam bi-Nashr Sura Ibnatiha bil-Hijab." 2011. *Al-Marsad al-Islami li-Muqawamat al-Tansir.* http://www.tanseerel.com/main/articles .aspx?selected_article_no=18529, accessed July 18, 2011.

Wardle, Huon. 2001. "Schismogenesis in a Belfast Urinal." *Anthropology Today* 17 (3): 24–25.

Weber, Donald. 1995. "From Limen to Border: A Meditation on the Legacy of Victor Turner for American Cultural Studies." *American Quarterly* 47 (3) (September 1995): 525–36.

Wickham, Carrie. 2013. *The Muslim Brotherhood: Evolution of an Islamist Movement.* Princeton, NJ: Princeton University Press.

Wickham-Crowley, Timothy. 1997. "Structural Theories of Revolution." In John Foran, ed., *Theorizing Revolutions.* London: Routledge, 36–70.

Williamson, John. 2004. "A Short History of the Washington Consensus." Publication of the Peterson Institute for International Economics. http://www.iie.com/publications /papers/williamson0904-2.pdf, accessed December 27, 2015.

Winegar, Jessica. 2006. *Creative Reckonings: The Politics or Art and Culture in Contemporary Egypt.* Stanford, CA: Stanford University Press.

———. 2009. "Culture Is the Solution: The Civilizing Mission of Egypt's Culture Palaces." *Review of Middle East Studies* 43 (2): 189–97.

———. 2011. "Taking Out the Trash: Youth Clean Up Egypt after Mubarak." *Middle East Report* 259: 32–35.

"WO/2011/116782." 2011. *World Intellectual Property Organization.* https://patentscope.wipo .int/search/en/detail.jsf?docId=WO2011116782&recNum=15, accessed August 13, 2016.

Woltering, Robert. 2013. "Unusual Suspects: 'Ultras' as Political Actors in the Egyptian Revolution." *Arab Studies Quarterly* 35 (3): 290–304.

Wynn, Lisa. 2007. *Pyramids and Nightclubs: A Travel Ethnography of Arab and Western Imaginations of Egypt.* Austin: University of Texas Press.

Yahia, Mohammed. 2014. "The False Science behind Egyptian Army's AIDS and HCV Cure." *House of Wisdom* (blog). http://blogs.nature.com/houseofwisdom/2014/03/the-false -science-behind-egyptian-armys-aids-and-hvc-cure.html, accessed August 13, 2016.

Yasin, Muhammad. 2010. *Al-Gamaʻa.* Cairo: Sharikat al-Batrus lil-Intag al-Fanni wa al-Tauziʻ (TV serial).

Youssef, Khaled. 2007. *Hina Maysara.* Cairo: al-Batrus lil-Intaj al-Sinimaʼi (film).

———. 2009. *Dukan Shahata.* Cairo: Misr lil-Sinima (film).

Zerubavel, Yael. 1994. "The Death of Memory and the Memory of Death: Masada and the Holocaust as Historical Metaphors." *Representations* 45: 72–100.

INDEX

References to images are in *italics*; references to notes are indicated by n.

Princeton Studies in Muslim Politics

John R. Bowen, *Can Islam Be French? Pluralism and Pragmatism in a Secularist State*

Roxanne L. Euben and Muhammad Qasim Zaman, eds., *Princeton Readings in Islamist Thought: Texts and Contexts from al-Banna to Bin Laden*

Irfan Ahmad, *Islamism and Democracy in India: The Transformation of Jamaat-e-Islami*

Thomas Barfield, *Afghanistan: A Cultural and Political History*

Sara Roy, *Hamas and Civil Society in Gaza: Engaging the Islamist Social Sector*

Michael Laffan, *The Makings of Indonesian Islam: Orientalism and the Narration of a Sufi Past*

Jonathan Laurence, *The Emancipation of Europe's Muslims: The State's Role in Minority Integration*

Jenny White, *Muslim Nationalism and the New Turks*

Lara Deeb and Mona Harb, *Leisurely Islam: Negotiating Geography and Morality in Shi'ite South Beirut*

Esra Özyürek, *Being German, Becoming Muslim: Race, Religion, and Conversion in the New Europe*

Ellen Anne McLarney, *Soft Force: Women in Egypt's Islamic Awakening*

Avi Max Spiegel, *Young Islam: The New Politics of Religion in Morocco and the Arab World*

Nadav Samin, *Of Sand or Soil: Genealogy and Tribal Belonging in Saudi Arabia*

Bernard Rougier, *The Sunni Tragedy in the Middle East: North Lebanon from al-Qaeda to ISIS*

Lihi Ben Shitrit, *Righteous Transgressions: Women's Activism on the Israeli and Palestinian Religious Right*

John R. Bowen, *On British Islam: Religion, Law, and Everyday Practice in Shari'a Councils*

Gilles Kepel, with Antoine Jardin, *Terror in France: The Rise of Jihad in the West*

Alexander Thurston, *Boko Haram: The History of an African Jihadist Movement*

David Kloos, *Becoming Better Muslims: Religious Authority and Ethical Improvement in Aceh, Indonesia*

Muhammad Qasim Zaman, *Islam in Pakistan: A History*

Walter Armbrust, *Martyrs and Tricksters: An Ethnography of the Egyptian Revolution*

A NOTE ON THE TYPE

{⁓⁓⁓⁓⁓}

THIS BOOK has been composed in Miller, a Scotch Roman typeface designed by Matthew Carter and first released by Font Bureau in 1997. It resembles Monticello, the typeface developed for The Papers of Thomas Jefferson in the 1940s by C. H. Griffith and P. J. Conkwright and reinterpreted in digital form by Carter in 2003.

Pleasant Jefferson ("P. J.") Conkwright (1905–1986) was Typographer at Princeton University Press from 1939 to 1970. He was an acclaimed book designer and AIGA Medalist.

The ornament used throughout this book was designed by Pierre Simon Fournier (1712–1768) and was a favorite of Conkwright's, used in his design of the *Princeton University Library Chronicle*.